Art Therapy Practice

Art Therapy Practice
Innovative Approaches
with Diverse Populations

Harriet Wadeson

JOHN WILEY & SONS, INC.
New York • Chichester • Weinheim • Brisbane • Singapore • Toronto

Library of Congress Cataloging-in-Publication Data:

Wadeson, Harriet, 1931–
    Art therapy practice: Innovative approaches with diverse populations / Harriet Wadeson.
        p. ; cm.
    Caption title: Art therapy.
    Includes bibliographical references and index.
    ISBN 0-471-33058-2 (cloth)
    1. Art therapy. 2. Psychotherapy. I. Title: Art therapy. II. Title.
    [DNLM: 1. Art Therapy. WM 450.5.A8 W121c 2000]
    RC489.A7 W33 2000
    616.89'1656—dc21   00-020708

10 9 8 7 6 5 4 3 2 1

This book is dedicated to my parents,
Max and Sophie Weisman.
During the writing of my first book, as they were nearing
their 80s, I hoped they would live long enough to see it in print.
It came to be displayed on their coffee table along with
three others their daughter published later.
Sadly, they are no longer here to welcome a fifth
addition to their coffee table. I miss them.

Contents

PART II: ADULTS

PART III: ART THERAPY PROJECTS

Introduction

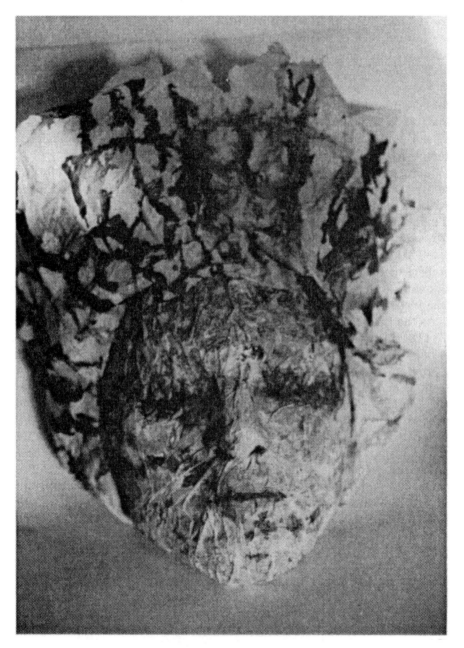

Mask made by the author.

Although writing this book has not been quite as arduous as my nine years of karate training, I am reminded of my introduction to the foundation white belt level when we learned our first kata. *Kata*, which means "shape" or "form," is a stylized choreographed sequence of moves that tells the story of a battle, a story that has been passed down from ancient masters. Our first kata was *Taikyoku*, meaning "the wide view," or being open to possibilities. It is a very symmetrical kata in which we move in all four directions, focusing our gaze toward each to be prepared for whatever we might encounter there. I could have titled this book *Taikyoku* if those outside Japan would have understood its meaning.

Art therapy has expanded exponentially in the last several decades. Many books continue to be written about its various facets. But I believe the time has come to take the wide view of this growing profession, in a sense to face the four corners of its great diversity and be open to possibilities. This book attempts to serve that purpose.

I have been privileged to be a part of the art therapy profession for more than 35 years. The changes that I have witnessed during this period of time have been monumental. My previous writings of the past several decades have led to this present book. When I wrote *Art Psychotherapy* (Wadeson, 1980) in the 1970s, art therapists worked primarily in mental health facilities and in special schools. At that time several books on work with children had been published, but there was little on art therapy with adults. *Art Psychotherapy* drew on my work with adult psychiatric patients at the National Institute of Mental Health in the 1960s and 1970s, as well as my private practice during those years.

As the field continued to grow, training programs were proliferating. In 1978 I became the director of an art therapy graduate program at the University of Houston, moving to Chicago in 1980 to develop an art therapy graduate program at the University of Illinois. Working with students raised many questions about why we do what we do. These reflections prompted me to write *The Dynamics of Art Psychotherapy* (Wadeson, 1987). One of my challenges as the director of training in a major city where art therapy was little developed was to expand the field by placing student interns at sites with populations not previously served by art therapy. Because *Art Psychotherapy* emphasized psychiatric work, the examples I chose for *Dynamics* were drawn from facilities for patients with developmental disabilities, the jails, rehabilitation programs for patients with chronic conditions, and work with older clients, immigrants, and victims of childhood sexual abuse.

As the field continued to broaden, I felt a book was needed to document the new populations and new ways in which art therapy was expanding. I invited others to join me in contributing chapters to *Advances in Art Therapy* (Wadeson, Durkin, & Perach, 1989). In response to an ongoing cry for research within the profession, I compiled and edited a research guide with chapters from a number of contributors, *A Guide to Conducting Art Therapy Research* (Wadeson, 1992) for the American Art Therapy Association. It was the first book the association published.

Now, in the new millennium, the picture art therapy presents is far different from that of its early development just a few decades ago. Even since *Advances in Art Therapy* in 1989, far-reaching changes have been shaping art therapy. AIDS became the plague of the 20th century at a time when we believed medical science had advanced beyond such catastrophes. Baby boomers reached middle age and began worrying about Alzheimer's disease among the increasing numbers of people living to increasingly advanced ages. Women's issues of family violence, victimization, childhood sexual abuse, and rape have continued to resist prevention. Crime, violence, and substance abuse are the everyday milieu for inner-city youth. Coupled with these problems is the changing face of health care delivery services and, to some extent, of social services, as well. In the light of these societal changes, art therapy continues to evolve and grow, often to accommodate the changes, sometimes to separate itself from them.

Like *The Dynamics of Art Psychotherapy*, this book has grown out of my work with art therapy students. In taking the wide view as an art therapy educator, I try to prepare students to work not only with needy populations of today, but with those of tomorrow, as well. Students must be prepared to work not only in the ways that are tried and true, but in innovative ways that will meet new needs in new ways. A training program can have a reciprocal relationship with the profession. It is fed by the knowledge accumulated in the collective wisdom that constitutes the profession, and it passes that wisdom to the next generation of practitioners. But it can also feed the profession. In my own commitment as an educator to the development of art therapy, I have tried to broaden the profession by placing students in internships in facilities working with populations new to art therapy. With new populations has come the need for new ways of working. New venues and new kinds of needs have also challenged art therapists to develop new ways of thinking about the work.

Taking the wide view in looking at the expansion of art therapy into new territory with new approaches in a society of changing health, social, and educational systems challenges us to articulate the directions we face. I have been fortunate that my wide view has encompassed the work of many innovative art therapists whose practice I have supervised. It is this work that constitutes the foundation of this book. Many of the art therapists represented here have been my students. It is with pride and pleasure that I bring their work to a larger audience. I appreciate the contributions of generous colleagues who have allowed me to include their work, as well.

Creativity is at the core of art therapy. We encourage it in our clients, both in approaching their art and in fashioning their lives. The examples of the work of many art therapists in this book give evidence of the enormously creative ways in which they bring creativity into the lives of their clients.

Because books have already been written about some of the populations discussed here, in attempting to present the broad spectrum of art therapy I have illustrated some innovative ways of working, rather than repeating what is already in print. Chapter designations are somewhat arbitrary in that various examples of work could easily fit into more than one chapter. It is my hope that readers will find inspiration in this work to stimulate their own creativity. I hope, as well, that the issues raised here will cause reflection, further questioning, and new solutions.

Art Therapy and the Elephant

An old Indian fable tells of the six learned blind men who argued over the nature of the elephant. One felt its side and said the elephant is like a wall. Another, feeling its tusk, said the elephant is like a spear. The third felt its trunk and said the elephant is like a snake. The fourth found the leg to be like a tree; the fifth, touching the ear, said the elephant is like a fan; and the sixth seized the tail and described the elephant as a rope. Each blind man was partly right, though all were wrong.

Five human service providers who work with art therapists attempt to explain what art therapy is. The first, who is a teacher at an elementary school, says art therapy helps her children with attention deficit disorder to settle down and concentrate. The second, who works with abused and neglected children, says that art therapy gives them a means to express the traumas that they cannot put into words. The third, who works on a hospital psychiatric unit, says that her patients overcome their isolation by painting their hallucinations and delusions so that she can share their private worlds. The fourth, who works with families at an outpatient clinic, says her families have gained insight through their drawings of their relationships and have made changes in their family dynamics. The fifth, who works at a nursing home, speaks of drawings for life review and socialization with the other residents. All are correct about what art therapy is, but each has a different picture. None has the big picture.

What is art therapy? Separately the blind men reply:

- It is the lonely child locked in a wordless prison creating sunshine with crayons.
- It is the pieces of a woman, shattered by rape, slowly melding together in a clay form of her intact body.
- It is the spiraling visions clashing and parting on paper painted by a man in a hospital who sees what others do not.
- It is the feeble scratching of an ancient woman whose words have failed, making her mark.

What is art therapy? Together the blind men grasp the whole:

- It is the legacy of the dying, the plottings of the living, and the pain made visible by those in between.

- It is the rivers of separate circumstances, private privations, and lonely hauntings flowing together in tides of shifting reflections streaming toward a deep sea of intermingled humanity.
- It is the fixity of the stars in which the evanescent dust of living is coalesced in images.

This book is an attempt to illustrate art therapy's great diversity—to show the elephant's massive bulk, tough skin, squirming trunk, sharp tusks, skinny tail, and flapping ears. This book is an attempt to draw the big picture.

PART I

Children and Adolescents

Art therapist's reaction to client, a 15-year-old mother. (*Reprinted from the* American Journal of Art Therapy, *Vol. 33, No. 1, pp. 14–20, by permission of Gladys Agell and Vermont College of Norwich University.*)

Working with children is the delight of many art therapists. They are often playful, open to new ideas, enthusiastic, and responsive to those who show an interest in them. Their feelings are close to the surface, not yet encrusted with the layers of defenses that characterize some adults. The vulnerability of children and the hope that they bring is touching to many who work with them. Their art expressions are often spontaneous and unencumbered by the performance fear that characterizes the work of many adults entering art therapy. However, many of the children art therapists see come from environments of neglect, abuse, violence, drugs, and crime. Unfortunately, many remain in economically disadvantaged neighborhoods where they are subject to the influence of gangs. Art therapists see children and adolescents in public schools, special schools, hospitals for both mental illness and physical illness, outpatient clinics, shelters, and family treatment settings.

Prolog

Art Development in Children

Kitty by 5-year-old girl.

Much has been written about the milestones in children's art development. In fact, the intelligence of young children has been measured by the correlation between the completeness of their drawings of the human figure and the expected norms for their age. Adults may become worried if children appear to be lagging behind in their drawing ability, and therapists have been quick to diagnose retardation, brain damage, trauma, and emotional problems on the basis of failure to meet expected developmental standards in drawing the human figure. In this area of art production more than any other, there is a standardization of drawing norms.

Although I offer some examples to challenge these practices, I do not attempt to repeat the seminal work by Lowenfeld and Brittain (1970) in describing children's artistic growth or the excellent study of the same by art therapist Judith Rubin (1978). The children's art I present here has the unusual benefit of a longitudinal view that follows the children into adulthood. From that vantage point, we can question the significance of art developmental milestones in an individual's life course.

The artwork that follows is by my own children and grandchildren, so naturally I have been a very close observer of their progress. Their drawings and paintings were made at home and at school, not in a treatment setting. Each has had a very different relationship to his or her own art making, and that has made all the difference.

Lisa and Eric were both bright, healthy children, but very different in their artistic development. Figure P.1, painted by Eric at age 3, is typical of a begin-

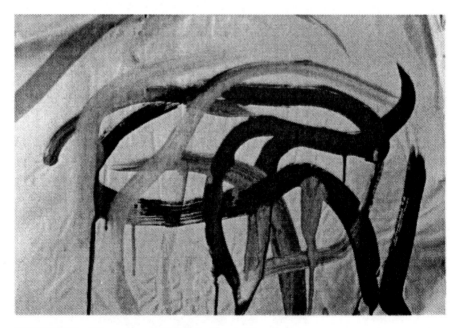

FIGURE P.1   Three-year-old boy's play with colors.

ning painting. He was playing with the colors, not trying to depict anything. We can see the rhythm of his motion in the strokes. He was standing before the easel with plenty of room to move around. Eric was a highly energetic child who was not happy sitting and engaging in quiet activity. He was always on the move, making noise. When he was 3 and 4, I helped out at his play school. I hardly saw him. He would be running around the playground with the other boys, pulling the wagon, riding the tricycle, climbing the jungle gym, and yelling out commands, while his more art-oriented mother would be sitting at a table drawing with the little girls and discussing the meaning of life. On the rare occasions when Eric was still and quiet, I knew he was sick. Adults sometimes make the mistake of asking young children what they are painting when they make pictures such as this. The children may take this to mean that they should be representing something that they are not yet able to do.

Lisa, in contrast with her brother Eric, enjoyed making art from an early age. At 3, she was already trying to represent forms (Figure P.2). Was she brighter or more mature than Eric? At 4, Eric was drawing the human form as the typical cephalopod (Figure P.3, left), but by 6, he gave his figure a body, arms, and details (Figure P.3, right). Lisa, on the other hand, would pore over her books and drawings, while Eric was too busy running around. Therefore, it is not surprising that the difference in their investment in their art is reflected in their drawing ability. Note how much more developed Lisa's art is at age 6. When her baby brother Keith was born, she wrote a book for him (Figure P.4). On the left is her mother (me) holding the baby on her lap as she sits in a chair. The pro-

FIGURE P.2   Three-year-old girl's representation of forms.

FIGURE P.3 Typical cephalopod by 4-year-old boy, left; development of the figure by the same boy at 6, right.

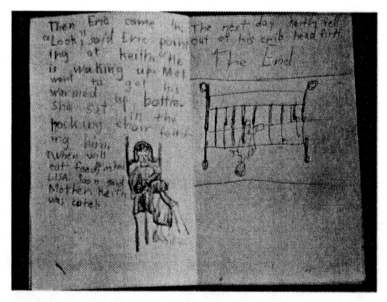

FIGURE P.4 Book by 6-year-old girl.

portions are very close to accurate, as are the relationships of mother, baby, and chair. On the right, the story ends with the baby falling out of the crib on his head. When Eric drew a picture of the family at six (Figure P.5), he found a solution to representing our varying heights by simply extending the legs. Note the difference in drawing maturity.

It is around this age, as children are able to depict differences in people and settings, that themes and even stories begin to emerge in their art. I do not have very many pictures by Eric because he seldom drew, but in school when he was 8 he had an assignment of composing "happiness books." He filled two spiral notebooks with pictures, each of which was titled "Happiness is. . . ." Figure P.6 is "Happiness is doing a headstand," at which Eric was very good. By this age his drawing of body proportions had become more accurate, even upside-down. Figure P.7 is "Happiness is going to camp." The log cabin is given more detail than Eric put into most of his pictures, and it shows that he had observed it accurately, including the round ends of the logs. The person on the right is proportioned well in relation to the cabin. Eric's final picture in the happiness books was "Happiness is finishing these booklets."

In addition to her book about her baby brother Keith, Lisa made a great many story pictures and often wrote down the stories. Children's fantasies can tell us much about their interests and concerns. For example, when Lisa and Eric were taking a bath together, she was the one who discovered that Eric was

FIGURE P.5 Extension of the legs to make height differentiations by 6-year-old boy.

FIGURE P.6 "Happiness book" picture by 8-year-old boy.

FIGURE P.7 "Happiness book" picture by 8-year-old boy.

showing a reaction to his tuberculin test. She did not seem particularly upset about this, but she wrote and drew a story about a girl rescuing her brother who was dying of tuberculosis. Most of her stories and drawings for the next several years, however, were about two girls; Figures P.8, P.9, and P.10 show examples drawn at ages 5, 7, and 10. Her major interest was her friendships.

FIGURE P.8 Two girls by 5-year-old girl.

FIGURE P.9   Two girls by 7-year-old girl.

FIGURE P.10   Two girls by 10-year-
old girl.

(When I spoke with her recently about these drawings, she said her friends are still extremely important to her.) At only 5, Lisa was attentive to detail in clothing. At 7, she placed the girls in a setting that shows distance. Note the perspective of the smaller pair of girls in the background, drawn from behind. At 10, she painted the girls with details of winter attire. When Lisa was 7, she attempted a profile showing the anatomy of her seated Barbie doll (Figure P.11), and at 8 she was able to draw a circus scene with many of the acts together in the ring, although she had probably seen them separately (Figure P.12). In another story, also drawn at 8, she has shown a group of children in the woods (Figure P.13). Note how she has been able to express that the children were a tight band by the way she has drawn one in front of the other. (Contrast this level of sophistication with Eric's drawings at this age.) Finally, Figure P.14 is Lisa's portrait of me drawn when she was 9, showing details of my hairstyle, dress, and jewelry. The folded hands are a challenging attempt at naturalism and individuality, rather than the stereotypical depiction of splayed fingers.

Although Eric's art development was slow and his interest in drawing minimal, by the time he was 8, when given an assignment to draw what interested him, he was able to do so adequately. When he was 4 to 6 years old and

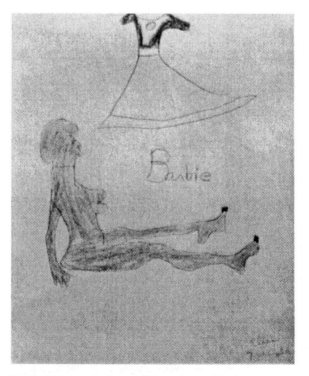

FIGURE P.11   Barbie doll by 7-year-old girl.

FIGURE P.12 Circus by 8-year-old girl.

FIGURE P.13 Story by 8-year-old girl.

FIGURE P.14   Portrait of the author by 9-year-old girl.

drawing the human form so much less maturely than his sister had, should I have been worried? Today Eric is a highly successful partner in a prestigious law firm and has published numerous cutting-edge legal articles. Lisa is also a lawyer, but she is in solo practice. Eric still doesn't like to draw, but his two daughters do, and their mother and grandmother (me) encourage them. Michaela, 6, wants to be an artist when she grows up and enjoys her grandmother's visits because of the art projects we do together. Her artwork has developed substantially in just one year, from the picture on page 3, drawn at age 5, to the two matted pictures she gave me for Christmas at age 6, Figures P.15 and P.16. Her younger sister Amanda, age 3, made a picture for me also, Figure P.17.

Most surprising is the artwork of my youngest child, Keith. Keith was born 2 months premature with an undeveloped eye and vision so limited in his functional eye that he was diagnosed as being legally blind. Skull X rays and electroencephalograms showed brain damage, as well. After thorough testing, I was told unequivocally by the director of the Johns Hopkins Center for the Diagnosis and Evaluation of Handicapped Children that he would

FIGURE P.15 Development in the art of a 6-year-old girl.

FIGURE P.16 Development in the art of a 6-year-old girl.

FIGURE P.17   Drawing by a 3-year-old girl.

never mature beyond an 8-year-old level. Additional testing at the National Institutes of Health confirmed the prognosis.

Even though Keith's vision was considerably impaired, he liked to draw. His human figures at age 4 (Figure P.18) were considerably more advanced than those of his "normal" brother (Figure P.3, left). Keith's development was very slow, so that at 4 he was just beginning to talk. Nevertheless, at that age he titled his drawing on the right in Figure P.18 as *Girl with Buttons*. He was very interested in vehicles, and at 4 drew them prodigiously. Despite his visual impairment, he studied details carefully and understood visual relationships at an early age. Note the rods on the wheels and the heads of people in the coaches of his train in Figure P.19. With crayon, Keith drew a similar train running all around the walls of his room. Although the children were not supposed to draw on the walls, his train was so captivating that I didn't wash it off, and it remained as a pleasant reminder until we moved to another house. At 4½, Keith's vehicles became more elaborate. Figure P.20 is a school bus with children in it. Note the fenders and other details on the bus, as well as the individuality of the children. Depicting the outside-inside relationships requires significant understanding of spatial relationships. With only one functional eye, Keith had impaired depth vision. A similar drawing shows the bus that brought our house cleaner (Figure P.21). She was an African American woman, and Keith colored her brown, as distinguished from the others. She is shown right above the door. Compare Keith's self-portrait at 4½ (Figure P.22), with that of his brother at age 4 (Figure P.3, left). Keith's has fingers, nostrils, a fairly well proportioned body, and even the slit of his undeveloped eye. When

FIGURE P.18   Figures by 4-year-old boy with visual impairment.

FIGURE P.19   Train by 4-year-old boy with visual impairment.

15

FIGURE P.20   School bus by 4-year-old boy with visual impairment.

Keith was 6, he taught himself to play the piano. Although we had only a spinet, at 8 he drew himself playing a baby grand (Figure P.23).

The development of this child, who was legally blind and diagnosed with a limitation of an 8-year-old level of intellectual and functional maturation, did not follow in the expected directions. Early on, it was evident that his comprehension and ability to represent spatial relations was precocious, despite

FIGURE P.21   Bus with housekeeper by 4-year-old boy with visual impairment.

FIGURE P.22   Self-portrait by 4-year-old boy with visual impairment.

FIGURE P.23   Self-portrait at the piano by 8-year-old boy with visual impairment.

extreme visual impairment. He went on to study computer science in college. Once again, overreaching his visual limitations, he developed a passion for photography. He taught himself the necessary skills and technical knowledge to the degree that the large university he attended commissioned him to photograph campus publicity shots. His computer work paid for his college education. After graduation he tried several computer jobs, but found that he did not like working in an office, so he retired. He is now doing contract work with a partner, combining his computer and photographic skills to do photo restoration. He has just completed a large assignment from Amtrak, altering photographs for advertising.

These examples of childhood art, in cases where it has been possible to follow the children into adulthood, challenge assumptions educators and therapists have made about the parallels between art development and intellectual potential. One formidable consideration that is often missing is *motivation*. In the examples presented here, we see the following:

- A girl with motivation to make art whose art was highly developed. She became a successful professional.
- A physically active boy with little interest in drawing whose art was rather undeveloped. Nevertheless, he grew up to become a very high achieving adult who is considered exceptionally bright and capable by his peers.
- A boy born with brain damage who was legally blind and whom experts predicted would never mature beyond an 8-year-old developmental level. Nevertheless, his art showed advanced ability at an early age. He has grown into a successful adult choosing to work in an area requiring visual acuity and an artistic sense.

One of my favorite examples of evaluating children's art comes from *Understanding Children's Art* by Rhoda Kellogg (1969), in which she shows pairs of figure drawings made within a week by each of 16 children. All the pairs show a large discrepancy in terms of completeness of the form, the major criterion for judging mental age. For example, one of the drawings by a particular child shows a 4-year-old developmental level, while the other, drawn within the same week, shows a 6-year-old level. This sort of divergence is seen in all 16 pairs.

These examples of my children's art testify to what is unique in human development. Although there are developmental milestones both in general maturation and in art making, the rate at which one progresses does not necessarily determine one's outcome. Motivation is a strong influence in art development, as is opportunity. I have been interested to observe that many school children from indigent backgrounds do not like to draw (see Chapters 1 to 3). This may have resulted from a lack of opportunity with art materials when they were younger.

Recently I was speaking to a preschool teacher about her work with

2-year-olds. Her goal was to enhance their development, including their drawing ability. I questioned working with them in this way. Unless they have severe impairments, children have a natural curiosity about their world and an innate drive toward mastery. If they did not, perhaps they would never learn to walk or talk. They don't have to be taught these things. Adults might be wise to provide stimulation and opportunity for development, but for the most part, if they just don't get in the way, children will develop on their own.

The children presented here were not art therapy clients, yet viewing their art is informative in understanding those with whom art therapists work. Whether seen in school or therapeutic settings, each child's art must be understood in the context of the child's life situation. The art can provide rich data around interests, fantasies, and life experiences. All the examples that follow in this book are taken from art therapy contexts, rather than the personal material I have presented here. This personal discourse on my own ongoing experience with the children closest to me and their art is intended to provide a baseline of understanding for the art expressions that follow.

Chapter 1

Children and Adolescents in Schools

Art therapist's reaction to work with a threatening teenage boy. *(Reprinted from* The Arts in Psychotherapy, *Vol. 24, No. 2, A. Coseo, Developing cultural awareness for creative arts therapists, pp. 145–147, copyright ©1997, with permission from Elsevier Science.)*

Leroy dips his brush in the blue tempera and adds the finishing touches to his star next to the yellow crescent moon and the pitchforks. Then he scrawls Big Man, *his gang name, across the bottom. (He's bigger than the other kids in junior high.) He steps back from the easel and smiles his patchy grin—his two front teeth have been knocked out. He asks the art therapist if he can hang his picture on the wall, but she tells him that he knows he can't hang up gang art. Leroy had hoped that José would see it when he comes to art therapy next period. He folds his picture and stuffs it in his pocket. He'll make sure José sees it anyway, just to let him know whose turf this school is.*

Art therapists see children in many different kinds of schools, but for the most part in special schools for children who are having difficulties. Often these are children who have been unable to progress in schools for the general population due to behavior disorders, Attention Deficit Disorder, delinquency, poor impulse control, and various emotional problems. Less frequently, art therapists are hired to work in public schools with problem children there.

Working in a school system can provide a treatment stability that often is not found in other settings. Hospitalizations tend to be short, whether for psychiatric or physical conditions. Although outpatient work in clinics is potentially of longer duration, parents may become threatened by a child's treatment that they perceive is implicating them as causal agents or that may upset the family homeostasis. As a result, they may remove the child before treatment is completed. Another gratifying aspect of work in schools is that most often children are happy to come to art therapy as a welcome relief from their schoolwork. Most enjoy making art, and some feel special in being selected to have art therapy.

Found Objects in Public School

Anita Yeh conducted art therapy in a city public school in which a majority of the students were of Hispanic descent and from economically disadvantaged families. This school is one of the few in the city with an established art therapy program that is separate physically and organizationally from the school's art classes. The art therapists (a full-time professional and a student intern) coordinated and planned services with school social workers and collaborated with two local hospital outpatient services. Problems faced by the children with whom Yeh worked included poverty, poor living conditions, family illnesses, loss of a family member, violence, and gang activity. They were referred to art therapy by teachers, counselors, and parents for aggressive behavior, failing grades, and isolation.

The goal of art therapy was to break the cycle of progressively negative patterns in which adverse circumstances provoke undesirable behaviors that elicit negative responses from others, leading to decreased motivation and failure, which, in turn, elicits more negative responses, and the cycle continues. Yeh recognized that the main advantage in incorporating art therapy into the school system is that emotional needs, imagination, fears, and fantasies become a part of the child's learning experience. Using children's creativity helps them to alleviate anxiety, find ways to get their needs met, develop problem-solving skills, express aggression safely, and have their expression of feeling understood and accepted nonjudgmentally.

In addition to using conventional art therapy methods with the children, Yeh discovered that they enjoyed creating with found objects. In *Exploring the Lost and Found: The Use of Found Objects in Art Therapy* (Yeh, 1997), she states, "I have always been intrigued by the items I find, things left behind, forgotten, or discarded by others" (p. 3). She believes that the transformative process of applying personal meaning and changing the emotional value of a found object can affect a child's self-concept and feelings of self-esteem. The transformation of something that already exists in concrete form from unwanted to worthy parallels changing the self in a similar direction. The found object can be a metaphor for the self that is changed through creative enhancement.

Yeh saw the children in twice-weekly individual sessions. Length of treatment was determined by progress, although most were seen throughout the school year. She asked them to bring items from home or things they found elsewhere. She also supplied two boxes of objects she collected, which were kept in two lockers outside the art therapy room. The children were invited to search the lockers for anything they would like to use. The children preferred searching the lockers to bringing in their own found objects. The emotional safety of the art therapy room and having the art therapist serve as witness to the search was more conducive to finding objects than searching elsewhere alone. Only one child brought in an object from home, although several talked about doing so.

Tony was an 11-year-old sixth-grader who used found objects as a vehicle for play. During the past year he had experienced a number of deaths in his family and was referred to art therapy for poor grades and misconduct. As Yeh walked him from his classroom to the art therapy room, he habitually complained of invisible sores and hurts. In his fourth session, he decided to build a birdhouse from precut, five-inch-square pieces of plywood. Constructing a box took the entire session. At the next session, he complained of being sick and did not want to make art. Nevertheless, he retrieved his box and said that he wanted to find a treasure for it. Yeh said that he didn't have to make art; he could go on a treasure hunt instead. He spent the rest of the session searching the found-object boxes and stopped complaining of feeling bad. His voice took on a playful tone as he chose several small animals for his box. As he placed the objects in the box with its open side toward himself (Figure 1.1), he identified them with various emotions: "The snake is scary, everyone is afraid of him. The clowns are afraid and frightened. And the mouse is afraid" (p. 13). Tony hung the tiger on the outside to be the night guard, and the duck on the top of the box would "take over and guard in the morning." Tony carefully placed his box on the shelf at the end of the session, positioning it in such a way that its contents would be hidden.

FIGURE 1.1 Found-object construction by 11-year-old boy.

The door to the art therapy room usually remained open several inches, but Tony had closed it when working on his box. During the next several sessions, he made another art piece and did not close the door, but did so again when he took out his box at his eighth session. This time he was even more playful with the objects. He sang songs and draped himself with beaded necklaces and lace. He found a key in the found-objects box and pretended to unlock cabinets in the room. Then he used it on the lid of the found-objects container and sang, "Unlock the magic!" Fantasy used in this way allows a child to imagine being able to cope with fears. Yeh was reminded of what Simic (1992) wrote of Robert Cornell's art, which is also comprised of collections of objects in boxes:

> A toy is a trap for dreamers. These are dreams that a child would know. Dreams in which objects are renamed and invested with imaginary lives that is what Cornell is after too. How to construct a vehicle of reverie, an object that would enrich the imagination of the viewer and keep him company forever. (p. 44)

Jerry, a 10-year-old Hispanic fourth-grader who was small for his age and cute and innocent looking, used found objects as a self-representation. His referral indicated that he needed constant supervision because he often provoked his classmates to anger and that he had difficulty verbalizing thoughts and feelings. In gluing together a small assemblage, he used a fuzzy bird, plastic eyes, and a cup, among several other objects. He said, "These eyes are watching and this cute little bird is pecking at them. It's small, cute, and it's fuzzy like me" (p. 16). In previous pictures, he had drawn birds that he described as mad and angry. Jerry tried to stuff gold tinsel into the small cup that was glued to his art piece, but the uncooperative nature of the material caused it to keep popping out as he tried to control it.

At his next session, Jerry was very intent on looking for something in the lockers. He let out a gasp when he discovered a large bundle of gold tinsel. He suggested decorating the room with it and chose a spot where it would catch the light from the window but could be seen only if one entered the room. Six- or seven-foot lengths of the tinsel were hung with the excess curled and draped on the floor. It was overwhelming and uncontrolled. Yeh quotes my work (Wadeson, 1987) in which I describe large art that can be impressive and overwhelming and small work that can be delicate and tentative. She states that both these kinds of attributes applied to Jerry's artwork. He had given the unruly tinsel of his first found-object piece full reign in the panel of hanging tinsel. At the next session, however, he quietly knelt down in front of the wall of bright, glittering tinsel and gently began to handle it. He then took the scissors and trimmed it so that it would not drag on the floor (Figure 1.2). Carefully he put the trimmings in a bag and tied it securely shut. A week later, Jerry announced that his family was moving and that he would no longer be attending this school. Although he could take any of his art with him that he wished, he chose only his small found-object piece. His tinsel wall remained hanging in the art therapy room. His working with the tinsel was a metaphor for his need for control.

(For further examples of art therapy in the public schools, see the work by

FIGURE 1.2   Tinsel panel by 10-year-old boy.

Leslie DeVera with adolescents around issues of ethnic pride in Chapter 9, "Displaced Persons." In the same chapter is work by Sue Lee on acculturation issues for adolescents born in Korea, though she saw them outside of school.)

Special Schools

The Education for All Children Act (Public Law 94-142), passed in 1975, guarantees all children the right to free and appropriate education, regardless of disabilities. Emotional and behavioral disabilities defined under this law include the following:

- An inability to learn that cannot be explained by intellectual, sensory, health, cultural, or linguistic factors
- An inability to develop or maintain satisfactory interpersonal relationships with peers and adults
- Inappropriate types of behavior or feelings under ordinary circumstances
- A pervasive mood of unhappiness, anxiety or depression
- A tendency to develop physical symptoms or fears associated with personal or school problems

A child exhibiting any of these problems for at least 6 months to the degree that the child's academic performance is adversely affected qualifies under this act. The 6-month time period may be waived if the behaviors exhibited are a danger to the self or others. Special public schools and programs have been developed to provide appropriate education for students who are considered emotionally or behaviorally disabled according to the act. Art therapy can be a valuable component of these programs.

Collage

Monique Prohaska developed an art therapy program for an alternative public special education day program for severely emotionally and behaviorally disabled students in grades 5 through 12. Referrals originate from the students' home school districts. The goals of the program are to increase self-esteem, motivation to learn, and self-control. Prohaska worked with adolescents who had suffered trauma and were afraid of exposing their vulnerabilities and weaknesses. Most suffered low self-esteem, and it was rare for them to experience a sense of accomplishment or pride. In order to overcome their resistance to creating a piece of art or revealing themselves, Prohaska introduced them to magazine collage (Prohaska, 1999). Students were seen in twice-weekly individual sessions. They used images and words from magazines to create self-collages, self-boxes, and body tracings. As they became more trusting and confident, they used other materials as well, including plaster, glitter, sponges, wire, paint, and tissue paper.

Margaret, 17, diagnosed with recurrent Bipolar Disorder with Psychosis, Attention Deficit Hyperactivity Disorder (ADHD), and learning delay, was referred by her homeroom teacher. She was on Ritalin, Depakote, and Risperdal to control her verbal and physical outbursts. As the only female in her class, she distanced herself from her peers and sat close to the teacher. At her first art therapy session, she was hyperactive, speaking rapidly and twirling her long hair around her fingers. She calmed down as Prohaska played some soft music in the background. Margaret made marker drawings of broken hearts, tears, and dead flowers with little comment. She was frustrated with her drawings, which she felt looked wrong. Nevertheless, she liked coming to art therapy because the sessions made her feel important. At her eighth session, she asked about the stacks of magazines. Prohaska suggested a magazine collage. With exuberance, Margaret cut frantically for the entire time. She could hardly wait for the next session to put her selections together. At the next session, she created her self-collage with words, faces, animals, flowers, and couples. She said, "I felt creative and liked using the different pictures and words to show how I felt. It was easier for me to focus on the collage because I wasn't so worried about how it looked" (p. 12). Prohaska commented to Margaret that she noticed a change in her demeanor and that she found her picture quite expressive.

Next she created a self-box (Figure 1.3). Up until then, she had rarely discussed personal issues and had spoken of relationships only superficially. While creating her inner self in the inside of the box, she expressed many of her hurts and spoke of them. She said she was ostracized because others saw her as crazy and a freak. On the outside she used words and symbols to convey that she had to put on a show to get others to accept her. Prohaska encouraged her to continue making art so that together they could understand her insecurities. Margaret replied that she felt lucky to have art therapy at school because it made her feel cared for.

After this session, Margaret took collage a step further. She made a body tracing (Figure 1.4). She painted in the clothes with the colors she was wearing. She wanted the tracing hung at eye level so she could look herself in the face. She stared at it and said that she couldn't believe it was herself. The next day, she grabbed magazines and cut out photos and words to glue on her portrait. Standing eye to eye with it, she smacked the photos and words in and around her figure, shouting, "*Yes!*" She said, "Sometimes when I smacked the picture, it was like giving myself a high-five. I felt confident, and I thought about some things I'm proud of, like wanting to go to college and being a nice person. Other times I guess I was angry and mad about all the things I'm bad at, like not being smart." She then listed her other failures. She began to understand the origins of her self-criticism and related her critical inner voice to people who had disappointed her, especially her mother, and realized that she herself was responsible for changing how she felt about herself.

FIGURE 1.3   Self-box by 17-year-old girl.

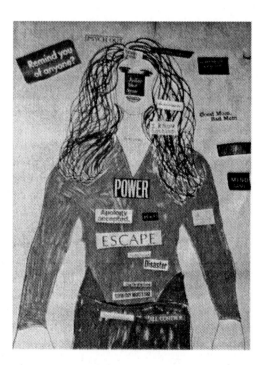

FIGURE 1.4   Body tracing by 17-
year-old girl.

After the school's winter break, Margaret became more talkative and out-going with other students. She smiled more and volunteered for school activities. At her first art therapy session after the break, she made a collage using feathers, glitter, paint, and tissue paper, rather than magazine images and words. She indicated that this collage represented her courage to take chances, such as visiting colleges, expressing how she felt to others, and keeping a daily journal in which she wrote poetry to learn more about herself. She described it as "feeling lighter . . . beginning a journey to the unknown, but feeling good about it . . . accomplishing goals if I put my mind to it" (p. 16). Through the course of art therapy, Margaret expressed herself more and more openly, and felt trusting of Prohaska. It is obvious that in addition to the facilitating function of magazine collage, Margaret's growth was supported by her sense that Prohaska cared for and valued her.

Franklin, 15, diagnosed with learning delay and an emotional and behavioral disability, had difficulty forming relationships. He was quiet and withdrawn, appearing very unhappy. His first sessions were spent in exploring the art materials, but he seemed very disinterested in them. At his fifth session, Prohaska suggested a self-collage. He used only words, most of them highly negative. Since he liked words, Prohaska suggested he write some stories to go with them. He continued making collages and started using pictures. He talked about the people in them, but did not relate them to himself. He enjoyed coming to art therapy and asked Prohaska if she would see him for the whole year. At his twelfth session he created a collage of feelings he had but didn't know how to express (Figure 1.5). He said that they looked mostly sad and mad. At the next session, when Prohaska took out his collage and asked him what made him sad or mad, he said, "Nobody cares about me at school. That makes me mad. The only person who cares is you because every Tuesday and Wednesday at eleven o'clock in the morning you bring me to art therapy and you're here. My social worker doesn't do that" (p. 20).

Franklin revealed more of the sources of his unhappiness and began experimenting with other art materials. He asked about the rolls of plaster gauze. He wanted to make a mask from a mold. He asked for Prohaska's help, another step on his road to building trust. At the next session he painted it and began assembling collage pictures he had set aside. He applied white glitter to the mask and cut a sponge in half for the ears. After gluing blue wires to the head for hair and centering it on his collage, he titled it *The Invisible Man*. Franklin explained that the pictures surrounding the face could be the invisible man's thoughts. He spoke of finding being laughed at painful. Using collage in art therapy enabled Franklin to come out of his shell, express his feelings, and even experiment with new art forms, such as his mask-collage.

Robert, a Hispanic 16-year-old who was diagnosed with Depressive Disorder and possible Attention Deficit Disorder (ADD), was considered emotionally and behaviorally disordered. He was medicated with Depakote, which slowed his impulsive aggression, and Albuterol for asthma. Although he could

FIGURE 1.5   Collage by 15-year-old boy.

work cooperatively with others, at times he became verbally and physically aggressive. In his first art therapy session, he threw away his drawing. His frustration mounted as he tried a second drawing. Prohaska suggested a self-collage to ease his frustration and showed him the collage box with precut magazine photos and words. Robert enjoyed choosing pictures and gluing them in place. At the next session, Prohaska took out his collage and asked him which picture caught his eye. He said it was the gun, and as he described the other pictures he spoke of the lack of control in his life (Figure 1.6). The bottle represents the drugs he takes, and the gun is pointing to the screaming man. At the next several sessions, Robert talked about his collage further. He felt like screaming, he said, because of the way his father made him feel. To explore their relationship, Prohaska suggested that he divide a piece of paper in half and make one side represent his father and the other himself. He chose to use collage again (Figure 1.7). He worked on his father's side first and searched for another screaming man because, he said, that's what his father did. On his own side was a large boxing glove. As he described his side, his anger grew. His father would repeatedly tell him he had no future, did not work hard enough, was lazy, and wasn't smart. The boxing glove represented Robert's wish to fight back. Prohaska told him that in art therapy he could fight back. Together they wrapped his fist in red tissue paper like the boxing glove, and he pounded his father's side of the picture with it. As he did it, he proclaimed, "I'm not stupid! I'm a good person! I am something!" (p. 28). Robert's insights from his col-

**FIGURE 1.6   Collage by 16-year-old boy showing
lack of control in his life.**

lages helped him to deal with his anger. He felt he was getting a lot out of art therapy and asked to continue for the school year.

These three examples illustrate how collage work in art therapy was able to help resistant special education students explore themselves and deal with disturbing feelings and maladaptive behavior. Margaret explored issues of self-esteem and her inner critic, leading to increased confidence and less withdrawal. Franklin came out of his shell and built a trusting relationship. Robert dealt with his anger.

Electively Mute Children

Elective mutism is a rare disorder. Although it seems only logical that nonverbal solutions be tried for nonverbal problems, art therapy has been used very little to treat this condition. Cheryl Koenig conducted art therapy with three such children at a therapeutic day school (Koenig, 1992). The school served

FIGURE 1.7   Collage by 16-year-old boy showing his relationship with his father.

children who were diagnosed with behavior disorders, emotional disturbances, autism, autism-like disorders, communicative disorders, and mental disabilities. These were all problems that precluded the children's attending public school, and the primary goals were to promote social and emotional growth to enable the children to reenter the public school system. Koenig saw the children in weekly individual 30-minute art therapy sessions throughout the school year. The art provided a way for them to communicate on their own terms without pressure to speak.

Todd was a 12-year-old boy who began speaking at a normal age, but only to his mother. He was diagnosed electively mute upon entering first grade at age 7. His mother was overprotective and overwhelming, doing everything for him, including undressing him for baths. Although he currently spoke to her in a clear voice, he did not respond to his father, though he sometimes initiated conversation with him in a low, raspy whisper. He also used this whisper when asked to respond in class. Todd exhibited motor tension and anxiety in shortness of breath and avoidance of eye contact. His initial drawings were constricted and controlled, usually small and detailed. His sculptures were made by carefully measuring and cutting pieces of clay perfectly to size. After a month, he made a puppet out of an empty towel roll, giving it an angry, fanged face. This spontaneous creation caused him to smile, and he began to experiment more. He became extremely protective of his artwork and would leave nothing in the art room, even when his piece was wet with paint. His art projects had become important to him. Along with his puppet, other valuable pieces were a three-dimensional secret place and a book with pictures of planets.

After two months, changes began to occur. Close to Halloween, Todd painted a picture of a pumpkin with the recurring angry, fanged face, but this time grinning. His work was becoming much more expressive. His use of the fluid tempera paints was much less constricted than in his early work. At the next session, he whispered his first words to Koenig, asking to use some plastic gemstones he noticed in someone else's sculpture. To encourage further communication, Koenig suggested that they also play a passing game, in which they took turns drawing on a picture. She drew a tree and the ground, and he drew the sun, clouds, and a rainbow. She drew a dinosaur on the right, and he asked her to draw another. Then he asked her to draw teeth and angry eyes on the dinosaur on the left to make it look mean. He also asked her to make two baby dinosaurs. From this session on, Todd increased his verbal interaction with Koenig, and he appeared less anxious. His classroom teacher reported a similar increase in verbalization and interaction with others. Todd felt positive about his art and often wanted to take his projects home. His relationship with Koenig continued to grow, as he talked to her more, made eye contact, and brought things from home to show her. Allowing Todd to proceed at his own pace, experimenting when he was ready, provided him a safe place for self-expression. His communication increased significantly throughout the school year.

Tracie was an 8-year-old girl whose impoverished family lived in cramped quarters. Her refusal to speak began in kindergarten after a pattern of normal speech development. At 7 she was diagnosed with elective mutism and was enrolled in the special school. Tracie appeared withdrawn and depressed, with poor hygiene. She spoke to her mother and selected siblings, but seldom in class. Unlike Todd, Tracie enjoyed getting messy. Although she would arrive at art therapy withdrawn, the art making relaxed her, and she would leave smiling, often jumping playfully down the stairs. Koenig suggested that she build a special place for herself, and Tracie spent the next 4 months working on it (Figure 1.8). She painted die-cut wooden people and placed them inside, sometimes moving them around. She wrote about her house and folded the paper and put it inside her house. Later, she glued it to the outside. At this session, when asked how many sisters and brothers she had, she answered Koenig for the first time using words instead of holding up fingers.

Renae, 14, had normal speech development until age 3, when her talking began to decrease. In second grade, she was placed in a classroom for children with learning disabilities. The family moved, and her mutism increased dramatically. Although undiagnosed, her mother was suspected of having a psychological disorder, staying in bed most of the time, acting childish, and expressing paranoid fears. Renae appeared isolated, withdrawn, and depressed. Nevertheless, she had recently begun speaking to her teachers and therapists, and spoke to Koenig in their first session. Renae explained the mask she drew as being half man and half woman, possessed by a demon

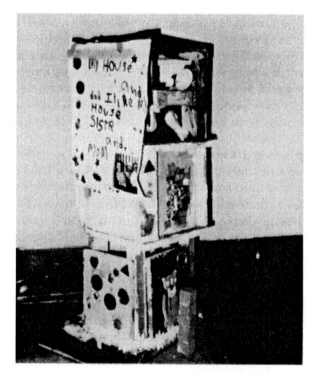

FIGURE 1.8   Special place for herself built by
8-year-old electively mute girl.

from hell. Its pronounced mouth appeared to be related to her obsession with food. She was always hungry and frequently asked Koenig to buy her food. All the figures she drew had grimacing faces. A common theme in her art was her anger. She often wondered about her mother's mental illness and questioned whether she, too, was mentally ill. After some time, however, she became less invested in her artwork and more withdrawn. She was not participating in the classroom and appeared more depressed. Her preoccupations and disorganized thoughts caused her diagnosis to be changed from elective mutism to schizophrenia. The art making provided her with an outlet for the outpouring of feelings that were surfacing.

From her work with these children, Koenig observed that there were strong feelings beneath their masks of being mute and that not speaking gave them power and control over those with whom they communicated. The art therapy allowed them to express themselves on their own terms.

Gangs

For the many neglected children whose parents are lost to poverty, drugs, crime, and imprisonment, gangs become their surrogate families. There they can find protection, identity, pride, camaraderie, and a sense of belonging. Unfortunately, they also find blind adherence to a rigid set of values and behavior, a warlike stance in the world, brutality, and violence. Their lives are filled with constant threats, real and imagined, to which they respond with assertions of power, symbolic and physical.

Kathy Neely endured a baptism by fire in her initiation into work at an alternative day school for children with behavioral and emotional disorders and adolescents who had been expelled from the public school system for unmanageable behavior. Most were gang-affiliated (Neely, 1984). As part of a larger urban social agency, the school provided weekly therapy sessions and milieu therapy activities to enable students to return to public school. Most, however, stayed at the school until age 18, when they dropped out. A few chose to remain until age 21. Located in an impoverished, crime-ridden, inner-city neighborhood, the school was poorly equipped, the heating in some of the rooms did not work, and there was frequent staff turnover. The student body consisted of 25 African American students and one Caucasian, mostly male. Neely found herself unable to understand their black dialect. More than half the students exhibited aggressive, acting-out behavior, while the rest were withdrawn. They had histories of repeated failures in the school system, having assaulted teachers or thrown furniture. Most were diagnosed with learning disabilities and had IQs between 75 and 85. Many had arrest records and came from multiple-problem families. Most of the mothers received public financial assistance, and the fathers were absent. The children were characterized by poor peer relations, low self-esteem, academic difficulty, problems with authority, depression, aggressive behavior, fighting, and stealing. Diagnoses included Conduct Disorder, Attention Deficit Disorder, Schizoid Disorder of childhood, and adjustment reaction to childhood. Half had not been clinically diagnosed.

As soon as Neely established an art therapy schedule, she met hard-core resistance. The most resistant students simply did not attend the sessions. Sometimes she followed them all over the building, with teachers and staff joining in, to no avail. Sometimes they would show up in her room after she had given up. Neely felt it was necessary to lay out some basic ground rules to ensure safety: no harming themselves or each other or each other's artwork; no mishandling the art materials. Much of the resistance took the form of disobeying the rules. As a result, instead of making the art room safe, the rules encouraged power struggles between the students and Neely. Resistance in the artwork took the form of gang imagery. Although many schools forbid students to depict gang symbols, Neely recognized that the gang culture was an important part of these children's lives. To prevent gang imagery would have been to reject some part of their identities, she felt. In the beginning, when she was just getting to know the kids and their culture, they could become her teachers in informing her about their pictures.

The school was chaotic and frequent fights broke out, particularly when older boys picked on younger ones. This happened often since the age groups weren't separated because of the lack of space caused by malfunctioning heating. The art therapy sessions were also chaotic, reflecting the general atmosphere of the school. Neely was constantly tested and found it almost impossible to enforce her simple rules for the art room. Physical restraint was often the only recourse, and many of the boys were bigger than she was.

Eddie and Gary, both 13, asked to come to art therapy the first week. They both painted gang pictures. Eddie's picture showed the moon and a five-pointed star, his gang's symbols, to which he added the sun and a car. Since the boys belonged to opposing gangs, the pictures could have been either a direct status threat or a simple assertion of identity. Gary's picture was similar, but it was subsequently destroyed by another student. Eddie talked about "kicking white people's asses" and said, "We hate white people." When Neely confronted him by asking their reaction to her being white, he said, "You're not white; you're black" (p. 10). Eddie was testing her, but asserting that she was black allowed him to save face and not have to back off from his assertion. The issue of race came up repeatedly. When it was time to clean up, Eddie cooperated, but Gary became obstinate. Not until they left did Neely discover they had left the rubber cement turned upside-down without the lid and had painted *G-Dog*, Gary's gang name, in three-foot-tall letters in the bathroom.

Tony was disruptive by defacing the drawings of the other students. Only when Neely got sufficiently angry to grab him and reprimand him did he become frightened and leave the room as she had requested. Her show of anger and strength had caught him off guard. The next day, he returned, sat down, and drew a fluid, abstract pastel drawing. For the first time he was able to talk about what was on his mind, though in a defensive and abusive way—sex and intimacy. He needed to know that Kathy could control the situation and protect him from himself and the havoc he could wreak before he felt safe enough to draw and talk about what was bothering him.

Neely saw Latroy and Gary together for regular art therapy sessions. Their backgrounds were relatively typical of gang-affiliated kids who cannot function in the public school system. Latroy, 11, lived with his mother, who was on public aid. He was hospitalized for illness and a car accident as a preschooler. At that time, he was so hyperactive and aggressive that his mother kept him away from the neighborhood children, sometimes locking him in the bathroom. He repeated first grade three times. He was expelled from public school for walking on a second-story ledge there, as well as repeated fighting and hyperactivity. He also beat his younger brother with a blunt instrument, tipped over the baby's crib, and poured gasoline on a cat. His IQ was tested to be low normal, and he was found to have problems with visual and motor integration. Projective tests showed a conception of parental figures as punitive and nonnurturing, and he saw his environment as barren and lacking comfort. After expulsion from school, his mother kept him home for a year and a half until his admission to the day school. He was diagnosed with Conduct Disorder and Attention Deficit Disorder. In individual art therapy, Neely had to limit his sessions to 30 minutes due to his hyperactivity. He habitually destroyed his artwork and that of others. Often he felt he had "messed up."

Gary was a husky 13-year-old who often was sullen and moody. He lived with his mother, who had given birth to him at age 14. She was on public aid. In the past 2 years he had lived with his mother's parents and a friend. Gary had been close to his grandfather, who had died some years earlier. Gary reported hearing his voice at times. Gary was diagnosed with Conduct Disorder and later with Schizoid Disorder of childhood. He had a history of running away, usually to his grandmother's house, and of setting fires. His mother described him as always overactive and "just plain evil" (p. 47). He was hospitalized at age 9 for running away, setting fires, breaking into cars, and fighting, all without remorse. Projective tests showed sadness and fear, and violence and lack of control were major themes. When his diagnosis was changed to Schizoid Disorder, his evaluation showed depression, anxiety, and lack of object constancy. Projection and denial were cited as his defenses. He had been expelled from four other schools, including a therapeutic school, before coming to the day school. Gary continued to have problems with enuresis. He was physically and verbally abusive, and Neely found him intimidating.

One day both boys came to the art room and made a picture together. Neely was impressed that they both behaved better together than they did individually, so she decided to schedule art therapy for them together. In an early session, they clamored to make plaster gauze masks. Latroy applied the plaster strips carefully to Gary's face, inventing a scenario in which Gary was in the hospital for a critical condition. Tony knocked on the door, and Gary opened it despite Neely's request that he not do so. With the wet mask still on his face, Gary and Latroy ran out to show the other students. The mask suffered in the expedition.

At another session, Latroy made a large painting of pitchforks extending downward from a central heart. In gang culture, this is called "throwing forks down," which constitutes a status threat to a member of an opposing gang. Gary threatened Latroy when he noticed the forks, and Latroy quickly changed them to arrows (Figure 1.9). Near the end of the session, Latroy's behavior deteriorated, and he painted on his skin. When he went into the bathroom to wash it off, he let the sink overflow. While the boys were cleaning up in the bathroom after another session, they went wild. When Neely went in to intervene, they locked her in the bathroom. Another disruptive session occurred when Eddie asked to join the group. The boys chose to work in ink, a medium coveted by gang members for homemade tattoos. Using ink quickly degenerated into jabbing each other with pens and defacing each other's artwork. Neely had to intervene to remove the materials. They began painting gang symbols on a wall mural, a large sheet of paper Neely left on the wall for anyone to use at any time in order to deescalate potential fights. She hoped it would be an outlet for aggressive impulses. Soon Eddie and Gary began to fight over their different gang representations. Latroy goaded them on. Then he made the bathroom sink overflow again.

FIGURE 1.9   Gang symbols by 11-year-old boy.

By this time, Neely was at her wits' end. Like many others working with this population, she was putting most of her effort into just trying to keep the peace. She had instigated rules to create safety so that therapy could take place. But the rules seemed to invite conflict, which then demanded disciplinary action, sometimes physically. These interventions were usually ineffective anyway. It struck her that safety was foreign to this population. Pretending to offer safety, she realized, was to base her therapy on a lie, since she was unable to provide the safety she had hoped for. If the boys were going to fight in the art room, she was no longer going to try to prevent it. She would try to help them to explore what was going on. She felt she had hit bottom and would change the meaningless rules to accepted anarchy to set the stage for constructive rebuilding.

Neely consulted Gail Wirtz, who had worked in a similar school (see Chapter 5 for her work with families). Wirtz suggested a token economy. Instead of punishing the boys, Neely inaugurated a reward system with points. Each point earned a piece of candy at the end of the session, with a possibility of earning 5 points per session. Ten points earned a Polaroid picture Neely would take of the student, which he could keep. This reward had the advantage of teaching the students to delay gratification and gave them visual feedback about their appearance. Points could be earned for the following behaviors:

- Coming to the art room promptly with good behavior
- Participating in the art activity

- Cleaning up
- Following the rules (2 points)

The rules were determined by the students themselves, thus making them responsible for helping to establish the therapeutic framework. They assessed their own behavior and reported on their own points at the end of the session. The students simply needed an incentive to control themselves. In my own work with adolescents, I have found that such tokens can also be a face-saving device. For two adolescent groups on a psychiatric unit, the members could choose to sign up or not after a trial period. All chose to remain in the hour-and-a-half sessions and cooperated fully, saying that they did so for the ginger ale we served during the break (Wadeson, 1980).

Gary and Latroy established the following rules: no fighting, no going into Neely's desk, no destroying others' artwork. They chose to work in pastels, and both made sad-looking faces suggested by a drawing Neely had made and hung on the wall after a bad day. Latroy drew Figure 1.10, and Gary made Figure 1.11, speaking about his grandfather's death. Both pictures are more expressive than anything they had done previously. At the next session, the boys came to the art room without having to be fetched. They drew pictures of Ironman (Figure 1.12, by Gary). They discussed whether Ironman had feelings and what he was like underneath his mask. Superhero drawings continued the identity theme that can also be seen in the gang drawings. The cartoonlike style shows the importance of hiding emotions, being cool, and maintaining a defended and threatening posture. Nevertheless, Ironman's facial expression is one of pain.

FIGURE 1.10   Sad face by 11-year-old boy.

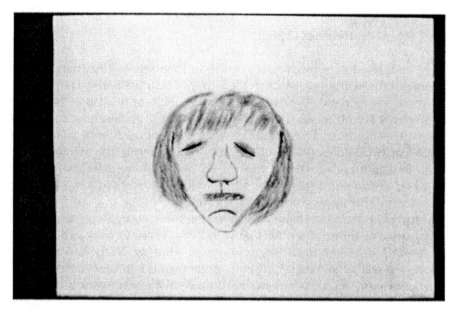

FIGURE 1.11   Sad face by 13-year-old boy.

FIGURE 1.12   *Ironman* by 13-year-old boy.

For these students with learning disabilities, for whom school can be very frustrating, art expression can be valuable, and the art room can be one place where success is possible and pride and self-esteem can be fortified. Defended gang art alternated with more open work, with the issue of identity usually the focus. Provoking teachers and therapists by showing their hostility and disrupting the general milieu—in other words, showing themselves at their worst—is one way for these students to test the staying power of caring people. If an adult can get through it all and still care, then perhaps there is the possibility for trust.

These children, who are among the most difficult to treat, pose the greatest threats to our society. Coming as they do from backgrounds of neglect, drugs, violence, and crime, they are the future generation of adults who will perpetuate what they have learned if interventions are not made. Schools for these youths provide our society's greatest opportunity and greatest challenge for change. Unfortunately, most of these youths receive too little too late. Art therapy can certainly play a part in making interventions, but a significant transformation will take much more than the work of a few dedicated therapists. A concerted societal effort is needed to break the cycle that afflicts the young people of our cities' poverty-ridden communities. (For art therapy with an adult with a significant gang history, see Vickie Polin's work in Chapter 11, "Sexual Abuse.")

Art Therapists' Self-Processing

Anne Coseo worked at a school with a student population similar to Kathy Neely's students. Like Neely, Coseo is a Caucasian middle-class young woman. This was her first experience in an African American environment. The therapeutic day school served 60 children, ages 5 to 18, who had severe emotional and behavioral disturbances. The goal of the school was to enable the child to remain in a family setting within the community while making gains to return to public school. Many of the children had neurological impairments; others had experienced physical and sexual abuse, neglect, and abandonment by their families. They exhibited developmental delays, Attention Deficit Disorder, hyperactivity, Conduct Disorder, autism, and learning disabilities. Approximately 80% were male, and 95% were African American. Art therapy referrals came from the clinical director, teachers, and social workers. Anne met with the children weekly in both group and individual art therapy sessions.

Having grown up in an all-white community, Coseo realized it was necessary for her to address her own cultural biases in working with this population (Coseo, 1997). She notes that therapists may impose their belief systems onto their clients through their own stereotypes and prejudices, whether consciously or unconsciously. This sort of cultural countertransference can negatively impact treatment. Most art therapists come from white, middle-class backgrounds, yet many treat various ethnic groups from disadvantaged communities, such as those with whom Coseo worked. As training programs are beginning to stress, cultural awareness, including examining one's own pre-conceptions, is essential for effective therapeutic relationships.

Coseo kept a visual sketchbook to log potent feelings and attitudes stimulated by her clients. Since she had little time between sessions, she often made quick sketches right after a particularly disturbing session. When issues or images recurred in her sketchbook or when they had a puzzling cultural content, she made larger mixed-media renditions to explore them at greater depth. She often combined oil pastels, acrylic paint, and chalk pastels with photocopies from magazines. To organize her exploration, she focused on three areas:

- She examined her experiences and beliefs about African Americans, including those communicated to her by her family, community, the media, and society at large.
- She read literature on African American culture, including similarities and differences between it and white mainstream cultural experiences.
- She tied the information together with her current clinical experiences.

Coseo tried to separate her current reactions to clients from responses previously learned from her culture. Michael, a large 13-year-old, is an example. With a history of violence and aggression, he was placed in the school for severe emotional and learning disabilities. He was referred to art therapy for impulsivity, low frustration tolerance, difficulty relating to others, and trouble expressing his feelings. Initially, he was friendly and cooperative, but became more demanding and was often hostile. He grabbed a pair of plastic scissors, which he stabbed into his stomach, yelling that he was going to kill himself. As Coseo walked him back to his classroom, he threatened her by coming very close with clenched fists and acting as though he was going to attack her. Although she remained calm, inside she was terrified. Several hours later, she was still panic-stricken and did not understand her powerful response. Still shaken, she had no idea what she would do when she sat down to draw. The result is the picture on page 21, which shocked and horrified her. She saw it as half human and half animal. Sharp scissors and knives project from the female-looking face, and fangs protrude from the lips. Hands and claws rest against her cheeks, and a collar binds her wrists. Coseo's first association was fear. That is what she had felt when Michael stabbed himself with the scissors and threatened her on the way to his classroom. She realized this was a feeling she had toward African Americans in general, that from her childhood she had been taught that they were dangerous, cunning, and violent. Many people in the white, middle-class suburb of Detroit in which she had been raised blamed African Americans for the city's high crime rate. They regarded African Americans as having aggressive, animal-like impulses. Like the creature in her picture, the only way to control them was seen to be by chaining or confining them. Coseo notes that from slavery in previous centuries to institutional racism today, African Americans have experienced many forms of control by the white American society. Coupled with her fear of Michael was Coseo's need to control him. She realized that he stirred up some embedded feelings and attitudes she carried toward blacks. This recognition helped her to reduce her anxiety in his presence by reminding herself that part of her intense reaction was coming from her fear of African American males. Returning to her image, she noticed that the beast looked like herself. Her association was that she, too, was bound—by her beliefs, biases, and prejudices. She felt awkward and unsure about putting racial issues on the table with clients. Her first inclination was often to deny or ignore the racial component of their relationship.

Kenny, an 11-year-old with a long history of abuse and neglect and physical disorders including seizures, bowel problems, and closed head injury, exhibited severe delays in social, cognitive, and communication skills. He had had several foster placements because of his extreme behavior problems. He was referred to individual art therapy for low frustration tolerance, impulsivity, and difficulty with verbal communication. He related to Coseo in a very needy way, hanging onto her arm and asking to be taken to art therapy when she saw him in other areas of the school, needing her to watch him closely during the sessions, and having difficulty leaving. She created her reaction to him in Figure 1.13. Three trees (hands) are reaching toward the sun. They represent Kenny's neediness in his struggle to grasp something unattainable. Coseo felt helpless and impotent in trying to meet his needs. She is represented by the mountain, which sits in a fixed position, unable to lift him to the sun. She realized that the mountain can support the trees, but they must create their own growth to reach the sun. The rings on the hands symbolize marriage for Coseo, the stable family life Kenny did not have. Along with his unstable home life, his head injury, emotional and cognitive delay, and experience of being an African American in a white-dominated society put him up against insurmountable odds, Coseo felt. Although her picture is about Kenny, Coseo realized that it expressed her feelings about the school's population as a whole. She saw the sun as the source of power that controls the trees' growth, just as the white-dominated society controls opportunities for African American people. The mountain also represents cultural barriers, such as stereotypes and prejudices, she brought to therapeutic relationships. She realized that she associated African Americans with welfare and handouts, although her reading had refuted this common misconception. Unfortunately, her belief that African American families tend to be dysfunctional and unstable, often accompanied by abuse, neglect, and drug addiction, was reinforced by the school children's social histories.

Coseo's readings on African American culture pointed out that all ethnic minorities must function in two cultures, their own and the white mainstream culture. This came home to her when one boy accused her of not liking him because he is black. To explore the bicultural experience, Coseo made a picture in which one individual appears torn between two worlds, with bands of color

FIGURE 1.13   Art therapist's response to needy 11-year-old boy. *(Reprinted from* **The Arts in Psychotherapy,** *Vol. 24, No. 2, A. Coseo, Developing cultural awareness for creative arts therapists, pp. 145–147, copyright ©1997, with permission from Elsevier Science.)*

ordered on one side and bending and twisting on the other. The ordered colors represent the white-dominated world, with clearly defined boundaries, rigid structure, and orderly divisions of roles. On the other side, the black experience is represented by blurred boundaries, flexible structure, and intersecting positions. From her readings she had learned that African American families often extend to the community, which is considered family. Family roles are flexible so that emotional, financial, and social support can come from various sources, such as extended family or community members. White family structure usually means the nuclear family. The interdependence of the extended family structure may come into conflict with the dominant culture's emphasis on independence and self-sufficiency.

An art therapy group for girls, age 13 and 14 focused Coseo's attention on communication styles. The group was very verbal, and conversation flowed easily among the members. Coseo, however, had difficulty communicating with them. She noticed how often it was necessary for her to repeat herself or to rephrase what she had said. From her reading, she realized that her difficulties stemmed from differences in African-American and white interaction styles. Figure 1.14 shows her large prominent mouth with a jumble of words issuing forth. Often she felt she was not making sense. Her body is small and restricted. The girls are turning cartwheels. Coseo recognized that the main difference between her communication and theirs was in body language. The four tumbling figures illustrate the importance of body language for them. In

FIGURE 1.14   **Art therapist's reaction to adolescent girls' group.** (*Reprinted from* **The Arts in Psychotherapy,** *Vol. 24, No. 2, A. Coseo, Developing cultural awareness for creative arts therapists, pp. 145–147, copyright ©1997, with permission from Elsevier Science.*)

contrast, highly verbal communication characterizes white interactions. The prominent mouth represents this characteristic, whereas the cut-off, tiny body symbolizes Coseo's lack of body language. As a result of this processing, Coseo began to pay closer attention to the nonverbal dynamics of the group interaction. She incorporated expressive hand movements into her comments, which caused the girls to ask her to repeat herself less often. She also used more facial expression and body movement. For example, she would cross her arms and lean back in her chair or stand up when the group became rowdy. These actions gained the group's attention and allowed her to communicate more fully.

In studying African American culture, Coseo discovered many strengths of which she had not been aware. In her work she hoped to help her clients draw strength from positive feelings about their heritage. Coseo has set an example that many art therapists would be wise to follow, both in examining her own preconceptions about an ethnic minority and in learning as much as she could about that culture. Using art making for our self-processing as art therapists brings to our own heightened self-awareness the same opportunity for self-exploration that we try to provide for our clients. Many examples throughout this book show the different ways of exploration and the different issues art therapists have explored through art made in the service of more fully understanding their work as therapists.

The year before Coseo's experience, Lexi Mitchell worked at the same therapeutic day school. She, too, experienced strong reactions to the children. She wrote poetry in addition to painting to address her countertransference (Mitchell, 1995). Mitchell agrees with Bean (1992) that "the poem, like the dream, realizes 'a knowing' that did not exist before its occurrence. A poem does not know what it is going to say until it says it, so that it is discovered by its own writing" (p. 349). Mitchell found that this was true for her painting, as well. For her, both modes of expression used imagery and metaphor to help bring form out of chaos. After having a session with a child that she found confusing, frightening, or overwhelming, she immediately jotted down words or phrases. Later she would look at the words and think about the session. She would then write a short poem. From the poem she would choose an image that interested her or that she wanted to understand more fully and begin to paint. She used acrylic paints for the layering, covering, and blending that their rich colors allowed.

Darien, a 9-year-old African American boy, sounds very similar to Coseo's description of Kenny. He fought constantly with his classmates, often requiring several adults to restrain him. His life had been chaotic from the start as his mother moved in and out of homes of various friends and acquaintances. In between, they stayed with her mother. There were reports of abuse and neglect. When the two women lived together, they fought over his care. Darien became quite adept at manipulating the situation. Mitchell saw him in individual art therapy sessions. Because his needs had been met so inconsistently, Darien craved the attention and nurturing he received in one-to-one sessions. He felt great anxiety, anger, and fear when sessions were about to end.

At the end of the second session, as they were preparing to leave the room, he yelled at Mitchell that he hated her and grabbed a package of rice cakes from her desk, stuffed one in his mouth, and ran into a corner, alternating between laughing and yelling that he would not go back to his class. She was flooded with feelings so strong and so conflicting that she felt paralyzed. Simultaneously, she experienced fear, anger, shame, hurt, love, and helplessness. She wanted both to punish Darien and to give him everything he needed to fill his hunger (similar to Coseo's feelings of helplessness in relation to satisfying Kenny). Mitchell wrote the following poem:

> You are in the corner, your mouth
> crammed full, your arms flailing,
> hands grasping at crumbs.
> You are giggling stars that
> sparkle and fall, turn to ash, sediment,
> something heavy at your feet.
> And I am before you dancing
> with milk in my hands.

The last two lines of the poem puzzled and intrigued her, so Mitchell painted them to try to understand them further (Figure 1.15). A part of her was in agreement with what Darien seemed to be saying to her, that what she was offering was inadequate. What she had drawn looked more like emptiness in her hands than the rich milk she had attempted to show. She felt anger and shame at witnessing his greediness. The part of herself that wanted to give and to nurture was the part she felt most comfortable with, and that is the only part she has shown in her picture. She began to realize that her anger toward Darien was connected with a part of herself she found unacceptable, her identification with his primitive needs. She wrote a poem to the hungry child within herself:

> You are a red wrinkled creature,
> a small-fisted something,
> a cactus in my soul,
> a word that means impossible.
> Your mouth is open wide,
> your lungs on fire,
> I wish you luck.
> I wish you gone.

Mitchell had hoped for a sense of acceptance from her poem, but it didn't come. In her accompanying painting, she appears to be trying to push the

FIGURE 1.15   Art therapist's image from her
poem about a needy adolescent boy.

baby down (Figure 1.16). When she was able to see the hand on the baby's head as an attempt to soothe the child within, she was better able to integrate her conflicting emotions. In acknowledging the hungry child within herself, she became more tolerant of Darien's needs. As their relationship continued, he became able to trust that she was reliable and able to manage the painful feelings projected into the therapeutic relationship.

Eddie, a 13-year-old African American, was referred to the school for constant fighting and aggression. His mother, a heroin addict since age 16, moved the family in and out of the grandmother's home, where they were abused and neglected. Eddie was beaten regularly and teased about his bed-wetting and about having teeth that protruded from thumb sucking. His mother would disappear for many months at a time with no contact. She had been arrested many times for stealing and for selling drugs, and once for stabbing someone. Eddie was reported as hiding under his bed, sometimes for an entire day, and hitting himself at night to help him get to sleep. He was often cruel to his peers, especially those younger and smaller than himself. In the past year

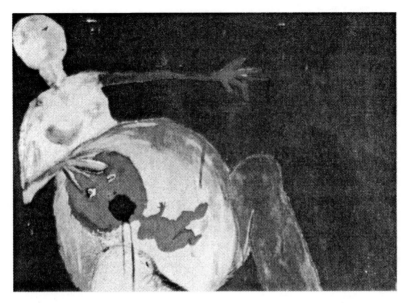

FIGURE 1.16 Art therapist's struggle to be accepting of difficult adolescent boy.

he had assaulted a bus driver, threatened his teacher with a broken bottle, and put his fist through plaster walls several times. Mitchell saw Eddie in individual sessions, where he presented a façade of extreme independence and competence, needing no one. Mitchell had a strong reaction to their first meeting and to reading his case history. She wrote a poem in his voice addressing his mother:

> My heart was cold like yours
> was cold each time you left. You
> delivered your love so directly, straight
> from your hands or the buckle of your belt to
> my head and my back and my heart. Your fists
> held the kinds of promises you could keep.
> I learned to hit myself to sleep and I hid
> And I am hidden still.

Eddie remained distant. Mitchell painted his face (Figure 1.17). She covered it with layers of wax to represent his defensive façade. She returned to the painting and began to scratch and scrape away the layers of wax, becoming aware of the violence contained in her action and the anger that lay behind it. Through her artwork, she became aware of her desire to rip away Eddie's defenses. She had to remind herself that he had built them for good reason and that they should be understood and respected. Although she sometimes

FIGURE 1.17   Art therapist's portrait of defensive adolescent boy.

glimpsed the playful child beneath the defenses, for the most part, Eddie continued to keep her at arm's length. He began to forget her name. His way of relating to her aroused in her a need to protect herself. He had started to try to scare her. He would come up behind her and yell to surprise her, or hide in the closet, or pretend he was going to throw paint at her. He told her about his assaults on other staff members. She found herself subtly withdrawing from him. Again Mitchell wrote a poem in Eddie's voice, this time addressed to herself:

> *If I could make*
> *you jump or wince, if I could make*
> *you dance, if I*
> *could only forget*
> *your name, then*
> *I could know, finally*
> *how they felt*
> *when I have done the same.*

Mitchell realized that by distancing herself she was only confirming Eddie's view of the world as a rejecting place. By writing in Eddie's voice, she was able to better understand his fears and needs. In her continuing work with him, she tried to remain a constant, accepting, empathic presence and to show the genuine positive regard she felt for him.

The combination of words and images was a powerful beacon for Mitchell, throwing light into the dark places of the fears, angers, needs, and vulnerabilities aroused in her through her work with these very difficult, needy, and damaged children.

Summary

Art therapists are called on to work with some of our society's most needy children, occasionally in public schools, but especially in special schools for children who cannot function in the public school system. Often these children have been the victims of neglect, abuse, violence, and crime. Many of the adolescents already have records of arrest. The material presented here includes the following:

- Anita Yeh's (1997) work with found objects in art therapy with children in a public school
- Monique Prohaska's (1999) use of collage in overcoming resistance by adolescents with behavioral disorders. Magazine images were also incorporated in self-boxes and backgrounds for masks (Prohaska, 1999).
- Cheryl Koenig's (1992) art therapy with children diagnosed with elective mutism
- Kathy Neely's (1984) implementation of structure in her work with gang-affiliated youth in a special education day school
- Anne Coseo's (1997) self-processing, through art making, of her own cultural biases that surfaced in her work with African American students in a school for children and adolescents with emotional and behavioral disorders
- Lexi Mitchell's (1995) self-processing, through writing poetry and painting, of her own strong reactions to the students at the same school

Conclusion

Hope is usually to be found in the new generation. Children bring the promise of a better life, a better world. Art therapists more often work with those for whom there is little hope, those who come from such desperate abuse and neglect that they appear doomed to follow in the footsteps of their parents, leading in circles of poverty, addiction, violence, and crime. The hope for a better society lies in changing these patterns. The schools offer us our greatest opportunity to reach these children. Art therapy can bring possibilities for self-expression, success, pride, positive relationships, and creativity. As important as these benefits are, for change to occur there must also be positive interventions in the living conditions and family structures of these children. Art therapy can offer these children part of what they need.

ART THERAPY PROJECTS

Projects discussed in this chapter are described further in Chapter 15, "Art Activities and Materials":

- Found objects (Yeh, 1997)
- Constructions (Yeh, 1997)
- Magazine collage (Prohaska, 1999)
- Self-boxes (Prohaska, 1999)
- Body tracings (Prohaska, 1999)
- Masks (Neely, 1984)
- Mixed media (Coseo, 1997)
- Writing poetry (Mitchell, 1995)

Chapter 2

Children and Adolescents in Psychiatric Hospitalization

Art therapist's attempt to help hopeless 13-year-old girl. *(Reprinted from the* **American Journal of Art Therapy,** *Vol. 33, No. 1, pp. 14–20, by permission of Gladys Agell and Vermont College of Norwich University.)*

Juanita stares at the blank paper before her on the table, but what she is seeing is the knife the art lady uses to cut mat board. The voice telling her to kill herself is more insistent than usual. She knows she is evil. If she weren't, Daddy wouldn't have left. Slowly Juanita draws the knife with the black marker, then she picks up the red and adds blood dripping from it. Now that she has drawn it, she doesn't have to use it. The voice has been silenced. Juanita asks for another piece of paper.

Children and adolescents who are more severely affected by problems similar to those experienced by students in therapeutic schools (described in Chapter 1) may be hospitalized for brief periods until their conditions are stabilized. Often they are in crisis. Shortened hospital stays seldom provide the long-term care that is needed by patients with psychiatric problems, whatever their age. Art therapists working in these settings must limit their goals to what can be accomplished in a week or two.

Brief Treatment

Ruth Evermann, who worked on the psychiatric unit of a major children's hospital where admissions ranged from 7 to 14 days, with few patients staying more than 10 days, found that applying structure to the art activities provided psychotic children with the boundaries needed to help them feel safe (Evermann, 1994). The children ranged in age from 4 to 13. The main purpose of hospitalization was stabilization. Most of the children were on psychotropic medication. They had suffered losses, such as the death of a parent, or abandonment; some had witnessed violent death, some had lived in one or more foster homes, and many were wards of the state.

Evermann spent time with the children outside art therapy in order to get to know them. Based on what she discovered in relating to the individual children, she was challenged to develop unique tasks for each child. She recorded her observations on a task analysis sheet for each art therapy session, using the following form:

1. Observation of the child upon entering
2. Description of task and materials
3. Description of interaction between the child and the art
4. Description of interaction between the child and the therapist
5. Observation of the child at the end of the session
6. Reactions from staff about the child after the session

Karl was a 6-year-old who had been hospitalized for self-destructive behavior following an automobile accident. He lived with his father in a neighborhood that the family considered unsafe. Karl had no friends because he fought with everyone. He had been hospitalized after jumping from a second-story window (he sustained no injuries). He said he had been told to kill himself, but he did not know who had told him. He had a history of sleep disorder, setting fires, and walking on window ledges.

In art therapy, he did not speak to Evermann or look at her. When she asked him to draw a house, he put his head down on his arm and colored the same spot over and over with markers until the ink soaked through the paper. She designed a project with more visible structure and support. She would ask Karl to draw windows and doors on precut house parts, then assemble the house and glue it onto a base, and finally make a tree to put by the house. At the next session, although his affect was flat and he did not appear to look at anything in the room, he immediately began to draw the windows and doors as Evermann had asked. He spent a long time drawing a figure on the house and appeared to be in a trancelike state. Together they folded and glued the parts to assemble the house. Evermann felt that he was beginning to trust her. He scribbled freely to make the leaves for the tree and tore them out and assembled the tree (Figure 2.1). He had seemed to relax. After the session, the charge nurse told Evermann that Karl had communicated real urgency to get back to the art room to get his house. She said that he calmed down after he had retrieved it. Later Evermann and the staff saw Karl throwing his blanket and toys out into the hall. Then he got his house and played with it for the remainder of the quiet time. He began to show his house to staff members and make eye contact with them, even though he remained nonverbal. Evermann said that it was as though he had awakened from a deep sleep. She felt that it had been a good task for Karl. He needed the visual and spatial containment it provided.

FIGURE 2.1   Pre-cut house made by 6-year-old boy.

Since most of the children on the unit refused to draw themselves, Evermann brought in a mirror. At the next session, Karl entered without speaking or making eye contact. Evermann startled him by holding up the mirror, and he established eye contact with her through the mirror. She asked him to touch various parts of his face as he watched his reflection. After doing so, he yelled that this was stupid. Evermann asked him to draw his face. He did so and said that the face was crying and that Evermann would cry when he was gone. Then he pasted sequins on the tears (Figure 2.2). He made a frame for the picture with strips of paper. In this session, he had shown his awareness of Evermann's feelings and had expressed his own. When he was discharged the next day, he took his house with him, but not his self-portrait.

Rosa was a Hispanic 11-year-old whose parents were substance abusers. Her mother had been treated for depression and a suicide attempt. Rosa had tried to kill herself with a knife after claiming she would kill a classmate, her hamster, and the cat. She insisted that someone inside her was telling her how peaceful death would be. When frustrated or angry, she banged her head.

Evermann devised a task for her made from foam rubber padding, plastic bottles, and decorative materials. At their first session, Rosa paced the floor,

FIGURE 2.2 Crying self-portrait by 6-year-old boy.

keeping her eyes on the floor. Evermann opened a cabinet and let some foam padding roll out. Rosa stopped pacing and watched it unfold. Evermann gave her some and asked her to trace her hands and feet on it. At the next session, Evermann explained how she could assemble her puppet, saying that she could make something like herself. Rosa said that would be impossible, but as Evermann demonstrated, she began to assemble parts herself. When finished, she measured it to her own size, walked and danced with it, and finally posed it in a chair. Then she said that she would dress it and fix its hair just like her own. Rosa described the puppet as beautiful, just like herself. Next she made jewelry for it. When finished, Rosa said she wanted to show her puppet to her mother and the other kids on the unit (Figure 2.3). Rosa had completed the construction in a very ordered way. She related to the puppet as a perception of herself in whom she felt pride instead of urges of self-destruction. She left the unit the next day with her puppet.

Chuck was a 12-year-old with auditory and visual hallucinations who had expressed intentions of killing himself. Both parents were substance abusers.

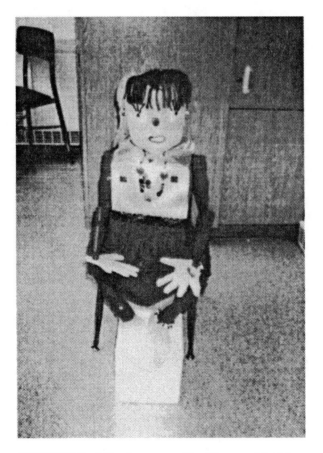

FIGURE 2.3   Life-size puppet by 11-year-old girl.

He and his father lived with his paternal grandparents, and his siblings lived with his mother. Chuck presented with flat affect, and as he scribbled rapidly, he seemed unconnected with anything or anyone. At the second session, Evermann presented Chuck with a collage task in which he could choose to glue as many magazine pictures as he wished onto a large piece of paper. He took a long time searching out specific sports pictures. After he had finished gluing them down, Evermann asked him to draw himself on another piece of paper. He turned red and slammed his fist on the table. First he made a very small figure, then turned the paper over and made a larger one. He colored it and glued it in front of a semicircle made from his large collage (Figure 2.4). Speaking in the third person, he described the piece as, "Chuck surrounded by all sports pictures since he was really interested in sports, especially baseball" (p. 24). He said that he really liked the good pictures on the table. When he placed his work on a shelf in the hall, several of the other children admired it. It was the first contact he had made with them, as he had previously isolated himself. Evermann felt that Chuck was able to reach out to others because he had related to himself in a genuine way through his art.

These children had all come from chaotic backgrounds. Evermann was able to provide them with a basic blueprint for a project to make building blocks for their own imagery and symbol formation at a time of crisis in their lives.

Recidivism

From her own work on the psychiatric unit of a major children's hospital where the goals were crisis stabilization, intensive evaluation, and short-term

FIGURE 2.4   Sports collage by 12-year-old boy.

treatment, Laura Jacob noted that shortened stays in psychiatric hospitals have led to a dramatic increase in recidivism (Jacob, 1995). The children in her study had all been hospitalized previously within the year and were currently hospitalized for further decompensation and suicidal ideation or behavior. She was able to work with some of them during partial hospitalization in between hospital admissions, as well. The children ranged in age from 3 to 13 and were considered to be a danger to themselves or others.

Kayla was an 11-year-old African American who seemed to want to please others. She had first been hospitalized for suicidal gestures and depression, which had begun after a 5-month stay with her grandmother 2 years earlier. She had been burdened by a secret that she finally told her therapist—that while at her grandmother's she had been sexually abused by a relative. She was discharged 12 days later. After 7 months she was hospitalized again when she was brought to an emergency room after holding a knife to her throat and screaming that she was going to kill herself. The family had not followed recommendations for outpatient treatment. Her primary therapist suspected Kayla's mother of abusing her. In art therapy she drew Figure 2.5, saying that it is a friendly cat who sometimes gets scared and hides in alleys. Nevertheless, blood is dripping from its claws. She titled it *Cat Claws*. She was discharged a few days later. Kayla was Jacob's first patient at the hospital. Jacob felt frustrated with the realization that the needs of this frightened child who was trying to be friendly had not even minimally been met.

Thirteen-year-old Maria, whose family had immigrated from Cuba, had initially been hospitalized when she confided to a friend that she wanted to die. She was discharged in 7 days. One month later, she was readmitted for suicidal ideation. Although resistant at first in group art therapy, she cried as she drew Figure 2.6. All around the sad face she wrote how she missed her

FIGURE 2.5   *Cat Claws* **by 11-year-old girl.**

FIGURE 2.6   Sad face by suicidal 13-year-old girl.

mother. She cried as she said that she did not want to be in the hospital again. Jacob did not see her again before her discharge. Afterward, her roommate told Jacob that Maria had said she would be back. One of the girls in the group told Jacob that the portion of Maria's picture that reads "Maria-N-Hippolita 4-Ever" refers to her being in love with her distant cousin. She said that Maria was afraid to tell Jacob that she was a lesbian and that she hadn't told her family, either. There are also pleadings to God in her picture. Maria seemed to Jacob to be immersed in struggles about her sexual preferences in relation both to her staunchly Catholic family and to her religion. Once again, Jacob felt discharge was premature.

Jacob observed that the art process helped her patients to reveal their issues more readily than did verbal therapy, but just as they did so, they were discharged. All returned a second or third time during the year she was there. She concluded that quality health care is being sacrificed for cost efficiency.

Garbage Pail Kids

Many of the children discussed in this book were abandoned by their mothers. In her work on an inpatient psychiatric unit, Mary Lou Hasara focused directly on the problems children were having as a result of having been given up by their mothers. Their mothers were either unable to care for a child or didn't want the responsibility. Although it is an accepted practice in the African American community for children to be raised by their grandmothers, these African American children could not accept being relinquished by their mothers. Most were angry and depressed. Hasara used art therapy to help them explore their feelings about living with their grandmothers instead of their mothers (Hasara, 1993). The patients were all hospitalized on an adolescent psychiatric unit in a general hospital. All came from lower socioeconomic backgrounds. They had trouble with school authorities and the law. One had been selling drugs; others had been suspended from school for fighting. Two had experienced auditory hallucinations telling them to hurt themselves or others. Depressive psychosis was the most common admitting diagnosis. Hasara saw the children in individual art therapy sessions, during which she asked them to make the following pictures:

- The patient and mother interacting
- The patient and grandparent interacting
- A speech/thought collage with a magazine photo of a dyad to which a spoken dialog is added
- An addition of the thoughts of the dyad
- The patient's feelings about his or her living arrangements,
- Good and bad aspects of living with Grandmother rather than Mother

Michelle was a 12-year-old African American girl who expressed her anger at her mother by acting out against her grandparents. She had been removed from her mother at age 5 due to her mother's physical abuse of her. She had been brought to the hospital because of oppositional behavior and because she was staying out late at night with men in their late teens and early 20s. She treated her grandparents with intense contempt because of the rules they tried to impose on her. She received negative feedback from both peers and staff at the hospital about her treatment of her grandparents, and after a month her art reflected her response. She drew a house with her grandparents and her grown-up self living in it. She said that she would be working three jobs to take care of them. Mother's house was miles away, Michelle said, and her grandparents were angry at her mother for the way she had treated her. She said that her grandparents were more like parents should be than her mother, even though she didn't obey them. She knew her grandparents deserved more respect, and she left the hospital resolving to make a successful life with them.

This was the second hospitalization for Clarence, age 15, an African American boy who had been given up by his mother at birth. She was an addict, and an older brother was a drug dealer. Clarence evidenced mental problems at age 3 and had been brought to the hospital this time for extreme sexual acting out. He was provocative toward people of all ages and both genders. Due to his large size and his grandmother's advanced age, he posed a threat to her, according to his aunt. When Clarence was asked to draw a picture of himself interacting with his grandmother, he drew them slow dancing. Clarence stated that he had never done this, but that he would like to. He denied any feelings of rejection, saying that Mom really loved him and they had great times together. When asked to draw himself interacting with her, he drew himself looking sad because he could not think of any interactions with his mother. He had drawn the image in pencil so lightly that Hasara could hardly see it. She asked him if he felt invisible, and he responded by darkening the outline on his sad-faced figure. He admitted that he hardly ever saw his mother. He remained on the unit 2 months, but his mother never visited, nor had she during his previous hospitalization. His speech/thought collage showed a pair of lovers expressing their love to one another.

Tasha was a 15-year-old African American girl who was the only patient to have been legally adopted by her grandmother. Until age 5 she lived with her addicted mother and the mother's drug dealer boyfriend, who used to beat her mother regularly and hide drugs in Tasha's underwear. Her mother had taught her how to steal food and clothing. When she was 5, the boyfriend kidnapped her and traveled from place to place with her for a month. Tasha believed that she had probably been sexually molested by him during that time. After her mother located them, she sent Tasha to live with her grandparents. When she drew a picture of herself and her mother, she erased her mother and moved her farther away. Then she drew a sketch of the two of them fighting, in which she is waving a knife. She has drawn herself smiling and her mother frowning. Tasha's speech/thought collage is a tender picture of a young mother holding an infant. She is telling her baby that she loves it and will protect it. The baby is thinking that everything will be all right because its mother loves it. Tasha said she was attracted to the picture because of the way the mother is engulfing the baby in her arms and protecting it. She said that these were the issues that hurt her the most. She asked to keep the picture because she was very pleased with it and wanted to have it to remind her of what a mother should do.

Most of the children and adolescents with whom Hasara worked were able to recognize that their feelings of distress, including those focused on their grandmothers, stemmed from feelings toward their mothers for abandoning them. These children all lived with their grandmothers, in contrast with many others discussed in this book who had either been given up by their mothers or were removed to become wards of the state, where they were moved from one foster care placement to another. Hasara tried to help her patients achieve a more comfortable relationship with their grandmothers.

Working Large

Robin Lee Garber taught scenic art in the theater department of a university before becoming an art therapist. She found that when painting scenery, where she worked on a grand scale, she felt more energized and experienced feelings of mastery, emotional release, and enhanced creativity. The problem-solving challenges she faced often promoted enthusiasm or sometimes intimidation. In working at a hospital, primarily with patients with Bipolar I Disorder, she hoped that by encouraging patients to work on a grand scale using the entire body, they might alleviate psychomotor retardation in depression or discover a venue for sublimating rage, tension, and anxiety (Garber, 1996). She also hoped to explore issues of mastery and body awareness. Florence Cane, a strong influence sparking the development of art therapy, writes that "Art may be inspired by feeling and conceived in thought, but it is executed through the body. Thus, the body is the instrument through which creative process occurs" (1951).

Garber worked on the adolescent unit of a private psychiatric hospital, where patients were admitted for 7 to 14 days. She saw patients in individual sessions. Most suffered anxiety and depression, low self-esteem, and poor social skills.

Garber laid down plastic drop cloths and taped a sheet of 4- by 6-foot mural paper to the floor. She poured tempera paint into large coffee cans and inserted paintbrushes into the open ends of 4-foot bamboo poles. The brushes ranged in size from 1- to 4-inch widths. They were secured inside the flared bamboo openings with rubber bands. The first session for each client was begun with some technical instruction. She demonstrated holding the bamboo horizontal while walking to prevent dripping and how to stand while painting, upright using the legs instead of the back and utilizing the upper arm and back muscles as well as the lower arm. She encouraged patients to approach the painting from all sides and to be conscious of their breathing and posture. Often, the patients enjoyed making sounds as they worked, and some sang as they painted. During the discussion, patients usually focused on their imagery first, but Garber also asked them how they felt about working in this way and if they wanted to again. If there was anxiety about the technical process, Garber suggested either drawing a smaller image on a grid and then expanding the grid to the mural paper or creating a smaller painting or drawing and then enlarging it or a part of it on the mural paper. Also, they could try out the extended brushes without paint so they could experiment with the movements before painting.

Shelly was a 15-year-old African American diagnosed with Bipolar I Disorder/depression, admitted by her mother for depression, angry outbursts, and threats of homicide and suicide. After 2 weeks in the hospital, Shelly was relinquished by her mother and placed in the custody of the Department of Child and Family Services (DCFS). Shelly remained on the unit for 4 months until the hospital could find placement for her in a long-term residential treatment program. In art therapy, Shelly's behavior vacillated between extreme exuberance and theatricality and self-depreciation and hostility. Garber hoped that by working large, Shelly would find some release from depression as well as a positive way to ventilate her anger and aggression.

At her first session, Shelly insisted that Garber paint with her on her mural. She had Shelly select the brush size, colors, and where Garber should stand. They mirrored each other's strokes and sang as they moved, sometimes in unison, sometimes in harmony. Shelly frequently exclaimed, "You sing like my mother" and "This is fun! I like painting like this!" (Garber, 1996, p. 14). Shelly painted freely, and soon the paper was filled with paint. As they began cleaning up, she dipped her hands in the paint and made two sets of hand-prints on one side of the paper. During cleanup, her mood changed dramatically. She kept repeating that she hated herself and asked why her mother didn't want her anymore. She said that the mural looked like hell, the pit of hell, and that she was the devil's wife. Then as quickly as her sadness had come, it disappeared, and she smiled and asked Garber if she liked the way she sang. She said she would like to do large art again. During the next 3 weeks, however, Shelly was on elopement and assault precautions and was not allowed to leave the unit. Because the mural room was on another floor, Garber had to meet with her in a small extra room on the unit, where she made drawings on 18- by 24-inch paper.

In her last large art session, 3 weeks after the first, Shelly was fairly labile, but she did not fall into depressed moodiness as she had before. She had made a smaller drawing on her own and enlarged it in her mural. The process stimulated a lively enactment. Since she seemed to work better when structure was provided, Garber suggested a theme: a window that showed the world she knew or as she would like it to be. As she dipped her extended brush, Shelly turned to Garber and in a loud falsetto announced, "Ladies and gentlemen, I shall introduce to you my window to the world!" (p. 15). As she painted the window shape, she asked if it wasn't the nicest window ever and answered herself by saying, "Of course it is, for I Shelly am the greatest painter of windows!" What happened next, Garber describes as "a combination of Masterpiece Theater (complete with Shelly's version of a British accent) and a hip hop musical review" (p. 16). In between singing, she described herself as an expert painter. She accented her singing with bounces of her extended brush. She began enacting two characters, a maidservant who served many glasses of water to Madame Shelly, the world's most famous expert artist. Between singing and painting, the maid would implore Madame Shelly not to work so hard. The madame would take imaginary glasses of water, drink from them loudly, and fling them back in the maid's direction. When she was finished, she remained stable while cleaning up. Shelly said she had had lots of fun making the mural. She identified items in her picture, including some abstract portions, as children playing. She was pleased with her picture and liked singing as she painted. She said that she felt better from having made her picture because art therapy helped her get her frustrations and aggressions out. Unlike the frequent warnings and punishments Shelly received for being too loud or outrageous on the unit, in art therapy she could let her songs, dances, and cast of characters come to life. Painting large was a much-needed energy release for her. It was a large enough container for her overflowing creativity.

Polaroid Photography

In her work on an adolescent impulse disorders unit of a private hospital, Claudia Clenard instituted the use of Polaroid photography in art therapy (Clenard, 1986). She felt it would provide the following advantages:

- The focus on the picture-taking process could diffuse the intensity of the one-to-one therapeutic relationship and give the patients a safe distance from their feelings.
- The picture provides a record and can be used in conjunction with other art media.
- The instant photograph provides immediate feedback and can help to engage the patient in the therapeutic process.
- It provides a nonthreatening way to look at aspects of the self that may have been lost in the confusion of impulsiveness.

Patients ranged in age from 12 to 18. Their problems included family difficulties, problems in school, legal difficulties, depression, aggression, substance abuse, and thoughts or acts of self-harm. The program had a defined system of behavioral requirements, a goal value system in which patients earned points for achieving positive goals. Numbers of points accumulated determined the level to which the patient was assigned, with greater privileges being granted for the higher levels. Patients remained on the unit for an average of 3 months, which would be unusually long in more recent times. Clenard worked with the patients in individual sessions in which they could take four photographs each session. Sometimes they elaborated the prints with art media. Usually the patients chose the subjects they shot, but sometimes Clenard gave them assignments.

Mark was a 16-year-old who had been admitted on a voluntary basis with symptoms of depression, poor school performance, and suicidal ideation. Although he was compliant and dependent and presented a nonaggressive façade, he was extremely labile. Mark's feelings of depression, emptiness, and loneliness were expressed through his photographs of relatively empty static scenes in and around the hospital. At his eighth session, 2 weeks before he was scheduled to be discharged, he decided he wanted to photograph the restraint bed where patients were put if they were uncontrollable. He had never been in restraints, but he saw the bed as the ultimate symbol of restriction on a locked unit. After photographing the bed, he wanted a picture of Clenard in restraints. Although Clenard was uncomfortable with his request, this was the first time he had requested a picture of her, and she thought it would be important for his termination. She decided to lie on the bed with the restraints unfastened (Figure 2.7). When she saw the photograph, she was embarrassed by the sexual overtones in the angle of the shot. To her the picture suggested sexual conquest and perhaps even sexual abuse. (When another patient requested a similar shot, Clenard refused.)

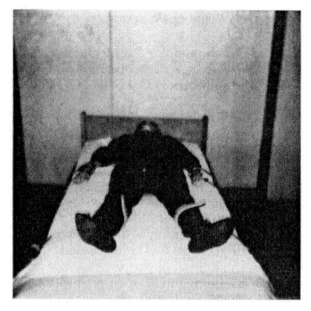

FIGURE 2.7   Polaroid of art therapist with re-straints taken by 16-year-old boy.

Sherry, 14, had jumped out of a second-story window of her house and sprained her foot. She had problems with truancy from school, anger, and getting into physical fights with her mother, and had complained of physical abuse by an older brother. She had also been in trouble for marijuana abuse, possession of cocaine, and breaking into a house, and had been arrested for breaking into a car. The Department of Child and Family Services (DCFS) had investigated the family for suspected child abuse or neglect, but found the claim of the brother's abuse to be unfounded. Sherry was diagnosed with depression and mixed personality disorder. At her first art therapy session, when Clenard asked her to shoot a picture that would represent her impressions of the hospital, she responded immediately with an idea. She walked back to her room, took a chair into the bathroom, stood on it and flushed the toilet (Figure 2.8; because of the flash, the swirling water cannot be seen.) Sherry's impression was negative, and she was delighted with the freedom to express it. Her next pictures were of staff members, which seemed to show a desire for affiliation. Sherry was eager to begin her next session. Her first picture was of the unit's locked doors, which she titled *Freedom*. At her fourth session, Clenard took her outside for photography. Her photograph of the cracked ice on the pond was titled *Testing Limits*. She said she imagined someone skating on thin ice and testing the limits. She said she would like to see her social worker out on the ice. They were in a power struggle. Clenard told Sherry that she thought her picture represented her main problem. Sherry was surprised, because she had not consciously intended to express herself this way. After six sessions, Clenard asked Sherry to make a collage of her pictures.

**FIGURE 2.8   Polaroid impression of the hospital
taken by 14-year-old girl.**

She titled it *My Moods,* saying that the toilet represented a disgusted mood, the
ice a rebellious mood, and the people pictures a good mood. The picture of her
social worker was placed between the toilet and the cracked ice. She said that
he reminded her of something that should go in the toilet and repeated that
she would like to see him out on the ice. Although Sherry had problems in
dealing with authority, the picture-taking process allowed her to express both
her rebellious anger as well as positive feelings in wanting to photograph a
number of the staff members. She and Clenard developed a positive relationship that could be both serious and playful.

Monica, 16, had been admitted voluntarily for communication problems
with her parents. She was diagnosed with a major depressive episode. Monica
was curious about what she expressed in her art and was motivated to understand herself better. She had run away from home and also used sex as a
means of escape. In this connection, she decided to pose by the unit doors as
though she was going to escape, and Clenard photographed her. In discussing
what she hoped to get out of her hospitalization, Monica said she wanted to
feel good about herself. To put this into a picture, she assumed a pose from a
dance number in a school production chorus line. She started to sing the
words, "I'm leaving today. . . ." She and Clenard made a paper top hat, bow
tie, and cane to complete the pose. She practiced the dance a few times and
decided on a pose in which she was facing the camera and kicking to the side.
In the picture, she is looking directly at the viewer, smiling, and waving her
hat. Her exuberance was contagious. Clenard felt that she was collaborating
with an artist.

At the next session, Clenard asked Monica to cut out her two photographed images of herself and arrange them on drawing paper to represent
the transition from one to the other graphically. (Clenard had Xeroxed the two
pictures because Monica did not want to destroy the originals.) Because Monica seemed to be in a quandary, Clenard suggested that she move kinestheti-
cally from one pose to the other. She pushed against the wall in her pose of
trying to escape. Slowly she turned, feeling along the wall until she came to an
imaginary door. She opened it and went through, closing it behind her. She
put a hand up to shield her eyes as though from bright lights. She had walked
onto a stage. She picked up her imaginary cane and top hat and began to
dance as in the second picture. She pasted her first figure in the upper left corner of the paper and drew a black hole, into which she was falling. Then she
made a long black diagonal wall across the page. The door in it that opens onto
the stage is yellow, as is a path leading to the stage. Yellow, she said, symbolizes happiness and light. The right half of the page is taken up by the stage,
with opened curtains and an audience before it. At center stage is the figure of
herself dancing and waving her top hat. At the top is the marquee, which
reads, "Presenting Monica in *Feeling Good about Myself.*" In reviewing her work
shortly before being discharged, Monica said that the turning point in her
treatment was when she found the door. She returned home, and she and her
mother continued to work on their relationship.

Adolescents with Neurobehavioral Brain Impairment

Remey Rozin conducted art therapy for adolescents in what may be a ground-
breaking project that postulates neurological impairment as the causative factor in frequently seen behavior disorders. She found it necessary to tailor the
art therapy to meet the special needs of these young people (Rozin, 1999).

The impulsive, aggressive, oppositional, and depressive behaviors we
have seen in the children and adolescents described in this chapter and in
those seen in art therapy in the schools are in the early investigative stages of
physiological study. The Comprehensive Neurobehavioral Systems Program
looks at adolescents with these behaviors, who often seem to be caught in a
revolving door in and out of psychiatric hospitals. The investigators believe
that many are misdiagnosed for psychiatric illness, particularly Conduct Disorder. The program uses the brain electrical activity mapping (BEAM) test to
determine neurobehavioral brain impairments, and it provides appropriate
medication and therapy. Fisher, Matthews, and Seals (1992) reported that fetal
exposure to drugs, alcohol, birth injuries, inadequate prenatal care, and
shaken baby syndrome produce organicity from brain trauma. Manifestations
of problems include impulsivity, explosive behavior, poor frustration tolerance, poor verbal and memory skills, and learning disabilities. The BEAM
measures which area of the brain has been affected. Damage causing frontal
lobe syndrome affects executive control systems that have a modulating effect

on behavior and emotions, causing impulsivity, poor frustration tolerance, and explosive outbursts. Temporal-limbic syndrome describes damage in regions that regulate emotional control, resulting in severe rage and depressive episodes. It is rare for only one of the brain areas to be affected. Matthews, Williamson, Seals, and Fisher (1993) believe that the milieu for this population should be quieter and less stimulating, with positive discipline rather than punishment. There should be limit setting and redirecting, but not punishment that might evoke violence. Since brain impairment usually leads to poor social development and limited communication skills, training in these areas should be implemented. Traditional verbal therapy is not recommended because so many patients exhibit poor language skills, poor attention span, and poor verbal memory. Matthews and Fisher (1992) contend that nonverbal therapies, such as art therapy, will be more beneficial because they are action oriented. Rozin notes that although art therapy is recommended, there are no suggestions as to how it should be structured.

Patients age 8 to 18 came to the unit to be evaluated for neurological impairment with the BEAM test, and if impaired, to have a trial of medication for a sufficient time to determine its effectiveness. The average hospital stay was 3 to 5 weeks. In her work in this program in twice-weekly 45-minute individual art therapy sessions, Rozin found the following:

- Paint and clay were very difficult for this population.
- Three-dimensional construction materials proved easier to control and more interesting to the patients.
- They did not respond well to therapist-directed art tasks.
- For those with low attention span or impulsive behavior, writing a plan for making a construction was helpful for concentration. It was not so helpful for those with explosive behaviors.

Dan, a 12-year-old Hispanic boy, had been hit in the head by a brick at age 4 and suffered an automobile accident at age 7. Since then, his mother reported, there had been personality changes, such as depression, impulsiveness, and violent, aggressive, oppositional, and defiant behavior, including setting fires and damaging property. He had also been hurting his sister, which caused his mother to place her in a residential setting to keep her safe from Dan. Dan's BEAM test showed damage to the temporal region with more impairment on the left side, which explained his unpredictable behavior of explosiveness and depression. After an initial session in which he had drawn the Joker from the *Batman* movie, Dan refused to come to art therapy. He told Rozin of his nightmares, and she offered him art materials in order to draw them. He then resumed art therapy. At his next session, Rozin gave him a cardboard box and told him to make whatever he wanted out of it. Without hesitation, he started cutting the box to make a house. He told Rozin how he had watched his house burn down several years before and had heard the cat screaming in the fire. He showed no emotion. When Dan had finished his house, Rozin commented that it had no windows or doors. He replied that it was a trap, just like the hospital. He then painted it, adding windows and a door (Figure 2.9). Dan was able to use the art materials in a focused way and complete the project he had begun.

Cord, 11, was an African American boy who had been relinquished to DCFS after it was discovered that his mother was a multiple drug user. He had lived with adoptive parents prior to hospitalization. His adoptive mother had called police to take him to the hospital after he had threatened to cut his own throat and had then cut her with a kitchen knife. He had a history of depression, emotional outbursts, somatic complaints, low frustration tolerance, and poor impulse control. He had sniffed glue and correction fluid in the past. His BEAM test indicated physiological dysfunction in the temporal region, which explained his impulsive behavior and temper tantrums. The test also showed physiological evidence of Attention Deficit Disorder. Cord had been tested on the unit and given medication 6 months earlier, but he had not been compliant with his medication. His second stay in the program was short, as he was discharged as soon as his medication was again regulated. Rozin saw him only twice. In art therapy he wanted to make a large chair, but his thoughts were scattered, and he did not seem to know where to begin. Rozin asked him to write a plan for his project, which he did. They discussed which part of the chair should be made first, which second, and so forth. As Cord constructed his chair, having a written plan to which he could refer helped him to organize his thoughts. Occasionally he asked what to do next, and Rozin told him to look at his plan. Although he did not have a chance to paint his chair before he was discharged, Cord took great pride in the successful completion of the construction (Figure 2.10).

FIGURE 2.9   House constructed by 12-year-old neurologically impaired boy.

FIGURE 2.10 Chair constructed by 11-year-old boy
with neurological impairment.

Sarah, a 15-year-old African American girl, had been adopted by her aunt and uncle, along with her six siblings. Six months prior to hospitalization, she had begun running away due to feeling unloved and having many verbal and physical fights with her aunt. She was missing for several months the first time, and remained at home for only 1 week before running away again for 2 months. She was picked up by the police and brought to the hospital. While living on the streets, she had experimented with drugs and prostitution. High on drugs with uncontrollable behavior on admission, Sarah also had a history of depression and oppositional defiant behavior. Her BEAM test indicated physiological dysfunction in the left frontal and temporal regions, causing depression and poor judgment. The damage to the frontal region was believed to cause her impulsive behavior in running away. She was also diagnosed with Attention Deficit Disorder.

When Sarah had difficulty choosing materials in her first session, Rozin realized that she would respond better to a smaller selection. Sarah wrote a plan for her project and worked very slowly on it. She completed two dolls, of herself and her boyfriend. She said that the plan had helped her to concentrate. She said that the girl figure shows her as sad because of something her boyfriend said to her on the phone. He is shown as happy because he didn't know he had made her sad.

Joe, a 15-year-old Hispanic boy who lived with his Mexican adoptive parents and two adopted siblings, had been referred by the juvenile detention center, where he had been detained for battery and theft. He had had three previous hospitalizations in 3 years. His symptoms included uncontrollable aggressive and impulsive behavior with poor judgment and difficulty in focusing and concentrating. He had attacked his family, attempted suicide when depressed, and complained of blackouts. The BEAM test showed impairment in the left temporal area and Attention Deficit Disorder.

Joe wanted to make a house, so Rozin gave him a box and some construction materials. Because she noticed his difficulty in concentrating, she asked him to write a plan. She quickly saw that he could not spell basic English words. Rozin spelled the words for him, and Joe wrote them down. He constructed the house from tongue depressors, but became frustrated that the glue would not dry fast enough. He solved the problem with masking tape. After the construction was completed, he wrote a new plan for painting the house. Next he decided to create a "scene" for his house and took the initiative in writing a plan, asking Rozin how to spell the words he needed. He refered to his plan often, and was very pleased with his *Winter Wonderland*, which he showed proudly to others (Figure 2.11).

FIGURE 2.11 *Winter Wonderland* constructed by 15-year-old boy with neurological impairment.

Rozin reports that adolescents who had difficulties controlling their impulses due to frontal lobe impairment or Attention Deficit Disorder said that the step-by-step plans were a reminder to keep their attention focused and helped them to control their impulses. On the other hand, those who were extremely explosive, aggressive, and hostile due to temporal lobe impairment did not respond well to writing a plan. Especially significant is her observation that adolescents who had difficulty communicating with others were able to communicate through their art.

Obviously, the patients were helped by their medication, as well. It is exciting to anticipate that the behaviors that get so many children and adolescents into trouble may be controllable with medication that can help these young people to break out of the patterns of aggression and depression that lead them to failure and, often, institutionalization. Hopefully, it will enable them to lead more fulfilling lives as adults. It is also sad, but not surprising, to realize that many of these children's problems may stem from their treatment by adults, in the form of fetal alcohol syndrome and physical abuse. In the course of their treatment, they learned to express themselves in art, to develop some coping and problem-solving skills, and to increase their frustration tolerance.

Art Therapists' Self-Processing

The powerful affect-laden behavior of many of these young people, particularly the adolescents, can have a reciprocally powerful effect on the art therapists who work with them. In some instances, student interns are not much older than their adolescent patients. At any age, art therapists may identify with their patient's adolescent struggles toward separation and individuation through strong reminders of their own adolescent struggles. On the other hand, the tragic realities of their patients' lives may come as a shock. As is stated throughout this book, it is important for therapists to recognize the sources of their own feelings in response to their clients. For art therapists, there is no better vehicle for exploration than their own artwork.

Terry Lavery, a young person himself, worked as a student intern on a hospital adolescent psychiatric unit. In addition to conducting art therapy, he also co-led verbal therapy groups. Coming from a middle-class suburban neighborhood, he was not prepared for the culture shock of hearing his patients' horror stories (Lavery, 1994). Because he usually felt tense after the verbal group, he developed a process to explore his feelings and find release from the painful negativity he had been hearing. Since the group met at the end of the day, he made quick postsession pastel drawings to release his immediate feelings before going home. Working on dark paper, he found that being able to cover the paper quickly with vibrant colors against a dark background captured the raw intensity of his feelings. Nevertheless, the relief was only temporary. He added a second step. He made a scribble drawing with his nondominant hand and developed it in pastels with his dominant hand. Lavery chose this technique to tap into his unconscious and to gain a deeper understanding of his own reactions. His third step was a longer, more reflective process. Prior to art therapy training, Lavery had been an illustrator. He chose a medium he had used to good advantage then, colored pencils, a more controlled medium. The time-consuming layering and finished detail work fulfilled Lavery's need to make art. The steady work allowed a more meditative, reflective process that enabled him to empathize with his patients more fully.

Fifteen-year-old Jane told the group that she had been living on the street with her 5-month-old baby after her father had sexually assaulted her while her mother watched. She had taken her baby to the hospital after being alarmed by a rash he had all over his face. She had been feeding him candy and soda pop, with no idea that they could be harmful to him. This was Lavery's first experience of hearing "such a gritty first-person account of adolescent life in the inner city" (p. 16). In the scribble he made, the face of a crying baby emerged. In addition to thinking of the baby, he thought of this young mother crying for help. Page 1 shows the third picture of the sequence, a crying baby holding a baby, Lavery's illustration of teen pregnancy. In his art sessions with Jane, he helped her to master the use of various art media to increase her self-confidence. They were then able to relate her frustrations and difficulties with the media to similar feelings regarding being a very young mother.

Belinda, a 13-year-old African American girl, had been admitted for depression and suicidal ideation. She lived with 14 siblings in a four-bedroom apartment housing 20 people. A brother was missing and a friend had recently been murdered. Her own future was uncertain, as plans were being considered for making her a ward of the state and placing her in a group home. She was very angry in the group and said, "It doesn't matter what happens. I'm gonna be six feet under anyway" (p. 16). Lavery recognized that survival was a full-time job for Belinda and others in her situation. He felt hopeless for her and distant from her. His postsession picture is of a person as she described herself, "six feet under" (Figure 2.12). However, the figure is sitting up, which made Terry feel better about Belinda's possibilities. He wanted to show the picture to Belinda, but he was afraid that it might overwhelm her. He decided instead to tell her he had drawn a picture about her in response to the group session. She replied that she didn't know anyone cared, that in the past people had either disbelieved or ignored her suicide threats. She recognized that Lavery's taking the time to draw about her and discuss it with her in their individual session showed that he did care. (Art therapists have a powerful tool in using their own art to communicate with their clients.) In the next step in Lavery's drawing and reflection process, his scribble developed into a hand holding a rope (Figure 2.13). He was reminded of a lifeline thrown to someone who had fallen out of a boat, which he saw as a metaphor for his work with Belinda. He could not calm her stormy seas, but he could offer her a line to

FIGURE 2.12   Art therapist's reaction to an adolescent girl who expected to be "six feet
under." *(Reprinted from the* American
Journal of Art Therapy, *Vol. 33, No. 1,
pp. 14–20, by permission of Gladys
Agell and Vermont College of Norwich
University.)*

hold onto to keep from drowning, which he developed into his final drawing, shown on page 53. The rope looks strong, and Lavery saw an innocent yet desperate look in the eyes of the child. This sequence helped him to become aware of the importance of his own feelings about patients in terms of what he was able to convey to them. His hopelessness about Belinda had changed, and she, in turn, became more positive in the group.

In contrast with the separation from his adolescent patients that Terry Lavery felt initially, Angela Tarasiewicz identified with the confusion and excitement of adolescence. She notes that creativity is in abundance at this stage, which makes art therapy a potential outlet for the strong feelings of these patients. In common with Lavery, she recognizes the wide range of feelings that can be evoked in the art therapist, as well (Tarasiewicz, 1997).

FIGURE 2.13 Art therapist's scribble reaction to hopeless 13-year-old girl. *(Reprinted from the* **American Journal of Art Therapy,** *Vol. 33, No. 1, pp. 14–20, by permission of Gladys Agell and Vermont College of Norwich University.)*

Tarasiewicz notes that Tessa Dalley explains that though considered an inappropriate response by psychoanalysts in the past, countertransference is now thought "to incorporate ideas of therapeutic empathy and identification" (Dalley et al., 1987, p. 18). Tarasiewicz has found this view particularly applicable to working with adolescents.

Working on two inpatient units in a psychiatric hospital for children age 4 to 12 and adolescents age 13 to 17, Tarasiewicz made art after particularly emotional or otherwise impactful sessions or when she felt confused and needed to make art about what had happened. She also made art for up to 8 months after her work with particular patients had ended when feelings about them resurfaced. In searching the art therapy literature, Tarasiewicz found no other reports of postsession art made over such a long period of time.

Length of hospital stay ranged from 2 weeks to 6 months, and patients' problems included behavior disorders, depression, physical and sexual abuse, gang involvement, and drug use. Some were diagnosed with personality disorders, a few had psychotic disorders, and some were violent. They participated in a weekly 1-hour art therapy group and individual 1-hour art therapy twice weekly.

Tony was a "twelve-year-old landmine going off every time some one stepped on him" (Tarasiewicz, 1997, p. 7). He had been sexually molested at age 5, had a learning disability, and was diagnosed with major depression. His temper was easily triggered, to the extent that his fits of anger resulted in his being hospitalized several times. In her work with him, Tarasiewicz's goals were for him to establish trust, increase self-esteem, learn patience, and recognize cues that could lead to outbursts. As Tony created stories about a boy being rescued, Tarasiewicz noticed that she was developing maternal feelings toward him. After an angry outburst in their first month of working together, Tony was placed in the Quiet Room (seclusion). He was angry at the staff for not letting him go to the bathroom, so he smeared his feces on the walls. When Tarasiewicz learned of this, she felt shame and sadness for Tony, as her motherly feelings were again awakened. She made art, using an image Tony drew frequently, a totem pole. He is a needy figure in the middle with arms open for help. The background is scribbled in brown, representing his smeared feces. Tarasiewicz saw Tony as being at the mercy of his own depression and anger in a cycle of sadness-fear-rage-consequence. Once she recognized her own wishes to nurture and rescue him, Tarasiewicz put her feelings to use in their sessions. She helped him build self-esteem by teaching him to spell, fold his clothes, and sort the art materials. Interspersed with art making, these simple learning activities helped Tony to feel a sense of accomplishment and satisfied Tarasiewicz's own need to nurture him.

Tarasiewicz recognized her maternal feelings in her sadness to see him leave, especially because his future was uncertain. It was unclear whether he would return to his parents, live with an aunt, or be transferred to a long-term residential facility. Figure 2.14 illustrates Tarasiewicz's feelings, showing her standing on an island that the two of them had constructed together in art therapy while Tony rows away on a choppy sea. Two months later, Tarasiewicz had a dream in which she adopted him and took him out for ice cream. She awoke missing him, but felt that her dream signaled her acceptance of his departure. She wrote a poem that helped her realize that although she couldn't adopt Tony, their time together had been well spent.

Fifteen-year-old Star was Tarasiewicz's first patient. She had been physically abused by her parents and raped, and was involved in satanic cult rituals in which she had almost been killed. With a history of anorexia, bulimia, and active drug use, she was diagnosed with learning disability and bipolar disorder, manic type. Tarasiewicz recognized Star's strengths in her creativity and straightforward self-assertiveness. Her hair was neon green in the front, and she wrote poetry. As Star spoke of her friends and how she was always on

FIGURE 2.14   Art therapist's feelings upon termination of work with 12-year-old boy.

the run and showed Tarasiewicz her extensive photo album of people she loved and hated, Tarasiewicz's head became filled with images of these people and the horror stories that Star told of her life. Tarasiewicz began to recognize that she was feeling "a reluctant envy for her exciting, unpredictable, wild, law-breaking life" (p. 13). Drawing a portrait of Star helped Tarasiewicz understand her feelings (Figure 2.15). The head floats amid a sea of psychedelic twists and turns that signify her drug-induced, surreal lifestyle and family history. Her eyes sparkle with silvery glitter. Tarasiewicz began to feel satisfied just hearing Star's stories; she realized that she did not want to live them. She recognized that she was vicariously participating in the events of Star's life.

In their individual sessions, Star began to show Tarasiewicz how to make plaster "friends" from plaster gauze strips. Tarasiewicz describes them as "stark white, doll-sized little mummies" (p. 15), each with its own personality. They made lots of them together. It was important for Star's sense of worth to be able to teach Tarasiewicz. Eventually, they even exchanged some of them as Star spoke more and more about her feelings surrounding the events in her life. They decorated the plaster dolls with glitter, and "they sparkled with new life" (p. 16). Star loved to use glitter and got the gluing technique down pat, never wasting a speck of glitter. Sometimes she happily dusted her hair with it. By the time she was ready for discharge, she had come a long way in developing trust and expressing her feelings in art therapy. After her last session, Tarasiewicz drew herself as one of the plaster dolls, limp and empty, with a hole in her chest to represent her loss of Star, her first patient. But subsequently, she developed a

FIGURE 2.15   Art therapist's portrait of 15-year-old girl.

liking for glitter and began using it in her own work. Star was still an influence. When she realized this, she decided to make a tribute to her from a plaster doll Tarasiewicz had made in one of their sessions. She decorated the "friend" with metallic paint, glitter, and sparkling beads, and replaced the hole in the chest she had drawn with a golden spiral (Figure 2.16).

Sixteen-year-old Ben had been hearing voices for 2 years. His mind was filled with fantastic images that flowed forth in his many creative drawings. Unlike most of the other patients, he came from a cohesive family with a strong religious faith, which he shared. His hallucinations, however, interfered with his struggle to be "good," telling him to pick fights and to join a gang. He had been involved in gang wars and robberies. His initial drawings centered on themes of yearning for inner peace. He told Tarasiewicz that he liked drawing together with friends and asked her if she would do one with him. The resulting picture "was filled with humor and deep metaphor" (p. 21). Joint drawings became their modus operandi, and a strong therapeutic relationship developed through their combined creativity. The contrast between Ben's humble presence and his wildly imaginative artwork, his low self-esteem, and lack of pride in his accomplishments all reminded Tarasiewicz of herself at his age. Enhancing his self-esteem became her goal in their sessions. During one session, he began feeling happy because he had not had an hallucination or headache all day. He lifted his head and squinted into the distance. He was hallucinating. After the hallucination left, he started to cry, saying that he felt like a freak. Tarasiewicz felt helpless because she could not identify with having hallucinations. She needed to draw after the session. Figure 2.17

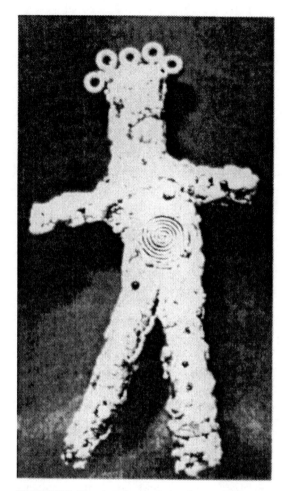

FIGURE 2.16   Art therapist's plaster doll made
in the style of a 15-year-old girl.

shows Ben on the left, hallucinating wildly, and herself on the right, getting a
tail of the experience.

As time passed, Ben progressed, making many drawings and decorating
his room with them. He was proud of his accomplishments. He advanced in
the unit's level system. A change in medication diminished his hallucinations.
As they planned for termination, they reviewed the highlights of past sessions
and created a joint picture of the loss both would feel. Tarasiewicz found it
important to share with Ben the loss that their termination would mean to her.
"Remaining in the role of therapist while experiencing the emotions of a friend
proved to be a challenge," Tarasiewicz reports (p. 25). During a workshop several months later, her identification with Ben resurfaced. She still needed further closure and drew Figure 2.18 to gain it. He is floating free, being kissed by
creativity, a gift they both shared.

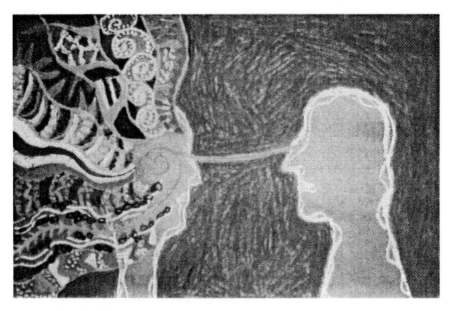

FIGURE 2.17   Art therapist's portrayal of 16-year-old boy hallucinating, left.

FIGURE 2.18   Art therapist's portrayal of 16-year-old boy being kissed by creativity.

Through her art responses, Tarasiewicz recognized her maternal impulses toward Tony, her envy of Star's exciting life, and her identification with Ben in relation to their shared creativity. Even months after the termination of work with some of her patients, she continued to process her reactions in her art and come to closure with their relationships. These patients were among Tarasiewicz's first, and the psychiatric hospital experience was new to her, as was also true for Terry Lavery. These are seminal experiences in the career of art therapists and are, therefore, of great impact. Exploring these experiences in their art was of great benefit to these young therapists.

Nina Kuzniak also had strong reactions. She was working at a private psychiatric hospital that was primarily a short-term facility, and her patients could be discharged earlier than expected because of termination of payment by insurance carriers. As a result, Kuzniak had no firm basis of projected length of treatment on which to design therapy goals and strategies in conducting individual art therapy. She saw some patients for as little as 3 sessions and others for 40. The possibility of arriving at the hospital and finding that a client had been discharged without even a chance to say goodbye is a condition many art therapists face in hospital work (Wadeson, Durkin, & Perach, 1989). From a previous position in a school setting in which she had unexpected difficulty with termination, Kuzniak realized that she had to deal with the powerful feelings that were churned up for her in this phase of treatment (Kuzniak, 1992). At the school, she had "fallen into the trap of believing that those students could not go on without our therapy sessions. I overestimated my importance and underestimated their ability to generalize their progress beyond our time together" (p. 10). Kuzniak made art every day at the hospital in order to process her adjustment to this new system of working. She found that it was difficult to sort out the feelings brought to the surface during termination into reactions to the patient, the hospital, the system, and her own issues. The art helped.

Kuzniak had been working with A., a 12-year-old girl, for a month. One hour before she was to leave for the day, she received a call from the unit informing her that A. would be discharged that evening. They had 15 minutes to talk. Kuzniak took 15 minutes to calm her anger before meeting with A. Kuzniak gave her the sculptures she had made and praised her for her progress. Afterward, Kuzniak sculpted three heads. One is the patient in pain, screaming for more help; another is the hospital, depicted as green and greedy, seeing only the need for payment; the third is Kuzniak, who must remain neutral and blank for the patient's benefit, not showing her anger. Kuzniak had made a mask that was shattered and pieced back together, showing the cracks and a large hole that had not been repaired. It became a representation of the hospital for her: "Piece the patient back together and don't worry about filling in all the gaps" (p. 19). Kuzniak felt she was not given sufficient time to work with each patient.

A 16-year-old boy who was discharged without even the benefit of a 15-minute termination session is a case in point. Figure 2.19 shows the sculpture

FIGURE 2.19   Art therapist's sculpture in reaction to sudden discharge of 16-year-old boy.

Kuzniak made in connection with her work with him. It enabled her to see that beyond the dark exterior of the tactics he had used to keep her at a distance, she still felt a connection, depicted in the bright interior. She shared these feelings with him. The art helped her to feel positive about her work with this patient even while feeling anger toward the institution. She had thought that art therapy could be of significant benefit to this patient, but by the time some of his defenses had been addressed, like the others, he was discharged.

Kuzniak made art about her termination feelings with many of her patients (see Chapter 7 for her work with adults). She came to realize that whereas she previously could not even imagine positive feelings unless a patient was markedly improved, she now was able to allow herself satisfaction in achieving small goals of understanding, symptom relief, and planning for change. Short-term work such as this poses a major challenge for art therapists (and other therapists, as well), because the reality of abbreviated treatment imposes limitations of minimal attainable goals, less interaction and involvement, and, ultimately, less satisfaction in taking part in the client's progress. Unfortunately, current economic conditions are dictating much shorter hospital stays than were the norm in the past. As discussed here and in the chapters on adult care (Part II), recidivism is often the result.

Summary

The psychiatrically hospitalized children and adolescents described in this chapter were in great need, but were often given only treatment sufficient to stabilize them or refer them onward. Art therapists have been creative in their efforts to work effectively within the limits of often restrictive conditions and conscientious in their self-exploration, through their own art, of the feelings engendered by working with these needy youngsters.

- Ruth Evermann (1994) developed highly structured tasks for children on a short-term psychiatric unit of a major children's hospital.
- Laura Jacob (1995), working in a similar setting, found that art heightens expression, but that short-term treatment leads to recidivism.
- Mary Lou Hasara (1993) focused her art therapy interventions on the feelings of adolescent patients around having been abandoned by their mothers or removed from their homes to live with their grandmothers.
- Robin Lee Garber (1996) instituted art on a grand scale (working very large) for adolescent patients.
- Claudia Clenard (1986) utilized Polaroid photography, sometimes embellished with other media, for adolescent patients to explore their feelings.
- Remey Rozin (1999) worked with adolescents with neurological impairment in a study to investigate brain damage as a causitive factor in behavior disorders and medication as a form of treatment.
- Because working with adolescent patients often arouses strong reactions in therapists, Terry Lavery (1994), Angela Tarasiewicz (1997), and Nina Kuzniak (1992) developed systems of using their own art for relief, release, and exploration of their reactions.
- Terry Lavery (1994) recognized the culture shock he experienced in response to his patients' inner-city lives.
- Angela Tarasiewicz (1997) explored her strong countertransference reactions in her art.
- Nina Kuzniak (1992) dealt with difficult termination issues through art making.

Conclusion

The treatment of severely impaired children and adolescents is of crucial importance in its own right. This is a population for whose members positive intervention can make a significant difference. Patterns are not so ingrained that they cannot be changed. But beyond the difference treatment can make in individual lives, the future of our society rests on decreasing (or more hopefully, eliminating) the cycles of drug abuse, violence, crime, and homelessness that impoverish and endanger the lives of citizens of our inner cities. These conditions are significant causal agents as well as results of the problems encountered by these young people. Art therapy is a natural outlet for the expression of feeling and the synthesizing of experience for children and adolescents. It can make a difference in individual cases, but these young people need more than short-term treatment to help them to grow up to have lives of hope and fulfillment.

ART THERAPY PROJECTS

Projects discussed in this chapter are described further in Chapter 15, "Art Activities and Materials":

- Paper house and tree (Evermann, 1994)
- Life-size dolls (Evermann, 1994)
- Verbal/thought collage (Hasara, 1993)
- Polaroid photography (Clenard, 1986)
- Construction (Rozin, 1999)
- Written project plans (Rozin, 1999)
- Plaster gauze dolls (Tarasiewicz, 1997)

Chapter 3

Outpatient, Shelter, and Residential Treatment

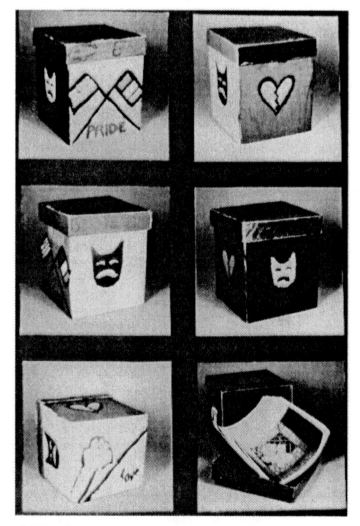

Self-box by 15-year-old girl.

David is looking through his folder to pick out his best picture, which the art therapist says he can hang in the spring art show. He's surprised at how thick the folder is. The way he decorated it last fall is really stupid, all those moons and stars. He smiles at the gooey Halloween jack-o'-lantern he drew. There's the book he made Mom for Christmas. He feels sad that they couldn't find her so he could give it to her. He brightens when he turns to Mechanical Man *with his gears and switches and the fire shooting out of his eyes. This is it. He waves his hand vigorously and calls to the art therapist to tell her he wants red matting. David writes his name in big uneven letters across* Mechanical Man's *chest.*

Outpatient Services

Children and adolescents who may have emotional problems, yet who are able to function while living at home and attending regular schools, are seen in outpatient clinics. In some cases, their life situations have imposed problems, such as those who have been sexually abused. Treatment may be time-limited. Art therapists have devised some innovative projects for reaching children who may respond better to the playful opportunities art activities can provide than to purely verbal therapy.

Photography

Alexandria Elliot-Prisco worked for a not-for-profit organization that provided counseling to women and children, primarily those who had been sexually assaulted (Elliot-Prisco, 1995; for a discussion of her work with women, see Chapter 11, "Sexual Abuse"). The central goal of counseling was empowerment. Elliot-Prisco offered her clients a variety of materials for their artwork, including the use of both Polaroid and automatic 35-mm cameras. Photography was useful in helping her clients to experience a sense of control and mastery. It provided distance and boundary definition, thus aiding intrapsychic integration.

Fifteen-year-old Kate had been gang-raped. Elliot-Prisco had initially met her in a family session, in which she learned that Kate had also been raped a year prior to the recent assault. Kate was dressed in oversized clothing to hide her obesity. She reported that she had been ridiculed for being overweight throughout her school years, causing her to have low self-esteem. Kate had a twin sister, whom she described as the "perfect, goody goody angel," and described herself as the "invisible one." She added, "I wear a mask; I shut [the family] out and I am evil, the opposite of my [twin]" (p. 14). Her diagnosis was major depression. When depressed, she had inflicted superficial cuts on her forearm with pins to draw blood as a release, "to let the pain out" (p. 15). After desisting from cutting behavior at her parents' insistence 2 years previously, Kate had accelerated her risk-taking, defiant actions, which eventually led to both rapes. She said that she was obsessed with finding intimacy and a sense of belonging with her peer offenders prior to the rapes. In both cases she was involved in risk-taking behavior, blacking out from alcohol at the time of the first rape and isolating herself with three volatile gang members who were intoxicated at the time of the gang rape.

Recognizing Kate's need for structure, boundaries, and containment, Elliot-Prisco offered her a choice of boxes for creating a self-box. Kate chose a sturdy one and spent five sessions completing it (see page 86). She painted the inside in dark blues, purples, and teals to represent her depression. The lid was covered in silver, black, blue, and green glossy papers. Each side of the box was painted to represent a feeling: pride in being an Irish American, symbolized by two flags; a broken heart on a background of blue for tears; two sorrowful masks; and on the bottom, where it doesn't show, a fist raised in anger. She made a diagonal dividing line and wrote *love* on the other side next to a small heart, for unrequited love. Elliot-Prisco gave Kate a camera and a role of film to shoot. At the next session, Kate returned the film to have it developed. Using objects from her environment, Kate created an image to represent her feelings of entrapment (Figure 3.1). "Deep inside," she said, "I am like my teddy who wears a happy mask but is in a jail cell. . . . He feels confusion, anger, frustration" (p. 16). She decided to put the photograph in her self-box as she was beginning to move toward self-containment.

Eleven-year-old Nancy had been molested an unknown number of times beginning at age 9 by an extended family member who was her baby-sitter. She suffered night terrors and chronic gastrointestinal problems, making her

FIGURE 3.1 Feelings of entrapment by 15-year-old girl.

school attendance inconsistent. Nancy's parents were divorced, and the family was impoverished. She lived with her mother and two siblings. The children slept on the floor. Elliot-Prisco observed that Nancy and her mother appeared to be fused: Nancy sat on her mother's lap and wrapped herself around her; they spoke for one another; and Nancy would look toward her mother before she could respond to anything Elliot-Prisco asked. Nancy had requested that her mother join her in the initial art therapy sessions. Although Elliot-Prisco gave them each a roll of film in order to shoot separate pictures of what they each considered to be personal safety, they both used the same roll. Nancy shot a picture for her mother that was almost identical to her own. It was a picture of the gravestone of Nancy's grandfather, to whom they both prayed for protection from material want and abuse by men. Nancy's mother maintained that a crack in the gravestone allowed him to hear their prayers. After her mother no longer came to the sessions, Nancy told Elliot-Prisco of her imaginary companions, Dog, Seal, Dolphin, and Kitty. They came to her, she said, when the sexual abuse happened, and they made her feel better. This dissociation was likely the result of the overwhelming helplessness she felt in dealing with the abuse. Elliot-Prisco entered Nancy's imaginary world through a multimedia art project in order to communicate with Nancy in a way that would feel comfortable to her. Nancy made paper dolls from Polaroid shots of herself that she had Elliot-Prisco snap in the poses she selected (Figure 3.2). (To protect confidentiality, the faces have been covered with drawn faces.) Her imaginary friends were constructed from self-hardening clay. She created a background with paint and markers for an enactment with her paper dolls

FIGURE 3.2 Polaroid paper doll dramatization by 11-year-old girl.

and clay animals. As she prepared her project, her problem-solving skills increased and her self-esteem rose. She requested Elliot-Prisco's assistance less and less. In directing the 10 different shots she wanted Elliot-Prisco to make of her, her sense of self-empowerment grew. Without direction, she organized and created a storyboard for her ensuing drama. Nancy said that all her animals are female. In elaborate stories, she told Elliot-Prisco of their origins, ages, and characteristics. They appeared to express aspects of her own identity. Nancy added a Bad Animal/Man to the group, represented by a Polaroid shot of a Big Bad Wolf toy, to stand for the evil threat in her drama. In her story, Kitty got taken away by the Bad Animal, and Nancy orchestrated the group in rescuing her. The Polaroid of herself kneeling shows her feelings of sadness and loss. In her next play, Dolphin was put in a dungeon by the Bad Animal/Man, where "the bad thing" (her way of referring to the sexual abuse) happened (p. 23). She addressed Kitty and said, "Kitty, what are we going to do today?" in imitation of the way Elliot-Prisco opened their art therapy sessions (p. 23). When the Bad Animal/Man returned to kidnap another of her companions, she protected them with the figure holding out her hands. The standing doll points her finger at him, and Nancy said, "You are bad. Never come near my friends again," and flung him at Elliot-Prisco, saying, "You take him. I have no use for him anymore" (p. 24). Creating art and ventilating feelings through its dramatic use enabled Nancy to recreate her victimization through a drama in which she herself was the rescuer, and the evil menace was eliminated.

Masks and Puppets

Holly Pumphrey also utilized art that could be used for dramatization in helping children to create masks and puppets (Pumphrey, 1999). Pumphrey utilized these projects as easy-to-make, successful activities that could help children feel a sense of power over their own lives. She felt they would also help in interaction, where one puppet could interact with another, perhaps more freely than the children might do otherwise. She expected their self-esteem to be enhanced as a result. Pumphrey worked in a community program for wards of the state who had been removed from their parents and placed in foster care due to parental abuse and neglect. She describes them as "uncontrollable children and adolescents who have absolutely no sense of who they are or how to feel good about themselves" (p. 2). Building self-esteem was a treatment goal for every child in the program.

Pumphrey demonstrated the mask-making process, using plaster gauze strips to cover a face mold. After making their own masks, the children painted and decorated them with a wide variety of materials. They were asked to make up an identity for the mask, with a personality and a history. They could make a book about the mask or write what they wished on a sheet of paper. The children were also encouraged to wear their masks and to interact with each other as their mask characters, creating a play and asking questions of the other masks.

Janelle, 16, was an African American girl diagnosed with Oppositional Defiant Disorder who had been court-ordered to receive therapy for recurrent aggressive behavior in which she attacked others. She had already spent time in a juvenile correction facility, to which she was to return if she attacked anyone again. Her typical behavior was to monopolize conversation, to yell over others' voices, to argue and provoke, and to hug, touch, and slap others inappropriately. She often skipped school. Since removal from her parents at age 8, she had had 10 different foster placements. Pumphrey saw her in an adolescent art therapy group, although her attendance was sporadic. Her investment in her art was minimal, and she had little awareness of her feelings. At her first mask-making session, however, she was invested in her work for the first time, taking great care to place the gauze strips evenly and to smooth them out. She was eager to come to the next session and began work on decorating her mask immediately. She was meticulous in her decoration of the mask. She asked Pumphrey what she thought of it, in Pumphrey's first glimpse of a softer, approval-seeking girl beneath the hardened teen who had usually told Pumphrey that she would not return after each session. When she spoke through her mask, she did not yell or insult anyone, as was her custom. She made a book about her mask, saying she was an Indian woman from Nebraska (where she knew Pumphrey was from). She shared her character's story with the group in a first attempt to communicate seriously with others. They reacted by letting her know they thought her work was very creative, and she obviously enjoyed the compliments.

Tiffany, an 8-year-old Puerto Rican/Mexican girl, had been referred for moodiness, hyperactivity, aggressiveness, lying, stealing, defiance, and low self-esteem. Her history included suicidal threats and self-injurious behavior. She had been removed from her mother due to drug abuse and neglect. Her mother had since quit using drugs and had complied with all DCFS referrals for counseling. As a result, Tiffany was soon to be returned to her mother's custody. Although Tiffany's symptoms were still present, they had decreased since learning that she would be returning to her mother within several months. Because she was easily frustrated, Tiffany was given an art directive that would not be too difficult, a plaster gauze mask. She responded enthusiastically. After a few frustrations along the way, she completed an Indian princess. She was unhappy with her mask, calling it ugly. Pumphrey was able to discuss with her the feelings she had when something was not perfect and why it had to be. This brought up issues of abandonment and how she got attention through throwing tantrums. Tiffany said her mask was the spirit of the dead. She did not want to share her mask with the group, but wore it on the van going home. She received a lot of praise for it. She returned with it to her individual art therapy session, saying how much her family had loved it. She asked for a string so she could attach it and wear the mask without holding it. Once again, she wore it home. Although Tiffany had been easily frustrated with her mask and had found many ways to reject it, in the end she was proud of it and, with difficulty, was able to ask the group members what they thought of her by speaking through her mask.

Tiffany began a puppet unenthusiastically, saying that it would not turn out well. She covered a Styrofoam ball attached to a cardboard cone with plaster gauze. She painted the head a flesh color and began making clothing. As she tackled the various steps of its creation, she developed confidence that she could do it and that she would like it even if it weren't perfect. She covered the face with black spots to indicate illness (Figure 3.3). As Tiffany decided that the puppet was recovering from its illness, she began painting over the spots. Each time she worked on it, she painted over a few more spots, healing herself one day at a time. Pumphrey could see her confidence blossoming. She kept the puppet in a special spot in the art room where it would be safe.

Cordelro, an overweight 12-year-old African American boy referred for unmanageable behavior at home and school leading to school suspension, had

FIGURE 3.3 Spots representing illness on replica
of puppet by 8-year-old girl.

been reported to have poor concentration and either to withdraw or to hold in anger until he exploded, resulting in constant fighting. He had been removed from his mother at age 2 due to her neglect, physical abuse, and drug use. He was living with his great aunt. Cordelro was diagnosed with ADHD, for which Ritalin was prescribed, but he was inconsistent in taking his medication. Having repeated several grades, he was older than his classmates in special education. He did not have any friends, probably due to being older than his peers, but also because he lived in a neighborhood too dangerous for him to be allowed to play outside. His only interests were watching television and drawing, the only activities on which he could concentrate. In individual art therapy, he was not hesitant to draw, but he remained very closed. Pumphrey introduced puppet-making to encourage him to open up, and he seized on the opportunity, immediately choosing to make a dragon (Figure 3.4). He began with a tube sock and glued two halves of a plastic cup to it to create a snout. He cut large fangs from cardboard and covered them with modge-podge to make them strong. He wanted his dragon to be able to bite. As he continued to work on it, he put the puppet on his hand at the beginning of each session and tried to bite Pumphrey with its sharp teeth. Foam formed the eyes, and cardboard inserts covered with felt became the roof and bottom of the inside of the large mouth. Finally, Cordelro added a long red tongue.

As he was working, he accidentally burned himself with the hot glue gun. He asked Pumphrey if the burn would scar like his other burns. When she asked him about them, he revealed that he had burned his hands and arms in

FIGURE 3.4   Replica of dragon puppet by 12-year-old boy.

the past to feel pain instead of the numbness he usually experienced. This revelation was a major step in Cordelro's building trust with Pumphrey.

Cordelro was very proud of his puppet and showed it to the other therapists and the children. He also used it for communication with Pumphrey. He put it on his hand at their subsequent sessions and spoke to her through it. Pumphrey took out a puppet she had made, and they had conversations through their puppets' voices. Sometimes Cordelro's dragon bit hers, and she would have to set some boundaries. This was an excellent way for them to deal with his aggression. He was able to share with her that he was teased a lot because of his age and weight, causing him to explode in anger as a way of dealing with his hurt feelings. Pumphrey used her puppet to model problem-solving behaviors, and he used his puppet to express the feelings that were difficult to verbalize directly. Pumphrey's puppet validated his feelings of loneliness, abandonment, self-consciousness, and anger. She helped him to see that these were normal feelings for a child his age in his circumstances. When it was time to say goodbye, they used their puppets to express their feelings, and the dragon gave Pumphrey a kiss on the cheek, affection he was not able to express as himself. Over the several months Pumphrey worked with him, Cordelro's problematic behavior decreased markedly, he developed more positive relationships with the other children, and he seemed a much happier boy. His angry, aggressive dragon had become a friendly creature.

Games

Marjory Hamilton worked at a not-for-profit suburban agency that provided outpatient services primarily for women and children who had been sexually abused or assaulted. Groups met for 90 minutes one evening weekly in cycles of 10 to 12 sessions. New members were added only at the beginning of a cycle, and most clients stayed for four cycles, or approximately 1 year. All were required to attend individual therapy as well. The agency served a primarily Caucasian lower socioeconomic class community.

Hamilton conducted an art therapy group for three sexually abused boys, age 8 to 11. In the first couple of sessions, they wanted to sit under the chairs, and when asked to find a safe place in the room, they fought for the same area under a table. Hamilton realized her challenge was to create a treatment plan to facilitate appropriate peer interaction among these boys, who tended to act out their anger. She developed a project for them to create their own communication board game (Hamilton, 1996). The boys were familiar with therapeutic board games, as several were often used at the agency. They would need to cooperate to create a game themselves, and they would have to develop problem-solving skills. The three boys in this group each showed some degree of social impairment and difficulty with peers. Goals for these boys included aggression management, frustration tolerance, increased assertiveness, and active group participation. Because sexual abuse victims are often defensive about being told what to do and fear being controlled, it was important to give the boys the bulk of control in developing the game. The project was presented in the following way:

> Together, as a team, you will design, plan, and create a therapeutic board game. The goal or theme of the game should have something to do with understanding sexual abuse and how to feel strong, powerful, and good about yourself. We will help you construct the project, but it is *your* project, so most of the decisions are up to all of you as a group. Remember, though, that the group has to agree with what each boy suggests. We want you to finish the project before the end of the cycle so that you can have the chance to play the game you have created. Also, if all members agree, the game can be used in the future by other children at the agency (p. 7).

The group consisted of the following boys:

- Ronnie, 8, who was small, quiet, and had difficulty speaking, for which he was teased. He had been molested by several family members, but was the only boy not to acknowledge his abuse. The individual goal for him was increased participation.
- Jeremy, 9, who was shy and was bullied by bigger kids. He had been molested by a neighbor, the only one of the three who was not a victim of incest. The individual goal for him was increased assertiveness.
- Mitch, 11, a self-described bully who experienced some dissociation. He had been abused by a brother 10 years older for about a year. The individual goal for him was management of frustration and aggression.

After hearing the group project proposal, the boys had an idea session and came up with a list of the materials they would need. They agreed on a theme about a boy who takes a journey on a pirate ship. Ronnie and Mitch had read Robert Louis Stevenson's *Treasure Island*, in which a boy meets a man whom he trusts but who turns out to be a treacherous pirate. Similarly, the perpetrator in abuse situations often tries to gain the victim's trust. Being in an incestuous family can be like being on a ship with no means of escape. As the boys discussed an obstacle or danger for the boy in the game, they decided on a crab with large pincers. Ronnie drew it while they were discussing it. The other boys were impressed with his drawing. This was Ronnie's first creative contribution.

At their first creative session, the boys were given a large sheet of paper to plan what the game board would look like. They drew boundaries, and each made his own design. Ronnie's plan was very rich and creative, revealing a complicated inner world. Jeremy did not want to work as a team member, but wanted to create his own game independently. Ronnie was absent at a subsequent session, and Jeremy and Mitch combined their designs for the game path. They painted it on a piece of 24-inch-square illustration board.

As the plan and painting proceeded in the following sessions, there were conflicts and compromises, challenges and resolutions. Mitch backed off from controlling. Jeremy became more assertive. When Ronnie and Jeremy teamed up against him, Mitch took himself out of the battle. The boys were able to learn from one another, as well. The oldest, Mitch, was impressed with the way the youngest, Ronnie, made his playing piece by using a pinch method with the clay. He asked Ronnie to teach him how to do it. Compromise and accommodation won out in what turned out to be creative solutions.

The board contained a painting of pirate ships, gold nuggets (made of clay and painted with metallic paint) for rewards, crab cards to be drawn when one landed on a crab space (from Ronnie's original design), star squares decorated with sequins, where the player had to say something positive about himself, and imaginative playing pieces made from clay (Figures 3.5 and 3.6). Crab cards included questions and directions related to abuse and peer relations, for example, "When might it be alright for a child to say 'no' to an adult?"; "Give an example of a bad secret"; and "Tell a bully to STOP." Hamilton helped the boys to develop the crab cards in order to encourage them to recognize dangerous situations and to learn possible useful reactions.

Following completion of the game, Hamilton asked the boys to make pictures of how they felt at the beginning and how they felt now. Mitch indicated that he was mad at the beginning but happy now. Ronnie didn't remember how he had felt, but drew himself with a big smile. Making the game taught the boys to work as a team, to solve problems together, to accept others' ideas,

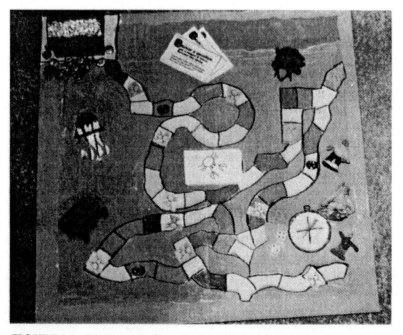

FIGURE 3.5   Pirate game board made by three sexually abused boys.

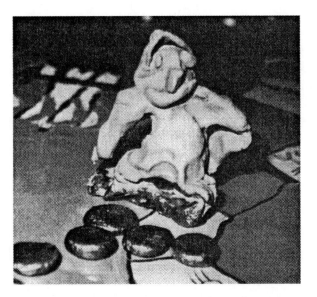

**FIGURE 3.6 Game piece and gold nuggets from
game by three sexually abused boys.**

and to negotiate. They realized that there were more fruitful ideas from the
three of them than any one of them could have come up with alone. The boys
played their game together and with other groups, as well as with their therapists. Other groups at the agency have played it, as well.

Shelters for Women and Children

Shelters provide temporary residential care for women and their children who
have been battered and abused in violent homes and for those who are homeless due to eviction. These families are in crisis. Treatment is short-term and,
for the children, is generally directed toward adjustment to their changing circumstances.

Children accompanying their mothers to a shelter from domestic violence
are in a state of crisis. They have lost their homes, parts of their families, and
most of what has been familiar in their lives. Generally, they stay at the shelter
until their mothers are ready to resume their lives outside the shelter. (For a
discussion of art therapy with mothers who are victims of domestic violence,
see Chapter 10, "Women.") It is important to help these children to deal with
the devastating aftereffects of the violence they have witnessed and, perhaps,
experienced directly. An investigation by Rosenbaum & O'Leary (1981) indicated that 82% of boys who witnessed spouse abuse were victims of physical
abuse by one or both parents. Because there is often a cross-generational cycle
of violence, interventions are needed to prevent these children from also
becoming violent as they grow older. Unfortunately, the mothers and their

children often return to their violent homes, only to return again to the shelter after a new bout of violence. It is estimated that women seek shelter an average of 5 to 7 times before they leave their attackers for good (Streeter & Bell, 1991). Some shelters also provide temporary residence for newly homeless women and their children. Loss and adjustment are significant factors for these children, as well.

Juliana Van der Ent-Zgoda worked with children at a community crisis center where 10 to 14 mothers and their 20 to 24 children stay for an average of 4 to 6 weeks. The center serves those who leave their homes due to domestic violence and who are temporarily homeless, usually because of eviction. These children face significant problems in fearing adults who are significant in their lives, in having permanent homes and consistency in school, and in having a parent who can care for them adequately. Nevertheless, due to the short term of their residence at the shelter, Van der Ent-Zgoda found that she needed to address their adjustment to living in the shelter and having lost their homes. During this time, the children's mothers were generally under extreme duress.

At individual 1-hour sessions, Van der Ent-Zgoda asked the children to draw where they lived (Van der Ent-Zgoda, 1990). Donald, 9, had been living with his mother and brothers in a church basement prior to coming to the crisis center. When asked to draw where he lived, he said, "I live here." He said he didn't know how to draw the center, so he drew a tree instead. Because of her own crisis, Donald's mother was not able to recognize his needs. In later sessions, Donald was able to recognize his anger and drew a volcano exploding in the direction of his mother and his younger brother.

Monique, 11, and her mother and sister were homeless. They had lived briefly with a friend until she, too, was evicted from her apartment. Monique drew a house with smoke coming from the chimney, where her mother made blueberry pies in the friend's apartment. They had lived there for two days. That had been her favorite of the many places where she had lived for a short time, and she worked diligently on her picture.

Maurice, 7, who came from a violent family, drew the projects where he had lived. He showed himself fighting with his cousins, which was how they had played. Van der Ent-Zgoda used art expression to help him learn more appropriate behavior and safer ways to play and to vent his anger.

Raven, 12, was afraid of her father because of witnessing his physical violence toward her mother. She drew the place where her mother was planning to move with two other women and their children, making a total of 14 people. Raven said there would be no boys in her picture, and that she didn't want her mother and her brother there.

Cindy, 8, her mother, and her older sister had lived in many shelters as a result of domestic violence. Cindy's sister had been raped by her father in her presence. She drew the crisis center, saying, "I am sad when we have to leave a place when we have been there so long and my friends leave me, I leave them" (pp. 28–29). In her final session, she wrote on her picture, "I HATE to leave" (p. 29). The disruption and turmoil in the lives of these children was evident in their artwork.

Anne Morrill worked in a family shelter service for women and children subjected to domestic violence. Among its services was a shelter for women and children. Often they arrived at the center in the middle of the night, sometimes with only the clothes on their backs. The focus of the shelter's program was education to empower women to avoid dangerous situations. The women and children stayed for an average of 3 weeks. Morrill conducted art therapy with the children. Their mothers were often too preoccupied with their own problems to attend to their children. The children were from 4 to 10 years old and either had been physically abused themselves or had witnessed violence in their homes. Morrill initially met with each child individually to introduce them to art therapy. They were then admitted to an art therapy group that met two or three times a week for 75 minutes (Morrill, 1992).

Aggression was addressed by asking the children to draw a time when they were angry. Discussion topics included children's right not to be hit and positive ways of dealing with conflict. Self-esteem tasks consisted of making life-size body tracings and books about themselves. The children made masks representing various feelings and used role-playing to assist them in sorting out confusing feelings and to encourage them to express their feelings. Family life was explored through family drawings, often reflecting a confusing situation for children from violent families.

Long-Term Residential Care

Children and adolescents who have not completed treatment in psychiatric hospitals, where care is usually short-term, or who need continued care but are unable to remain at home (including children removed from their homes because of abuse or neglect) are often referred to a long-term residential facility. Most often, these institutions are designated as schools because they must provide for the education of the children, but some hospitals also have long-term programs. What they all have in common, however, is a comprehensive program that provides both treatment and special education. Although psychiatric hospitals refer patients needing long-term treatment to residential care, the opposite is also true: Youngsters in residential care are referred for hospitalization when more acute care is needed. Art therapists working in residential settings are able to integrate their work into their clients' total life picture and develop an ongoing therapeutic relationship for the course of the child or adolescent's residency. In most cases, the length of stay is at least for the academic year. Many may stay several years. Most of these facilities have summer programs, as well. Those placed in long-term residential treatment usually have severe emotional disturbances.

Establishing Art Therapy

Establishing an art therapy service at any facility requires thought, planning, and usually some education of the staff. In a long-term residential setting, the art therapy treatment must fit into the total program for the children's daily lives. When I moved to Chicago in 1981, I met the director of a prestigious long-term residential facility for children and adolescents with severe emotional disturbances, which is associated with a major university. It is a world-renowned institution seeking to treat the untreatable, and much had been written by its famous director about treatment. Unlike many other treatment settings for young people, which use a behavior modification approach, the school utilized psychoanalytic milieu rehabilitation therapy by facilitating ego growth. (It has since changed to a more behavioral approach.) Maximum enrollment was 15 girls and 15 boys, age 6 to 15. The average classroom size was 6 students. All received individual therapy twice each week. Many of the children stayed for a number of years. The staff was very protective of the children, so the director was reluctant to have an art therapy intern because she felt the yearly turnover of interns would be too disruptive to the children. After I had known her for 6 years, we were having lunch one day, and I was speaking about the work of students in the art therapy graduate program I direct at the University of Illinois. She became very interested in arranging for an art therapy intern for the school. I visited the school on a carefully arranged tour that allowed me to view the beautiful, art-filled building while the children were at lunch so that I could see their classrooms and other facilities. (The children themselves were protected from strangers' visits.) In order to build a solid relationship and establish what I expected would be an excellent learning opportunity for students, I carefully selected the intern to be placed there. She was subsequently hired by the school. In the following years, more of our students interned there and were also hired. At present, the school has had a continuous art therapy program for 12 years.

Susan Kowalczyk has written about her experience as the school's first art therapist (Kowalczyk, 1988). Her first assignment was to reshape the art classes into groups that embodied aspects of art therapy. Teachers attended these 1-hour classes with their students once a week. The art classes were taught by a social worker who presented art fundamentals and instruction. She had been associated with the school for 28 years and had been teaching art there for 1½ years. Kowalczyk felt she needed to address whether there should be designated art activities for the classes in order to encourage self-expression and disclosure and what the roles would be for the social worker, the teacher, sometimes a teacher's aide, and herself. There were five classroom groups, and thus five art groups. Kowalczyk arranged to meet with each teacher every week to receive their feedback and to tell them of her plans for their art group.

She also arranged a quarterly review of the art with each student. One teacher had a strong negative reaction, questioning whether Kowalczyk and the social worker knew the students well enough to assist them in deciding on the disposal of their artwork. There appeared to be competition for the students' loyalty, and what subsequently developed into a rebellious attitude toward the art sessions on the part of one student may have been the result of subtle sabotage on the teacher's part.

Initially, the art classes continued as art education with the only change being Kowalczyk's presence. In one group, behavior problems were handled by the teacher, who had been at the school only a short time and had unrealistic expectations. The students had little investment in the art activities and resented being monitored constantly. Their behavior became very unruly. The teacher approached Kowalczyk almost in a panic and asked her to do something about the class, to add more structure. At this point, Kowalczyk tried to divide the class so that each leader would be responsible for two children. This plan did not work, however, as the teacher continued to monitor the whole group, and the social worker had difficulty hearing the children's questions due to a hearing problem, so Kowalczyk would jump in with a response. Out of frustration with the ensuing chaos, Kowalczyk took charge of the whole group. She also established rules: The children were to remain in their seats; they were not to touch one another's artwork; and they were to talk one at a time without interrupting. The teacher and the social worker were to participate in the artwork. The rules helped to organize the environment so that it was conducive to creating art. The organizational structure Kowalczyk developed was comfortable for the three leaders, and it remained the mode of operation for the remainder of her internship.

Kowalczyk also added structured activities, including group projects, such as a "musical drawing," in which everyone passed their pictures to the person to the right when the music stopped (like musical chairs), until each picture had been worked on by all the students. All the drawing had to conform to the picture's original theme, and no one was to draw on top of another's image. Several art sessions were devoted to life-size stuffed self-portraits (Figure 3.7). Large sheets of paper were folded in half longitudinally, and the children's bodies were traced on them. The outlines were then colored in, and the two sides of the paper were partially stapled together, stuffed with newspapers, and stapled closed. The students then introduced their "people" to each other.

The other groups, each with its own unique composition and set of needs, created their own special dilemmas. Three succeeded with an unstructured "art as therapy" framework. The fifth group, however, required a more complex design due to the divergence in the ages of its students. The class was divided into two groups of older and younger children, with the older two students working independently, attended to by the social worker, who chatted socially with them. Kowalczyk organized the younger three students into making a structured art project each week. The teacher fluctuated in her involvement with the group, rarely engaging in artwork.

Kowalczyk's next assignment was to integrate individual art therapy into

FIGURE 3.7 Life-size stuffed self-portraits.

the students' schedules. If sessions were to be scheduled during school hours, they were likely to be viewed as more important than if they were scheduled after school, when they would be considered more recreational. Teachers objected to the students being taken from class. Counselors, who were responsible for them outside the classroom, objected to after-school scheduling. Kowalczyk's role was unclear as well. Was she a teacher or a counselor? There was resistance from a teacher and a counselor who appeared to be threatened by Kowalczyk's involvement with their charges. After initial positive responses to the sessions, two boys in their charge became desultory in one case and resistant in the other. After discussions with each child and his counselor together, the problems were worked out, and the boys resumed art therapy. Kowalczyk notes that because art therapists have concrete results from their work (the art), other therapists may be envious of this advantage, in addition to the personal competition for the child's loyalty.

Her third assignment was to educate the staff about art therapy. To this end, she gave three in-service sessions. At the first, she informed the staff about art therapy, her educational background and experience, and her conception of her role at the school. She illustrated art therapy with examples of the students' work. At her next in-service session, she presented a case from the school. At the final session, she conducted a similar case presentation, but rather than offering her own comments about the work, she asked the staff to respond to the artwork. Responses to the first two sessions were minimal (except on the part of the counselor of the student whose case she presented; the counselor asked to meet with her on a regular basis). At the third session, however, when she requested that they guess whose sculpture she was displaying, there was much interest. The child's counselor was certain it had not been made by one of his clients. He was then amazed at the amount of information Kowalczyk was able to convey about the child and was slightly embarrassed that he had never seen this side of the child in therapy. The senior clinician admired the aesthetic value of the piece and said that it made her want to try sculpture herself. At this point, Kowalczyk began to receive acceptance and respect from the staff for the valuable role she was playing in the school's program. At first, Kowalczyk had felt alienated from the rest of the staff, as she was not a part of either the counselor group or the teacher group. (Such is the case for many art therapists, who are often the only art therapist at a given facility.) Her efforts to inform them and to interact with them eventually paid off, however.

Kowalczyk also participated in school activities as an "art person." She photographed the Halloween party and made a collage of the pictures for display, and she held an art show at the end of her internship, 9 months after her arrival. The former, early in her internship, brought her recognition as an artist, but did not further the staff's understanding of her work as an art therapist. The art show, however, was a great success on many levels. Although it had been scheduled to last only half an hour, because that was the usual amount of time that the entire school could be together without chaos breaking loose, the students remained interested in the event for 45 minutes. They interacted with each other and with the staff in a very appropriate way. The students were clearly very pleased to see their work matted and hung, feeling a sense of worth that their creations were treated with such recognition and respect. The show also provided a new way for the students and the staff to interact. The senior clinician stated that she thought it also brought the staff closer together.

The established, traditionally oriented structure of the school was perhaps more resistant to change and the introduction of a new way of working than would be the case at many institutions. Nevertheless, the integration of art therapy into a treatment setting as a new modality should be thought out carefully, with allowance for trial and error. Especially in settings where there is already an art program, the art therapist needs to be careful not to step on toes and to try to collaborate with the other art people. Kowalczyk offers the following suggestions:

- Allow time to get a sense of the philosophy of the facility before initiating changes.
- Educate the staff as soon as possible about art therapy to reduce feelings of alienation. Presenting in-service sessions, displaying client artwork, sharing the art experience, and holding individual meetings are ways to do so.

- Expose the staff to artwork as soon as possible in order to help them gain an understanding of the creative process and to minimize their resistance.
- Try not to hide in the unfamiliarity of the art therapist's role.
- Take advantage of the special kind of communication the art can offer.
- Seek support from external sources, especially other art therapists.
- Use art to clarify art therapy for yourself.

As a student intern, Kowalczyk found that by integrating art therapy into the school, she also integrated the profession within herself, clarifying how her own value system, personal goals, and self-image interacted with her professional learning in shaping her work as an art therapist. Establishing a new art therapy service is a challenging enterprise that calls forth creativity and insight. The art therapist must create a program that will fit into an existing treatment framework; gain the support of the rest of the staff members, who may initially be suspicious or threatened; and try to motivate the clients.

Junk Art

Michele Drucker is an art therapist at a special education school that is a part of a social service agency for youth age 6 to 21. In addition to being a residential facility, the school also serves day students. Most of the students are children and adolescents who have been unable to function in public schools. Almost all come from disadvantaged areas, and many have been involved with the juvenile courts. Most have learning disabilities. They are referred for art therapy by their social worker, a teacher, or sometimes at their own request. Drucker observes that special education students are often disruptive in their art classes when given conventional drawing materials. Therefore, she decided to use junk materials to engage them (Drucker, 1995). Although Drucker has found that engagement is less difficult in individual art therapy sessions, she organized some groups in order to help the students learn to work together. She formed two groups, one for elementary school children and the other for high school students.

The elementary school group was composed of eight boys and girls. The group met weekly for 45 minutes, with most of the time devoted to art making and only a short discussion period because these children had difficulty staying focused while listening to others. At one session Drucker gave each child a bag full of assorted junk materials and a Styrofoam base on which to build. The children responded quite differently from their behavior with two-dimensional media. For example, Tony had stormed into the room saying that he did not want to make art because he was mad at his teacher. At first he tried to distract the others, but as they were looking through their bags, he soon desisted and looked in his own bag. He built a large volcano out of wood pieces and cardboard tubing. He placed rubble made from little pieces of junk around the base. He said that there were people under the rubble who had been destroyed by the volcano. He seemed less angry as he channeled his feelings into his construction.

Mary, who usually demanded one-on-one attention, did not seem to know how to go about building with her bag of materials. James asked if he could work with her, probably because he liked her materials. Mary arranged the objects, and James glued them down. They worked well together and completed a scene with a tunnel and roads.

Steve was loud and demanding of attention. His attention span was short, and he had never completed a project. With assistance from Drucker, however, he was able to finish his abstract junk sculpture. He was proud of his creation and wanted to show it to his teacher.

At another session, Drucker gave each of the children a cardboard cone with a Styrofoam ball on top to make into puppets. This time, they were to share the other materials with the group, rather than having their own bags. Raymond made a magic lady (Figure 3.8), who could do magic to get what-

FIGURE 3.8   Magic lady made from junk materials by elementary school boy.

ever she wanted. The children were proud of their creations and elected to place them on a shelf in the art therapy room and bring others in to see them.

The high school group consisted of eight boys who had difficulty getting started. They were disruptive, interfering with each others' projects and throwing materials at each other. Two were designated as "artists" by the school's art teacher. In order to help the group become more focused on the art making and to bring them to the same level, Michele introduced the junk materials, which none of them had used before. She told them that they could either work individually or create a group project. After coming up with many ideas, they decided to build a house, with each one making a room. At the end, they would put all their rooms together. Half the boys lived at the facility. The day students lived at home. Most came from cramped apartments in disadvantaged neighborhoods. While building the project, they spoke of how it felt to live at the facility or in their own homes.

Tom, a residential student, said that he did not have a bedroom at home and did not know what he would want to put in one. He began building his room at the school. Although he had to share his room with three other boys, the room he created had space for only one. He decided it would be his ideal room, where he didn't have to share his space. He spoke of his problems with his roommates.

Dan, another resident, was having a difficult time at the residence, but could not go home because his mother didn't want him there. He decided to build his fantasy room. He said he understood how Tom felt in having no privacy at the residence. He gave his room a lot of attention, making a rug for the floor, pictures for the wall, a blanket for the bed, a plant, a television set, and a stereo. David, a day student, worked meticulously on the kitchen. He said that his family never ate together. He usually ate by himself in front of the television.

In the end, the boys decided to keep their rooms rather than putting them together. They had become very attached to them and made sure the art therapy room was locked after each session so that no one would disturb their rooms. Though there was some arguing over sharing the materials and occasional rowdy remarks, for the most part the boys cooperated and discussed many personal issues about home life, their families, and living at the residence.

Drucker found that the students who seldom completed art projects did so when using the junk materials. She notes that drawing and painting require conceptualization, whereas the junk allowed the students to experiment with assembling materials and to create a little at a time. Also, she felt that the tactile qualities of the materials were engaging. In supervising Drucker's work for several years, I was also struck by the lively three-dimensional creations the students made, whereas most were reluctant to try drawing. Because most of them came from impoverished inner-city backgrounds, I have wondered if they had had little previous exposure to art materials and therefore found the idea of transforming experience from a three-dimensional world into a two-dimensional picture to be foreign to their conceptualization processes.

Guided Imagery

Holly Rugland, who works with Drucker, also has found the children resistant to making art. Many state that they have no idea what to draw or that they do not know how to draw. To overcome these barriers, she introduced guided imagery (Rugland, 1999). She has found that beginning the sessions with this process promotes physical relaxation, self-awareness, emotional expression, and creativity. Rugland saw the children in weekly individual art therapy sessions. She began with relaxation exercises, in which they were asked to focus on their breathing and muscle tensions. After they were relaxed, she supplied guided imagery by telling a story that consisted of primarily visual images, but involved other senses, as well. They then spent the remainder of the session creating art from their imaginative experiences.

Richard, a 12-year-old residential elementary school student, had been removed from his home due to sexual abuse by his father. While living with his aunt and her husband, he was physically abused, and he was returned to his mother, who was no longer living with his father. He stayed there until his behavior became violent and he was expelled from school for threatening to kill his teacher. Rugland's first art therapy session with Richard occurred immediately after she had broken up a fight in which he had attacked another boy. But in contrast with the behavior she had just witnessed, Richard was quiet and reserved in art therapy. Although he was intrigued by the junk materials, he chose to make a beaded necklace. At the next session, he did the same. At the third session, Rugland introduced guided imagery to encourage his creativity. The scenario was about creating a safe place. Richard wanted to tell Rugland what he "envisioned," but he stumbled over his words. She suggested that he construct it. Using a cardboard tray, he created a duck pond with magic rocks, where he could wish for whatever he wanted. On the side he made clay figures of his mother and himself having a picnic on the grass. When Rugland asked him if he had made a wish, he said he did and that it came true because his mother came to have a picnic with him next to the ducks. He described a time when they had visited the duck pond at the zoo. He said that he missed her very much and that he cried when he went back to his residential unit. By the end of the session, Richard seemed relieved to have expressed his sadness.

At the next session, Rugland used guided imagery about discovering a door and observing what is behind it. She gave Richard a piece of paper with a door taped on it. He drew a picture of seeing his aunt on the other side of the door. She is an angel now, he said, as he drew her on top of a car with red smeared underneath it (Figure 3.9). He explained that she had been killed in a

FIGURE 3.9   Guided imagery door exercise by 12-year-old boy.

car accident. He spoke of his sadness and of missing her, saying he wished he could be an angel with her. He added doorknobs on both sides of the door so he could visit her whenever he wanted.

Charles, a 14-year-old junior high school student, lived at home with his mother and siblings and commuted to school. After he became frustrated with drawing, crumpling his picture and throwing it away, Rugland introduced guided imagery. Charles was excited about the process, saying he wanted to take a vacation in his brain. Rugland used guided imagery about traveling to another planet. Charles created a planet with a gun and jets made from cones so the planet could be protected and fly away from Earth. There were two separate compartments, which Charles explained as being for good people and bad people, respectively. The good people were those who would never hurt anyone, and the bad people didn't care about others. After completing the planet, he decided to make a good person to live there. He asked for a guided imagery about aliens, so Rugland created one about traveling to Charles's special planet to meet aliens. He made an alien puppet out of a cardboard cone and a Styrofoam ball. The good people in his imagination were likely the people he needed in his life.

Angel brought an arrogant attitude to art therapy, saying he thought it was stupid. He resisted making art. At his second session, Rugland tried guided imagery with a scenario of space exploration. As soon as he opened his eyes, he began searching through the bins of recycled material. He made a spaceship with cardboard cones for jets to blast him far, far away as fast as possible. Angel wished to return to public school and was embarrassed to be in special education. At the next session, he painted his spaceship blue so that it would be invisible in outer space and in the ocean (it could transform into a submarine), so that no one would see him leave; he would just blend in with everyone else.

At his next session, Angel came in furious with his teacher and asked to do just the relaxation part of the guided imagery. Rugland agreed, and when that was finished she suggested that he concentrate on a blank screen behind his eyes to notice any images that appeared. He became very excited and raced around the room looking for the largest drawing paper he could find. With markers, he drew an erupting volcano. He said the lava exploded the way he did in class. Frustrated with his drawing, however, he crumpled it up and threw it away. He then asked Rugland how to build a volcano. She suggested plaster and newspaper. Angel worked hard on his project, and asked for extra sessions. Each session was begun with the blank-screen guided imagery, and Angel made a point of gauging his mood by the volcanic states. His emotions ranged from angry, like a volcano on the verge of eruption; to excited, like an exploding volcano; to peaceful, like the aftermath of a volcanic eruption. This project helped him to identify and deal with his emotions.

Lakeysha, a 16-year-old African American girl who lived at the facility, was in the agency's independent living skills program. The oldest of eight children, all of whom had been removed from their mother's care because of her neglect and narcotics abuse, she had witnessed the murder of her father when she was quite young. Diagnosed with Dysthymic Disorder, she had been hospitalized numerous times. She had suffered physical and sexual abuse and had engaged in self-injurious behavior. She exhibited poor impulse control and threw tantrums, but was also capable of insight. Lakeysha took pride in her artistic ability and had won citywide recognition for her artwork. As a result, she was overly focused on artistic success. With this in mind, Rugland began their first session with guided imagery about being a robot in order to encourage her to explore being controlled by others (i.e., the art teacher who urged her to compete). She immediately grabbed some wood and constructed an image of herself as a robot (Figure 3.10). She added a brain that could be opened and closed. She said that others had programmed memories into her brain that could not be deleted. She created the memories out of construction paper and placed them in the robot's head (shown at the bottom of Figure 3.10). Most are tragic, including the broken heart for the abuse she endured, gravestones for the deaths of her father and grandfather, and a child with its mother to symbolize the trust she never had as a child. The book represents her knowledge and schoolwork, and the intact heart the positive relationships she has. She said that it is not fair that she has to walk around with these bad memories. With markers, she added scars to the robot. Lakeysha was able to express many of her very painful issues through her robot figure.

Rugland notes that the school's program is highly structured, and that when given an opportunity to experience the loose, imaginative activity of art making, the children were often inhibited. Guided imagery opened a window

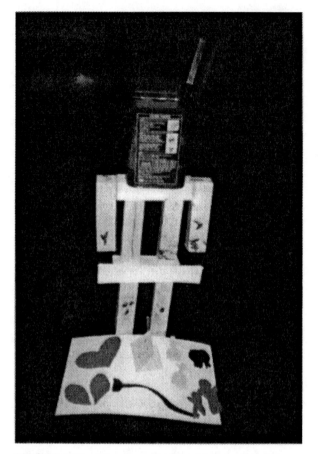

FIGURE 3.10   Wooden robot by 16-year-old girl.

to their imaginations that allowed them more free expression. It also helped them to remember details. For example, when Richard imagined lying in the grass with his mother, he remembered feeling rocks under his shoulders. The first thing he searched for among the recycled materials was something that felt like a rock. Then the rocks in his creation became magic instruments to fulfill his wishes.

Art Therapists' Self-Processing

The relationships with children and adolescents in long-term treatment are often very intense. Using their own art for reflection has been very helpful to art therapists in these settings. Rita Nathanson worked on a state psychiatric hospital adolescent unit where patients remained for 2 to 4 years. The luxury of being able to sustain long-term work such as this is extremely rare in a hospital setting, and this hospital has since been closed. Nathanson's patients were difficult-to-reach adolescents who were mistrustful, hostile, angry, and sometimes violent. All had been physically or sexually abused, and they defended themselves by lying, manipulating others, and turning to delinquent behavior. Many had been abused by treatment staff members as well as by their parents. Nathanson questioned whether she would be able to empathize with patients who were so hostile and guarded in relating to others. She devised a process to utilize art making through a series of images to lead her to awareness of her own issues in relation to her patients and to gain a fuller understanding of their issues (Nathanson, 1994). She utilized a "pursuit of the image" approach from my own work (Wadeson, 1987), in which I suggest that art makers "refrain from explaining and instead search for what they find exciting, surprising, puzzling, or intriguing in their own work (images)" (p. 265). Out of this response a subsequent image is then developed, which is then viewed in the same way, and another image is made. This process can continue indefinitely, but usually three pictures are created. Nathanson found that through this process she could understand her own issues in relating to her patients, which "made the way clear for empathy" (Nathanson, 1994, p. 1). She drew when she felt confused in her interaction with a patient or had intense feelings and when she was not clear how to proceed in treatment.

Thirteen-year-old Len suffered Post-Traumatic Stress Disorder (PTSD) as a result of paternal incest and neglect. Both parents abused drugs. He had made a serious suicide attempt, had had multiple foster home placements and hospitalizations, and was a ward of DCFS. Len was agitated in his art therapy sessions, had difficulty remaining in his chair, and drew violent pictures about which he told violent stories ending in death. Nathanson found herself spending most of the sessions setting limits on Len and feeling confused about his anxious, aggressive behavior. In her first picture of a sequence of drawings in response to Len, he is shown exploding in all directions while she is off to the side, only half in the picture. She felt unable to connect with him. Blue hands surrounding his figure are a metaphor for the consistency and clear expectations she needed to provide to help Len feel safe in their relationship. With her increasing understanding, he began to become calmer in the sessions. He attempted to make a papier-mâché animal out of tissue paper and failed. She did not know where Len was trying to lead her and felt that a drawing would help her find the way. Nathanson's next picture of Len shows him smiling proudly at a large paper mache animal he has made. It brought her back to her first experience with clay in elementary school and her love of the feel of it and the control she felt in forming it. (Nathanson is an accomplished ceramist.) Len had little control over his physical and emotional needs, which had not been met in early childhood. Being able to control and manipulate art materials could provide an important corrective emotional experience for him, Nathanson realized. She felt a strong connection with him. Creatively, Len built a green dinosaur, then a plaster gauze castle with a moat where he would live alone. Through her own connection with the art materials, Nathanson gained insight into Len's needs, which enabled her to help him to achieve a stronger sense of himself in art therapy.

Krista was a 15-year-old Hispanic girl diagnosed with chronic schizophrenia. Having suffered sexual abuse at an early age, she had had six unsuccessful foster placements and a previous psychiatric hospitalization for a suicide attempt. She had a history of polysubstance abuse beginning at 9 and of prostitution beginning at 11. She was tall and obese. Although most of the patients on the adolescent unit were initially unfriendly, Krista was friendly until Nathanson gave her a restriction in her second session that evoked much anger, and she then refused to speak to Nathanson. Worried about how to respond to Krista, she drew Figure 3.11. Although Krista looks innocent, the second face in her torso is bizarre and frightening. In the next picture in Nathanson's series, the image of the inside face becomes a large egg shape with cracks and heavy-lidded eyes (Figure 3.12). Nathanson saw the cracks as giving it a fragile brittle appearance and was reminded of feeling intense anger herself that she felt would split her open and explode out of her. She saw

FIGURE 3.11   Art therapist's depiction of 15-year-old girl with a face in her belly.

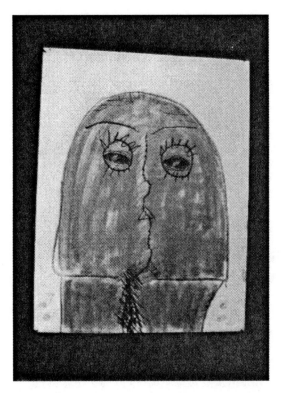

FIGURE 3.12   **Art therapist's development of
the inside face from Figure 3.11.**

the picture as reflecting Krista's efforts to control her rage. Nathanson remembered her own rage at her parents when she felt unfairly treated.

For several sessions Krista painted quietly, interacting very little with
Nathanson. Feeling superfluous to her art making and her therapy, Nathanson
asked Krista what she got out of art therapy. Krista replied, "I get to be a kid"
(p. 12). Nathanson felt rejected and incompetent as an art therapist. She drew
Figure 3.13 to understand her reaction and her role in Krista's treatment.
Nathanson is holding a large balloon that is Krista's face. There is a small child
behind bars in her mouth. Nathanson saw herself as looking confused and
frightened. The child behind bars is Krista's childhood. Nathanson recalled
how wonderful she had felt in losing herself in her own creativity in playing
with clay and empathized with Krista's need simply to make art as a child, to
compensate for the childhood she didn't get to have. The sewn-up wound on
Nathanson's figure of herself represents a close relationship in which she realized she was not allowing the other person to grow but had wanted to keep
her dependent. The ropes that hold the balloon face are Nathanson's attempts
to hold onto Krista, but this image made her realize that what Krista needed
was support for her own autonomy, not dependency. Nathanson recognized
and empathized with Krista's use of art to reclaim her childhood.

FIGURE 3.13   Art therapist's exploration of relationship with 15-
year-old girl.

Nathanson's art responses were quick and spontaneous, more primitive in
their form and content than the finished illustrations made by Terry Lavery in
the final pictures of his series to process his reactions to his adolescent patients
(see Chapter 2, "Children and Adolescents in Psychiatric Hospitalization"). Immediate reactions without preconceptions can tap into unconscious processes
that surface in the art. The slower development of a finished piece can be a
meditative experience that deepens reflection and understanding. Both are
useful processes. Each of the art therapists used a serial method whereby one
picture led to another.

Polly Cullen worked at a school that provided long-term residential treatment. In trying to understand the complex dynamics of her clients and her
relationships with them, she utilized her own artwork to examine her countertransference (Cullen, 1992). Cullen was particularly interested in projective
identification. She states that Cashdon (1998) captured the essence of her experience: "Individuals who rely on projective identification engage in subtle but
nonetheless powerful manipulations to induce those about them to behave in
prescribed ways" (p. 56). Cullen used a powerful dream, an overly strong
emotional reaction to a client, a repeated visual image she experienced in relation to a client, a preoccupation, or avoidance of a client as indicators that she
needed to make art about her relationship with a client.

Eleven-year-old Melissa looked more like 4. She had been hospitalized at
age 9 after alleged sexual abuse by her father and brother. She was placed in
custody with her grandparents, who gave her up due to her unmanageable
behavior. Melissa sucked her thumb and often talked like a baby. She related
to Cullen on a symbiotic level, claiming that Cullen's artwork was her own

and that Cullen knew what she was thinking. Her provocative behavior was often sexualized. Reports indicated that her mother treated her like a baby.

Cullen drew a dream she had about Melissa in which they were in her office (Figure 3.14). Cullen is curled up in the lower right corner, naked, and Melissa is standing across the room in a position of victory, with her hands over her head, cheering. Her teacher is looking in the window at the "boundary violation and my victimization by Melissa" (p. 13). Until this dream and picture, Cullen had not realized how deeply her difficult relationship with this child was affecting her. She herself was feeling as if she were a victim of sexual abuse. Her dream and the resulting artwork, symbols of Melissa's projective identification, enabled her to empathize with Melissa's position as a victim. Difficulties in Cullen's relationship with the teacher surfaced in her appearance in the dream as a judge witnessing the therapeutic relationship. Cullen was feeling responsible, as though she was causing Melissa's behavior. In further art with construction pieces and in her interactions with Melissa, Cullen struggled to foster a healthier relationship where appropriate boundaries were fixed. Eventually Melissa accepted these boundaries and began to voice them in terms of "mine" and "yours."

Deborah Haugh worked at the school two years later under Cullen's supervision. She, too, utilized postsession art to work out relationships with her clients (Haugh, 1994). First, she made a spontaneous art piece in order to

FIGURE 3.14   Art therapist's dream about 11-year-old girl.

center herself. Then she copied the client's art piece, even sitting in the client's chair and trying to mimic the client's body position while working on it. In the next two steps, she engaged in the "pursuit of the image" approach—she included the client's original imagery, which she progressively manipulated by the distortion, addition, or deletion of visual elements.

Eleven-year-old Evan was an African American boy who had been placed in protective custody after he and his siblings were found in a housing project, filthy and eating garbage. His mother, a drug abuser, refused to cooperate with DCFS and subsequently lost her parental rights. Two years later, she died of an overdose. Evan's father was incarcerated for selling drugs. During the 3 years Evan was in foster care, he was hospitalized three times for suicidal and homicidal behaviors. He was diagnosed with schizophrenia, childhood type with depressive features, and severe Narcissistic Personality Disorder. Haugh met with him twice weekly in art therapy as his primary therapist. His behavior alternated between being charming in one session and hostile and manipulative in another. In his artwork, he often created very original heroes and villains.

In reproducing one of Evan's pictures, Haugh sat in his chair and assumed his position and movements. She copied Itchy Fingers, a superhero who fights crime. In applying many layers of transparent tape to the red construction paper to form the frame, she felt that it provided containment and safety. She drew the figure carefully in pencil, filled it in with markers as he had done, and watched the color bleed through and distort the detail (Figure 3.15). The process annoyed her, and she felt disorganized, fragmented, and trapped. The drawing looked empty to her, and she had the urge to give it a baseline and an environment. In her development of this picture, she did just that. She asked herself where she would be in the picture and added herself observing in the background. She was surprised to discover herself in Itchy Fingers' line of fire. She became aware of Evan's fear of victimization and his need to defend himself. She suspected that he was afraid of killing someone or of being killed himself. Haugh's next drawing shows the two of them contained in a yellow force-field sphere that Evan had drawn in one of his comics. Itchy Fingers floats above and points his gun at Haugh (Figure 3.16). She no longer fears this part of Evan. This exploration helped Haugh to see that she had been attempting to control Evan's expression of aggression. She felt freed from her fears and her need for control. Rather than confronting his manipulative behaviors, she stressed his fear of being attacked by refocusing him on the art process. He seemed empowered as a result.

Needy, attention-seeking Laura was a 10-year-old child who had been placed in foster care after being found roaming unsupervised and malnourished. She had had three foster placements and three hospitalizations for aggressive behavior toward peers and animals and for suicidal ideation. She had attempted suicide by running in front of cars. As her primary therapist, Haugh met with her twice weekly in individual art therapy. She also saw her

FIGURE 3.15   Art therapist's development of client's image to process her reactions.

in two weekly groups. Laura told Haugh she resembled her mother, and Haugh felt a reciprocal maternal countertransference. Creative and invested in the art at first, Laura's depression surfaced after a while, and her energy flagged. Haugh made several art pieces indicating her wish to nourish Laura. She quotes my advice to her in a supervision group, "to listen, be with Laura, and hold her symbolically" (p. 23). Haugh created a mask on a mold in the same way as Laura had (Figure 3.17). While making it, Haugh felt frustrated, sad, numb, and empty. She then turned it over and created a nest in it with birds she sculpted to represent Laura and herself (Figure 3.18). She saw them as together but separate. Laura could sit in her depression as long as she needed, and when she was ready, she could fly out. Making the art enabled Haugh to feel greater empathy for Laura and to recognize that she was stuck in a symbiotic phase of development. Haugh also realized that she needed to step back from Laura's symbiotic orbit.

FIGURE 3.16   Further development of client's image from Figure 3.15.

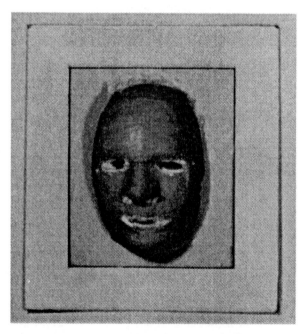

FIGURE 3.17   Art therapist's mask, made by methods used by her client.

FIGURE 3.18   Art therapist's nest in mask from Figure 3.17.

Summary

Children with less severe problems may be seen in outpatient art therapy while continuing to live at home and attend their regular schools. At some facilities, outpatient services are organized in cycles of treatment. Art therapists have been innovative in developing various therapeutic art projects to suit the particular needs of these children. Children in residential shelters for women and children who have been victims of domestic violence or homelessness receive short-term treatment, generally directed toward adjustment to their changed living situations. Long-term treatment in residential settings offers therapists the opportunity to develop a therapeutic relationship and the possibility of seeing substantial improvement. The children and adolescents in residential treatment, however, are among those who have been the most severely damaged and may be the most difficult to treat. The intense long-term therapeutic relationships with these clients have motivated art therapists to utilize their own art making to process their strong reactions. The following are some innovative ways of working in these settings art therapists have devised:

- Alexandria Elliot-Prisco (1995) used photography in work with sexually abused girls.
- Holly Pumphrey (1999) designed puppet- and mask-making projects to build self-esteem and identity formation for foster children. Speaking through the masks and puppets also aided authentic communication among the children.

- Marjory Hamilton (1996) worked with sexually abused boys by facilitating their building a therapeutic board game.
- Juliana Van der Ent-Zgoda (1990) helped children to adjust to being in a shelter for women and children by asking them to draw where they lived.
- Anne Morrill (1992) worked with children in a shelter for women and children who had suffered domestic violence.
- Susan Kowalczyk (1988) described establishing an art therapy program in a residential school where there was resistance to her work.
- Michele Drucker (1995) found that utilization of innovative materials stimulated the children and adolescents who had previously been disruptive.
- Holly Rugland (1999) inaugurated guided imagery to stimulate art production among resistant children.
- Rita Nathanson (1994) used her own art to help her to develop empathy for the difficult-to-reach adolescents on a long-term hospital psychiatric unit.
- Polly Cullen (1992) and Deborah Haugh (1994) used their own art in exploring their reactions to children in a psychoanalytic milieu treatment setting.

Conclusion

Children who are able to function at home and at school, yet who show signs of having problems or who have been in situations where problems are likely to develop, are often treated in outpatient facilities. Many have experienced sexual abuse or neglect. These children may be living with parents or foster parents, and some may have had numerous foster placements. Art therapists are often able to reach these children through projects that involve them much more than verbal discussions are likely to do.

Children in shelters with their mothers receive only short-term treatment there, even though they have suffered violent or deprived home lives. Follow-up therapy to help them to adjust to their new living arrangements—or, too often, to their unfortunate return to their violent homes—would be beneficial. Ongoing work with these children to help them learn nonviolent ways of coping, in order to interrupt the perpetuation of the intergenerational cycle of violence, would be advisable.

Providing long-term care for disturbed youths is extremely important work. Many of these children and adolescents have met with successive failures. Coming from disadvantaged communities, they may have experienced abuse or neglect, expulsions from other schools, psychiatric hospitalizations, and, in some cases, conflict with the law. Those who have been given up by their parents or removed from parental custody have swelled the numbers of youths who are wards of the state. In Illinois, wards of the state are more likely to go to jail than to college, and most face serious obstacles in achieving future independence. Half the young women sign up for welfare benefits immediately after they turn 21, trading one system of dependency for another. University of Wisconsin researchers checked on former wards a year after they grew out of the system and found that more than a quarter of the young men had already spent time behind bars. "Policymakers interested in crime prevention would be hard pressed to find a group at higher risk of incarceration than the males in our sample," the study reported ("Graduating from State Care," 1999, p. 12). It is clear from these studies that long-term treatment can be a significant resource in preventing some of the gravest ills our society faces.

ART THERAPY PROJECTS

Projects discussed in this chapter are described further in Chapter 15, "Art Therapy Activities and Materials":

- Polaroid photography (Elliot-Prisco, 1995)
- Self-boxes (Elliot-Prisco, 1995)
- Environment (Elliot-Prisco, 1995)
- Puppets (Pumphrey, 1999)
- Masks (Morrill, 1992; Pumphrey, 1999)
- Board game (Hamilton, 1996)
- Body tracings (Morrill, 1992)
- Books (Morrill, 1992)
- Life-size stuffed dolls (Kowalczyk, 1988)
- Musical drawing (round robin; Kowalczyk, 1988)
- Art exhibit (Kowalczyk, 1988)
- Junk art (Drucker, 1995)
- Construction (Drucker, 1995; Rugland, 1999)
- Guided imagery (Rugland, 1999)
- Construction in mask (Haugh, 1994)

Chapter 4

Physically Ill and Dying Children

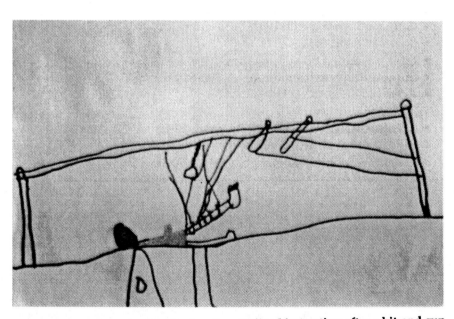

"Traction reaction" drawing by boy hospitalized in traction after a hit-and-run accident.

Danny presses the button to raise his bed so he can sit. He reaches for the pad of paper and box of markers the art therapist gave him. Looking around the room at all his pictures she hung on the walls for him, he's unsure what he wants to draw next. He still feels weak from the surgery, and the place they cut him open under all the bandages on his stomach hurts. At least he isn't still hooked up to the IV, so he can draw now. He looks at his last picture, a painting he made in the playroom right before they did it. It shows the doctor cutting him open and red blood spurting everywhere. He starts to draw himself all sewn up. He can hear some kid crying down the hall, and then the sound of the art therapist's cart rolling toward his room. He smiles and draws big stitches down his abdomen.

Children receiving hospital treatment face a great many challenges. They may be in a weakened or painful condition. They are often subjected to frightening, invasive, painful procedures that they do not understand. They have been removed from all that is familiar—home, family, school, and friends. They are often isolated in hospital rooms. The environment of the hospital itself may be strange and frightening to them. They may have lost control of their bodies to a large extent, and certainly they are at the mercy of those prescribing the procedures they must undergo, often at unexpected intervals. They often feel extremely vulnerable. Vulnerability to stress depends on many factors, including the child's chronological and developmental age as it relates to the ability to understand what is happening; responses to previous hospitalizations and separations; emotional support, especially from the family; coping and communication skills, especially with caretakers; cultural definitions of illness and views of modern medical treatment; and, of course, the child's physical condition. The latter encompasses diagnosis and prognosis—that is, whether the condition is acute, chronic, disfiguring, life threatening, or terminal. The prognosis assesses the degree to which current and future symptoms interfere with normal functions and comfort levels, the risks and side effects of treatment and their duration, and the probable course of recovery or deterioration.

Given the helplessness and confinement that many children experience in the hospital, art therapy can provide an important outlet for the ventilation of feelings, as well as offering one arena in which the child can take control. Art therapists are often associated with hospital child life programs that attempt to meet young patients' psychosocial needs during their stays. Many hospitals have a playroom or recreation room for children who are mobile. For those who are not, art therapists have utilized various devices to enable children to make art in bed (see Wadeson, Durkin, & Perach, 1989). Since children come to the hospital for outpatient tests and other procedures, art therapists also work in hospital waiting rooms with children waiting to be seen, as well as with the siblings who often accompany them on these visits to the hospital. (Children testing positive for human immunodeficiency virus [HIV] and those with acquired immunodeficiency syndrome [AIDS] are discussed in Chapter 12, "Sexual Orientation and AIDS.")

Child Life Program

Diane Evans worked in a large inner-city children's hospital. Children stayed from a few days to several months. Each had a private room, which tended to increase their isolation. The hospital had a large playroom that included medical equipment so that the children could become familiar with it and could use it on dolls and staff members. There was also a teen lounge, as well as a kitchen and a play kitchen. When Evans visited patients in their rooms, she carried a large basket of supplies and a plastic cafeteria tray with paper taped to it so patients could work on their laps. Evans worked in the Department of Child Life and Family Education, whose mission was based on the belief that all children have the need to play and that through play children can gain some control over their environment. Even so, Evans still felt depressed by the hospital's atmosphere in which she saw children placed near the nursing station crying and others in their steel cribs all alone and hooked up to intravenous (IV) apparatus poles and other machinery (Evans, 1985). Because this was a teaching hospital, daily rounds were made by residents, nurses, and both medical and nursing students. The children were often seen by as many as 50 different strangers in one day. Blood was drawn by one person, X rays taken by another. As their art therapist, Evans became a constant presence in the children's lives at the hospital, and one person who did not administer pain. Many of the children thought they were in the hospital as punishment. Some stayed too briefly for a relationship to be built. Others were too ill or too constantly involved in medical procedures to participate in art therapy

Almost all the children with whom she worked, no matter what their age, drew a picture of home in their first or second session. Figure 4.1, drawn by 15-year-old Anissia, is an example. Hospitalized to have surgery for Crohn's disease, she seemed to contain her preoperative anxiety in this detailed rendering, which she colored with fine markers. She said it was the apartment house where she lived.

Art therapy became an important means for children to tell their stories. Both Dominique and Temisha were victims of hit-and-run automobile accidents, and both spent 8 weeks in the hospital with a leg in traction. Daily art therapy visits were important in giving them at least one activity where they could be active. They each drew a picture of what had happened to them. After Dominique drew a map of the scene of the accident (Figure 4.2), he reenacted it with toy cars and people. As he told and retold the story, the people and cars he selected got bigger and bigger. Both children were able to discuss their fear of crossing the street after discharge. Whereas Dominique's drawing depicts a scene, Temisha's is more personal (Figure 4.3). In what Evans labels the "traction reaction" (p. 66), she observes that these children usually feel healthy aside from having a broken bone. She describes them as generally engaging and quick to learn how to get people to stay and to come back to their rooms. After a few days, however, they become restless, bored, less responsive, and more demanding, with generally shorter attention spans.

FIGURE 4.1   *Home* by 15-year-old girl.

Their initial art therapy generally addresses their traumas, as was the case with Dominique and Temisha. After several false starts that disappointed him, Dominique drew himself in traction (see page 122). Eight-year-old Pharies was in head and neck traction as a result of a child falling from a building onto his head. He made many fantasy picture stories in art therapy, some of which

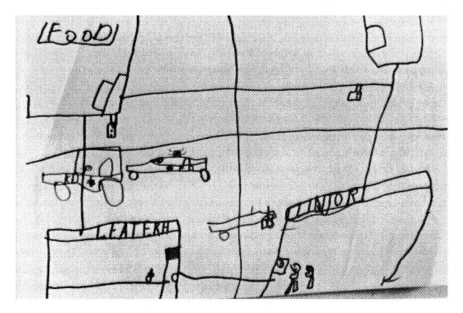

FIGURE 4.2   Map of hit-and-run accident by boy hospitalized in traction.

FIGURE 4.3   Being hit by a car by child hospitalized after a hit-and-run accident.

looked as though one person was falling onto another from a building. When his attention span grew shorter, Evans suggested some joint picture making. In a sequence drawing, they drew his head, ending with it in traction, in the drawing. Pharies then wanted to look in the mirror to see what he was feeling really looked like to others.

Johnnie, a 15-year-old African American boy, was hospitalized to undergo kidney tests and was due to be discharged the next day. Nevertheless, his one art therapy session was meaningful to him. His anxiety level was high, but he was impressed with the technology of the machinery in the testing room (Figure 4.4). He drew another picture of how his kidney looked on the monitor, coloring it bluish green, as he remembered it looked. He spoke of how awful it was to be waiting for the test results. Nevertheless, this experience led him to consider a career in medical technology. The single art therapy session helped him to gain some sense of mastery over his unpredictable situation.

In contrast, David, who was hospitalized for 3 months, is an example of a long-term relationship. A 20-year-old African American with paraplegia, David was hospitalized for repair of anal ulcers. He was also dialyzed three times a week. Having to stay in bed at all times on a sand-air mattress, he was understandably depressed, but appeared to expend all his energy on keeping the lid on his anger. Because David did not want to do any art, Evans made things for him. Slowly a relationship began to build, and David would ask for Evans from other staff. They designed a bulletin board together and decorated his room. He tended to be very passive. Evans was appalled when a doctor came into his room and began examining David's rectum in her presence. She

FIGURE 4.4   **Testing room machinery by 15-year-old boy.**

excused herself and later began educating David to use his own power, so that by the time he was nearing discharge he was able to tell the doctor to wait until she left and to ask her to close the door.

Ledonne, 15, was hospitalized for colitis, which may have been a somatic manifestation of his emotional problems. He believed he had extraordinary mental powers and could control his IV pump with his mind. He drew a picture of the operating room doors and spoke of his fear of surgery. He said that is where doctors cut people up. His next picture was of his IV pole, which made him angry even though he showed it off to others. After making this picture, Ledonne did not want any more art therapy. Evans discussed her concerns about his sense of reality with a psychiatric resident, and after an evaluation the child psychiatry staff became involved in his case. Unfortunately, the discharge plans were not communicated to them, so no psychiatric treatment was continued. Evans remarked that this sort of interdepartmental failure in cooperation was one of the frustrating realities she encountered in working in a medical setting.

Yolanda, a 13-year-old African-American girl, was hospitalized for corrective surgery for scoliosis. Harrington rods were inserted alongside her spinal column to elongate and straighten her spine, and she was placed in a body cast to be worn for 6 to 8 weeks following surgery. After drawing her room at home, she began to cry, saying she wanted to go home. When Evans suggested she put her feelings into a picture, she drew *The Fixed Up Clown* and talked about how scary it was to be in the hospital, but that it felt good to put her feelings on the paper. In a joint sequence drawing, Yolanda began to communicate about her crooked spine. Her bodies always leaned. Evans deliberately exaggerated the crooked body image in one panel. In the next panel, Yolanda straightened it out. Her last picture was titled *The Sad Room*. She was in a room across from the parents' waiting area for the intensive care unit. She was alarmed by all the crying that kept her awake at night. She drew two figures next to a phone, with one telling the other not to cry. Yolanda had formed a strong attachment to Evans and used the art to deal with her difficult feelings.

Thirteen-year-old Adan overheard doctors discussing the progress of his Hodgkin's disease—it had reached stage 4, the most critical stage—before he was told of his condition directly. This provoked a lot of anger and anxiety in an already frightened boy. He liked markers and drew a picture series about a father who arrives from another planet to find his son, who is in prison. Adan thought he was in the hospital with stage-4 Hodgkin's as a punishment for some wrongdoing. Another picture expresses his anger through showing planes bombing his school. Adan felt victimized, which was exacerbated by the promise of discharge several times, only to have his discharge repeatedly delayed by the staff. In another series, a moving van goes to his house in the country (where he lived) and takes all his possessions away to the big city (where the hospital is). Evans notes that his drawing of his bedroom at home resembles his room in the hospital. During a later hospitalization, Adan received a catheter directly into his heart that administered chemotherapy more easily and eliminated the need for an IV pole. He knew his stay at the hospital this time would be short, and he drew a happy family picture. Adan was able to use art therapy to create metaphors for his real-life experience.

Tamur, age 6, came to the United States from Iraq with his mother for treatment after having ingested a cup of bleach that damaged his esophagus so severely that he couldn't eat. Treatment in Iraq had been unsuccessful. Neither he nor his mother had ever been out of Iraq before. Both spoke only Arabic, so Evans found verbal communication impossible. The hospital experience is frightening at best, but in this case it was not even possible to explain the procedures or offer reassurance. Tamur loved the markers and drew pictures of his country. On his final day at the hospital, he and Evans traded pictures of their country's flags. She observes that the two figures in his picture look frightened. Art making was an important means of communication where there was no common language.

Renal Failure

Whereas Diane Evans worked with patients having a variety of medical problems, Mark Hollinger worked in a hospital pediatric dialysis unit where children receiving long-term hemodialysis must come for 4-hour treatments 3 days every week in order to survive. These treatments must be continued for life or until a kidney donor can be found (Hollinger, 1997). There are more than 160,000 patients being maintained on dialysis in the United States, and the number of children undergoing maintenance dialysis is expected to rise dramatically (U.S. Renal Data System, 1991; Port, 1993). This end-stage renal disease is diagnosed when individuals suffer from chronic renal failure. Hemodialysis is an artificial simulation of the kidney's function of filtering waste products from the blood. The treatment requires repeated venipunctures, severe dietary restrictions, restricted access to normal childhood activities, and dependence on medical caregivers. Because of the amount of time spent in dialysis, children cannot attend regularly scheduled schooling. Children in dialysis face many problems directly attributable to their illness: body image concerns, developmental delays, low self-esteem, anxiety, feelings of loss of control, dependency, and depression. Depression has been identified as the most prevalent psychological problem for end-stage renal patients treated with hemodialysis. According to Kimmel, Weihs, and Peterson, (1993), depression may complicate immunologic function, nutrition, and compliance with treatment. Physical side effects of dialysis can include cramping, nausea, irritability, drowsiness, and intense pain. Children receiving dialysis leave normal life behind and enter a life of illness, recurrent hospitalization, and heightened vulnerability. There can be a profound effect on their psychosocial development.

At the hospital where Hollinger worked, the pediatric dialysis unit was set up to treat four children at a time, each receiving 4 hours of treatment per session, and each having three sessions per week. The unit was equipped to treat 16 children in a week by operating on two shifts, 6 days each week. Before Hollinger's arrival, the only activity provided for the children during their long hours of treatment was television. Although the hospital was meeting the children's medical needs, there were no provisions other than art therapy for attending to their very substantial emotional and psychosocial needs.

Hollinger conducted art therapy with each child twice weekly, if possible. The art-making process allowed the children to be expressive and creative while undergoing dialysis instead of passively watching television. These 1-hour individual sessions also provided opportunities for interaction instead of isolation. If problematic physical reactions made art engagement impossible, Hollinger tried to reschedule the session for a later dialysis time in the same week. During the first few sessions, he offered the materials to the child and tried to establish a safe atmosphere for self-expression. After sufficient trust was developed, he encouraged the child to address issues of body image, anxiety, loss of control, dependency, and depression. Naturally, Hollinger followed the child's lead in the direction the artwork took. His objectives were as follows:

- Identify the children's the emotional and developmental needs.
- Decrease the children's negative psychosocial adaptation.
- Increase the children's adaptation to issues directly attributable to dialysis.
- Increase the children's imaginal expression of both illness and health.

John was a 14-year-old African American boy who had been receiving hemodialysis for 5 years. His initial art making consisted of quick, random pencil marks on small sheets of paper. He became frustrated easily, but did not verbalize his feelings about his art. After working with Hollinger for several months, he began to express himself actively through his art and use it as an avenue to discuss his feelings surrounding his illness. Expressive outlets for children in dialysis may be limited, so expression through art and the trusting relationship where the expression of all feelings is encouraged is very important for these patients.

Styrofoam Heads

In addition to serving a kidney dialysis unit as did Mark Hollinger, Anastasia Limperis, as a member of the hospital's child life department, also served the pediatric, neurology, and cardiac transplant inpatient units. Most of the children with whom she worked were severely ill with chronic, lifelong diseases that were often life threatening and sometimes terminal. Most pediatric stays were short term, averaging 3 days to a week. Chronic conditions, however, necessitated frequent hospitalization. Sometimes art therapy sessions were interrupted for medical procedures, and sometimes the child's severe pain or drowsiness from medication made therapy sessions impossible. The length of sessions depended on the child's condition. When a child was uncomfortable, Limperis sometimes encouraged artwork that would be a distraction. At other times, she encouraged expressing the pain through the art. Art therapy took place in either the recreation room, which was preferable in order to counter isolation, or bedside if the child was immobile. Sometimes Limperis rolled the child down the hall to the recreation room in a bed or reclining chair. A stop sign was posted on the recreation room door to warn physicians, nurses, and technicians that medical procedures were prohibited inside. It became a safe haven where the children could not be examined, invaded, or otherwise subjected to pain.

Limperis's routine was to look through the census each day and visit each newly admitted child age 7 to 19. After reviewing each child's medical assessment, she would return later in the day, when the children were likely to be less drowsy from medication or more rested from early procedures. She encouraged each child to explore the art cart. In addition to the usual art supplies, she provided life-size Styrofoam heads of the type used to hold wigs (Limperis, 1996). She carried both blank heads and some that had been completed to show examples of what could be done with them. There were also some completed heads displayed in the recreation room. Work on these forms provided several advantages for physically ill children. Because the children began with preformed heads, they were practically guaranteed a recognizable finished product. Completion could be accomplished in one session, which was the total art therapy available for those hospitalized only briefly. The Styrofoam surface allowed both painting and easy attachment of objects, either with glue or by sticking material into the surface. Finally, the end result of a life-size head was often impressive, giving the children a sense of accomplishment and mastery.

Terrell was a 9-year-old African American boy diagnosed with an inoperable malignant tumor that wrapped around his stomach. Radiation and chemotherapy were used to diminish the tumor's size and to prevent the cancer from spreading. He was admitted to the hospital every 3 weeks for treatment. His family had not told him of his prognosis, but his many hospitalizations made him aware that his illness was serious. Limperis had met with him during previous hospitalizations in both group and individual art therapy. A frail and quiet child, he had been hesitant to make anything for fear that he was incapable of doing so. After asking Limperis to cut out geometric shapes for him, he eventually cut some of his own, which he made into Christmas presents for his family. He told Limperis that his brothers destroyed all his artwork and any presents from the staff that he took home from the hospital. Terrell rarely received visitors, and the staff expressed disapproval of his family's absence, increasing his anxiety and feelings of isolation. He experienced homesickness and roamed the halls, rolling his IV chemotherapy apparatus alongside him, looking for someone to invite him into a room for company. The Styrofoam head resembled his own bald head and small features. In working on it, he was quick to select paints and yarn he wanted to use. As he painted, he spoke of his family situation for the first time—their financial problems, his mother's two jobs, and her boyfriend. He named his head Cherrise after his mother, saying that the yarn simulated her braids and the mouth was painted to match her shade of lipstick. The beard and mustache, however, were clearly male (Figure 4.5). Terrell's father visited him that same evening, and Limperis noticed the similarity between his own beard, thin mustache, and hairline and those of the Styrofoam head. Terrell told him that he was going to give the head to his mother, and his father seemed quite pleased. Combining their features as he did may have represented Terrell's wish for them to reunite. His father's approval brought a smile to Terrell's face, the first Limperis had ever seen. He became more animated in the session as he worked on the head; he spoke more personally, and his affect improved. After making the head, he came to the recreation room of his own volition, immediately digging into the art materials without hesitation or requests for assistance. The premolded Styrofoam head gave him an opportunity to create a successful and impressive product of which he could be proud. Making it heightened his self-esteem and encouraged his expressiveness and risk taking with other art materials.

Nancy was a 7-year-old child admitted for congenital scoliosis, whose spine was in danger of becoming more crooked as she grew. A metal halo had been drilled into her skull on both sides of her head in order to lift its weight and hold it in a stationary position while the vertebrae of her spine were realigned. The mechanism extended laterally past her shoulders to her waist,

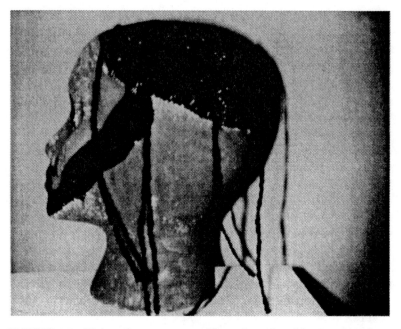

FIGURE 4.5   Bisexual appearance of Styrofoam head by 9-year-old
boy with a stomach tumor.

keeping her torso in place. She was very uncomfortable and had limited mobility. She could raise her hands only from her elbows, to a maximum angle of 45 degrees. When she saw a Styrofoam head with a crown that Limperis had made, she said she wanted to make one like it. At first she wanted Limperis to paint it for her, but after Limperis moved the head lower, to where she could reach it within her forearm's range of motion, she painted it herself. She began to talk freely for the first time, saying how much fun she was having. She said she wanted to make her face look sad, however. When Limperis asked her if she ever felt that way, she answered with an emphatic no. She became noticeably anxious as Limperis took the wire for making the crown out of the cart. Limperis asked her if she still wanted it, and Nancy insisted that the head have a crown. Limperis demonstrated how pliable the wire was and how to cut it, but Nancy did not want to look at it. She asked Limperis to "sink" it into the head, and she could not tear her eyes away from watching the process. As Limperis sank it in, Nancy yelled "Ouch!" (p. 22). She spoke of how she had cried when the halo was placed in her head, how much she hated the hospital, and how frightening it was at night. Both of them held the hot glue gun to affix yarn and feathers to the crown, and Nancy became intrigued with the residual strands of glue and asked to make a web on the crown. Limperis describes the result (Figure 4.6) as "a dazzling array of glossy strands that seemed like jewels decorating the head piece" (p. 22). Nancy said that the hospital was not such a bad place after all, and that it could even be fun. By working on the Sty-

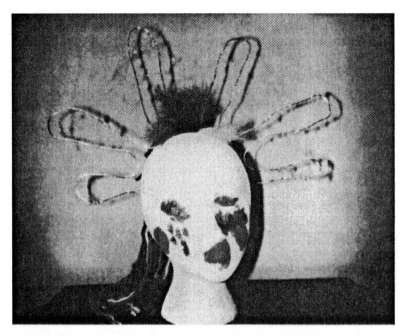

FIGURE 4.6 Metal skull brace "halo" by 7-year-old girl with scoliosis.

rofoam head, she controlled the re-creation of a painful and frightening experience. She had directed Limperis in shaping the wire and looked away when it was too uncomfortable for her. Being able to use her arms to create, even with a limited range of motion, improved her mood within minutes of beginning to paint. Her final product had transformed an imprisoning, painful experience into something poignant and beautiful.

Daphne, an 11-year-old girl with end-stage renal disease receiving dialysis three times a week, had been hospitalized for fever and infection complications. She had been in and out of hospitals for renal problems, and finally for renal failure, since birth. Daphne always smiled and never voiced anything negative. As a result, the hospital seemed to be the place where she received the most support. She was always ready to help others, and Limperis noticed Daphne's ongoing efforts to please her. Limperis tried to convey permission to do and be whatever she wanted while they were in the recreation room. Her family was comprised of her mother and 10 children, all living in a three-bedroom apartment. Daphne often did not receive her medications at home, because her chemically dependent mother would forget to give them to her. Daphne had often missed school or attended without having been fed. As a result, Daphne no longer attended school but received her schooling from the hospital's tutoring program. Her friendships consisted of relationships with other children at the hospital; all of them were dialysis patients also. Since the growth processes of children with long-term kidney dysfunction tend to slow down, Daphne, like her friends, appeared to be 3 or 4 years younger than her age.

In prior sessions, Daphne had made happy pictures of smiley faces, butterflies, and hearts. Her interactions with Limperis were playful; they sometimes conversed in various accents. Her images were usually imaginative and fantastic, but when she saw the Styrofoam head, she wanted to make it as realistic as possible. She chose textured yarn that resembled her own hair. She used a mirror to mix a shade of paint that matched her lips. Daphne kept saying how cute she wanted to make the head, just like herself. Finally she added three long, thick eyelashes for each eye, resembling her own long curly lashes. She named the head for herself, because it looked like her. Daphne said that it was fun to be in the hospital because she got to see her friends and she got better, but when she looked at the head from a distance, she said that it did not look very happy. Limperis asked her if there was anything she disliked about the hospital, and she replied with an emphatic yes. She did not like being stuck with needles every time she came in. Her Styrofoam head appeared to be a more genuine expression of her feelings and more personally rewarding than her previous art.

For each of the three children described here, making the Styrofoam head was a pivotal experience. Terrell gained confidence and expressed his separation anxiety; Nancy mastered her painful experience of being fitted with a metal halo and gained a new perspective of her hospital experience; and Daphne expressed some of her negative feelings instead of being only positive as before. The children who created these heads felt a sense of accomplishment and mastery. They showed them off to staff members and visitors and wanted them to be displayed.

Terminally Ill Children

Susan Gasman worked on an oncology and hematology unit for children 18 and younger at a children's hospital. All had various types of cancer. Incorporating art therapy into their treatment plans had the goal of helping them to clarify the emotional, physical, and psychological ramifications they encountered in the progressive stages of their illness. The art therapy promoted self-discovery and enhanced self-esteem. Anxieties and concerns often gained a stronger focus in images, Gasman reports (1989). For many, this included deeper perceptions regarding death and their own dying. Gasman saw patients when they were hospitalized for diagnosis or medication; she saw them through fevers, low blood counts, anemia, and bone marrow transplants. After discharge, she was able to stay in contact with them as they periodically returned for treatment in the outpatient clinic. Often they were accompanied by a parent and sometimes by siblings, as well. Newly diagnosed patients were often asked to draw their reactions to their hospitalization. Children in later stages were often asked to draw some of their disease-related experiences, such as drug effects, radiation, and hair loss. At other times, no directives were given, and the children's spontaneity was encouraged. Gasman found the spontaneous drawings to be more helpful in gaining an understanding of what the children were experiencing. Often a second drawing was suggested in response to what was expressed in the first.

Thomas, age 16, had been living with acute lymphocytic leukemia that had been diagnosed when he was 10. Gasman saw him in the outpatient clinic waiting room. It was difficult for him to draw because of the IV lines in both his hands. He had come for a spinal tap, a painful procedure in which cerebrospinal fluid is withdrawn from the spinal canal by a needle inserted between the bones of the vertebrae. He appeared nervous about the procedure, which was scheduled for later in the day. Gasman commented that it was too bad that the doctors couldn't gain the information they needed in a less painful way. Thomas agreed and began talking about inventing a machine that could scan spinal fluid with laser technology. Gasman suggested that perhaps he could draw his machine. Thomas was very interested and drew his machine with much investment of effort, from four different angles (Figure 4.7). He explained its operation in great detail, and to be sure it was understood, he drew it from four different perspectives. He wanted his doctor to see it, because he thought the doctor would appreciate the chance to offer a pain-free test for a change. Thomas used the art experience to relieve some of the tension he felt in anticipation of the upcoming procedure. When his doctor was shown the drawing, he was surprised to see that Thomas had so much anxiety from past spinal taps, yet had never told him so directly.

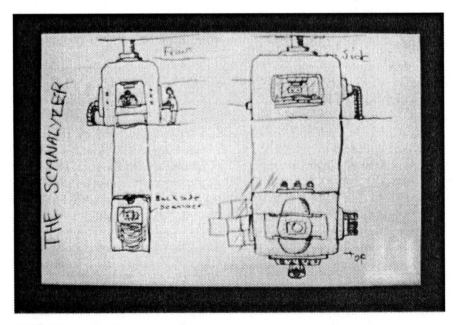

FIGURE 4.7   Painless spinal fluid scanner by 16-year-old boy with leukemia.

Gasman saw Billy, age 10, in individual art therapy sessions in his hospital room. He had been admitted for a relapse in his leukemia after a 4-year remission. He was reluctant to draw at first, so he and Gasman made some joint pictures together. Billy enlarged the mouth and arm joints on the figure they drew, parts of his body that were causing him pain. Two days later, when Gasman stopped by his room to remind him of their session, he expressed distress over losing his hair and brushed his hand across the top, causing large amounts of hair to fall on the bed. Billy titled the picture they made together later that day *The Sunny Day That Turned into a Bad One.* What began as a nice day on the beach turned into a fight for control between two sharks, as other fish and birds fear for their lives and call out to be saved. Gasman drew the balloons from their mouths, and Billy filled them in with dialog, mostly calling for help. He appeared to be using the drawing to vent his anger at having no control over the frightening return of his leukemia.

Eight-year-old Louis had been diagnosed with Wilm's tumor (cancer of the kidney usually found in very young children) 3 years earlier. He now had a tumor in his lung, as well. He was being treated with chemotherapy to shrink the tumor until it was small enough to be removed surgically. He painted a picture of his dream house. Three weeks later, he was hospitalized again for chemotherapy. He was too nauseated to be able to draw, so Gasman asked him if he would like to hear a story. During this portion of his treatment, he expressed only happy emotions. This round of chemotherapy was stronger than the previous two, which had not been effective. Gasman's goal in their sessions was to provide an outlet for the expression of all his feelings. During his next hospitalization, she saw him before his treatment, and he made an aggressive picture with planes, guns, and bombs that he titled *Scary.* He was detained after his next hospital visit due to a fever. His mother was unable to visit him for most of his stay, but finally came the day before his art therapy session. Louis drew a picture of the two of them watching television. He said he did not like the shows unless someone in them was dying. He related a dream in which he had died all alone in a snow avalanche. He had screamed for help, but no one came. He did not understand the reasons for having to remain in the hospital and for his apparent abandonment by his mother. Finally, a discharge date was set, and his surgery was scheduled for 2 weeks later. Louis showed Gasman a picture he had made with the markers she had left for him (Figure 4.8). He described it as a monster that gets its power from thunderstorms. The lightning goes into his chest, where it is stored as power. The fingers are sharp claws that can kill people. When Gasman showed him this picture at a later session, he appeared overwhelmed by it and would not talk about it. The surgery was not successful, and Louis was put on a new course of chemotherapy to try to maintain the size of the tumor. Nevertheless, the tumor continued to grow at a rapid rate, so he was sent home with palliative medication to allow him to spend some quality time with his family.

Gasman worked with Lucy, age 11, for 5 weeks while she was hospitalized for a bone marrow transplant. She was full of creative ideas and was especially

FIGURE 4.8   Monster that gets power from thunderstorms by 8-year-old boy with a kidney tumor.

interested in working three-dimensionally. She made a doll family (Figure 4.9) and a house for them to live in. The figures were made from pipe cleaners, beads, felt, sequins, and other scraps of material. Their house, with separate rooms, was created from a shoebox. Lucy received a lot of praise for her project from the staff and visitors. Gasman saw her role in her work with Lucy as

FIGURE 4.9   Doll family made by 11-year-old girl hospitalized for a bone marrow transplant.

one of support for Lucy's industry and her sense of self. When Gasman returned from her Christmas vacation, Lucy was in the intensive care unit suffering from pneumonia and other serious complications. She had been placed on a ventilator, which inhibited her ability to speak or create art. Gasman hung some of the tissue paper snowflakes Lucy had made around her room to help her recall some positive memories. Unable to fight off infection, Lucy died 2 weeks later. Gasman had an opportunity to tell her how wonderful it had been to know her and that she missed their time together creating projects.

Art Therapists' Self-Processing

Working with seriously ill and dying children obviously evokes very strong reactions. Art therapists' own art has been very beneficial in helping them to deal with their difficult and painful feelings. When Lucy died, Susan Gasman felt that "Her strong desire and talent to create left a hole that was impossible to ignore" (Gasman, 1989, p. 25). She made a drawing to express her grief and to reflect on how personally meaningful their relationship had been to her. The picture incorporated Lucy's images, including her dolls and snowflakes, and shows compassion for her family, especially her brother, who had donated bone marrow in an unsuccessful attempt to save her. Gasman's artwork was helpful to her in reviewing what she and Lucy had accomplished together in the final stage of Lucy's life. The dolls and their house now resided with Lucy's family, who looked on them with similar sentiments.

Figure 4.10 shows a collage Gasman made to help herself understand her feelings when Louis was discharged to receive palliative care. Most of the paper shapes were torn, which she said expressed how torn she felt from her work with him. Her profile is on the left, facing Louis on the right. Within her mind are images of herself, now traveling alone on a road and wondering how much time is left for Louis. Out of her head floats sadness and pain about his inevitable death. Out of her mouth come words of praise for Louis about how hard he worked with her and what it was like to know him. The newsprint represents their talking about the reality of his situation, that it is good for him to spend his last days with his family and what it will be like to die. She tells him of her sadness at not seeing him anymore. Within his mind, he sees her as a friend who went to many places with him, who helped him to become an artist, and who supported his range of feelings. Gasman's artwork clarified for her how much she and Louis had meant to each other.

After working with Billy for two sessions, Gasman noticed a drop in her energy level. By the week's end, she was exhausted and questioned her ability to work on an oncology unit with such ill children. She made art to explore these physical warning signs (Figure 4.11). She began with a watercolor wash of dark, "tragic" colors. On the left is her own profile, and on the right is Billy, from whom a large wing unfolds, representing his future struggle with leukemia and its possible outcome of death. Gasman portrayed herself with

FIGURE 4.10   Art therapist's collage in reaction to terminally ill child's discharge.

FIGURE 4.11   Art therapist's painting in reaction to feelings of despair about a patient with leukemia.

no ears to listen to him, and her lack of hair, she felt, conveys how much she was identifying with his symptoms. She is not looking at him, but beyond him. Gasman realized that the picture shows how transfixed she was on how poor Billy's prognosis could be and how traumatized she felt by this possibility. These feelings were unacceptable to her. With further reflection, she realized that she was also confronting the inevitability of her own death. Becoming aware of her distressing personal emotions through her art made her feelings more manageable for her. "With this," she says, "came a great sense of internal freedom from no longer working so hard to hold them at bay and sharpened sensitivities towards Billy's current needs" (p. 17).

Working in a treatment setting with severely ill young people can arouse strong responses even to patients with whom one hasn't worked. Julie Marchand was assigned to a hospital floor where treatment for many medical conditions was offered to a diverse population of children, adolescents, and young adults. Some were terminally ill. There were no other therapists to deal with patients' emotional issues. Marchand established a routine for herself of using colored markers to create a scribble or cartoon after each session (Marchand, 1993). She chose markers because they are easily transportable and because she was aware of her own tendency to blur boundaries. In addition to the sharp edges that markers produce, she used black ink for outlining in order to maintain clear boundaries in her drawings. Her response to reading the diagnosis of a 2-year-old boy, who was the roommate of an older child with whom she was working, was particularly intense. His chart read, "colostomy, post-trauma to rectum" (p. 11). She understood that his condition was caused by repeated sexual abuse. She immediately sought time alone to draw Figure 4.12. "The monster gripped, punctured, and mutilated him physically and spiritually from behind, as if the life in him (represented by droplets and a small puddle beneath him) pooled on the ground. I felt the urge to destroy this molesting creature as the only means to make it stop. . . . I drew a gun blasting and a spear about to impale the head" (pp. 11–12). She added "I hate you" in red. After creating this "vengeance," she felt exhausted and wanted to find a way to protect this patient and the others in her life who were too small to protect themselves. Marchand drew a nurturing woman to protect them. Nevertheless, she was concerned about what she might be able to do for this particular child, who was about to be transferred to another hospital. In her next drawing (Figure 4.13), she has drawn him with various life-support systems attached. His hospital bed has become a circus wagon to symbolize the various relocations he will undergo, like the travels of circus performers. She wondered if the bars of the cage would protect him or keep him prisoner. His mattress is represented by a thin line resembling a tightrope, indicating that the child would remain at high risk for the rest of his life. She then drew herself waving goodbye. Marchand added a poem to comfort the child. Making the art helped her to contain her powerful, murderous feelings toward the perpetrator of the child's abuse.

Holly, age 17, had been diagnosed with anorexia nervosa. Her schizo-

FIGURE 4.12　Art therapist's reaction to sexual abuse of a 2-year-old boy.

phrenic, abusive mother, unavailable father, and emotionally remote sister were physically disgusting to her because they were all overweight. At 5 feet, 8 inches, she had weighed 230 pounds and had dropped to 120 pounds by purging with diuretics and laxatives and exercising, often walking 30 miles a day. Upon admission, she was physically exhausted and dehydrated. One of her pictures was an underwater scene of herself diving with a shark. In working on a scribble immediately after the session, Marchand recognized that she, too, often used a shark as a symbol. In creating her own shark, she was able to separate, acknowledge, and validate similarities and differences between their sharks and the use they each made of them. This was important to Marchand in recognizing how she overidentified with some of her patients. Holly was able to utilize the art therapy sessions as a safe place to express and contain some very traumatic childhood memories and the present feelings associated with them. Holly said that it was easier to draw these memories than to talk about them. In response to a picture of a particularly vivid memory of Holly's

FIGURE 4.13   Art therapist's drawing and poem in reaction to anger about the transfer of the patient depicted in Figure 4.12.

mother chasing her with a knife, Marchand made a scribble. At first, she saw no images in it, but after turning it several times, she saw the face of a sobbing child. Marchand developed it with color and surrounded it with "threatening, pointy, invasive shapes" (p. 26). Marchand's drawing helped her to empathize with Holly.

Heavy emotional demands are placed on art therapists who work with physically ill and dying children. They certainly require an outlet for the expression of reactions of grief for those who are dying and of horror for those who have been badly mistreated. As stated elsewhere in this book, art making is a most significant resource for helping art therapists to deal with the powerful feelings aroused by their work. (For a discussion of art processing by those working with HIV-positive children, see Chapter 12, "Sexual Orientation and AIDS.")

Summary

Art therapists who work with physically ill and dying children may be assigned to child life programs designed to aid in children's psychosocial development and adjustment to hospitalization. These programs administer to children coming to the hospital for medical procedures; they may be carried out in a special playroom or waiting room. Art therapists also see children who are hospitalized for short and long periods of time, some of whom may come to the hospital on a regular basis for treatment. Those who are mobile are often seen in a playroom or recreation room; those who are not are seen bedside. In addition to working in child life programs, art therapists may be assigned to pediatric, oncology, dialysis, or general medical units. Examples presented include the following:

- Diane Evans (1985) worked in a large children's hospital with patients hospitalized for broken bones, kidney testing, Crohn's disease, scoliosis, colitis, anal ulcers, Hodgkin's disease, and esophageal damage.
- Mark Hollinger (1997) worked on a hemodialysis unit with children while they were receiving treatment for 4 hours three times a week.
- Stacey Limperis (1996) developed a project using preformed Styrofoam heads for the oncology, scoliosis, and dialysis patients with whom she worked.
- Susan Gasman (1989) worked on an oncology unit with children who were dying. She used her own art to help herself deal with her feelings of sadness, grief, and loss.
- Julie Marchand (1993) also used her own art to help herself process her reactions to the horrific background stories of the patients with whom she worked on a general medical unit.

Conclusion

Working with physically ill and dying children can be both gratifying and saddening in confronting the tragedies of their young lives and, in some cases, their deaths. Certainly, art therapy is a beneficial outlet in helping children to express the fears that hospitalization can engender, both in its frightening procedures and in their removal from the familiarity of home and family. Many children don't understand what is happening to them as they undergo pain from the illness itself, pain from invasive medical procedures, and often physical deterioration, as well. Some suffer immobilization and its resultant discomfort and boredom. Art making and a trusting relationship with an art therapist who does not administer medications or painful tests can help to alleviate the difficulties they are facing. As a vehicle for the expression of feeling, it can also serve as a release for anger. At other times, it can be a much-needed distraction. Art therapists who work with physically ill and dying children and adolescents must be prepared for the emotional toll such work can take. Using one's own art as a means to deal with these tragedies can be immensely beneficial.

ART THERAPY PROJECTS

Projects discussed in this chapter are described further in Chapter 15, "Art Activities and Materials":

- Styrofoam heads (Limperis, 1996)
- Dolls (Gasman, 1989)
- Scribble drawing (Marchand, 1993)

Chapter 5

Family Art Therapy

Heads drawn weekly by 9-year-old boy.

The Rodriguez family enters in pieces: Mr. Rodriguez first, seating himself stiffly in the chair where he can look out the window; Mrs. Rodriguez, dragging Hector and admonishing him in rapid Spanish; Maria, walking quietly; and Julio, lagging behind. The pieces coalesce in a mural they make together of their home in Mexico. Here is Mama hanging out the laundry with Maria at her side. Here is Papa building a fence. Julio hits a baseball, and Hector sleeps in his carriage because he is still a baby. The sun has a smiling face.

Family art therapy is most often sought when a child is brought to treatment and it becomes evident that it is the family, not just the child, that is in need of help. Often the child's difficulties are symptoms of problematic family dynamics. The demand for art therapists in large urban centers, however, comes from facilities with the most needy populations—those suffering from chronic mental illness, impoverishment, imprisonment, abuse, and addiction. These clients often live marginal lives and seldom have the support of their families. When there are family members in the picture, frequently they are unwilling to participate in therapy. Even when they bring their children for treatment, these parents' work schedules, responsibilities for other children, and transportation difficulties, as well as suspicion of therapy, often mitigate against full family participation.

Examples of family, couple, and multifamily art therapy in cases where there is family cooperation have been presented in *Art Psychotherapy* (Wadeson, 1980). The families described were comprised primarily of white middle-class clients. In addition to such work, the major portion of this chapter illustrates art therapy with more needy families and some creative responses that art therapists have developed in working with them.

Concurrent Family and Individual Art Therapy

Frequently, family therapy is instigated as a result of the referral of a child for treatment. The family therapy may take many configurations, depending on the issues and needs of the family. The family may be seen as a whole or in segments. Often the parents are seen together, to work on problems in their relationship as they impact upon the family. A child may be seen individually and in conjunction with the family, as in the example presented here.

Nine-year-old Michael was brought to art therapist Gail Wirtz by his family as a result of problems his teachers reported at school (personal communication, 1999). Apparently, he did not understand much of what was presented to him there, and teachers found his responses to be rude and inappropriate. It was clear that he had antagonized them. Wirtz saw Michael alone first. She immediately became aware of his communication problems, as he grew angry when she didn't understand his needs. He made a foam-core house (Figure 5.1). Rather remarkably, the house was not held together by glue or tape, but rather with slits to make the pieces fit into one another. Michael said he did not

FIGURE 5.1   Foam-core house by 9-year-
old boy.

want to give the house any windows or doors, and Wirtz saw the image as representing the way he felt boxed in. Without tape, it was also quite fragile. The house became a metaphor for Michael's condition. Wirtz remarked on Michael's skill to both him and his mother. At the next session, he made another house, but this time he decided to use tape. Wirtz tore it for him according to his instructions, helping him to articulate his needs. They began to connect to one another, and at the same time, Michael began making some connections with his teachers.

After working with Michael for 2 months and establishing a strong relationship with him, Wirtz saw the family together: Michael, his father, his mother, and two older sisters. They sat around a table that was covered with a sheet of mural paper. The children began to argue about wanting more space on the paper, and Michael ended up running to another part of the room, crying that no one understood him and that he felt like dying. His mother wanted to comfort him, but Wirtz did not want her to jump in and rescue him, so she asked one of the sisters to do so instead. At various points in the family therapy, Wirtz utilized strategic family therapy methods in restructuring the family relationships. Michael's sister apologized to him, and Michael responded with an immediate smile. The father had been rather isolated from the interaction, and when Wirtz asked him how he felt about this, he said he felt lonely. Wirtz asked the family to make another mural, this time with rules about respecting each other's space and asking permission to enter it. Once again, she utilized the strategic family therapy model to intervene in the family's system and restructure it. In this mural, there was genuine sharing, with respect for each member.

Next, Wirtz set up a session with the parents to review the family meeting. It was clear that the father felt left out and found that the limits he tried to set for the children did not work. The mother felt overworked with four children (a 4-year-old had been left at home during the family session) and needed some help. For the next several months, there were ongoing sessions in various configurations—father and Michael, mother and Michael, and the parents together. Work continued with the school, as well, dealing with miscommunications and crises as they arose. Michael's foam-core house served as a helpful metaphor in explaining to his teachers the need for some "tape" to help him adjust in getting from one class to another.

In her weekly work with Michael, Wirtz put out mural paper for him to draw on before starting a project. Each week, he drew a head (see page 145). Although each head was unique, Michael was unable to connect them with any feelings. After a number of weeks, he asked Wirtz to draw with him. She echoed his head theme, and following her lead, he asked if it showed how she was feeling. She assented and asked him how it looked to him. He said it looked happy and asked if that was how she was feeling. She said yes, and asked him about his feelings. He began to associate the faces he drew with his inner state. He was also beginning to communicate his feelings to someone other than his mother. Nevertheless, Wirtz was concerned that Michael was not drawing bodies. When she commented on this, he drew a very tiny body at the bottom of the page. She talked with him about how big bodies are in relation to heads, and helped him to see the relationship by using a yardstick. She rolled out some mural paper, and Michael climbed on it and asked her to draw him, which she did. She suggested that they make a cloth person from it. At the next session, he traced the body onto fabric. As he drew the legs, he told her of breaking a leg when he was 4, which had kept him in a body cast for a long time. He explained that this was why one leg in his picture was shorter and thinner than the other. He asked Wirtz to fix it on the fabric. Together, they used the sewing machine, with Wirtz moving the fabric and Michael controlling the pedal as she asked him to go fast or slow or to stop. Michael said that the fabric boy was himself (Figure 5.2). He took it home, where the doll had a place at the dinner table and said things that Michael did not feel able to say. Wirtz continued to work with Michael and his family. She saw him as a boy who communicated more on the level of a 4-year-old than of a 9-year-old. Although he had difficulty articulating himself verbally, his art was very expressive. He began to catch up.

A very interesting and beneficial aspect of Wirtz's family work has been her use of digital photography. The digital camera uses a computer disk rather than film, and the photographer can see the picture on a screen at the back of the camera, both before and after shooting. In the therapy sessions, the children took much delight in taking photographs of their own artwork. Interruptions for shooting were part of the mural-making process with Michael's family. Michael took multiple shots of his own work, sometimes including Wirtz or himself. The immediacy of the image was satisfying, as was the

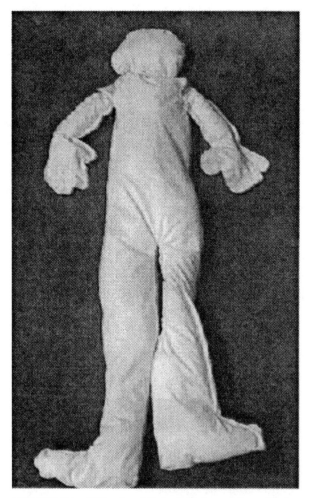

**FIGURE 5.2 Life-size fabric doll drawn from body
tracing by 9-year-old boy.**

importance that immortalizing the art process gave to his work. At present, Michael is putting together a portfolio of the photos of his art. Wirtz hopes that this collection will become a significant link in helping Michael to share himself with his teachers at school.

Wirtz has also used digital photography for her own notes and for reviewing client artwork. After each session, she transfers the disk to her computer; she can then compare pictures by looking at them together, as shown on page 145. She prints them out, writing her notes on one copy and giving another copy to the client. In fact, Michael's fragile foam-core house (Figure 5.1) eventually fell apart, but he still has a picture of it. It is from these prints that Michael is putting together his portfolio.

Conjoint Art Projects

As discussed in *Art Psychotherapy* (Wadeson, 1980), family art therapy provides the family a forum for doing something together, often allows them to have fun together (which may be a rare experience in some families), and provides a leveling experience through participation in an activity where young children are as articulate as the adults (or more so).

Families Involved Together (FIT) is a program developed by a city child and family counseling center, intended primarily to teach parenting skills. While working there, Kama Schulte developed a family body-tracing project in which families worked together on a large mural containing life-size images of each member (Schulte, 1991). The process illuminated family dynamics, decision-making processes, boundaries, alliances, and conflicts. First, the family members chose the size of paper needed to accommodate them, then decided whether to hang it on the wall or place it on the floor for the tracings. Each family member was traced on the paper. Once again, a number of choices was possible, such as the order of the tracings, who traced whom, body positions, and arrangement of the figures on the paper. Using crayons and markers, family members found many possibilities in embellishing the figures. Schulte added to the families' comfort by providing magazine cutouts for them to affix to their figures in case they were hesitant to draw. She utilized this project with individual families, family dyads, and multifamily groups.

The magazine pictures were useful in the work with a Caucasian woman and her two daughters, age 4 and 2, referred because of the 4-year-old's aggressive behavior. The father, who was African American, was not present because the parents were in the process of divorcing. The 4-year-old found a picture of a black man, saying, "This looks like Daddy." She glued it within the confines of her mother's body in the tracing. At cleanup time the mother removed it. From this Schulte was able to explore the children's relationships with their father and coparenting issues.

Kimberly Rakestraw found clay to be a useful medium in examining family dynamics (Rakestraw, 1997). The malleable quality of clay allows family members to move the material around and change its proportions if desired. Working the clay can parallel changes in a family system through therapy. The following example is from work Rakestraw undertook with a husband and wife and their two foster children at the request of the Department of Child and Family Services (DCFS). Her goal was to explore issues of adoption and to increase communication within the family. Rachel, 10, and Sarah, 7, had lived with their foster parents for 4 years. Both had received individual therapy after being abused and subsequently removed from their biological mother's custody.

After 10 weeks of family art therapy in which there had been resistance to drawing and dissatisfaction with the results, Rakestraw asked each member to create a clay self-representation. There was much less resistance to working in clay, probably as a result of the medium's forgiving nature, allowing one to make endless changes in the creation. Rachel explained her piece first, saying that she is smart. Previously, as well as in this instance, she sought confirmation from her foster parents in her ongoing struggle to form a positive perception of herself. Sarah, who tended to be very outspoken, immediately made a bid for her turn and explained the three pieces she made. The first was "machine-o-saurus," half dinosaur and half machine, which wildly ate buildings and houses, "chomp, chomp, chomp." The next was her bunny-self, also eating, and the third was herself as a person. The bunny, her playful side, was less formed than the others. Although Sarah had expressed her anger and frustration in her previous drawings, the clay enabled her to create a more complete being in the form of "machine-o-saurus" in order to communicate her aggressive feelings. Catherine, the foster mother, initially claimed that her red lumpy figure was not her. She asked the children if it looked like her, and they giggled yes. As a result of Sarah's expression of aggression, she said, Catherine put her hands on her hips, like the figure's, and admitted that it did look like her when she got mad. It was difficult for her to accept this part of herself. All her drawings of herself had portrayed a calm, spiritual person. William, the foster father, spoke about his two clay figures last. One of them was praying, which was how he usually portrayed himself. He felt more confident in working the clay than he had in drawing. In forming their self-images from clay, the members of this family were able to explore their self-perceptions and increase communication.

Formal Games and Puppets

Gian Luca Ferme points out that therapy with families with young children requires resourcefulness and creativity (Ferme, 1996). It is difficult for young children to participate in conventional "talk" therapy. Although formal games and crafted puppets have been used in family therapy previously, these methods have relied on premade materials. Ferme's work focused on creating games and puppets with the family, thus heightening the members' identification with the objects. In developing treatment plans, Ferme drew on his earlier experience in conducting workshops for low-income families in which they created board games and musical instruments from found objects. The purpose had been to teach skills and increase feelings of competence. The workshops also provided opportunities for the families to play together.

The family therapy Ferme subsequently conducted was held at a family health center that serves Chicago's large Puerto Rican and Mexican American communities. Most clients are low-income Hispanics. Families usually come for medical services; some are then referred for mental health services by the medical staff. Art therapy is the treatment of choice for those with children, because it allows simultaneous treatment of the children and their parents. Because Ferme is fluent in Spanish, he was able to conduct sessions for those who could not speak English. (For additional discussion on work with immigrants, see Chapter 9, "Displaced Persons.")

After an initial art assessment, using varieties of conjoint drawing, families were asked to craft puppets from cardboard tubes, fabric, construction paper, and crepe paper (Figure 5.3). A resultant example of self-revelation can be seen from Ferme's interview of a Zorro puppet created by Mr. Peron, who sabotaged his wife's attempts to discipline their daughter in order to win the daughter's favor. He said, "My name is Zorro and I am rich . . . I decided to get me an outfit so I won't be recognized and I started taking money from the soldiers and the rich and give them out to the poor" (p. 11). This was an apt representation of his activity within the family. He wanted his daughter to see him as a superhero. Ferme's work with this family focused on building an alliance between the parents.

In the Salgado family, 9-year-old José was diagnosed with Attention Deficit Hyperactivity Disorder (ADHD). The puppet-making activity enabled him to be assertive instead of being dominated by his 12-year-old brother, as was usually the case. In introducing his puppet, José said, "My name is Juan and I get in fights with other children and then I beat them up like the Power Rangers. I am really bad!" (p. 16). His mother became dismayed, confessing that in her frustration with him she calls him "bad." The family discussed other ways of dealing with frustration. It was unusual for José to make a powerful statement as talking through his puppet had enabled him to do.

For the Diaz family, in which there was a conflict in leadership between the parents, Ferme created a joint problem-solving task of building a house together. Ferme wanted to see how the family distributed responsibilities. He supplied a cardboard box, glue, scissors and an X-Acto knife. Mr. Diaz decided to delegate activities and to assemble the parts himself while the others watched. After his protracted unsuccessful attempt, his wife asked for the box. In a few seconds, she succeeded where he had failed, and the children joined in (Figure 5.4). Although Mrs. Diaz was the family's most resourceful member,

FIGURE 5.3   Puppets made by family from cardboard tubes, paper, and fabric.

FIGURE 5.4   Polaroid portrait puppets and house made by family from a
cardboard box.

for cultural reasons the father was the designated leader. The presenting problem of the inappropriate hyperactive behavior of the 7-year-old son appeared
to be a distraction from worries over the father's recent illness, which had
caused him to lose his job. At the beginning of treatment he was taking no
steps to seek employment.

After the house was completed, Ferme suggested that it needed residents
and introduced a puppet activity combined with photography. The family
members took Polaroid pictures of one another, and each created an animal
shape and glued it to the back of the portrait (Figure 5.4). They then made up
a story together about their animals. The story was short and evidenced their
resistance and difficulty in communicating. Ferme asked them to turn their
animals over so their photographs faced them and to introduce their animals
beginning with "I am. . . ." Mr. Diaz had chosen a donkey to represent himself,
a *burro,* which in Spanish also means "fool." He spoke of the hard-working
animal and was able to share with his family that he sometimes got tired of
having to bear the burden of work.

In creating formal games and constructions for families, Ferme selected
particular issues and methods to address them. Nevertheless, he did not use
games with all families. Where there were urgent needs for the discussion of
feelings, he utilized more direct expression through drawing.

For 9-year-old José Salgado, the boy with ADHD previously described,
Ferme devised a game to help prevent him from getting lost in detail to the
extent that he was unable to complete a project, a problem that had bogged him
down in the initial assessment. He also had difficulty following directions. The

game involved a short well-defined activity with clear rules. José had a great interest in airplanes, so Ferme asked him to make as many airplane outlines as he could while Ferme timed him (Figure 5.5). He liked the challenge and quickly learned how to focus on the outline without becoming mired in detail.

In subsequent games for the Salgado family, Ferme assigned Mrs. Salgado the role of assisting him in running the activities for the children instead of participating in them. Her husband, who refused to attend family therapy, blamed her for José's disability and their children's disrespect for her. Ferme discussed decisions with her in front of the children, thus boosting her authority in their eyes. The nature of the games for the family's six children helped reduce the negative focus on José, because they all had to follow the same rules. In one game, each child created a drawing and copied it on 5-by-7-inch cards placed for each child around the room. The first to finish could color cartoon characters Ferme had photocopied. Because the children all created original drawings to copy, they could choose their degree of difficulty, and all

FIGURE 5.5 Game devised to help 9-year-old boy complete a project without getting bogged down in details.

finished at about the same time. The result of Ferme's work with this family was that the negative focus was removed from José, and the children stopped opposing the mother so much. It should be noted that the father's participation probably would have provided further significant areas for work. Nevertheless, his resistance did not prevent Ferme from working effectively with the family issues that were presented.

Ferme also utilized board games, such as the goose game for the Diaz family, whose 7-year-old, Tito, threw temper tantrums whenever he lost a game. The game was crafted by the family, with moveable pieces made of clay, dice made from cardboard, and a board drawn with 64 squares in a spiraling pattern. Each square contained an object to be named in order to enable the 4-year-old daughter, who spoke very little, to acquire a vocabulary. In playing the game, Mrs. Diaz, the family's most resourceful member, won, and Mr. Diaz, who felt like a failure, came in last. Tito did not throw a tantrum, but said he wanted to win. Ferme helped him to see that sometimes he would win and sometimes he wouldn't. The family created more board games, and through them explored some of their problems. Eventually, Mr. Diaz returned to work, and the family reached a more comfortable equilibrium.

Ferme was able to apply the inventiveness he had used with low-income children to teach them skills and boost their feeling of competence. These techniques worked well for families with young children. All could participate together as a family unit in creating the puppets and the games. Utilizing them then brought out much expression that may not have surfaced otherwise, and patterns of family interaction became apparent. These activities also provided the means for developing solutions to family problems. This work highlights both the flexibility possible in art therapy and its potential for providing observation of family interaction. The importance of the opportunities for families to create together, to enjoy one another, and to have fun together cannot be overestimated.

Family Art Therapy for Problem Prevention

For 9 years, Beth Gonzalez-Dolginko has worked at the Child Research Development Center in New York, where prevention is the goal of treatment (personal communication, 1999). Much of this work involves parent education. The treatment is usually short term and problem oriented. Gonzalez-Dolginko begins her sessions with the kinetic family drawing technique, in which each family member draws a picture of the family doing something together. If the family has come for a problem they see in the child, Gonzalez-Dolginko generally meets with the parents after the initial session to discuss a treatment plan for the child. She often refers to the kinetic family drawings to advance the parents' insight into their interactions with the child and the overall family dynamics.

Gonzalez-Dolginko's work with families of children who are dually sensory impaired, usually with legally defined levels of deafness and blindness, has been particularly interesting. Treatment consists of weekend-long retreats in which she meets with small groups of parents all day long. In addition to working on kinetic family drawings, these parents focus on their feelings toward their disabled child. Gonzalez-Dolginko asks them to draw an image of the "perfect baby" they had anticipated and hoped for, followed by a picture of the reality of their child with disabilities. Although it is always acknowledged that there is no such thing as a perfect baby, it is nevertheless important to mourn the loss of an anticipated "perfect baby." The actual art-making process in creating these images is extremely beneficial in enabling the parents to process their grief and more readily accept their feelings toward their child. They are also better able to understand how this grief is played out in family dynamics and how it colors all family relationships and interactions.

Gonzalez-Dolginko has adapted the mourning process used for families of disabled children to work with adoptive parents. She has found that mourning the "perfect baby" can be generalized to mourning the "perfect family." These parents are asked to draw their ideal family, followed by a drawing of their family today. Mourning the loss of their hoped-for family helps them to embrace the actual family they have.

Figure 5.6 was drawn by Peggy, a freelance artist who works from home to be available to her school-age daughter. It shows her ideal family as consisting of herself, happily working on her art; two perfect children, playing at her feet; and her husband, returning from work, happily greeting the family. The scenery outside is prominent in both her drawings, here depicting the warm climate in which she would like to live. Figure 5.7 represents her actual family.

FIGURE 5.6   Ideal family by a woman.

FIGURE 5.7 Actual family by woman who drew Figure 5.6.

All the members are facing away. Peggy reported that she feels like the maid in the house, and has shown herself washing dishes as her husband demands his dinner. The tree outside the window is a northern tree, in contrast to the palm tree in her ideal family picture, and she spoke of disliking living in a cold climate, necessitated by her husband's job. Peggy was very unhappy that she was unable to conceive a child, but said that her adopted daughter from a different culture is the light of her life. Nevertheless, in the picture the daughter is distant from her mother, working on her computer. The group noted the parrot in both pictures, and Peggy explained that it was the last vestige of her ideal life. She said she regrets that too much time has gone by so that she and her husband are now too old to adopt more children.

Although Rita's family is very different from her ideal, she appears to be more accepting of the way things are than is Peggy. In her ideal family, titled *Father Knows Best* (Figure 5.8), she has depicted the sort of family shown on television when she was a child. The group commented on the explicit gender identifications in her picture. They noted the contrast with her actual family, shown in Figure 5.9. The exaggerated gender roles are gone. Although she felt grateful to be able to be a stay-at-home mom, she was sorry her husband had to work long hours. When her two sons were in high school, the family adopted a daughter from a different culture. There is an additional figure drawn in the family, as well. When Rita's younger son was in college, he announced that he was gay. He is drawn here with his partner. She described how she and her husband had gone into mourning for the ideal life they had wished for their son. But "after about six months," Rita said, "I told myself it

FIGURE 5.8   *Father Knows Best*, ideal family by a woman.

was time to get over it." The family had a big wedding for them, and Rita has included her son's partner in her family portrait. Gonzalez-Dolginko reports that Rita is very sensitive to comments that reflect traditional gender relationships. She enjoys hearing her daughter correct people who tell her she'll marry a nice man someday by saying, "Maybe I'll marry a nice woman!"

FIGURE 5.9   Actual family by woman who drew Figure 5.8.

In helping families to adjust to unanticipated circumstances characterized by loss, Gonzalez-Dolginko has enabled them to gain clarity about their present lives by visualizing the loss of their dreams and concretizing it in an image. As exemplified by Rita, grieving and coming to terms with loss can help people to embrace the present and form more productive and positive family relationships.

Family Home Treatment

An effective solution to the problem of families' resistance to participation in therapy is home-based treatment. Beth Black and Lorelie Swanson have set up the Family Art Therapy Center in a rural southern community to provide home treatment for at-risk families in several rural counties through contractual arrangements with the DCFS. They conceptualize their work in a systems framework which recognizes the triangular relationship among the family, the Family Art Therapy Center, and the DCFS (personal communication, 1998). In order to avoid disadvantageous triangulation, they maintain close communication with the DCFS caseworker, who is very much a part of their treatment planning.

Throughout treatment, which is contracted for a maximum of 24 weeks with two or three sessions weekly, Black and Swanson are very respectful of the family's needs, with special courtesies regarding the use of the family's home. A home venue provides a significantly different context for therapy from that of an office or an art studio, with attendant influences on the work. In the first place, the therapists are in the clients' territory, where the comfort level may be the reverse of the office situation for both parties. On the other hand, at least initially, the family members, particularly the parents, may be self-conscious about the appearance of their home. This may lead to major housecleaning or pressure on the children to straighten up. Black and Swanson discourage hosting activities, such as serving refreshments, because they want to convey that this is a professional visit for family work rather than a social occasion. Of course, seeing the home and how the family members utilize the space gives the therapists abundant information they might not have otherwise. There may be interruptions by the telephone or visitors that would not be a part of an office visit. Black and Swanson try to be respectful of these family conditions as well, even though they encourage the family to set aside the therapy time and discourage interruptions. Nevertheless, they remain flexible, and if the family is interrupted a lot or appears to be too fatigued at a session, they will suggest rescheduling. They negotiate the initial schedule with the family, as well as any need to change the schedule.

Black and Swanson have found that the art activities are empowering to the family in this context, so they begin them right away. Often the family is in a state of chaos at the beginning of therapy, and the art helps everyone to settle down. Usually the therapists sit on the floor with the family and spread out the art materials for all to reach. Working in this way to create art has a generational leveling effect on the family (Wadeson, 1980). As opposed to processes involving "grown-up talk," young children can interact as comfortably or more so than the adults.

In the initial family session, the family art therapist creates a genogram from information the family provides. The therapist tries to emphasize the positives in the family history. The therapist then consults with the family members about what they would like to change in their system. Often DCFS sets goals, as well. Black and Swanson have found that concrete, measurable goals are the most successful.

Early in treatment the family is presented with *image cards,* large magazine photos mounted on stiff paper. An abundant variety of pictures is arranged on the floor or table, and each family member is asked to select one. This is a non-threatening way to introduce the family to working with images. The cards can be geared to a number of responses: a picture to represent how each member views the family and another to represent how they would like the family to be; how each feels now or at a specific time, and so on. Each member might be asked to enact or discuss how it feels to be the chosen image or what attracted each to the selected image. Sometimes the family as a whole is asked to make up a story together, round-robin style, with each person supplying a sentence in turn about his or her image. Working in this way, communication among family members is instigated; they begin talking about feelings, and start to create the family's "healing story."

In another early project, the family places its designated problem in the center of a large piece of paper. It may be written or drawn, or one of the magazine photos may be glued on. Around the problem, family members write or draw everything that has led to the problem. From this, the therapist formulates goals with the family and develops a treatment plan.

Many of the families with whom Black and Swanson work have very unclear ideas of personal space and boundaries. This is especially evident in frequent hitting. In order to develop conceptualizations of claiming space and being sensitive to and respecting the space of others, the therapists have developed *boundary mats.* Each family member stands in the center of a discarded sheet, with the others on the perimeter. One by one, they advance toward the center until the central individual stops them at the point where they become too close for comfort. The spot is marked on the sheet. After all family members' places have been marked, the central person cuts away the sheet outside the marks so that what is left is a boundary mat of his or her own personal space. This can then be decorated. Each family member makes such a mat, with the others advancing slowly to circumscribe the mat's perimeter. (Figure 5.10 shows students and teacher trying the exercise.)

The making of the mats leads to much discussion about relations between the individual family members. Body language is pointed out in response to the approaches, and the meaning of boundaries is discussed. For example, issues of privacy and special possessions belonging to each member are

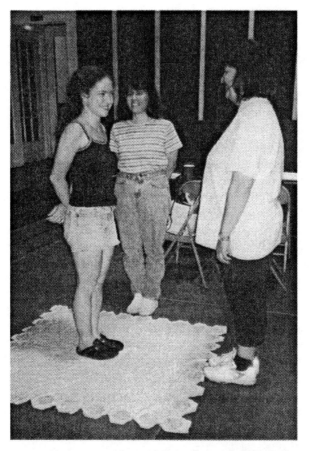

FIGURE 5.10   **Students and teacher trying boundary mat exercise.**

brought up. The project gives each person the opportunity to control his or her own personal space, which may be a rare occurrence in the family. The mats are referred to frequently throughout treatment, especially by the children, who may call others on violating their space. For many of them, this is their first recognition of their own personal space. The family members are taught to use assertiveness rather than aggression to protect their personal space and to ask permission before entering the space of another. They become responsible for their own space and come to respect that of the others. Often they need guidance in learning how to do this. Ultimately they become aware of the boundaries (or lack of them) that have existed in the family and learn to make them more appropriate.

In moving toward an integration of the family members' individual needs, each member makes a clay animal to represent himself or herself. The family discusses each animal's characteristics and needs. Their task is then to create an environment, using a box, colored paper, glue, fabric, and other materials, where all the animals can live in harmony such that their different needs are met and they are all safe (Figure 5.11).

A project that elicits lots of affect is making dolls from stuffed socks, fabric, wool, felt, buttons, beads, feathers, and similar materials. These dolls are easily made by tying, gluing, or sewing. They can be very expressive, taking either human or animal form (Figure 5.12). They can be named and moved. Clients often speak their minds and hearts more easily through their dolls than in speaking directly. How they handle them—lovingly, angrily, roughly, indifferently—is usually very telling.

When the family members are ready to complete treatment, Black and Swanson create a celebration with them, according to their wishes. Often they choose pizza. The Family Art Therapy Center reports a high degree of success with at-risk families in which DCFS is considering removing the children. Their treatment is very structured and utilizes a variety of art projects within the family's home. The therapists are careful to respect the family's wishes throughout. Given the complexity and difficulty of family work, it is noteworthy that the combination of art activities within the family's home has shown effective results.

A different form of home-based family art therapy has been practiced by Alicia Contreras (1993). In contrast with the Family Art Therapy Center in the rural south, Contreras had intended to meet with families at an urban treatment center that served a predominantly Latino community, not in their homes. It was necessity that brought her into their homes. The families were of a lower socioeconomic status. Usually, both parents and, often, adolescent

FIGURE 5.11   Family's environment for clay animals made by each individual member.

FIGURE 5.12   Stuffed sock doll.

children had to work outside the home. The conflicting schedules often impacted on family unity, and the varying work schedules also prevented family members from coming to the treatment center together. Moreover, resistance to revealing family matters to outsiders is characteristic of the Hispanic culture. Being sensitive to the culture through her own Mexican American heritage, Contreras allowed the families to treat her as a guest in their homes. Like Black and Swanson, she attempted to be as respectful of the family's needs and wishes as possible. The process was different, however.

Families worked together in all sessions with simple, easy-to-use media. Contreras began with a family mural of an enjoyable family activity, which the family members then discussed. This was a unifying activity. At the second session, they made individual drawings of their roles and their feelings about their move to the United States.

An example is provided by the Palacios family. They came to the United States to seek help for their 3-year-old boy, who had been diagnosed with cerebral palsy and seizure disorder. Their mural was of happy times in Mexico. The family included three sons, one daughter, the mother, the father, and the mother's brother. They met for four 2-hour sessions in their home. During the sessions, it was difficult to predict who might visit the Palacios. The family was careful to attend to visitors briefly in order to continue the art therapy. Sometimes guests were invited to join in. At the end, Contreras was always offered something to drink, and she shared some of her own memories of Mexico. Contreras became a role model for the children in the parents' hope that their children could develop productive lives in this country. In approaching the individual pictures, Contreras encouraged the family members to work in different parts of the house in order to foster concentration and reflection on their feelings. Most of the pictures centered on missing their home and way of life in Mexico.

At the third session, the family members made progression drawings—each picture grew out of the previous one, and the others responded to each without explanation from the artist. They enjoyed guessing about the pictures' meanings and praised the creativity of one of the boys, who drew their house in Mexico. Mr. Palacios drew his workplace at the supermarket (Figure 5.13). There was much guessing and laughing at the depiction of the people there. One of the boys depicted himself as a musician, his dream in Mexico, which was now becoming a reality (Figure 5.14). At the end of the session, he played a tape made by his band. The three-year-old child with cerebral palsy, who could not sit up, joined in singing, and the others followed him. They sat closely on the couch with their arms around each other in a very cozy interchange, with many smiles and much laughter. Mr. Palacios held the 3-year-old, who laughed whenever the others did. The family thought the girl's picture of herself in Mexico looked like a mother teaching a child to walk, the family's dream for the 3-year-old. This led to a discussion of his condition and

FIGURE 5.13   Father's workplace.

FIGURE 5.14 Son's dream of becoming a musician.

of their hopes and love for him. In comparing the pictures, Contreras noticed that although there were expressions of missing other family members, friends, and the way of life in Mexico, there were also depictions of opportunities in this country.

Like many other Mexican immigrant families, the Palacios had not all come to the United States together. First came Mr. Palacios and one of the sons, and the others followed later. Mrs. Palacios made a picture she titled *Esta es una familia unida* (This is a united family). She showed herself as responsible for holding the family together. She complained that on weekends, when they had some free time to be together, they all went their separate ways. Contreras helped her to realize that this situation would likely have come about as the children grew up regardless of the country in which they were living. The boys laughed about the broom she had drawn, saying it was a weapon to keep them together. At the end of the session, they were very excited to show Contreras their Mexican home. They played a home video of their town in Mexico. The house looked very much like a drawing of it by one of the boys.

For a final project, the family made a piñata together. Mrs. Palacios showed her daughter how to cut the tissue paper. They filled the piñata with representations of memories and reminisced about special town feasts. They said that the colors symbolized their different feelings, some bright and some dark. The piñata turned out to be aesthetically pleasing. They planned to display it in their home as a reminder of the successful completion of their therapy (Figure 5.15).

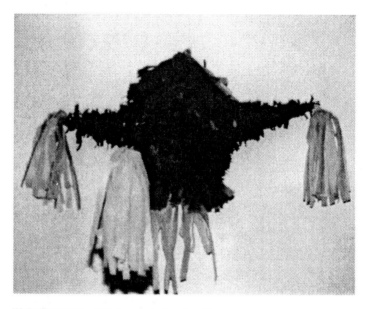

FIGURE 5.15   Piñata made by family.

This short-term home-based approach of four 2-hour sessions afforded the Palacios family the opportunity to relax from their busy and conflicting schedules and to enjoy one another. The home setting facilitated their openness. They took some risks and shared their feelings, including their losses and gains in their move to a new country and a new culture. They experienced the support of other family members as they became aware of their own conflicts, and they were eager to communicate their observations to one another. Perhaps most important was the reinforcement of family solidarity the short-term home-based art therapy provided. (For further discussion of art therapy with immigrants, see Chapter 9, "Displaced Persons.")

Art Therapists' Self-Processing

Working with the complexities of a family system is confusing enough in its own right, but add to this the inevitable distortions, biases, projections, and identifications that the therapist carries from his or her own family, and it is a wonder that there can be any clarity at all. It is necessary, therefore, for family therapists to try to understand their own family systems of origin so that they are able to focus on the dynamics of the family in treatment without reliving their own family issues.

As in other contexts, art expression can bring clarity and a sharper focus. Not only can the art expression help a family to see itself, it can enable family art therapists to sort out their own family issues as they may be stimulated by their work with families.

Courageously, Kathy Osler created a family scrapbook to promote her own differentiation from her family of origin in order to help herself better understand the family systems she was confronting in her work (Osler, 1996). She begins with a quote from Murray Bowen, the "father" of family therapy:

> I believe and teach that the family therapist usually has the very same problems in his own family that are present in families he sees professionally, and that he has a responsibility to define himself in his own family if he is to function adequately in his professional work. (Bowen, 1978, p. 468)

Osler describes her work as forming "a bridge of understanding between the two family system experiences: the one from which I came and the ones with which I am working" at a community mental health center (Osler, 1996, p. 2). The center provides family sessions for children referred there. At intake, Osler conducted family art therapy assessments to determine what services would most effectively benefit the families.

Osler began her scrapbook by collecting family photos, letters, newspaper clippings, and childhood drawings, which she then discussed with other members of her family. She photocopied the photographs and arranged them in collages to illustrate family alliances and separations. Some of the systems concepts she explored in her own family were individuality versus togetherness, emotional reactiveness, and triangulation. For example, in one collage she noticed how she distanced herself from other family members with a road cutting diagonally across the picture, leading her away from her family on her journey toward differentiation. She realized this was how she coped with her emotional reactiveness. From this picture she made other collages, drawing over photocopied family photos to show her emotional responses to various family members, particularly her parents. She also drew triangles illustrating how she got pulled into the emotional triangles in her family, helping her to understand the triangulations in her clients' family systems.

In undertaking this project, Osler recognized her own resistance to making art and writing about her family. She put these feelings into a picture showing her family in a bubble, floating above her, and herself holding a needle representing her fear of provoking conflict by probing, and perhaps popping, the bubble (Figure 5.16). The red brick wall stands as a barrier of resistance. Seeing her own resistance so clearly displayed helped Osler to empathize with her clients' resistance.

In what is an excellent model for art therapists, Osler was able to weave back and forth between her own family exploration and her work with client families. Twelve-year-old Lisa's family is an example. The oldest of three children, Lisa felt responsible for her family's problems and adjusted her behavior to try to preserve family harmony. When her parents separated and then divorced, she exhibited behavior problems. In a family art therapy assessment, she drew the family, with her own face looming very large behind the

FIGURE 5.16   Art therapist's reaction to studying her own family's dynamics.

others (Figure 5.17). She said she drew herself this way because she was the whole reason everyone was there in the family session.

Prior to the family assessment, Osler had been seeing Lisa in individual sessions in which she was becoming more and more able to express her feelings of anger and loss at the family breakup. Lisa's father, Bob, said he didn't think these sessions were helping her and that, in fact, her behavior was getting worse. She was acting out toward his girlfriend. Osler felt distraught and questioned herself about how he could so easily shake her confidence as a therapist. She drew a picture of how she perceived Bob—calm above the table,

FIGURE 5.17   Family portrait by 12-year-old girl.

with angry red fists below it. He had seemed angry yet removed and passive. He gave no information about his drawings, and Osler surmised that the session was threatening to him, as he was trying to move on to a new relationship with his girlfriend. Osler's drawing showed him keeping his anger and vulnerability under the table.

To explore her reaction to Bob, Osler drew Figure 5.18 in order to understand how she had learned to deal with anger in her own family. Her family pattern was one of distancing—either physically, by leaving the room, or emotionally, by withdrawing to avoid conflict. To change the pattern she has drawn herself as a rock hitting the very solid wall of her family. The powerful rock has cracked the solid wall. In relating her picture to Bob and Lisa, Osler saw that just as her change in confronting her own family was causing cracks in the family, she was stirring things up for Bob by encouraging Lisa to express her feelings. Osler's own artwork enabled her to move beyond her diminished confidence as a therapist, and Bob began to participate more fully in treatment,

In her work with Barbara, a 38-year-old woman with depression, Osler was able to help Barbara see the connections between her anger and depression and her relationship with her mother, who was also needy and dependent. Osler could see that the neediness and resultant disappointments in current relationships that Barbara experienced resulted from insufficient nurturing by her alcoholic mother, who had been preoccupied with caring for her own alcoholic husband. The dynamics became clear to Osler as a result of

FIGURE 5.18 Art therapist's reaction to her own family's pattern of dealing with anger.

exploring her own family through art. Figure 5.19 shows Osler at the bottom of the page holding up a red hand to distance herself from her own emotional needs while she gives of herself with the other hand, spreading blue and green leaves to fulfill the emotional needs of others. Above her is her mother doing the same thing. At the top is a faded image of her mother's mother doing the same. Osler discovered that what distanced her from others, not allowing them to know her needs, also distanced her from her mother, explaining why she felt that she could not give back to her mother what her mother had given her. As Osler understood her own pattern of family repetition, Barbara's sessions became more focused, and Barbara was able to find her own connection between the emotional dynamics in her relationship with her mother and her current relationships with friends and relatives.

The Garcia family, consisting of a single mother and four children, was a study in chaos in which each was highly reactive to the others. At the initial art therapy family assessment, most of the pictures were disorganized, and the session felt unsafe. Kathy noticed many interlocking triangles in the family interaction preventing direct one-to-one communication.

FIGURE 5.19   Art therapist's reaction to distancing herself from her own emotional needs.

In looking at the triangulation within her own family, Osler recognized how powerful the pull from other family members can be. For example, she became aware of the anger that could arise in her when talking to her father. Often he would pull another family member into their conversation and criticize or make fun of him or her. Probably it was easier for him to do this than to confront the family member directly. To illustrate her reaction, Osler created a collage. At the bottom is a blue and green figure representing the other family member, who is reaching out to Osler, above, represented by a photo of a woman about to shoot an arrow. She felt she had to defend this person against her father. Her anger is represented by red paint spilling out of the woman's head toward her father. Osler recognized that she had to remove the third party from her relationship with her father and relate to him directly. As she became aware of the triggers of her emotional reactivity within her family, Osler was able to make changes in her own patterns of relating and begin to see their reverberations in her family system.

The Garcia family also needed to unlock themselves from the destructive emotional patterns that caused their heightened reactivity to one another. Osler encouraged them to relate directly in order to cut through the triangulations that were part of their family dynamics. She arranged for them to create art in dyads and to discuss the experience one-to-one. The artwork itself also provided opportunities for family members to share their perspectives without interruption and to express themselves to one another directly, bypassing the triangular relationships that had prevented direct communication.

Osler realized that making art about her own family issues had been invaluable to her in achieving clarity. Professionally, the recognition of such concepts as triangulation and multigenerational emotional processes within her own family vivified her real-life grasp of these dynamics in client families and enabled her to understand the complexity of client family dynamics more readily. As a result of working through some of her own family issues and having seen the impact of her own efforts to change both on herself and on her family, Osler felt more confident as a therapist in promoting change in her clients. What Osler describes as the messy business of trying to understand her own emotional system of origin is certainly a difficult and often painful process, in which one holds a mirror up to images of oneself that one might prefer to hide. Like other self-examinations described in this book, Osler's took honesty and courage. Her work is another illustration of art's effectiveness in revealing and clarifying, another model of the conscientious art therapist's continuing self-examination.

Summary

Conducting family art therapy often poses considerable challenges. Among them are obtaining full family cooperation, working with young children, and understanding the complexities of family dynamics.

- Gail Wirtz (personal communication, 1999) worked with a child and his family around developmental problems in the child and structural problems within the family. Digital photography served therapeutic ends for the family members and served as a reference source for the therapist.
- Kama Schulte (1991) developed a family body-tracing project for a child and family counseling center program focused on teaching parenting skills.
- Kimberly Rakestraw (1997) utilized clay for self-representations in family work to increase communication and awareness within the family.
- Gian Luca Ferme (1996) created games and puppet projects at a family health center serving Puerto Rican and Mexican American communities. The projects, which could be used with young children, were geared to the families' needs. They often increased skills and competence, brought out much expressiveness, identified interactional patterns, and provided opportunities for the families to create together and have fun.
- In preventative work with parents of disabled and adopted children, Beth Gonzalez-Dolginko (personal communication, 1999) focused on mourning the loss of the "perfect baby" or "ideal family" these parents had hoped to have. In contrasting the dream with the reality, parents were able to grieve what was lost to them, accept their present family, and understand more fully how their grief impacted their family dynamics.
- Beth Black and Lorelie Swanson's Family Art Therapy Center utilizes a systems framework in a highly structured home-based treatment program that includes a large variety of art therapy projects for rural southern families (personal communication, 1998). The program has been highly successful in work with difficult-to-reach families.
- Alicia Contreras (1993) also conducted home-based family art therapy. Hers was a short-term approach for urban Mexican American immigrant families who were unable to come to the community center where she worked.
- Kathy Osler (1996) created a family scrapbook of photographs, drawings, and collages to explore her own family in order to achieve clarity in recognizing dynamics such as triangulation and multigenerational processes in client families.

Conclusion

Family art therapy can be a very effective treatment modality. The possibilities for families to create together, have fun together, and communicate clearly with one another open doors of interaction that may have been closed previously. Young children may be included in novel ways that are unavailable in purely verbal therapy. On the other hand, family art therapy may be threatening to some or all family members. Cooperation and participation may be difficult to obtain. Factors other than resistance may intrude as well, especially scheduling problems. One avenue around this impasse is home-based family therapy, which also provides the many advantages of seeing the family in situ. Family therapy may be threatening to the therapist as well, plunging him or her into family dynamics that may feel all too familiar. As in other dark places, the therapist's own artwork can be a beacon of illumination, clarifying the therapist's own family dynamics and increasing his or her understanding of the client family's dynamics.

ART THERAPY PROJECTS

Projects discussed in this chapter are described further in Chapter 15, "Art Activities and Materials":

- Foam-core construction (Wirtz, personal communication, 1999)
- Murals (Wirtz, personal communication, 1999)
- Life-size dolls (Wirtz, personal communication, 1999)
- Digital photography (Wirtz, personal communication, 1999)
- Body tracings (Schulte, 1991)
- Clay family figures (Rakestraw, 1997)
- Puppets (Ferme, 1996)
- Polaroid puppets (Ferme, 1996)
- Cardboard box house construction (Ferme, 1996)
- Games (Ferme, 1996)
- Directive drawing of ideal and reality pictures (Gonzalez-Dolginko, personal communication, 1999)
- Magazine collage image cards (Black and Swanson, personal communication, 1998)
- Boundary mats (Black and Swanson, personal communication, 1998)
- Sock dolls (Black and Swanson, personal communication, 1998)
- Piñatas (Contreras, 1993)
- Therapist's postsession family scrapbook (Osler, 1996)
- Collage (Osler, 1996)

Chapter 6

Developmental Delay

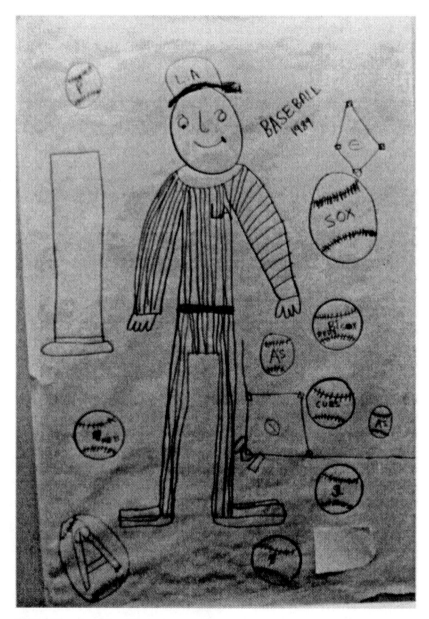

Me by 30-year-old man.

Marvin is rocking and slapping his head. There are food stains on his shirt. When the markers and paper are placed on the table in front of him, his rhythmic movements slow down. He picks up the red marker and starts to draw a truck. His brows knit in concentration as he bends over the paper, squinting to see his marks. When he's finished he smiles broadly and holds up his picture.

We have been viewing the life cycle from the perspective of expected intellectual development. This chapter is a detour in the direction of those who are chronologically adults, but developmentally are much younger. They are characterized by the less visible, often overlooked, and frequently misunderstood condition of developmental delay. The limitations imposed by this condition can lead to an overlay of emotional difficulties, as well.

There can be as much individual difference among the members of this population as in any other, not only in functional level and particular talents and gifts, but in emotional state, as well. Sometimes it is difficult to distinguish the underlying condition from the influence of the environment, such as institutionalization, rejection by family and peers, the stigma of difference, experience of abuse, and discouragement of autonomy and independence. Low self-esteem is a frequent result.

Case management for individuals with developmental delay is often directed exclusively toward learning appropriate behavior and social and vocational skills. Such individuals are seldom given opportunities to make independent judgments or to function autonomously. People with developmental delay have traditionally been considered incapable of abstract thought and therefore incapable of truly creative expression. They have also been considered incapable of the sort of insight that psychotherapy can stimulate.

Art therapy has proven otherwise. A particularly dramatic example is provided by Ellen Sontag in her work with Dobie (Wadeson, 1987). A 21-year-old woman with an IQ of 34, Dobie had lived in a large state institution since she was 8. Her verbal ability was almost nonexistent, and her aggressive behavior was injurious to both herself and others. Yet her artistic ability was remarkable, exhibiting perspective, understanding of complex spatial relationships, accurate depiction of detail, and personal expressiveness that conveyed her feelings meaningfully (see Wadeson, 1987, pp. 204–211 for illustrations). Through art therapy she was able to come to terms with her present life situation, accept the loss of her family, establish a strong relationship with her art therapist, and effect a positive termination of this relationship when Sontag completed her internship at the facility where Dobie was being treated.

Client Art Exhibits

Dobie was an exceptional art therapy client. Art therapy is beneficial for unexceptional individuals with developmental delay, as well. In the early 1980s, the University of Illinois at Chicago (UIC) art therapy graduate program began placing student interns at its Institute for the Study of Developmental Disabilities (ISDD; now the Institute for Disability and Human Development [IDHD]). Sontag was its first art therapy intern. Then geared to the treatment of the emotional difficulties and psychiatric diagnoses in this population, its clients were transported from residential facilities, sheltered workshops, and family homes. From the beginning, at Sontag's instigation, the students produced a culminating art show at the end of the academic year. These were significant events in the lives of the "artists." Some years the shows were videotaped. Refreshments were served and family and friends were invited. The characteristic feature of my attendance as the UIC art therapy director was the tours given by the individual exhibitors. Their pride in their work was almost boundless. The interest of others was obviously immensely gratifying to people who so often experience social isolation. What was most impressive was the opportunity for success and recognition with the resultant elevation of self-esteem provided by art therapy. For them, it was more than just learning or mastering a new skill. It was more than just approval of their behavior by the people important to them. They valued their own unique personal self-expression. Their art on display was its tangible representation.

Art and Movement

An example of the sort of progress in personal expression that can be seen in art therapy is provided by Susan O'Boyle (1989). Her client, Richard, a 30-year old man referred to ISDD for help in controlling his anger, tended to deny his feelings in an attempt to control his angry destructive outbursts. He was a member of the movement and art group that O'Boyle co-led with a movement therapy intern. The 1½-hour sessions began with movement followed by art making and then verbal processing. During the movement portion, Richard moved freely and seemed to feel safe in expressing his aggression. Nevertheless, during the drawing segment he almost always drew baseballs, which had been a repeated theme for several years.

At the beginning of a particular session everyone in the group appeared to be angry, so they were encouraged to shout, punch and kick the air, and throw a ball against a wall. To continue the release of anger in the art part, the group members were given 6- by 3-foot paper taped to the walls and colored chalks and markers, with which they were asked to scribble a depiction of the movement without attempting to draw a picture. At first, Richard moved his marker around in the air, but did not touch the paper. The uncontrolled scribbling was too threatening to what O'Boyle describes as his energy-draining task of maintaining continuous control. She had hoped that if he gained experience in expressing his anger safely, he might become able to cope with his anger more adaptively. He drew another one of his repetitive themes, a very controlled looking geometric wrestling ring. Eventually, however, without pressure to change his picture, Richard became more relaxed, his movements became more fluid, and on his own initiative he began scribbling over his wrestling ring, drawing with several different colored markers at once. He received immediate positive feedback from the group. He then made another large scribble, showing satisfaction with both of his scribbles, and participated in making the group mural, as well.

At the next session, Richard again chose to work standing up, and he made another scribble drawing. This appeared to loosen him up. Then, for the first time, he drew a human figure, shown on page 174, which he titled *Me.* Here he's a professional baseball player surrounded by baseballs, a bat, and several baseball diamonds. In reviewing Richard's record, O'Boyle discovered that when his grandmother had first sought treatment for him at ISDD, she was worried that no one had been caring for him, saying that he had never been taken to a baseball game and that it wasn't right for a 24-year-old boy just to sit at home. During his time at ISDD he was taken to baseball games and wrestling matches. Like many others in our society, he was then able to release aggression as part of the crowd at spectator sports. His personal identification with the baseball player is a significant advance in self-expression over the perseverative baseballs he had been drawing. The opportunity art making affords for the safe release of anger can be an important benefit for individuals with developmental delay who may have few other acceptable avenues for the expression of aggression.

Another example of expanded expression from O'Boyle is her work with Thomas, a 29-year-old man who had been referred for debilitating anxiety. He had only mild retardation, making him sensitive to his deficiencies. He held unrealistic expectations for himself, resulting in low self-esteem and a sense of personal failure. As he gained self-confidence in the art group, he was able to control his anxiety, and his artwork became increasingly imaginative and expressive. His drawing of a tiger, in addition to showing his skill and imagination, suggests power and strength, even though the feet don't touch the ground (Figure 6.1).

Bookmaking

Anita Glover (1991) developed picture-book-making projects for her clients at ISDD. One client evolved a seasonal theme as he made pictures for his book throughout the year. Especially interesting was a group book project to which each individual contributed a chapter. The group members generally had a borderline level of functioning; several were quite isolated and had no friends. Consisting of five men of various ethnic backgrounds (two African Americans, two Caucasians, and one Hispanic American), the group provided a structure and a focus for interaction and self-expression.

In the first group project, each member made a self-portrait to introduce

FIGURE 6.1 Tiger by 29-year-old man suggests power and strength.

himself. Sam reached out in his, drawing a characature of his plump face and titling it *This Is Your Friend Sam*. In order to keep the chapters consistent and to heighten shared experience, the group was given a common directive for each page. At times they chose their own directives, for example, *My Favorite Room in My House*, chosen by Jason, who depicted his bedroom in his group home. He explained that it was the only place where he could be alone and have peace and privacy.

At the end of a session in which Ron was unusually quiet, he spoke of feeling safe in the group and told of the death of his father the previous weekend. At the next session, the group members discussed what death meant to each of them and included their imagery of death in their respective chapters. As the group was drawing to a close for the year, Sam linked death to the ending of the group. They drew pictures of the art room and images of the group. Upon completion, the book was bound. They found that looking through it brought back significant memories of their individual expressions and shared experience.

In her work with the same population, Vickie Scescke (1990) also utilized creating bound books, but in a different way. Scescke's clients often came to the session with a story to tell. She wrote them down and read them back to the clients. Sometimes the stories were stimulated by the pictures of other clients hanging in the art room. Some stories described direct experience; others were highly imaginative. Claudette told stories of her family's activities, drew pictures of them, and named the pictorial elements. Scescke photographed her art, transcribed the stories, and bound them in a book that she gave to Claudette at the end of therapy. There were empty pages for her to fill later.

Lenore presented a placid exterior, but drew a rattlesnake hiding under a bush. This became a metaphor for the part of herself she kept hidden. She felt like a rattlesnake when she was very angry, she said, but she hid it because she didn't want to be evil. Another picture shows an ocean with a smooth surface and many currents beneath it. Scescke helped Lenore to bind a book of her images and stories. Their juxtaposition told a more complete tale of Lenore than any one of them did singly.

Puppets

Another method Scescke used to bring her group together for art and stories was making puppets to enact the storytelling. Other group members were often involved in a client's story by enacting a character, operating a puppet, focusing a light, or being a part of the audience that interacted with the puppets. The first puppets were made from socks and decorated with yarn, feathers, buttons, sequins, markers, and felt. As the group became more experienced, heads were formed from clay and covered with plaster gauze; a felt body that could slip over the hand and arm was then added (Figure 6.2). The group members then gave them names and stories.

FIGURE 6.2 Puppets made from plaster-gauze-covered clay heads and fabric, about which stories were created.

With help, Rosalind, a very shy girl who never made eye contact, created a puppet she called Sheba the Wild Dog, which resembles a person more than a dog (Figure 6.3). In the process, the dog became female. Rosalind made up the following story:

> This is a dog named Sheba. Sheba lived in the woods. Sheba was a wild dog. She roamed all over the woods. But she was also a lonely dog. One day in the woods she met another dog, and she made a good friend with this other dog. And then she wasn't lonely anymore. (p. 26)

At the next session, Rosalind drew a picture of the forest in which Sheba lived. She drew the other dog and mounted it on cardboard. Rosalind enacted the meeting of Sheba and the other dog in front of the forest background. Usually painfully quiet, Rosalind laughed through her puppet during the enactment. Subsequently, she also ventured into new ways of making art. Scescke's group created two stages for their puppets, one that Scescke designed and one they designed themselves.

FIGURE 6.3   Sheba the Wild Dog puppet.

Group Work and Sensory Stimulation

Vivian Ragis, another UIC art therapy intern, stresses the importance of group work and sensory enrichment in her work at ISDD (Ragis, 1987). She notes that this population often experiences environmental and cultural deprivation in addition to social deprivation (i.e., isolation). To address the latter, Ragis developed such projects as group mural making. Each member completed a portion of the mural individually, and each portion was then joined to the others to form a composite. Members were encouraged to help one another, which was often necessary because there were physical disabilities, as well. Ragis realized that individuals have richer experiences when more than one sense is stimulated. Therefore, to address environmental deprivation, she played music and introduced scents to be sampled, both of which were then discussed; provided fruit for a still life, which was eaten after the painting was finished; and read poetry and other literature for visualization exercises. The group made collages from both manufactured objects and natural materials such as coffee beans, lentils, rice, pasta, shells, and wool made into yarn.

Mask Making

A particularly engrossing project Ragis developed brought cultural awareness to her two groups, as well. Because almost all the members were African Americans, she created a 3-week Black History Month project of mask making. Precut cardboard shapes were provided for those who could not make their own. Some chose to alter the shapes. They were given assistance in cutting out facial features if they needed it. Throwaway materials such as toilet paper tubes, small boxes, plastic egg-shaped panty hose containers, poster board pieces, and ribbon spools were available to build up the masks. After taping on these items, members covered them with plaster gauze. Smoothing out the wet plaster was often a soothing experience. The final step was to paint the masks after they had dried. Tapes of African music and music it has influenced were played during the sessions. Ragis read African folk tales to her groups, as well.

One group visited a gallery to view an exhibit of African masks, and the other group was shown photographs of Ragis's trip to Egypt because the members had expressed an interest in Egyptian art. Some were so inspired that they made their own "Egyptian art." The members' masks were displayed in the clinic waiting room, where they were a source of interest to clients, staff members, and visitors (Figure 6.4).

The group members showed great enthusiasm for the mask making. The few members who were usually resistant to trying anything new showed no resistance to this project. One dependent member with a withered arm who had always asked for help said he could create the entire project by himself,

FIGURE 6.4 "Egyptian art" masks.

and he did. Interest in the throwaway materials later prompted junk art sculptures, with each member designing a unique piece. Painting the masks brought forth a lot of interest in one another's creations.

Constructing the masks elicited revealing evidence of some of the members' hidden problems. One did not know the position of her facial features. The mask making provided a tactile and visual activity to help her kinesthetic orientation in this regard. Another member, who said that his brain was hurting him, began to exhibit psychotic behavior. In this way the masks became indicators of the group members' cognitive and emotional states.

The gallery tour was a great success also. The curator of the exhibit was the guide for the group. Despite some worrisome behavior by two members, most were attentive and asked relevant questions. The group was invited back for the next year's Black History Month exhibition. On the way home there were spontaneous discussions of the show. They noted some similarities to their own masks. Long after the gallery visit, the members were still discussing it and expressing interest in future visits to other galleries. The success of Ragis's two groups increased the demand for art therapy to the extent that she established three additional groups.

Sensory Stimulation to Prevent Self-Injurious Behavior

The members of the population with developmental delay with whom Dee Ann Foss worked were women who had been institutionalized most of their lives. Many of these individuals exhibited self-stimulatory behaviors that were often self-injurious, including rocking, head nodding, hand flapping, tapping or shaking objects, and gazing at lights. Performed sufficiently often and intensely, these behaviors resulted in bruising, bleeding, or other tissue damage. More severe behavior included scratching, biting, head banging, pinching, and face slapping. Hypothesizing that this activity was due primarily to underarousal for which self-stimulation was an effort to compensate, Foss developed art therapy projects with sensory-stimulating materials (Foss, 1999). Projects utilized tactile materials such as fabric swatches, tissue paper, pasta, potpourri, pom-poms, feathers, modeling compound, and Plasticine, in addition to the usual paints and drawing materials. Large paintings and drawings provided opportunities for kinesthetic activity through large sweeping motions. Music was played for auditory stimulation, according to clients' personal tastes. The room was scented with potpourri and scented candles for olfactory stimulation, as well.

Michele, a 26-year-old woman diagnosed with Profound Mental Retardation, severe Attention Deficit Disorder, and autism, had lived at the residence for 12 years. Although able to walk, feed herself, and dress with minimal help, her mental age was estimated at 18 months. In addition to running agitatedly, ripping paper, knocking over objects, attacking others, biting herself, screaming, and throwing herself on the floor, Michele also performed such self-stimulatory behaviors as rubbing her eyes, neck and shoulders; poking her eyes; and putting pebbles, ants, and bees in her ears. In providing materials to give her added stimulation, Foss noticed that Michele seemed to have a fondness for collage. In attaching materials to the paper, she evidenced a much higher level of motor ability than that of an 18-month-old as she squeezed glue and placed objects on the paper. She was also able to choose the objects independently. She glued the somewhat difficult pom-poms and feathers and arranged and rearranged her composition to suit herself. Foss noted a dramatic decrease in Michele's self-injurious behaviors during the art therapy sessions, decreasing from 20 to 30 occurrences in the first sessions to 1 to 10 times in later sessions.

April, a 24-year-old woman diagnosed with Severe Mental Retardation, Bipolar Disorder, and severe allergies, complicated by fetal alcohol syndrome and early neglect and abuse, was estimated to have a mental age of 3 years, 2 months. She was able to communicate verbally but behaved inappropriately in hugging, touching, pinching, and scratching others. Her self-injurious behavior took the form of picking her fingers until they bled. She had lived at the facility since she was 9. Although April's artistic ability was consistent with her mental age for the most part, there were exceptions. She was making a crayon border for a large painting when the crayon slipped and marked the wet paint, revealing layers of paint underneath. April liked the effect and continued to use the crayon to expose the paint beneath. Although in her residence April was observed to perform self-injurious behavior almost constantly, she averaged only about three incidences in each art therapy session.

Kelly, age 34, was diagnosed with Profound Mental Retardation and seizure disorder. Her mental age was estimated at 18 months. She was functionally nonverbal with an extremely short attention span. She had lived at the facility for 11 years. She hit herself as many as five times within 30 minutes and often bruised herself. While the residence staff had difficulty in keeping Kelly engaged in an activity for more than a few minutes, she worked consistently and quietly with Foss for up to 30 minutes. Foss had intended to introduce her to sponge painting, but before she had an opportunity to do so, Kelly grabbed the materials and began working on her own. Apparently she had done sponge painting a few months before and remembered the process. This demonstrated more cognitive ability than she had been estimated to have. Her self-injurious behavior, which initially occurred approximately five times per session, disappeared altogether during her later art therapy sessions.

An obvious observation Foss made was that using their hands as they did in art therapy prevented these women from engaging in self-injurious behaviors. Very likely, however, art therapy provided creative stimulation, decreasing the need for self-stimulation. Foss had hoped that the effect would carry over into other areas of their lives, but there was no evidence that it did so. Nevertheless, Foss's work raises questions about how the days of individuals with Profound Mental Retardation should be organized.

Film Animation

The most amazing project I have seen in work with people with developmental delay is *The Belles of St. Mary,* an animated film created by UIC student Monica Dougherty and four residents of St. Mary's of Providence, a school and residence for people with developmental delay (Dougherty, 1991). The complexity of film animation—the necessary planning, teamwork, technical skill, and perseverance—is beyond the capacity of many art therapy groups. To expect success, or even a positive experience, for a group of individuals with developmental delay took great confidence, courage, and trust on Dougherty's part.

The four women selected to participate were Dori, 25, with a diagnosis of Mild Mental Retardation, seizure disorder and congenital hydrocephalus, a St. Mary's resident since the age of 4; Margaret, 32, diagnosed with Mild Mental Retardation and Down syndrome, at St. Mary's since 8 months of age; Roberta, 25, diagnosed with Moderate Mental Retardation and Down syndrome, placed in foster care at 3 and at St. Mary's at 7; Mary Ann, 27, diagnosed with Moderate Mental Retardation, Down syndrome, delayed language disorder, and limited vision in both eyes, placed at St. Mary's at 11. The women tended to be isolated, spending most of their leisure time alone. As is evident, this was not a group from which one would have great expectations.

Dougherty's goals were to establish an animation team whose members would learn to interrelate with one another, to trust themselves and each other, to learn and master new skills, to develop their personal expression, and to make choices and decisions independent of the institution. All these would be new challenges for individuals in an institution where life was so totally regulated that the women did not even select their own clothes to wear each day. Dougherty also hoped the project would provide an exciting experience for these women.

The first couple of months were spent in planning. During this time group cohesion was beginning to build, and the women started spending leisure time with one another outside the animation team's sessions, which were held three times a week for 1½-hour sessions. Discussions centered on proposed themes; they finally settled on a day in their own lives at St. Mary's, oriented around the seasons, beginning with fall because that was the time of year the project began. Initially, Dougherty had to do a lot of the organizing in the face of the learned helplessness and other limitations the women experienced. She brought in books on animation and explained the parts of the camera, but it was a spontaneous demonstration that proved most useful in illustrating the process. Margaret was the first to grasp the concept and brought in a drawing she had made of her parents meeting her at the airport (she visited her family on holidays). She said she wanted to animate it. Dougherty showed her how to cut out the figures and move them across the background. Various members volunteered to draw the first images: the front doors of St. Mary's, morning coffee, and a face with a separate toothbrush to move. There was a problem in creating the title, so the original plan was abandoned in favor of a simpler one. Another problem was deciding how to portray the women, because they were having difficulty in drawing themselves. Dougherty made cutout paper doll shapes, which the women personalized. This way they were all the same size. They dressed them in day clothes, pajamas, winter coats, and summer clothes (Figure 6.5).

Two months into the project they began shooting their images (Figure 6.6), with Margaret as camera person and the others as prop people. First the title was shot, then the doors. Next, autumn leaves that had been drawn and real ones that had been collected were very carefully and gradually added to simulate the blowing leaves of fall. The group counted off the number of single frames together as the camera person clicked the cable release. This initial filming was very exciting to the team, pulling together all the planning and drawing. They had finally reached the "lights, camera, action" phase.

A couple of months later, in the middle phase of the work, the filming

FIGURE 6.5   Film animation characters.

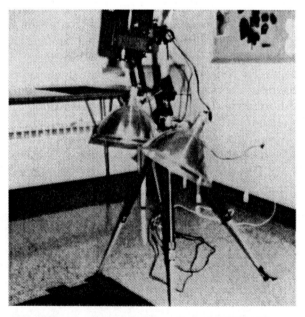

FIGURE 6.6   Equipment for photographing film
animation.

process became tedious. Roberta began missing sessions. Although the others always tried to include her, her resistance may have been partly due to her comparison of her own art to that of the others. Dougherty gave her the more practical tasks of cutting out images and moving the drawings and photographs across the filming surface.

In the course of the 6 months of the project, each woman shared something personal about herself and her difficulties with the others. Each learned to operate the camera and set up the animation area. Given the rigidity of their lives in the institution for so long, it is not surprising that they did not make much headway with independent decision making. Obviously, there is not support for this in the institution.

Previewing the completed *Belles of St. Mary* was a revelation to the women. Its premier was well received by the audience of other residents and staff members, especially the administrative director. I was truly amazed at how charming the film is. It is a wonderful accomplishment reflecting the creativity, personal expression, and teamwork of the women who made it. Working with a very limited budget and less than adequate equipment, Dougherty enabled the women to tell their story in their own personal images, and to work together to produce a documentary of which they can be proud, judged by any standards. There is much to be learned about limitations and transcending them in this project.

Dehumanization and Hopelessness

In spite of the impressive projects art therapists have been able to facilitate among the developmentally delayed, there is another side to this work that is important to note. In reflecting on her experience with this population, Riv Stein (1994) has written honestly and courageously of her difficulties.

For 6 months, Stein kept a journal and made art after each session in order to confront her "unacceptable" feelings. She often felt fear, disgust, and confusion in relation to her clients and then guilt for harboring such feelings. She discovered herself not to be the accepting therapist that was her ideal, but often found herself wishing to avoid her clients. Through her art work and journal, Stein recognized that she was dehumanizing her clients by speaking to them as if they were children, was avoiding physical and sometimes even eye contact with them because she was so repulsed, and was pitying them and comparing their lives to her own. Her hopelessness in working with them resulted from being unable to see past their limitations and deficiencies and from projecting her own fears of loneliness and isolation onto them.

In writing of her experience, Stein focused on three clients. Robert, 54, had mild retardation with various medical problems, antagonistic behavior, and poor temper control. His unkempt appearance repulsed her. To her surprise, he said he thought she was scared of him. In time, however, a relationship developed between them, and Stein began to see Robert with a degree of affection and admiration, as a whole person (Figure 6.7). She saw the sad lonely man behind the strange facade. Stein has noted that these feelings expressed in her art could not have been expressed verbally.

Jake, 32, had severe to profound retardation and Down syndrome. He could not speak, and he alternated between chewing and sucking his enlarged, protruding tongue. He jerked his body and grunted to express himself. Stein felt no contact with him and could see no human spirit there, only an empty vessel. During a session in which they were making a collage together, Stein got glue on her finger, and Jake wiped it off. She felt they had finally connected and recognized each other. Her art helped her to see their relationship and the powerful influence each had on the other more clearly.

Elijah, also 32, was diagnosed with Moderate Mental Retardation and autism. He had a speech and language handicap and was unresponsive and lifeless. Stein saw him in a group. In contrast with his lifelessness, sometimes

FIGURE 6.7 **Art therapist's portrait of a sad, lonely client.**

he bolted from the room, rocked, or jumped up and down, often disrupting the group. Stein was afraid he might hurt her. Eventually, she realized she was projecting her own anger. At one session, when she was angry at him for making her feel so out of control and helpless and at herself for not being able to control the situation, Elijah lay on the floor refusing to get up. The group was making a mural, and Stein ignored him. He then stood up on a table and copied one of her images, a heart. This was the first evidence that he noticed her. In the following sessions, he was less disruptive. Stein became able to allow Elijah his own space and his occasional disruptions, and he was able to participate more fully.

Through keeping a journal and making art of her fear, anger, disgust, and confusion, Stein was able to accept her initial discomfort with her clients as natural instead of feeling guilty about it. She learned to see past their limitations to their unique abilities and to respect their own pace of growth.

By making art and writing about it, Stein has provided an honest self-exploration of feelings that other therapists may experience but seldom discuss. Her courage and honesty in documenting this difficult passage can serve as a model for dealing with the negative feelings all of us have toward our clients at one time or another.

Summary

Art therapy has demonstrated that individuals with developmental delay are capable of creative expression.

- Ellen Sontag initiated an annual exhibit of art by participants in a program addressing the emotional difficulties of clients with developmental delay (Wadeson, 1987).
- Susan O'Boyle (1989) combined art and movement to enhance self-expression.
- Anita Glover (1991) developed picture-book projects.
- Vickie Scescke (1990) utilized storytelling, bookmaking, puppet making, and enacting to integrate clients' stories with their art.
- Vivian Ragis (1987) encouraged group mural making and provided sensory stimulation incorporating both natural and manufactured objects in collage work.
- Vivian Ragis (1987) developed African American cultural awareness through mask making and a gallery visit to view African masks.
- Dee Ann Foss (1999) utilized sensory-stimulating art materials to decrease the self-injurious behaviors of women institutionalized with Profound Mental Retardation.
- Monica Dougherty (1991) created a film animation project for women who had been institutionalized for most of their lives.
- Riv Stein (1994) kept a journal and made art after each art therapy ses-

sion to process her own feelings of hopelessness and dehumanization in relation to her clients.

Conclusion

As a group, individuals with developmental delay attract little societal attention and are relatively easily managed compared to those who promulgate danger to society through violence, drug peddling, spreading disease through multiple sexual contacts, and the like. Nor do they require treatment as do those who are afflicted with mental or physical illness, substance abuse, neglect, or life-crisis disasters. Services to this population, therefore, tend to be primarily custodial in nature, with an emphasis on conformity to appropriate behavior norms, learning basic social skills, and low-level vocational training. Although care is usually humane and often even nurturing, there is little encouragement of individual self-expression and creativity. The art therapy work with persons with developmental delay, both individually and in groups, has demonstrated some surprising possibilities. Art therapists who consider work with individuals with developmental delay to be pedestrian might discover unique challenges and rewards in the creativity, pleasure, and personal growth art therapy provides these clients. Their often immense appreciation of art therapy is especially gratifying.

ART THERAPY PROJECTS

Projects discussed in this chapter are described further in Chapter 15, "Art Activities and Materials":

- Art exhibits (Sontag; described in Wadeson, 1987)
- Art and movement (O'Boyle, 1989)
- Scribble drawing (O'Boyle, 1989)
- Bookmaking (Glover, 1991)
- Bookmaking and stories (Scescke, 1990)
- Puppet making and enactment (Scescke, 1990)
- Group murals (Ragis, 1987)
- Sensory stimulation (Ragis, 1987)
- Mask making for cultural awareness (Ragis, 1987)
- Gallery visit for cultural awareness (Ragis, 1987)
- Collage (Foss, 1999)
- Crayon with paint (Foss, 1999)
- Sponge painting (Foss, 1999)
- Film animation (Dougherty, 1991)
- Therapist's postsession journal writing and art (Stein, 1994)

PART II

Adults

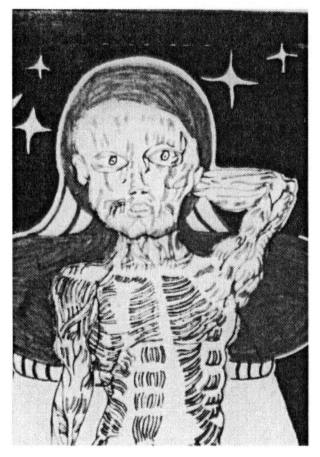

Alien by 41-year-old male aftercare client with
Borderline Personality Disorder.

What will become of many of the forlorn children described in Part I? In Part II, we meet their past—their parents—and their future—what they are likely to become. Those born to poverty, neglect, abuse, violence, drugs, and crime may remain in the communities to which they were born. Some will be removed to foster care and will face similar conditions. Consequently, as these children are moved into a succession of foster families, many will develop a long Department of Child and Family Services (DCFS) history that, for some, leads to eventual institutionalization. Along the way are gangs, violence, and crime. Nevertheless, as adults they will have the ability to influence and change their environments and their lives in ways that dependent children are unable to do.

Art therapy with adults presents new challenges and opportunities. Possibilities for insight and intentional change are greater. The wherewithal to direct one's life is more accessible. On the other hand, entrenched patterns may be more crippling. Adults are often more removed from the free play of fantasy and experimentation that art making provides than are children. Where there are opportunities for long-term work, however, art therapists have been able to help kindle sparks of creativity in their clients. Art therapy with some of the most needy adult populations can be extremely poignant. It has changed the lives of many.

Chapter 7

Inpatient Psychiatric Care

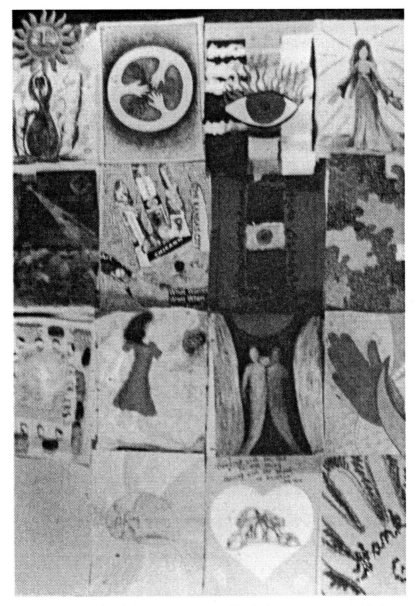

Paper "quilt" by group, in which individual pictures are assembled.

"That's my usin' self," says Billy, holding up the plaster gauze mask shaped from his own face. He has painted red rims around the eyeholes and a scar with stitches on the cheek. "When I'm high, I fight a lot," he explains. He puts on the mask and staggers around the room. Some in the group laugh. Billy's a clown. Others wonder how many times he'll be back before he takes off the mask for good.

Art therapy originated with psychiatric patients. The nature of psychiatric hospitalization, however, has changed markedly since the early days of the profession. Even since I wrote *Art Psychotherapy* (Wadeson, 1980) in the 1970s, hospital treatment has undergone significant transformation. When I first began art therapy with hospitalized patients with psychoses several decades ago, it was possible to work with them over a period of months and to witness dramatic improvement. Psychoses cleared, suicidal patients wanted to live, most returned to their homes and families. Treatment now is short term, usually for crisis intervention, and recidivism is high, particularly on psychiatric units serving low-income areas. These unfortunate conditions often limit treatment to Band-Aid care, rather than providing lasting improvement. Complicating many psychiatric problems are social issues, such as extreme poverty, lack of family or community support, and the effects of substance abuse. The latter is such a major factor among treatment considerations that it is discussed separately in this chapter.

Art therapists working on short-term psychiatric units are limited in what they can accomplish. For those who run groups (as many are required to do in order to see as many patients as possible), the constant patient turnover makes group consistency an impossibility. Even in individual treatment, a long stay is seldom more than 3 weeks, allowing little opportunity for the natural unfolding of image exploration and the building of trust. (However, whereas interventions are limited in short-term psychiatric treatment, art therapy has expanded considerably in long-term work with chronic populations, as discussed in Chapter 8, "Aftercare for Chronic Psychiatric Clients.")

Debra Paskind, who has worked for many years at a public psychiatric hospital, reports that the average length of stay there has decreased from 90 days to 14 days. In the past, there were walk-in patients and those brought by their families or the police. These occurrences are rare these days. Now, most patients are referred by community hospitals, which perform triage and send them on with a petition and a certificate. Most are identified with Axis I diagnoses of Major Depressive Disorder, substance-induced Mood Disorder, Schizophrenia, Bipolar Disorder, and various personality disorders (personal communication, 1999). They are certified by a qualified examiner to be a danger to themselves or others or to be unable to care for themselves.

Art Tasks

Paskind uses art therapy to effect more direct expression of feeling and involvement in the creative process, as well as to generate energy. She finds that the art itself is less amenable to control and censure (Wadeson, 1980). In group work, art therapy fosters socialization and allows patients with a wide range of functional levels to participate together. Although Paskind continues to wrestle with decisions about using a directive or nondirective approach in groups, the rapid turnover of patients on the unit necessitates structure, so she often gives the group a directive for the art making. Group members are always given the option of making something more personally meaningful than the directive suggests, if they wish to do so. Group size is a factor, too, in that although 5 to 10 members would be a more workable size, Paskind's groups usually include 12 to 15, because of the limited number of groups that can be held. Mostly as a result of the size problem, she facilitates the work of the patients and does not make art herself unless she is demonstrating the use of new media. At times, Paskind may make art to convey her understanding of a patient's feeling. She drew a two-headed figure looking in opposite directions in response to a female patient who was leaving and acting out ambivalent feelings that she could not voice. When the patient saw the image, she acknowledged that it showed just how she was feeling.

Chronically ill patients often display inappropriate social behavior due to lack of awareness of others' needs, failure to recognize their impact on others, or response to paranoid ideation. To promote socialization and the acquisition of social skills, Paskind introduces tasks that force interaction, as well as attending to interactions in encouraging the patients to hand out supplies, share materials, and clean up. These include round robins in drawing with different colors or making a collage. In some instances, each person uses a different color of construction paper for tearing shapes and gluing them to the sheets of white paper that are passed around. On other occasions, they use precut magazine images they have selected. The round-robin approach is also used for mural making. Each person rotates around the mural, working on a particular space for a minute. The groups also make murals with tempera paint, often deciding together on a topic. Dyad drawing, in which two people share the paper and are asked to communicate without speaking, is another exercise that promotes interpersonal engagement.

For increasing self-awareness, Paskind encourages the development of an observing ego. Frequently, her patients are either overly self-deprecatory or grandiose in demeanor. She utilizes the art for reality testing. Patients make self-boxes, in which the inside represents the private or inner self and the outside represents the persona or public self.

Because difficulty in both identifying and expressing strong feelings often contributes to the aggressive, hostile behavior of these patients, and to substance abuse or isolation for some of them, Paskind has developed several tasks to help with this problem. One is to select from her collection of photocopied affect-laden words one that describes recent feelings and to make a picture about it. Another is to choose a picture from Paskind's face file, a collection of ethnically diverse faces showing various expressions. Patients are encouraged to customize the face they have chosen by altering it to make it more expressive of their own feeling state, gluing it onto a sheet of paper, and drawing a background to tell its story. Wanda, who had selected *grumpy* in the earlier exercise, picked many faces to show how she had felt at different times in her life. This was a significant activity for her in that it opened the door for her to start looking at her early life and her pattern of substance abuse.

Because recidivism is high among these chronic patients, particularly those with issues of substance abuse, Paskind has developed a task to help them look at the triggers that evoke behavior that gets them hospitalized again. They fold a large piece of paper into eight frames or cells. Paskind asks them to begin with the eighth and draw themselves at the hospital's central intake office. She explains that in order to understand the relapse, they are to work backwards, drawing next in cell 7 what happened right before coming to the hospital, and in cell 6 what happened right before that, and so forth. Figure 7.1 shows Don's rendition. A 39-year-old man diagnosed with Schizoaffective Disorder, he was a well-educated professional who had had a late onset of the disease. Through this exercise, he became aware that having money was a trigger for relapse for him. He drew himself at a private hospital picking up his stipend upon discharge, found himself with money in his hand, was off to find his dealer, used drugs, was beaten up and robbed, and ended up back at the hospital. Although shortened hospital stays are seldom sufficient to produce significant curative changes in chronic patients, art therapy can help them gain coping skills and increased awareness.

Delusions

Susan Johnson was interested in exploring delusions in art therapy (Johnson, 1985). She questioned the relationship between patients' making visual repre-

FIGURE 7.1   Reverse sequence drawing of relapse
triggers by 39-year-old man.

sentations of their delusions in art therapy and their willingness to reveal delusions through verbal discussions. Mary, a woman with schizophrenia who had had repeated hospitalizations in her 31 years, was the mother of two children. She drew herself as the mother of "thousands of children." She believed she had been chosen by God. When Johnson tried to ask her about her delusions (describing beliefs that others don't share, rather than using the word *delusion*), Mary refused to answer and also refused to do any more artwork. It was evident that for this patient, expressing delusions in art felt natural, whereas being asked to speak about them made her defensive.

Ann, a 51-year-old woman diagnosed with bipolar affective disorder, had also had recurrent hospitalizations. Ordinarily, she lived with her husband; her four children were now grown and living away from home. Ann was an enthusiastic member of the art therapy group. She believed she was pregnant with "the baby Lord Jesus" and that she was married to the unit's activity therapist. In a scribble drawing she saw the lines as representing dance steps that would bring her together with the activity therapist. Eventually, her behavior became so regressed that she could no longer attend the group. With a change in medication, she regained her previous level of functioning and returned to the art therapy group. She abandoned her delusional beliefs, looked forward to her visits home with her husband, and explained her former beliefs about the activity therapist as feeling loved during a period when she was lonely. In a drawing of her reunion with her husband, they appear rather distant.

Howard, a 29-year-old African American man, had been in an agitated, combative state when admitted. He claimed that "Chinese and white boys are out to get black boys and cut off their penises" (p. 33). He also spoke of "words inside other words" (p. 36). In response, Johnson offered him materials to make a magazine collage so that he might use preformed words. In his first collage, Howard selected words and images with special meanings to him. He explained that *reaching* contained the word *ching*, which was Chinese, and that *warrant* contained *war*. The letter *E*, he said, represented a man because it looks like "two legs and the other part, you know, that a man has" (p. 36). Howard believed that a spirit had entered him. He said that his illness had begun with feelings that female newscasters on television were touching him in "private places" (p. 38), and he began to hear the "newsladies" talking to him. Howard refused to make art about his sexual preoccupations, which seemed central to his delusions, and Johnson felt it would be best to focus his art therapy on reality-based art assignments. Prior to discharge, Howard indicated that he had become more comfortable in his relationships and in expressing his feelings.

Johnson worked in both group and individual art therapy with Willie, a 34-year-old African American who had spent most of his life since age 16 in hospitals. Willie appeared malnourished and complained of hearing voices, especially when there were family arguments. In the art therapy group, he was grandiose, as shown by the Cadillac and dollar signs he drew. He said that he owned many luxury cars and that he was very wealthy. It was impossible to communicate with Willie except through his grandiose beliefs. Although Johnson encouraged Willie to draw other subjects, he refused. Even in making a magazine collage, he cut out a picture of a dollar bill, and he wrote *Mafia* on his collage. At one group session, Willie suggested that everyone draw a car, and he proceeded to try to grade people on their renditions. Willie's life was characterized by repeated transitions from hospital to hospital with brief intervals at his brother's family home, so that he had had little opportunity to try to establish relationships. Following termination of the art therapy group, Johnson continued to meet with Willie individually. She hoped to help him to establish a relationship with her. It seemed, however, that his art was stimulating his delusions, and his artwork was becoming more disorganized. Eventually, he was discharged to a day treatment program.

Johnson felt that the delusional patients with whom she worked suffered from loneliness and alienation. Their delusions further distanced them from others. She found that group art therapy was especially useful in helping them to relate to one another. Although individual art therapy uncovered some issues, it was too short in duration to achieve a reintegration for her fragmented patients. Nevertheless, Johnson came to see that "art expression is one of the only ways the delusional patient can bridge the isolation of living in a private world" (p. 65). This has certainly been my own experience as well, as described in detail in *Art Psychotherapy* (Wadeson, 1980), which also includes comprehensive presentations of work with patients diagnosed with schizophrenia and affective disorders.

Group Murals

Working with less severely impaired patients, Nina Benson was able to form a mural group (Benson, 1983). The short-term residencies of the patients on the psychiatric unit (2 to 3 weeks) caused the composition of the group to change from session to session. All the patients selected for the group were diagnosed with depression and functioned at a level sufficient to utilize insight. None had psychoses. Benson began by structuring the initial group sessions with a suggested theme, but in time allowed the group to choose its own mural theme. The mural paper was placed on a large table, and Benson encouraged the group members to move around it rather than drawing in only one space, so their work could be more interactive. To warm the group up to mural interaction, Benson cut the paper into giant puzzle pieces prior to the first session so that each member could take a piece to work on and then fit it back together with the others when finished. Rather than removing the pieces, however, the group left them in place and drew on them. As the constellation of members changed, so did the murals and the interaction around them. Figure 7.2, made in the third session, is an example of a mural in which the patients worked in a very isolated fashion. Growing out of an initial discussion about what one patient wanted from her daughter, Benson suggested that the theme be "wants."

FIGURE 7.2   Group mural on which patients worked in
an isolated fashion.

The mural from the next session shows much more energy and interaction (Figure 7.3). Though hesitant at first, the group chose a theme of pain and revenge. Benson strongly encouraged them to move around the paper; as a result, the patients became concerned about each other's pain, asking questions and offering support. They had become much more invested in the production of the mural. In the discussion afterward, they decided to step on it to make it uglier. They came to recognize not only their pain, but also the causes of both it and their anger. One patient spoke of internalizing her anger, which she thought had led to her hospitalization, and others agreed that they did the same. The group ended with a discussion of some alternatives to internalizing anger and some means for coping with problems. The next mural focused on fears. Out of it came expressions of fear of loneliness, death, and suicide.

FIGURE 7.3   Group mural showing energy and interaction.

Benson continued the mural group for 12 sessions. Except for one session, each was composed of a different group of patients. Although there was some carryover, as members participated for several weeks, in a sense each was a completely new group with new members. Benson found that individual art expression was more useful for helping patients to deal with their individual problems that had been brought to a crisis and necessitated their hospitalization. Nevertheless, the mural making reinforced feelings of universality and support from others in like situations. (For additional work with hospitalized patients, see the discussion of art therapy for pregnant patients with mental illness in Chapter 10, "Women.")

Showing Videos

Gail Roy has discovered movie videotapes to be an effective therapeutic tool in the partial hospitalization program where she works. Recently she reminded me of how the idea came to her. She recalled my response to her when she applied to the University of Illinois at Chicago art therapy graduate program in 1987. She was teaching full-time in five schools located in the most impoverished community in the nation, was struggling with family responsibilities for three children, and was about to undertake the demanding schedule of a full-time graduate student. "You sound like Shirley Valentine," I exclaimed. So Roy rented a video of *Shirley Valentine* and realized affirmation in feeling stuck in roles that were becoming increasingly unsatisfying. That was her first encounter with the power of videos in effecting dynamic life changes. In more recent years, that lesson has influenced Roy's work, both as an art therapy educator and in her work in a partial hospitalization program. Patients are referred to her by a staff psychiatrist if they either are ready for discharge from the inpatient psychiatric unit or are currently in need of more intense treatment than outpatient visits can provide. As in full hospitalization, therapy is brief.

Videos are shown for group viewing and discussion or as homework assignments. In addition to *Shirley Valentine*, she has found these others to be especially evocative for her patients:

- *Ordinary People*, showing life after a suicide attempt, complicated grief, and how therapy operates
- *Dolores Claiborne*, showing family violence, substance abuse, and flashbacks
- *She-Devil*, showing emotional abuse, self-esteem issues, and motivation for change, with humor
- *Home for the Holidays*, showing dysfunctional family roles and holiday stress
- *The Breakfast Club*, showing group building and intimate sharing
- *How to Make an American Quilt*, discussed in the following paragraphs

No doubt, there are many others that could be used, and the list will grow as more movies with which patients can identify are made.

Sandra, a 35-year-old divorced nurse who had been hospitalized for a serious suicide attempt, was referred for art therapy and had four sessions before being discharged. Her suicidal ideation had continued in the hospital. Prior to hospitalization, she had ended a long-term relationship due to her partner's infidelity and discovered that she was left responsible for exorbitant charge card debts incurred in the relationship. She had faced pending foreclosure on her home, bankruptcy, the recent deaths of both parents, numerous physical problems, the imminent loss of her job, and the loss of her children, who had elected to move to the home of their biological father, to whom she would now have to pay child support. This was Sandra's first treatment for depression and her first trial of antidepressant medication.

Sandra joined the art therapy group and enjoyed several of the listed videos and the ensuing discussions. Her medication and intensive group therapy were beginning to have a positive effect on her mood and outlook. On her last day of hospitalization, the art therapy group viewed *How to Make an American Quilt*. The film showed how each of the quilters' choices in young adulthood, regardless of ensuing difficulties, became incorporated into the person each became. These choices took on different meanings when the transition or crisis had passed. In observing that many people with depression are so sunk in current miseries that they have no perspective on their life situations, Roy felt that the women's stories in the video could encourage a more long-term perspective. Another emphasis of the film was the support that remained among the group of women long after their male partners were gone. After reviewing the video and discussing these issues, the art therapy group members were given squares of paper and art materials in order to depict some aspect of their life on a "quilt square." Sandra's quilt square illustrated her connection with nature. The group discussed the meanings of the objects depicted in the squares on multiple levels. They saw Sandra's prominent flower as heavy and childlike, but the only object that was grounded. A leaf was disconnected from its source, a tree, and a feather, also disconnected, was lighter and more free than the leaf. Sandra said, "I realize I must find that middle ground that has been missing in all of my chaos. I am no longer stuck in the ground; neither am I without substance, able to be tossed around by threatening winds. The middle is my safe place" (Roy, personal communication, 1999). Sandra was excited about new employment options, an upcoming appointment with an outpatient therapist, and medication management with her doctor. She praised the role that video and art therapy had played in her search for meaning as she emerged from a life-threatening depression. Page 193 shows an example of a paper quilt made by another group.

Roy believes that the videos allow patients to step back and observe life dilemmas similar to their own from a safe viewing distance. Roy introduces such questions as "How did you feel when the character . . . ," moving toward more personal exploration, such as "Can you identify with that character?"

The awareness that comes from viewing the film and participating in the discussion is then expressed in art and often carried further as the patients use their own imagery to understand and change their lives.

Substance Abuse

A major portion of this chapter is devoted to substance abuse because it is such a significant factor in psychiatric hospitalization. Substance abuse is one of the most destructive conditions art therapists treat. Because of its addictive nature, it is also one of the most difficult to treat. Art therapy is usually conducted in conjunction with other forms of treatment, which include detoxification, medication, education, and social services as part of a rigorous program.

The magnitude of the substance abuse problem in this country is shown by research that supports the following conclusions: There is a correlation between crime, including family violence and child abuse, and alcohol and other drug abuse. One-third of all hospital admissions are alcohol related. It is estimated that 20 percent of the American people are affected by their own substance abuse or by that of others. Self-reports have shown that 10 percent of Americans have alcohol abuse problems. Alcoholism manifests an intergenerational dynamic: Children of alcoholics are at 4 times greater risk of developing alcoholism than are children of nonalcoholics. Multiple drug use and abuse frequently are evident among drug-abusing populations. The combined problems associated with alcoholism have been estimated to cost the American public $120 billion annually (Center for Substance Abuse Prevention, 1995).

The illegality of various addictive drugs has given rise to enormous black-market economic enterprises in drug trafficking, often Mafia or gang controlled. Life for many addicts has been taken over by the necessity of supporting their very expensive habit, which may mean resorting to crime. Because withdrawal symptoms are often very disagreeable, and the addiction is usually both physical and emotional, quitting is extremely difficult.

A maladaptive pattern of substance abuse leading to clinical impairment or distress is diagnosed when one or more of the following conditions is present:

- Recurrent use leading to failure to fulfill obligations in work, home, or school
- Recurrent danger caused by substance use, such as in driving or operating machinery
- Recurrent related legal problems, such as citations for disorderly conduct
- Recurrent interpersonal problems resulting from substance use, such as fights and arguments

---

ALCOHOL ABUSE STATISTICS

- One-third of hospital admissions are alcohol related.
- An estimated 20 percent of the American people are affected by their own or others' alcoholism.
- Ten percent of the American people are alcoholics (based on self-reports).
- Children of alcoholics are at 4 times greater risk of developing alcoholism than are children of nonalcoholics.
- Problems associated with alcoholism cost the American public $120 billion annually.

Source: Center for Substance Abuse Prevention (1995).

Therapists should check to determine if substance abuse is a cause when any of these problems are seen in a client's present life. Although substance abuse therapists usually work in rigorous programs aimed at eliminating substance use, it is important that therapists be aware of possible substance abuse among clients seeking therapy for other conditions. Evidence of use of drugs is particularly insidious because denial, both conscious and unconscious, is so strong among users. Although addiction is usually associated with such illegal substances as heroin, it is important to keep in mind that an especially harmful substance is both legal and widely used in our society—alcohol. Although harmless in small amounts, it is both addictive and physically damaging in larger quantities imbibed over time. Alcoholism, left untreated, leads to death.

The necessity of determining if the client has a substance abuse problem results from the next-to-impossible task of treating a client who is using. Whatever gains may be made in therapy are usually abolished by the drug. Obviously, the motivation to give up the habit must surmount the need for the drug, which can be a very difficult row to hoe for those who are strongly addicted. In most instances, successful treatment requires a commitment to total abstinence. Residential detoxification and treatment programs make accessibility to drugs impossible during the period of the program, often 28 days (the limit of Medicare coverage).

Although giving up the drug is necessary for the client to be amenable to therapy, it is not the only step. Some individuals may become addicted due to unfortunate circumstances (such as gang influence in the case of an adolescent), but many others initiate drug use to fulfill a significant need. Drugs may be an escape from loneliness, low self-esteem, or some other painful conditions of one's life. Therefore, it is not surprising that a dual diagnosis of substance abuse and mental illness characterizes a large proportion of those admitted for psychiatric hospitalization.

One of the most successful programs to combat substance abuse has been Alcoholics Anonymous (AA). AA reports indicate abstinence rates as high as 45 to 75 percent (Center for Substance Abuse Prevention, 1995). Based on the experience of its members, rather than on professional expertise, AA is a self-help group falling between the natural systems of families and neighborhoods and the formal systems of social agencies; as such, it provides services at no charge. Although AA has been criticized for its spiritual component and the rigidity of its 12 Steps, it appears to offer some significant benefits to its members that may have been lacking in their lives. It provides a community, a buddy, a doctrine to live by, and a forgiving approach to transgressions. Its goals are realistic, "one day at a time."

Karrie Stevanus, who conducted art therapy on a hospital chemical dependency unit, worked with her patients on the first of the AA 12 Steps, accepting that they have a drug problem and that they are powerless over it (Stevanus, 1997). Most of her patients were very resistant in the program, and some flirted with her inappropriately. She found that they worked on their own issues more readily in individual sessions than in group art therapy.

Sam attempted to please the staff, and in his artwork identified himself as happy. He claimed that he had his life in control. Three days after his discharge, he readmitted himself. He told Stevanus that he had thought about killing himself to end the pain and failure. He drew himself (Figure 7.4) and said, "I didn't surrender completely. I was sure I could control it and that I had the power, but the drugs had it. I need to admit I'm powerless to the drugs" (p. 19). This was

FIGURE 7.4   Self-portrait by male substance abuse patient.

a turning point in Sam's recovery. He had not been so honest in sharing his feelings before. In his next session, Sam drew a tornado (Figure 7.5), moving his arms furiously as his tornado grew. With strong emotion he described his picture: "The tornado is my addiction. It made a mess of my life. It destroyed my home, took my work, my money, and my family. I need to get out of its way. It has a lot of power. I know I can't fight its power" (p. 20). Upon completing the program, Sam moved to a halfway house, continued in the hospital's chemical dependency day program, attended AA and Cocaine Anonymous meetings, began going to church, and started attending educational classes. Stevanus continued to work with him in the day program, helping him focus on his daily improvement, keeping himself safe from drugs, and identifying his emotions.

Also conducting art therapy on a hospital chemical dependency unit, Edward Foss developed a unique approach in his work with resistant patients (personal communication, 1999). These were people who self-medicated their feelings outside the hospital, so in art therapy their work was very controlled in order to defend against experiencing feelings. Foss observed that they frequently used pencils, erasers, and rulers to draw "correctly" or else used words instead of images. Their art was superficial and stereotypical, and often they told Foss what they thought he would want to hear.

His solution to these problems was to introduce the patients to working with clay, which helped to facilitate emotional release. He taught the patients the basic building skills of the slab, pinch, and coil methods. This educational framework relaxed some of their anxiety around having their art analyzed or

FIGURE 7.5   Tornado representing male substance abuse patient's addiction.

interpreted. Foss used the clay-working process as a metaphor for the patients' lives. For example, if a patient got frustrated and smashed a piece, he would talk about frustration and explore less destructive ways of coping with it. There were also discussions of controlling the medium and experiencing feelings of loss of control. In dealing with these here-and-now experiences, the patients weren't able to give the "right" answer, which they often sought to do in their treatment.

Foss taught his patients to make clay heads by forming two equal sized pinch pots that could be fused together to create an egg-shaped ball. A hole was made in the ball to allow air to escape during firing, so that the head wouldn't explode. Sometimes the hole formed the mouth or an eye, or it could be made on the bottom surface where it would not show. Since the form was hollow from the outset, there was no need to hollow it out for firing, as would be necessary if the head had been carved from a solid ball of clay. The patients also learned how to wedge the clay to eliminate air bubbles that could explode their pieces in the kiln and how to add and subtract material from the surface to form facial features. They had access to sharp metal styluses, wooden tools, sharpened pencils, and an assortment of kitchen implements for carving and smoothing the clay. Most enjoyed the process and without intention explored self-images, sometimes creating their "using selves." After the heads were bisque fired, the patients painted them with various glazes for a final firing.

An example can be seen in the head made by 29-year-old Lenny, an African American with a cocaine addiction who had been a gang member but claimed no longer to have gang involvement. It was clear that Lenny had been exposed to 12-step programs in the past, as he "talked the talk" of recovery. He presented his experience with little depth of emotion and a superficial range of affect. He often used the words of others to express himself, and his gestures were waxy and mannered. As Foss put it, much of his speech sounded like a gangsta rap song with many rhymes. In the art therapy group, he responded to questions with riddles and more questions. His communication kept others at a distance. Lenny was excited about using the clay. At first he had difficulty knowing how much pressure to use, and parts of his sphere collapsed under too much pressure. Nevertheless, Lenny ingeniously saved the integrity of the piece by creating ears and cheekbones from the indentations. He worked long and hard on his clay head, eventually giving it a scarred face. Initially, Lenny was unwilling to risk cutting into the sphere to straighten out the collapsed portions for fear of failure, but his creativity was evident in the way he incorporated his mistakes into his finished project. His painting was meticulous. Once again, he displayed the fear of risk by declining Foss's suggestion of filling the scar with an abundance of glaze and then wiping it off so that it would remain only in the grooves of the scar and stitches. He used a tiny brush instead. Figure 7.6 shows a sketch Foss made of Lenny's clay head. Lenny told the art therapy group that his relationship to violence and gang life could have come out in the sculpture, but his intention was to save others who would see

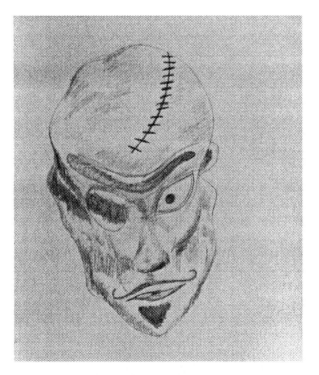

FIGURE 7.6 Art therapist's sketch of male substance abuse patient's clay head.

it from the painful experiences he had had. He was exceedingly pleased with
his piece. Lenny had found an outlet for his emotions, a sense of accomplishment, and a means for working through his frustrations with the recovery
process. Foss relates that Lenny's clay head was "a startling image of fear and
victimization."

Dual Diagnoses

Lori Hannigan Blocher's investigations have indicated that 20 to 50 percent of
any psychiatric population has a coexisting substance abuse problem (Hannigan Blocher, 1988). In the past the dual disorders were treated independently,
which neglected to address the many interrelated problems of the two conditions. Current approaches give more recognition to patients with dual diagnoses, although diagnosis is often complicated and difficult to determine.
Treatment of each condition poses considerable problems, and the combination is a major challenge.

Hannigan Blocher conducted individual art therapy with structured art
tasks with this population over an 8-week period. The sessions included pictures of the following themes in the order presented:

1. How your substance abuse began
2. A family portrait including substance abuse and mental illness
3. A self-portrait collage
4. What it is like to be under the influence of drugs or intoxicated
5. What it is like to be sober
6. How substance abuse has affected your health
7. What you can do to deal with problems of substance abuse and mental illness
8. How art making and talking about it has been for you

In his first session, 41-year-old David, diagnosed with major depression, recalled his family's frequent fights over his mother's alcoholism. His picture of how his substance abuse began shows his mother on the left drinking whiskey (Figure 7.7). On the right is his father, who had a history of mental illness. David felt rejected by his father because of his mental illness and alcoholism. He also recalled drinking heavily in the navy due to peer pressure. Figure 7.8 shows how he thought he would look if he continued drinking (session 4). He believed he would die or go insane. The furrows in the forehead represent his problems, the red eyes are bloodshot, and the red nose blowing brown smoke symbolizes the tingly feeling he got from drinking. He is smiling because of happy feelings he also got while drinking. David said that he drank because he got bored and isolated. He described the bar in his building as a place to go where he felt welcome and shielded and had a sense of belonging. (This is the sort of venue that AA members describe as slippery places that

FIGURE 7.7 Mother drinking whiskey by male substance abuse patient.

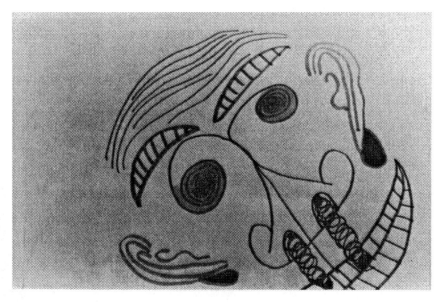

FIGURE 7.8   Male substance abuse patient's drawing of how he believes he will look if he continues drinking.

should be avoided. Unfortunately, for many lonely members of our society, bars become social centers.) In Figure 7.9, David drew how drinking affected his health. He worried about how alcohol would mix with Haldol, the antipsychotic medication he was taking. At the end of the session, he said it felt good to express his feelings. In subsequent sessions with Hannigan Blocher, he discussed ways he could continue his medication and keep out of the bar by concentrating on his daily tasks. They discussed sources for support, including AA, and Mentally Ill Recovering Alcoholics (MIRA) and outpatient drug treatment.

Hannigan Blocher found that those who could benefit most from the sort of program she had established were patients who were higher functioning, motivated, emotionally stable, chemically stable, and medication compliant, and who have a capacity for insight. This observation is not surprising. Unfortunately, too many patients with dual diagnoses do not fit this picture. Nevertheless, for many, art therapy can provide a less threatening way to express themselves than in the verbal therapies that are part of their programs.

Individuals with dual diagnoses may suffer delusions and hallucinations from either or both of the diagnosed conditions. As illustrated in *Art Psychotherapy* (Wadeson, 1980), art expression can be a useful means for communicating these very idiosyncratic experiences. One member of a group for patients with dual diagnoses that Susan O'Bryan conducted at an inpatient acute care facility provides an example (O'Bryan, 1989). Greg was a 24-year-old African American man with a history of multiple hospitalizations and a diagnosis of chronic schizophrenia and polysubstance abuse. He tended to

FIGURE 7.9   Male substance abuse patient's drawing of worry about mixing
alcohol with antipsychotic medication.

isolate himself and found social settings stressful. Nevertheless, he became
quite invested in drawing and was the first in the group to discuss his picture.
Initially, half the group had been discussing feeling scared, and the other half
had been talking about being high. Combining the two, O'Bryan suggested
that they draw a scary time when they were drunk or high. Greg's picture represented a time when he had smoked marijuana or used PCP. His drawing
shows a light bulb and a smaller sun. He explained that he saw a bug on the
floor that kept appearing and disappearing. It generated a tremendous
amount of heat, which Greg felt in his ankles. "I was trying to draw the heat in
my picture," he told the group (p. 33). This isolated, resistant patient was able
to participate productively in the group through creating and sharing his art.
He seemed eager to show in imagery what must have been a disturbing hallucination.

Working with groups of patients with dual diagnoses in a residential treatment center, Betty Wolff designed some unique art therapy projects with the
primary objective of confronting the denial of substance abuse that is common
among users (Wolff, 1993). One was the "addiction monster." For this directive, most of the patients chose an animal, such as the vulture in Figure 7.10,
which the patient described as symbolizing the ugliness and evilness of his
addiction. The body of the bird, however, contains warm bright colors that
show the ever-present lure of the drugs. Members of the group commented
that the vulture is always hungry, just as the addict is always craving the high
from drugs. A woman who was new to the group was afraid of appearing
inadequate in drawing, but eventually made a small black-and-white striped

**FIGURE 7.10   The "addiction monster," a vulture,
by a male substance abuse patient.**

animal. She said it was a zebra (hardly a monster). The zebra had just seemed to emerge on her paper, she said, and she was amazed by its significance to her. She became tearful as she described how her addiction had led to a jail sentence, and said that the stripes reminded her of the bars on her cell. She said she would remember this zebra in times of weakness.

Another directive Wolff used was a past environment drawing. Rather than the hospital settings previously described, Wolff worked in a relatively luxurious private facility, where she felt that patients could easily forget the sordid circumstances and surroundings of their binges. Many members of the group readily related to one member's drawing of a filthy room with cockroaches where he is lying on a bed being serviced by two junkies. The room is filled with other addicts who are trading sexual favors for drugs. The patient found his picture disgusting, saying that the only time he could have sex without cutting his genitals was when he was high. The picture immersed this patient, and the group as well, in the degradation to which drugs had brought him. Another patient drew a room full of smoke from a time he had passed out on the couch while his dinner was burning on the stove. His family had returned home to find the house on fire and him asleep on the couch. He recognized that he had put his family in danger through his drug use.

Wolff also created a message in a box project. Her original idea had been a message in a bottle, but she realized that would be too provocative. She gave patients various boxes and other materials, such as scrap wood, beads, buttons, fabric, and string, in addition to the usual art supplies. She asked them to create a message about their recovery to someone important to them outside the hospital and not to use words in doing so. These patients were very good at verbal manipulation, and she hoped this project would provide them a more direct means of expression. She hoped also that those resistant to drawing would find this sort of assembling less threatening. Wolff turned on a song by World Party titled "A Message in a Box." One woman made her box for her husband because he had been hurt the most by her illness. She chose a box with a slot in the top and covered it with colored paper and hearts to symbolize her love. The slot represented opening her heart to let her feelings in. Inside she placed scraps of wood, two that were interlocking to represent her marriage and two that were cut down the middle to represent the split her alcoholism had caused. Another patient tied ribbon around a small jewelry box and strung two buttons on the ribbon loops to represent himself and a drinking buddy. He realized that he could now no longer get together with this friend and wished to send him a message so that he would understand. He said that the box was a coffin in which they would end up if they continued to let alcohol control their lives. Although the themes of the patients' work were very serious, the materials lent a playful atmosphere to the session.

Art Therapists' Self-Processing

Working in short-term care can be frustrating, particularly in dealing with the abrupt termination of patients with whom one has invested hard work. Nina Kuzniak made art daily to deal with her strong reactions to the often premature termination of her patients in a private hospital when insurance payments were curtailed (Kuzniak, 1992).

Although most patients were hospitalized for a few weeks at most and were discharged with little advance planning, Kuzniak had been working with P. for 4 months. She was a 41-year-old woman who had been diagnosed with Major Depressive Disorder and Personality Disorder. Discharge dates were scheduled several times, but relapses extended P.'s hospitalization. Kuzniak made two clay masks to deal with her strong reactions to her work with P. (Figure 7.11). The smaller one was colored brightly to express Kuzniak's happiness at P.'s progress, which had led to discharge planning. The larger mask was made after a hospital incident that led to P.'s relapse. It represents P.'s monsters and the past abuse she had experienced that was always with her. Kuzniak felt frustration and disappointment over their hard work

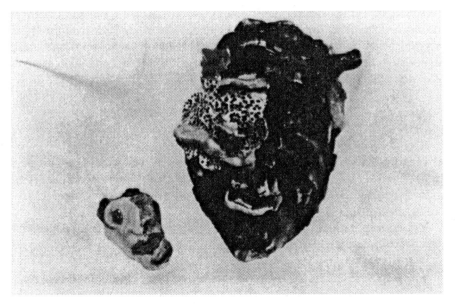

FIGURE 7.11   Art therapist's clay heads made in reaction to patient's improvement (small head) and relapse (large head).

together for so long being set back months by one incident. She was angry because she believed the incident could have been avoided had it not been for staff irresponsibility. She saw the large mask as expressing her anger, as well. In reviewing an art piece she had made earlier of P. and herself, Kuzniak saw herself as wanting desperately to have a successful termination with P., to the extent that she had been willing to overlook some of the cracks in the image of P., which shows her in pain. Kuzniak realized that her own needs and wishes were blocking her view of P.'s condition, which required further work.

In contrast, Kuzniak had a very different reaction to the termination of L., a 26-year-old woman diagnosed with Borderline Personality Disorder. As is often the case with such patients, L. was very manipulative. Kuzniak found her to be a needy and difficult patient who benefited little from art therapy. Sometimes she used it as a weapon against the staff, refusing to attend in order to get more attention. When termination was scheduled, Kuzniak felt relief. She was disturbed, however, because she thought a therapist should not feel as she did. Her art showed her that she "was tired of what felt like two-dimensional therapy where no amount of empathy seemed to change their relationship" (p. 13). Because L. kept much hidden, Kuzniak depicted her as a clay mask. She created an image of herself worn out by their sessions. Her art helped her to accept her feelings and to recognize that some patients are defeating, despite one's best efforts. It is important that therapists recognize their negative feelings toward clients, as an aid both to understanding clients' interactive patterns and to maintaining sincerity in relating to them. Kuzniak was courageous in confronting both her positive and negative feelings toward patients, particularly those aroused in termination, and in recognizing her own needs as a therapist. (For Kuzniak's art reactions to terminating therapy with children and adolescents, see Chapter 2, "Children and Adolescents in Psychiatric Hospitalization.")

Summary

Art therapists have met the challenge of working with patients with severe mental illness, substance abuse problems, and dual diagnoses in short-term inpatient settings in the following ways:

- Deborah Paskind (personal communication, 1999) developed a number of approaches to aid in socialization and self-awareness for hospitalized chronic patients.
- Susan Johnson (1985) found that psychotic patients more readily expressed their delusions in their art than when questioned about them verbally.
- Nina Benson (1983) formed mural groups for higher functioning hospitalized patients diagnosed with major depression.
- Gail Roy (personal communication, 1999) showed videos of movies with material relevant to her patients' problems in order to promote discussion and understanding of their issues, which they then explored further in art responses to the videos.
- Karrie Stevanus (1997), working on a chemical dependency unit, constructed art therapy around the first of the AA 12 Steps: admission of one's powerlessness to manage alcohol.
- Edward Foss (personal communication, 1999) developed a project of making clay heads using a pinch-pot technique for self-exploration among resistant addicts.
- Lori Hannigan Blocher (1988) encouraged dually diagnosed mental patients to examine their substance abuse through their art.
- Susan O'Bryan (1989) helped patients with dual diagnoses to utilize art therapy for expression of delusional material.
- Betty Wolff (1993) developed some unique art therapy projects for patients with dual diagnoses.
- Nina Kuzniak (1992) used her own art to explore her feelings in reaction to patient termination.

Conclusion

Inpatient art therapy in psychiatric settings is limited by short-term stays and the low functional levels of many of the patients. Factors complicating recovery are severe poverty in some cases and minimal patient support from families and the community. For a very large number of inpatients, substance abuse is a major problem as well. At many inpatient institutions, the majority of patients suffer from chemical dependence, and a dual diagnosis of substance abuse and mental illness is widely prevalent. These conditions are very difficult to treat. Alcoholics Anonymous, a nonprofessional self-help organization with chapters throughout the world, has been more successful than many other approaches.

Although art therapists work primarily in rigorous chemical dependence programs, they should also be alert to the possibility of substance abuse in patients in treatment for other conditions, due to the denial that often accompanies drug use. Despite the difficulties in working with patients with severe mental illness, substance abuse problems, and dual diagnoses, and in spite of the short time of treatment in inpatient settings, art therapists have developed some innovative ways of working with this population. (For a discussion of art therapy with pregnant women hospitalized for psychosis, see Chapter 10, "Women.")

ART THERAPY PROJECTS

Projects discussed in this chapter are described further in Chapter 15, "Art Activities and Materials":

- Round robin (Paskind, personal communication, 1999)
- Mural round robin (Paskind, personal communication, 1999)
- Sequence drawing of relapse triggers (Paskind, personal communication, 1999)
- Scribble drawing (Johnson, 1985)
- Magazine collage (Johnson, 1985)
- Group murals (Benson, 1983)
- Viewing videos (Roy, personal communication, 1999)
- Paper quilt (Roy, personal communication, 1999)
- Clay heads (Foss, personal communication, 1999; Kuzniak, 1992)
- Directive drawing of "Addiction Monster" (Wolff, 1993)
- Past environment drawing (Wolff, 1993)
- Message in a box (Wolff, 1993)

Chapter 8

Aftercare for Chronic Psychiatric Clients

Queen Bee by 41-year-old man with Borderline Personality Disorder illustrates a poem of the same title (The Thresholds Lakeview Club, 1991).

Maggie is wearing lipstick and earrings. Donald is wearing a tie. Even Edward has put on a clean shirt, and it is tucked into his jeans. Their pictures may be in the paper. Along with the other agency "artists," they have worked all day helping to hang the annual agency art show at a gallery for outsider art. Maggie steps up to the wall of the small jewel-encrusted figures she has made from Sculpey. They glitter here more than in the agency studio. Donald steps back from the wall, which is papered end to end with his multicolored portraits of spacemen and monsters. He thinks about how many he will sell. Edward admires his banner hanging from the high ceiling and wonders if it's okay to grab a glass of wine from the table before all the guests and reporters arrive.

Whereas art therapy services for psychiatric inpatients have been severely curtailed in recent years due to greatly shortened hospitalizations, this slack has been taken up by extended art therapy services at aftercare facilities. Both the quantity and the innovative quality of art therapy for aftercare make work with clients with chronic conditions one of the most interesting growth areas in the profession. In the past, art therapists had the luxury of working with hospitalized psychiatric patients for several months, and in some cases even years, and were, therefore, able to see the impact of their work in the change and growth in their patients. Now hospitalizations are crisis oriented, and those who cannot function adequately are no longer cared for in hospital until they can do so. They are discharged to live on their own if possible, with family to care for them if available, but more often are released to halfway houses, some other sheltered living arrangement, or onto the streets. Homeless persons may find services and shelter in facilities such as those described in Chapter 9, "Displaced Persons." Some may participate in partial hospitalization programs during the day, but this is generally only temporary treatment until patients can function on their own.

Aftercare programs, on the other hand, provide day care over the course of years for those with chronic mental illness. Some very innovative art therapy projects have been developed in these facilities, where clients often attend for several full days each week. Although there may be stability in attendance by many of the participants, there are also individuals who are on a sort of round robin of various care facilities. The pool of individuals with chronic conditions in a particular area becomes a part of its mental health system. I have found it interesting to observe that students in a supervision group interning at various facilities may discover they have worked with one another's clients, as a particular patient may be hospitalized, then be discharged to attend a mental health clinic, be part of a rehabilitation program, perhaps become homeless and attend a shelter, be hospitalized again, and so forth. Some individuals go through a number of revolving doors in the mental health system.

Most of the art therapy described here comes from two different kinds of agencies serving the population of clients with chronic mental illness. One is a city Department of Public Health mental health outpatient clinic serving the adult population of a specific geographical area. Clients must present with a *Diagnostic and Statistical Manual of Mental Disorders, Fourth Edition (DSM-IV)*

Axis I disorder (American Psychiatric Association, 1994) and be without private healthcare resources. Deborah Behnke established an art therapy program there a number of years ago that continues to offer various innovative groups, individual art therapy, and an open studio. The other is a large private psychosocial rehabilitation agency. Joanne Ramseyer began an art therapy program there, which has continued to expand with the hiring of additional art therapists at the agency's various locations. Operated on a clubhouse model in which participants are considered members rather than patients or clients, the members sign up for groups that interest them. (For additional discussion of this model, see Wadeson, 1987.) Art therapists have initiated some very innovative programs for these groups with an emphasis on creativity, cultural awareness, self-discovery and expression, and in some cases learning new skills. These art therapy groups form the core of the daily programming for many of the members.

The opportunity to work with clients over a long period of time has enabled art therapists to try creative new approaches. Some of these have been within the realm of traditional art therapy, whereas others have reached beyond traditional borders into art history, photography, and writing.

Three-Dimensional Art

In working with a population with chronic mental illness, Sally Lindberg became interested in construction work, which she defined as the assemblage of a three-dimensional image from multiple materials. She notes two levels to the process, the physical and the symbolic. The physical process involves a "touch space," rather than the "sight space" of two-dimensional art, encompassing tactile and haptic sensations, originating initially from early experiences of touching and being touched when being cared for as an infant. Symbolically, gradually building forms is an excellent metaphor for the reparative building and transformation that occurs throughout healing (Lindberg, 1991, p. 8).

Lindberg worked in a psychosocial rehabilitation program in a large outpatient clinic for adults with chronic mental illness. The day treatment services included a number of art therapy groups, so that a client might attend several different groups within a week. The community the clinic serves is in an area with much poverty, ethnic diversity, drug trafficking and crime. For many, the clinic is a welcome refuge from a dangerous environment. Lindberg's groups initially experimented with materials, trying out balsa wood, fabric, wire, boxes, glue, and tape. They created mobiles, addressing problems of balance and movement. They also created environments, venturing out into the neighborhood to collect junk and organic substances. Lindberg also worked in individual art therapy sessions in which clients created constructions.

Lindberg encouraged those in her construction group to play as though they were children in order to familiarize themselves with the materials and just to have fun. In the building process, some of the members worked through their low tolerance for frustration. Making mobiles was challenging, requiring the execution of a moveable balanced piece suspended from the ceiling. After this experience, the group searched the neighborhood for junk. This activity stimulated a lot of socialization as clients negotiated with one another for their found objects. Building with these materials enhanced the expression of fantasies and the creation of stories.

Clients constructed environments, which in some cases became a vehicle for exploring the therapeutic relationship. Lindberg worked individually with some of the clients in constructing an environment of their relationship together—quite literally from foil, masking tape, and paint. The construction process became a dialog in which they communicated their feelings toward one another. Some of the clients became so enamored of building environments that they created more of them on their own. They began to feel more capable, and they applied some of their construction problem-solving skills to life issues.

In general, Lindberg found that the slow process of finding and selecting materials, building an image by securing forms together, and decorating the completed construction was a soothing operation that gave clients a kinesthetic experience of solidity and groundedness.

John Bolde, himself a sculptor, questioned the limited amount of three-dimensional work used in art therapy. He speculates that art therapists find two-dimensional work easier in terms of storage, space, cleanup, and use for assessment (Bolde, 1989). He used clay and other structural materials in his work with clients with chronic mental illness at a city mental health clinic. Located in an area of high crime, the clinic serves mostly low-income individuals from a wide range of ethnic backgrounds. He formed a group of higher-functioning clients with diagnoses of Schizophrenia, in remission; Schizophrenia, Paranoid type; and Schizoaffective Disorder. Bolde observed the lack of affect and interaction among the members and the general air of lethargy that pervaded the group. With the use of three-dimensional materials, Bolde hoped to promote interaction among the group members and improve their overall affect. He initiated the following projects for the group:

- *Four feelings.* Group members were asked to draw four feelings they had experienced and then, at home, to draw another picture of one that had given them difficulty. They then made a clay rendition at the following session.
- *Family clay sculpture.* Group members were asked to close their eyes and think back to when they were between 2 and 8 years old, then write names of family members, adjectives to describe them, and their own emotional responses to them. They then made a clay representation of each family member and arranged them according to emotional closeness and distance.
- *Wood sculpture.* Group members made constructions with scraps of wood and glue, then painted them at the next session.

- *Personal mobiles.*   Group members were asked to bring in small objects from home that had personal meaning for them, as well as sticks and hangers for the structure. Bolde provided rope, string, yarn, more twigs, and other found objects. String was hung from the ceiling to facilitate visualization of the final product. The group members were asked to make mobiles that would reflect who they were.

Some of the clients' depictions of feelings, both two-dimensional and in clay, were very minimal. However, they invested more in their family sculptures. Bonnie, a 40-year-old woman who had been diagnosed with Schizoaffective Disorder and tardive dyskinesia, was extremely labile and resistant. She referred to her clay family often in the ensuing sessions (Figure 8.1). She first made three adults lying down, then her brother sitting with arms outstretched toward them. She explained that she didn't feel herself there, that she was lost, so she wouldn't make a clay piece of herself. Bolde suggested that she convey that lost feeling with the clay. She made a seated figure of herself hunched over with outstretched arms, her back to her family. Her parents, who divorced when she was 3, were both alcoholics. Her first stepfather had died when she was 7, and her mother had always been unavailable because she was sick or drunk.

Sometimes the way the clay is worked is as important as the end result. Helen, an incest survivor whom Bolde saw in individual art therapy, made an image of her family by taking a small piece of clay to represent herself and

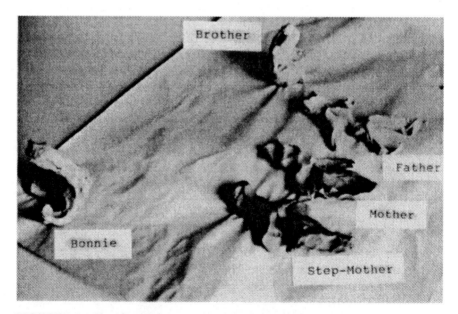

FIGURE 8.1   Clay family by 40-year-old woman with Schizoaffective Disorder.

crushing it with a larger hunk, stating, "This is my family." In her next piece, she reversed the process and put herself on top, saying, "I did feel special and favored at times." Bolde saw this as representing both her feelings of power-lessness and of power. Through pounding the clay, she was also able to access her anger at her father for the incest he had perpetrated on her. Although timid at first, she finally pounded so hard that the clay splattered on the wall and she hurt her hand slightly. Helen molded a tombstone from the clay, which sym-bolized the sexuality her father had taken from her. While working the clay, she was reminded of her father's hands touching her. She told Bolde of her guilt over masturbation and the shame she felt because she had enjoyed the contact and attention from her father.

Juanita, a 32-year-old woman diagnosed with Bipolar Disorder, had had a psychotic break requiring hospitalization the previous year. Her family sculp-ture changed significantly as it developed. Initially, her mother looked crazed, screaming, with her mouth wide open, wild hair, and a dress blowing all around her. Her father, with a cigar in his mouth, had his arms wrapped around the family, and she and her sister were barely recognizable, squashed between their parents. "I felt lost in the shuffle," Juanita said (p. 24). She titled her sculpture *Family from Hell*. At the next session, she reworked her sculpture so that she and her sister became more recognizable and her mother looked less crazed, although now her arms were around the family in a choking hold. In the course of completing her sculpture, Juanita became less angry at this very enmeshed family and more accepting of them. She spent a long time working and reworking the clay, and in the process reworked some of her feel-ings as well.

Bonnie used her wood sculpture to vent some of her anger about the no-smoking rule in the art therapy group, which she described as "Hitlerism." In the next session, however, she apologized for carrying on about it, but after painting her wood mask she said, "If it had a mouth, it would have a cigarette in it" (p. 28). Bonnie enjoyed making her personal mobile (Figure 8.2). It included two soapboxes that had been Christmas gifts from the clinic, a pic-ture of Man Ray's *Glass Tears*, and a card from her mother, in addition to very carefully selected twigs. The others enjoyed this project also, and when they had finished, the room looked like a forest with all the tree limbs hanging down. This was a much more light-hearted, fun-filled project than the family sculpture had been. I visited the clinic for their art show, and the mobile room was very impressive. The clients were quite proud of their work.

Bolde observed that the scrap wood project didn't seem to evoke the feel-ings that clay did, and that the family sculpture was so intense that he found it worked better with clients seen individually rather than in the group.

Bonnie Bluestein also worked at the mental health clinic. Some years before, she had bought a large Victorian dollhouse at a rummage sale. Having recently renovated the Victorian building in which she lived and had her stu-dio, Bluestein thought that fixing up the dollhouse might be meaningful to the clients in the same way that the renovation had been meaningful to her.

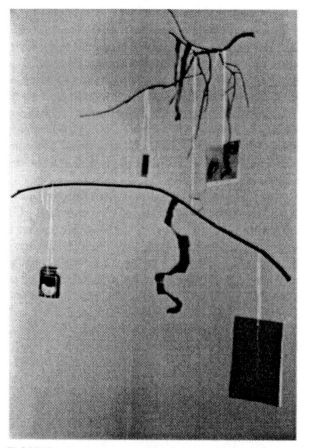

FIGURE 8.2   Mobile by 32-year-old woman with
Bipolar Disorder, made from personal
items and twigs.

Juanita became enthralled with the dollhouse and helped Bluestein repair it
and wash it out. Bluestein's idea was that by having control and shaping an
environment on the microlevel of the dollhouse, the clients might learn that
they could have a positive effect on the larger environment in which they live
(Bluestein, 1995). She provided three environment projects:

- *Self-object box.*   In the first session, clients created a plant or animal
  from clay; in the second session, they painted it. In the next session or
  two, they created environments for their objects from boxes and other
  materials.
- *Dollhouse.*   Clients could make a dream room, a fantasy room, or any
  other kind of room for the dollhouse, with removable cardboard walls,
  ceilings, and floors that could be worked on at a table. These could be
  decorated with felt, paint, wood scraps, ceramic tile, wallpaper, Styrofoam, and cardboard tubes and taken home when finished.

- *Model railroad track on plywood base.* Clients could create a landscape showing the past, the present, and wishes for the future in a journey analogous to therapy. The same materials used in the dollhouse could be used for the train track.

Clients also initiated some of their own environments.

Lana, an attractive young woman in her early 20s, diagnosed with chronic depression, had been abandoned in a trash can by her mentally ill mother. She had a history of abuse in foster care and often had been locked out of her house to roam the streets for hours. She had been raped four times and used drugs and alcohol. She fantasized about getting back together with the father of her child. She made a room in the dollhouse with white walls, a fireplace, and white felt carpeting (Figure 8.3). She adorned the room with flowerpots and planned to hang stars from the blue ceiling. She fashioned a man, woman, and child from beads to represent her fantasy. Lana also used the railroad track to represent where she had been and where she was going. Railroad tracks held a special poignancy for her, because she used to walk the tracks when locked out of the house as a child. They helped her to find her way back. To symbolize the obstacles she had faced, Lana painted a paper towel tube black to make a tunnel and made fire on the tracks at each end from red fuzzy material. A Styrofoam tombstone painted black and bearing the initials RIP reflected her suicidal ideation. Garbage and cigarette butts littered the ground. "There's garbage on my grave," Lana said (p. 17). A flimsy house made of

FIGURE 8.3 Dollhouse room by woman in her 20s with chronic depression who wished to return to her child and its father.

paper and wire built over a pool of red blood represented trauma and her lack of a stable home life. She made a hill of green felt, a felt swimming pool, and a tree house, which she had wanted as a child. She moved the toy family from her dollhouse room to stand by the ideal side of her environment. Christmas garlands separated the miserable side from the ideal side of her landscape. Bluestein tried to encourage her to seek a middle ground where she could meet her own needs instead of hoping to be given all that she had not received as a child. Although Lana improved, she still had thoughts of harming herself. She told her doctor that the only thing she liked was art therapy.

Roberta, a tough-acting well-dressed woman of 30, complained of loneliness after her friends moved out of the group home where she lived. She had a part-time job and hoped to start her own business with her boyfriend. If it were successful, she would move into her own apartment. Initially declining Bluestein's invitation to work on the dollhouse, at her third session she decided that she would give it a try. The room she constructed was to be her longed-for apartment. She painted the walls, made a sofa from wood, used fabrics for the rug and curtains, and included a mosaic tile table and a lamp. Throughout the process of construction over several sessions, Roberta discussed her living situation with Bluestein. Her thought disorder often led to misperceptions about those with whom she was living and working, sometimes leading to angry outbursts. At one point she thought the staff at her group home was going to make her move to a nursing home. Eventually, however, some new people moved in, and Roberta made new friends. Her chronic condition made the possibility of living on her own questionable, but creating her own space in the dollhouse concretized an important goal for her.

Carla had been coming to the agency for many years when Bluestein began work with her. She had been making art there for a long time and found it a relaxing and peaceful experience. When she came to Bluestein's open studio session, she decided to create a bathroom for the dollhouse. She used an aluminum container filled with green Styrofoam popcorn to make a bubble bath. She described her bathroom as a place where she could get away from everyone and relax. From her long-term experience, Carla was able to work the materials very adroitly. She also made a winter retreat environment with a shrine to reflect her religious beliefs. Although Carla became delusional at times, Bluestein reported that she had found a way to live with her condition. Making art that was soothing to her helped.

Bluestein observed that working on the dollhouse and other environments gave clients direct control over their environments in model form. The dollhouse, especially, provided an excellent microcosm for their living situations and a metaphor for what was needed in their lives.

Melissa Kistner, who worked at the same agency, created projects to affect the clients' home environments in an even more direct way. As she worked with clients in hour-long sessions, she began to wonder about the rest of their lives spent away from the clinic. It was important, she felt, for them to integrate what they took from their therapy into their home lives. She developed projects to help them alter their home environments in ways they wished (Kistner, 1999). Her group was advertised at the center as the "furniture transformation" art therapy group. Those who signed up had been diagnosed with Bipolar Disorder, Schizoaffective Disorder, Major Depressive Disorder, Schizophrenia, and Psychotic Disorder NOS.

The first few sessions were spent in discussing the clients' current home environments, and Kistner encouraged them to make maps of their apartments. The group members had difficulty with this task, however. They discussed the use of furniture and color in their apartments. Kistner brought in furniture she had picked up at thrift stores that they could transform; they could also bring their own furniture. She introduced a mosaic tiling technique and showed them paints and other materials they could use. One client brought in a desk, one requested a particular kind of chair, and the rest used the furniture Kistner supplied. She hoped that working on a functional object would encourage the clients to stay more focused on the present. The group worked on the furniture for 4 months.

Paula, a 41-year-old woman diagnosed with Psychotic Disorder NOS and who had a history of alcohol abuse, was often confrontational to other clients and disruptive in the open studio sessions. She talked constantly of her religious beliefs and would ask for drawing materials, but then would leave due to a headache. At her first session with the furniture group, she refused to participate. But at the second session, she said she wanted to make a plant stand. Kistner brought in an old stool from the thrift shop, and Paula began covering it with ceramic tiles. As she worked, she discussed her auditory hallucinations with other group members. She told them of a time that neighbors had reported her to the police for yelling out the window. This was the first time Paula had spoken of her illness. She said she would paint the stool and put it in her apartment. Although her apartment was large and she liked it, she felt sad there, often waking up crying and depressed. While working on her furniture piece, she also discussed her past, her alcoholism, and her family problems. During this same period, she continued to be disruptive in the open studio. Transforming the stool into a plant stand grounded her. She spoke of positive aspects of her life and changes she could make. She also built a trusting relationship with Kistner. After all the tiles were laid down, Paula was afraid to apply the grout, skeptical that it could be washed off the tiles. Despite her reluctance, Kistner was able to encourage her to try it. She screamed with excitement when she saw her finished product (Figure 8.4). She couldn't believe how beautiful it was. The experience showed her the rewards of seeing a project through, taking a risk, and trusting others. The completed piece made her very proud of herself.

Carol, a 56-year old woman diagnosed with Schizophrenia, lived alone in a studio apartment. In addition to her part-time job, she made quilts. She said that the chair she had at her sewing machine was uncomfortable and that she needed one with a high back to relax, read, and work on her quilts. The only place she had for relaxation was her bed, she said. She thought the high-back

FIGURE 8.4   Mosaic on stool by 41-year-old woman with Psychotic Disorder NOS and alcoholism.

chair could help her to relax without feeling depressed and falling asleep. She drew a picture of the kind of chair she wanted. The next week Kistner was able to find one like it at the thrift store. Although Carol's attendance had previously been sporadic, she concentrated on the design for her chair and was pleased to find that she was able to cut the ceramic tile into the shapes she wanted to use to decorate her chair.

Kistner's furniture transformation group was interspersed among more traditional art therapy activities that she and the other art therapists conducted at the clinic. Ordinarily, furniture refinishing would be considered a craft project. However, Kistner made use of this work to help her clients relate to the reality of their living situations and to ground them in their present experience. The successful completion of the projects they had requested and designed added to their self-esteem, as well.

Utilizing Art History

Because the conceptual foundation of art therapy is based on the importance of self-expression, it is almost antithetical to use the work of the old masters to stimulate clients. Yet, in working with specialized groups of clients with chronic mental illness, some art therapists have utilized slides, books, and museum trips in interesting ways.

Laura Safar, a psychiatrist who was undertaking art therapy training, established a structured art therapy group for aftercare clients with chronic mental illness at a private social service agency whose programs are based on a psychosocial model (Safar, 1998). She followed a five-session sequence. In the first session, she showed slides of works representing people in action or interacting with one another and showing meaningful expression. The purpose was to stimulate the clients' interest in art. After viewing the slides, the clients made art in response. At the next three sessions, the group members worked on individual projects, using images from art books as catalysts. The final session was a slide show of a selection of the clients' art, with commentary by them on their creative processes. Similar in format to the first session, this slide show brought closure to the experience and served to reinforce the message given throughout the sessions that what the group members did in the clinic studio belonged to the world of art.

In the first session, Safar encouraged the clients to react to the works by famous artists that she showed, rather than giving them information herself. The woman in Matisse's *Harmony in Red* was seen as gentle by Rose and lonely by Theresa. Amy speculated that she could be a housewife or mother who was preparing the table for her children. *Into Bondage* by Aaron Douglas provoked comments about slavery and ultimate death by some, whereas the star in the picture was seen as hopeful by others. The tenderness of a mother toward her child was seen by group members in both *The Bath* by Mary Cassat and *Self Portrait with her Daughter* by Louise Vigee-Lebrun. In the work that followed the viewing, clients began to depict human figures more frequently than they had done in the art therapy group before Safar began the project.

Figure 8.5, inspired by the Vigee-Lebrun painting, was painted by Rose, a 52-year old woman diagnosed with Schizoaffective Disorder. It is a self-portrait with her daughter leaning on her shoulder. Her daughter lived too far away to see very often, and Rose said that painting her image was a way of being with her. Prior to creating this painting, Rose had usually made wavy designs that seemed to soothe her when she felt anxious. She seldom drew people. Martin, age 34, who had been diagnosed with Schizoaffective Disorder and had a history of hospitalizations since age 18, gained increasing technical ability and independence in his artwork. After imitating several works by famous artists, he began painting people from his everyday reality (Figure 8.6). He imitated Degas's *Achille de Gas*, explaining that a coworker was about to join the army. He was very proud of his work.

FIGURE 8.5 **Self-portrait with daughter by 52-year-old woman with Schizoaffective Disorder, inspired by Vigee-Lebrun painting.**

Deborah, a 39-year-old African American woman diagnosed with Major Depressive Disorder and Borderline Personality Disorder, had a history of childhood emotional and physical abuse, substance abuse, and several suicide attempts. She had a long-standing relationship with the mental health system. Due to her symptoms of low interest and energy level and poor concentration, her attendance at art therapy had been irregular. Otherwise, she was an intelligent woman who had completed 2 years of college and had held a secretarial job for 6 years. After viewing the slides, her art included consistent use of human figures and African American themes. Figure 8.7 shows a slave being shot while trying to escape. She also made paintings of African masks. Deborah became completely absorbed in her work and spoke of her satisfaction with it. Safar brought in a book on art by black people, and Deborah made a

FIGURE 8.6   **Painting by 34-year-old man with
Schizoaffective Disorder, inspired by
Degas painting.**

playful collage inspired by the characters in William H. Johnson's *The Musicians* (Figure 8.8). She said she needed to make something fun. Figure 8.9, on the other hand, shows her despair. Inspired by Elizabeth Catlett's print, *I Have a Special Fear for My Loved Ones*, Deborah's painting is much more confused. Group members saw it as someone falling in a hole, and Deborah identified the image with her feelings of falling endlessly into hopelessness when depressed. With stimulation from art by famous artists, Deborah was able to express her suffering, joy, and sadness in the context of her racial heritage through her art.

Theresa, a 47-year-old woman diagnosed with Schizoaffective Disorder, had a history of childhood physical and sexual abuse and more than 20 psychiatric hospitalizations. She had attended art school and had held a few art-

FIGURE 8.7   Slave being shot while trying to escape by 39-year-old woman with Major Depressive Disorder and Borderline Personality Disorder.

related jobs. She was disappointed in her present painting ability, which she felt was inferior to what she had done when she was young. She felt that she needed to learn how to cope with her anxiety, so Safar suggested that she put her anxiety into a painting. She made a tornado and felt relieved. When working on a portrait, she once again felt anxious, so she made another tornado. Theresa spoke of her husband's abusive behavior and related the lines in the tornado to all that it drags away. Finally, she was able to control her anxiety and complete her portrait, a modification of Renoir's *Woman Playing the Guitar* (Figure 8.10). She saw her woman as looking passive. After the final slide viewing, Theresa painted another woman, inspired by Matisse's *Spanish Woman with Tambourine* (Figure 8.11). Theresa gave her a much more vivid facial expression and an intense gaze. She was very satisfied with this piece. Through her paintings, Theresa was able to reclaim her past as an artist and her present as a woman with mental illness who was trying to gain power.

Art therapists might question Safar's use of art for copying, but the message she intended to give her clients was that they could identify with the themes in the work of famous artists, which could stimulate their own expression. Rather than daunting them with their originality and technical excellence, these works helped to stimulate the group members' interest in art and encouraged their own creativity.

Judith Podmore, who was working with Spanish-speaking clients in the psychosocial rehabilitation program, put her own museum education experience to use in introducing her group to the work of famous artists (Podmore,

FIGURE 8.8 Collage by woman who made Figure
8.7, inspired by Johnson painting.

1991). Because her clients' primary language, Spanish, was different from her
own, she wanted to focus on the art as a major vehicle of communication with
the group and use museum visits as a stimulus for art making. She selected
exhibits that would speak to her clients' cultural heritage and enhance their
ethnic pride. The aftercare agency provided a co-leader who was fluent in
Spanish and a small bus for the trips. Podmore gave a short preparatory talk
before each visit. She found that museum education departments welcomed
her small group and usually waived admission fees. Over a period of 5
months, she took her group to five different museums. All were chosen for
exhibits that related to an immigrant population. After discussing the exhibits
they had viewed, the group members made their own art in response.

The first visit was to the natural history museum to tour an exhibition of
masks made by Indian peoples from Alaska to Guatemala. Podmore also
brought in masks from her own collection, with examples from Mexico,
Ecuador, the Dominican Republic, and New Guinea. She wanted the group

FIGURE 8.9   Feelings of depression and hopelessness by woman who made Figures 8.7
and 8.8, inspired by Catlett print.

members to feel the different materials used. The group members discussed
how the facial expressions showed various emotions. They also discussed
how masks could hide one's true self or disguise and distort reality. Figure
8.12 shows the group's art responses. They dealt with the project in a decorative way, rather than using it to examine the darker sides of themselves. The
mask making was appropriate for the season, as Halloween was approaching.

The next visit was to a collection of Christmas trees from around the
world. Because most of the clients spent the holidays alone, Podmore planned
to decorate their room, get a tree, and have a Christmas party. At the exhibition, members were able to seek out the trees from their ancestral countries.
The group was able to organize itself around decorating its own tree back at
the clinic. A group spirit that had begun to develop during the first project

FIGURE 8.10   Painting by 47-year-old woman with
anxiety and Schizoaffective Disorder,
inspired by Renoir painting.

accelerated during the process of decorating the room, culminating in a party with food made by some of the members.

An exhibition of the art of Ruffino Tamayo at a Mexican museum gave the group the opportunity to view the accomplishments of a 92-year-old artist who made difficult and monumental symmetrical sculptural figures and large-scale prints. The group members discussed how Tamayo worked with assistants whom he directed and how the seemingly impossible can be accomplished with the help of others. In response to the exhibit, the group members made large cardboard figures. Podmore showed them how symmetical shapes could be cut out using folded newsprint as a pattern. Individuals paired up to cut their large corrugated cardboard figures. They also experimented together in mixing earth tones like Tamayo's colors. Podmore encour-

FIGURE 8.11   Painting by woman who painted
Figure 8.10, inspired by Matisse
painting.

aged them to make figures showing feelings. The clients enjoyed forming
pairs to help each other and the childlike feeling of playing (Figure 8.13).

Next was a contemporary Cuban-American show that focused the
group's attention on the cultural roots of all the members. All the artists had
been exiled from Cuba as young children. They communicated their loss and
yearning for their homeland. Group members identified strongly with the
theme of the show. They created environments representing their own home-
lands. Some began their projects at home. Zulma, a 41-year-old woman with
chronic depression, created a vacation resort in her Puerto Rican homeland.
She made three flags, one American, one Puerto Rican, and one with a frog to
symbolize her happy childhood. She had a foot in both countries, she said.
Zulma invested a lot of time and effort in her project and said that concentrating on working on it at home and at the agency studio helped her to forget her
problems.

Music was incorporated into the final visit, which was to an African

FIGURE 8.12 Masks made by a group in response to a museum tour of masks of various Indian peoples.

FIGURE 8.13 Life-size cardboard figures by a group that visited a museum of Mexican art, inspired by Tamayo prints and sculpture.

American history museum. There the group listened to African music and played with African musical instruments. The visit was arranged in response to a group discussion about what the members would like to make next. One Spanish-speaking 56-year-old man could play many instruments. The group decided to take advantage of his talent and make instruments to create their own rhythm band. They planned a music month, during which they would make instruments at their Tuesday meetings and play them at their Thursday meetings. Podmore suggested that they end the year with a farewell concert and an art exhibit for friends and family members. After the museum visit, she brought in pieces of wood, plastic, and metal and urged the members to look around the agency, outside, and at home for anything that could be used as a noisemaker. The first session was devoted to making a maraca, a rattle made from two plastic, foam, or paper cups taped together, with nails, rice, sugar, or nuts inside. The clients decorated their instruments to reflect their own individuality (Figure 8.14). At subsequent sessions, the clients painted rhythm sticks and created some imaginative noisemakers. As they worked, they listened to different kinds of music. When they played their instruments, there was much laughter, singing, and dancing.

One might question whether, strictly speaking, Podmore's work with her clients was therapy. The language barrier was a factor in her decision to focus primarily on the art. Whether art therapy is defined narrowly or broadly, it is clear that this group of Spanish-speaking clients, who otherwise were often isolated and depressed, formed a cohesive group around their museum visits

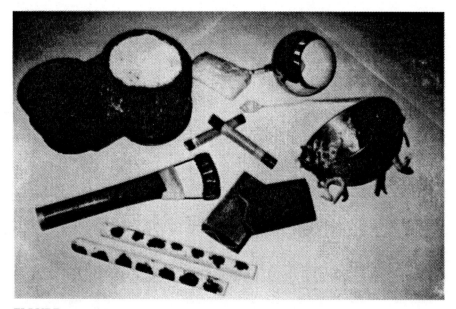

FIGURE 8.14   Musical instruments made by a group that saw and played instruments at an African American museum.

and art responses and enjoyed themselves thoroughly. This result is no small accomplishment in working with a population with chronic mental illness.

Gender Issues

Colleen McNally, an artist, art teacher, and feminist, was all too aware of the lack of female role models in the art world. As she redirected her professional life toward art therapy, she wondered if the lives and works of female artists who had figured significantly in her own life could be of value to the women with chronic mental illness with whom she was working. Like Safar, she showed slides of works by famous artists, but her purpose was to empower women with mental illness by exposing them to historical images by and about women (McNally, 1996). Like Safar, she also invited them to give artistic expression to the responses triggered by these images. McNally's clients were members of a women's expressive arts group that was a part of an aftercare program for individuals with chronic mental illness. Most had histories of childhood physical or sexual abuse. She hoped to help them see how their struggles as women living in a patriarchal culture could impact or trigger mental illness.

The group visited a local gallery where McNally had mounted an installation of her sculptural work, *Ritual Circle.* Inspired by ancient Celtic stone circles, it was composed of seven cedar forms echoing ancient standing stones. These were encircled by a wall that represented a well, which referred to the prehistoric goddess presently incarnated as St. Brigit. An inscription noting a tragic consequence of patriarchy was burned into each of the seven forms. The installation invited viewers to pass through the pain and suffering of females in patriarchy to the source of female strength signified by Brigit, the Irish saint/goddess. The women were very pleased to see the exhibit, and one of them said she felt validated in seeing pain she had herself experienced written in wood. Another said that seeing a sculpture created by a woman made her proud to be a woman. One of the injustices condemned in the writing burned into the wood was sexual assault. This opened the door for discussion of the women's own lives. One revealed for the first time that her father had abused her. For the next several sessions, the women dealt with this theme.

McNally found it appropriate to show slides of works by Artemisia Gentileschi, *Susanna and the Elders* (1610) and *Judith Beheading the Holofernes* (1612–1613). The former depicts a scene from a biblical narrative in which two elders are trying to seduce the wife of Joachim as she bathes in her garden. They are clothed while she is naked. One rape and incest survivor commented that it hurt to look at the picture. Others noted how vulnerable Susanna looks. Some saw shame in her expression. One spoke of her own shame over her numerous sexual experiences. McNally told the women that Gentileschi was seventeen when she created the painting and that she was being pressured to have sex with her painting tutor. Eventually, he succeeded. McNally then showed them *Judith Beheading the Holofernes,* in which the biblical heroine and her maidservants decapitate an Assyrian general to save their town from destruction. McNally hoped this painting would validate the anger the women in the group felt as a result of their abuse by men more powerful than themselves. One said it felt good to see the tables turned.

At the next session, the women made art responses to the slides. Janet made a bright, happy picture with an inscription of positive female qualities to defend against her powerful feelings. She told the group that she had had such a strong reaction during the showing of the slides that she had almost walked out. She was reminded of the time that she had purchased a gun to kill her father and herself after being sexually abused by him during her adolescence. Corrine, 40, had been sexually abused by her father and brother until she was 30. She suffered dissociation and disorientation from being traumatized and had been diagnosed with Avoidant Personality Disorder and Dysthymic Disorder. After seeing the slides, she had a dream, which she then painted. A male is leaving one torture chamber filled with torture devices to enter another. She said that she wanted to make him feel trapped the way she did. She felt that her father and brother had used her as a nonhuman. She, too, had experienced homicidal and suicidal ideation. In a ceramics group, she made two primitive-looking masks. The *Judith* painting allowed her to express angry feelings in her art, she said. It was now "okay to take ugly feelings and make beautiful art out of them" (p. 14).

Kathy, in her late 20s, had first attempted suicide at 14. At 4 she had been molested by a male babysitter and at 8 by her stepfather and his son. She had suffered anorexia and alcoholism and had been diagnosed with Depressive Disorder NOS, Bipolar I Disorder and Borderline Personality Disorder. Kathy had hated both the slides, which reminded her of her murderous thoughts toward her stepfather. She saw Susanna as vulnerable and frail, with fear, shock, and disbelief in her face. She said that it wasn't going to stop with one or two incidents, that Susanna would be stained for the rest of her life, and her life would be ruined the way incest had ruined Kathy's own life. Kathy splattered, dripped, and rapidly brushed paint over a board. A large red line that runs throughout signifies danger, deception, and blood, she said. Shorter lines are the aftermath that follows an incest victim for the rest of her life. She said she splattered the paint in frustration. "It's still with me. It won't go away" (p. 17).

About a month after seeing the Gentileschi slides, when the group was addressing loss, McNally thought it would be appropriate to show some of Frida Kahlo's art. She chose *Memory* (1937), *The Two Fridas* (1939), *Self-Portrait* (1940), and *Tree of Hope* (1946). The first three show loss and the last the artist's strength and determination despite her pain. Like Kahlo, Janet painted an image of physical pain and scars resulting from an automobile accident 11 years earlier. She spoke of emotional pain, as well—the desertion by her fiancée and then by her family. Kathy depicted a woman whose legs were being pulled apart by a ball and chain attached to each ankle. Kathy said she covered the woman's eyes because she is ashamed. She folded her drawing because she could no longer look at it.

The art of Gentileschi and Kahlo validated the women's suffering as they found expressions of vulnerability, powerlessness, shame, guilt, and anger in the artists' work and in their own art. (See Chapters 10 and 11, "Women" and "Sexual Abuse," for additional material on specific problems of women.)

Erik Engel notes that men are often inexpressive and have difficulty empathizing with others, perpetuating a pattern that is recycled from generation to generation. Many of the men with chronic mental illness with whom he worked had been raised by a single female and lacked a positive masculine role model (Engle, 1992). Engel worked in the ethnic services unit of a psychosocial rehabilitation mental health center. This unit served the ethnocultural needs of clients with chronic mental illness, predominantly migrant and first-generation Hispanics. The staff members were mostly Hispanic and bilingual. Engel formed a male art therapy group with a male case manager co-leader who had migrated from Mexico and was naturally fluent in Spanish. Engel is an American of Ecuadorian decent who speaks school-taught Spanish. The leaders presented the group as only for men in order to address issues of sexuality, intimacy, and emotions through creative expression. Their purpose was to model healthy relationships among men. Many of the clients had absent or inaccessible fathers, were isolated from their families, were unable to maintain a wife or children, and had no job. As a result of isolation from their families, male interactions made up most of their relationships. Diagnoses were predominantly schizophrenia and depression.

One of the group projects was mural making. Hispanic background music with English vocals was played as the group members painted themselves doing something together. Each worked in his own space. One by one, they then enacted and directed the others in what they had drawn. Pedro had made a man with his tongue sticking out, so the group members all stuck out their tongues. Engel's co-leader positioned all the group members to represent the sailboat he had drawn. Engel had depicted all the members of the group dancing to the music. He positioned them as he had drawn them, being careful to ask permission before touching them. The music was played and everyone danced. The enactment and the dancing had evolved spontaneously, and it worked well because the leaders trusted one another to lead the group in unanticipated ways. The usually resistant men enjoyed the experience and thanked the leaders. The leaders' supportive, companionable relationship modeled nurturing and intimacy. This was probably the first time that some of the clients had ever witnessed these more traditionally feminine qualities in a relationship between men. The leaders modeled a relationship that showed intimacy without feelings of devaluation.

To foster further intimacy, the leaders suggested partner portrait painting. Initially, the partners sat across the table from each other, not side by side. Subsequently, however, they varied their seating arrangements to include sitting next to each other. Body tracing was another exercise in intimacy, in which partners traced each other's bodies and sometimes worked together on the resulting life-size picture. The partner task they enjoyed most was wood construction using a hot glue gun. Murals made during later sessions indicated the changes that had occurred. Members worked in closer proximity to one another. When a new member entered the group, the leaders feared he might feel isolated from the comfort that the others had built together. They suggested a mural in which each would work in his own space for a few minutes, then move to the right in a round-robin fashion. When they had all drawn in each space and returned to the spaces where they had started, they would then work wherever they wanted to finish up the mural. The new member, working in a structured way on each person's image and then the mural as a whole, was readily integrated into the group.

Engel also worked individually with some of the agency's male clients. R.S. was a 27-year-old man diagnosed with Depressive Disorder NOS and Personality Disorder NOS. He and Engel agreed that the focus of their work would be to help him manage his depression better. In drawing his family of origin, he depicted and described his father as decidedly different from the others, explaining that he was distant and strict. He described himself as sad in the picture. Afterward, he drew *The Depression House*. It's the place where people go for help with depression, he explained. At the next session, he began a construction of it. He had a great deal of trouble with the X-Acto knife and needed a lot of guidance from Engel. R.S. was very self-critical. Although he became more independent in his construction, he was having difficulties elsewhere. R.S. reached a crisis point and told Engel of his suicide plans. Although Engel suggested that he bring up some of his problem issues in their sessions, R.S. said he liked working on *The Depression House* with Engel and that he planned to build a roof for it and add some people. During the course of their work together, Engel visited R.S. at home in a crisis period, and at one of their sessions he read him a story that was a metaphor for the nurturing in their relationship. They had evolved a way of working that had become comfortable for R.S. There were elements of ritual in it, and R.S. appeared to benefit from having a male in his life who was not strict like his father but was supportive and understanding. This relationship is a good example of an indirect way of working that does not necessarily focus on problem issues, but provides what the client needs through the relationship.

Combining Writing with Art

Drawing on her own experience in writing poetry and making art since childhood, Deva Suckerman sought to provide the benefits she had derived to the clients with chronic mental illness with whom she worked. The combination of the two, she found, balanced one another, with writing adding the order of language to imagery and imagery saying what cannot always be expressed in words. This dual process not only allows for a strong emotional release, but also can give meaning to what is expressed (Suckerman, 1999). In order to establish a safe environment for personal revelation and to model authentic self-expression, Suckerman joined her clients in making art and writing poetry.

Suckerman worked at a mental health clinic for adult clients with chronic mental illness where treatment goals were socialization, problem solving, and empowerment through self-expression. Her art and writing group met weekly for 2 hours and consisted of clients diagnosed with Schizophrenia and Schizoaffective Disorder. Members made art, then exchanged their pictures and responded to one another's art through writing. Sometimes this sequence was reversed, and members would respond in art to one another's writing. Because isolation and impoverished relatedness were common to this population, these exercises helped to overcome the distance between the clients and led toward building cohesion within the group. In the early group sessions, some joint poems were created, and although some were disorganized, the members enjoyed the collaborative process. The following is an example:

> *The candle's flame flickers*
> *My Bic lighter stopped working*
> *I stopped working years ago*
> *What happened next . . .*
> *I will not play my radio*
> *It's broken*
> *I'm broken and I can't get up*
> *What does it mean to be broken anyway (p. 6)*

Suckerman also experimented with using catalyst poems by famous poets to direct sessions toward themes relating to the human condition, such as isolation, struggle, and control. After a discussion of the poem, group members were encouraged to respond to it in both art and writing, or however they wished. The group was more structured in the initial phases of these activities. In time, the clients became more self-directed, and the structure was relaxed. Throughout, however, time was spent looking and listening to the works so that each member was bearing witness to the creative process of all the others.

Craig, a 50-year-old man diagnosed with Schizoaffective Disorder and Personality Disorder NOS, felt low self-esteem, anxiety, and inadequacy in personal relationships. In response to Robert Frost's "The Road Not Taken," Craig concluded that the author had regretted taking the wrong path, which was how he viewed his own life. He wrote the following poem:

> *A while ago, I was like a butterfly*
> *In a cocoon.*
> *I did not let anybody enter my*
> *Mind or my thoughts, or my emotions.*
> *I was concerned only in myself,*

Self-centered, egotistical, selfish.
I have had to make the
Constant effort to care about others. . . .
Slowly, I am letting others
Into my own little world . . .
Slowly I am pushing the feelings of
Malice out of my mind. (p. 12)

Craig's art was dark and stormy, representing his internal conflict in the gap between the reality of his life and how he wanted it to be. Writing and making art provided him some relief. At a later stage in the group, he began to recognize his own abilities:

In the depths of depression,
When all seems hopeless,
I paint my picture.
When the colors blend to
Produce shading, I look at
It and tell myself that
I have done a good job. . . .
I will be able to continue
With life as before.
And my oil paints will dry. (pp. 15, 16)

He explained that his art piece reflected his mood swings. The storm was balanced by movement and sunshine. Over time, Craig became less critical and more able to integrate reality-based perceptions into his work to create a sense of peace and well-being. Through his art and writing, he found a source of internal strength.

Tim, a 43-year-old man diagnosed with Schizoaffective Disorder who had a history of suicidal and homicidal ideation, also wrote about his experience in the group. He created more than 60 poems in 15 weeks, often bringing them from home to the group. The following is titled "I Am an Artist":

I am an artist. Painting the canvas
Of choice with words.
I am a poet. Using words as tools
To shape abstract thoughts and images
I write to move to stir to evoke
Emotions and bring back memories.
It's a form of magic. Conjuring
Up poems out of thin air.
Poems let my soul speak and give
It form. I am an artist, a poet,
A magician. (p. 23)

As the group came to a close, Suckerman expressed her own feelings, as well:

As we come to the end I'm at a loss for words
Where to go and what to take with
I've been given so much.
As we come to the end
I wonder how to describe it
How to express adequately
All that has been accomplished
All that we've learned
And then it changes and collides and moves
One path leads to another
As we come to an end
There is always a beginning (p. 10)

She made a drawing of the crossing paths and the spaces left to fill in their lives with people and events.

Jutta Ohl also used writing in her work at a psychosocial rehabilitation agency. A stop-by center had been operating for a number of years to provide services to individuals with chronic mental illness who were unable to tolerate the higher degree of structure and expectations found in other outpatient psychosocial programs. The center required that all members participate in the maintenance of the program by cleaning the facility, answering phones, and preparing meals. Ohl's goal was to demonstrate the abilities of people with mental illness. She noted that professionals write about clients, but she felt it was important that the clients write about themselves (Ohl, 1992). Specifically, her objective was to publish a magazine containing art and writing. Ohl's role in the magazine group was to help the individual members to stay focused. They consulted her about their feelings, their ideas, and their projects. Because English is not her native language, sometimes they had to explain slang and idioms to her; they enjoyed becoming her teacher. After the work was completed, the group members reviewed the material together, often with admiration for one another's creations, with much fun and laughter. They became serious when making the final selections. Then they undertook the mockup and key lining for the printer. The members did not like this part of the process, and attendance decreased. The magazine then had to be pasted up, proofread, and corrected. It was the members' responsibility to get it to the printer. When it was returned, they collated and stapled it and had a party to celebrate its completion. It was now ready for distribution. An issue of *The Musing Place* (The Thresholds Lakeview Club, 1991), was given free to those who attended the agency, but sold to the public for $2. It was placed on consignment at coffeehouses and bookstores. The magazine developed a readership.

White Deer, a 52-year-old Native American with a diagnosis of Bipolar

Disorder and Alcohol Abuse, drew warriors surrounded by rainbows as spiritual messages symbolic of life and harmony (Figure 8.15). He had difficulty living in an urban environment, and he felt his art was his only ticket out of his isolation. Through it, he could speak for his tribe and find pride, self-esteem, and recognition.

Alex, a 41-year-old man diagnosed with Borderline Personality Disorder, suffered from asthma and paralysis, as well. He had difficulty developing relationships. He expressed his loneliness in his art (page 191, and Figure 8.16) and in a poem titled "Alien to My Own Planet":

> *I am an alien to my own*
> *Planet, the black coldness*
> *Of space and stars' heat*
> *Are closer to me than love. . . .*
> *The horrors of human behavior*
> *Often rival the danger of anyone*
> *From the worst of our nightmares.*
> *We don't always get what we see. . . .*
> *Often before I go to sleep at*
> *Night, my own lullaby is one*
> *Of visiting aliens in some*
> *Field come to whisk me away. (The Thresholds Lakeview Club, 1991, p. 20)*

FIGURE 8.15 Native American themes in painting by a 52-year-old Native American man diagnosed with Bipolar Disorder and Alcohol Abuse.

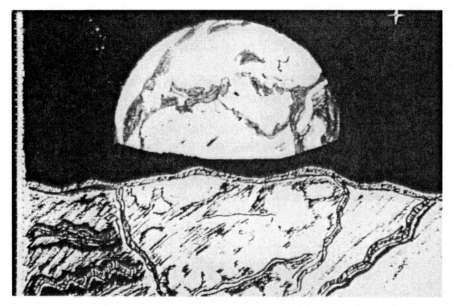

FIGURE 8.16   *Alien to My Own Planet* **by 41-year-old man with Borderline Personality Disorder illustrates a poem of the same title.**

Other group members admitted to similar feelings and gave him positive feedback, lessening his loneliness and helping him to feel understood and accepted. Alex channeled his sexual frustration into his art and poetry about his dream woman, "Queen Bee" (see page 216):

> *. . . Beneath her tough open leather*
> *Jacket she flaunts her bustier*
> *To match her crimson crest*
> *Of sparse hair, high mohawk. . . .*
> *Chalk cliffs of her face declare*
> *Her mastery of the night, her*
> *Fierce leadership of the street.*
> *The boom box howls her disdain. (The Thresholds Lakeview Club, 1991, p. 28)*

Dan, a 40-year-old man diagnosed with Narcissistic Personality Disorder with psychotic episodes, held graduate degrees in both art and literature. His work is full of humor. Haunted by bugs and "creepy critters," Dan relegated them to a poem:

> *Creeping Critters everywhere here and there*
> *Even in my underwear. . . .*
> *I scream out loud, "You nasty little vermin!*
> *Skedaddle, Vamoose, no cheese for you, no tidbits,*
> *   no crumbs for you."*

I see thousands of feelers scurrying out of sight,
Now that I have a can of ant and roach killer—
          So much for you tonight. (The Thresholds Lakeview Club, 1991, p. 24)

Dan titled Figure 8.17 *Monster Sleeping on a Couch*. It was his metaphor for his depression. He was able to express his fear and fight it through his art and poetry.

Ohl concludes that we all wish to tell our story; to have someone listen, understand, and accept us. The magazine gave these people with chronic mental illness an opportunity for just that. They saw their personal expressions published, and they had an audience that actually paid money for their work. The magazine was a tangible base in reality for recognition and self-esteem.

Photography

Bettina Thorn combined writing with photography in a therapy group she established at a psychosocial rehabilitation facility. The major emphasis in this group, however, was the photography (Thorn, 1998). At their first meeting, the group members recognized that although they had varying diagnoses and functional levels, and had been coming to the clinic for differing lengths of time, they all shared apprehension about their skills as photographers, each

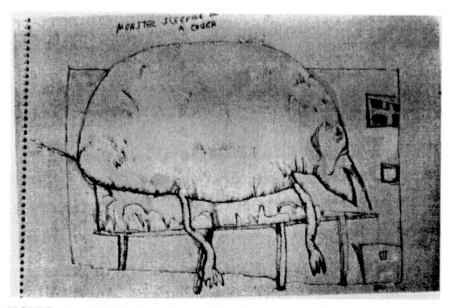

FIGURE 8.17   *Monster Sleeping on a Couch* by 40-year-old man with Narcissistic Personality Disorder symbolizes depression.

having had only minimal experience with the medium. The group members were given disposable cameras with 27 exposures and were shown how to operate them. Members were encouraged to ask each other for assistance and to offer it when needed in order to promote socialization. The group chose the locations around the city for their photography, with each member encouraged to select at least one. Thorn asked them what drew them to a particular spot, in order to foster reflection and self-awareness. Practicality was addressed as well, and members often worked together to determine the best bus routes and possible side trips along the way.

The particular location choices gave rise to self-disclosure: Going to the lake brought back childhood memories of trips to the beach; visiting Chinatown sparked a discussion of culture and fears of being harassed by gangs there, resulting in plans to watch out for one another; the cemetery provoked feelings of loss and fear of death. After all the excursions, Thorn had the film processed, and the group members shared their reactions to their photographs. They noted differences in shooting styles. There was an evident sense of accomplishment as the group members presented their favorite shots.

Each person was given two copies of all his or her photos, so that one could be kept as it was and the other could be utilized in artwork. Thorn gave the group members a number of directives for incorporating their photos into artwork, each taking several sessions:

- The first directive was simply to alter a photo in any way.
- Next, she asked them to create a story from a photo.
- For their third activity, they each selected a photograph to be photocopied and enlarged. Each copy was then given to another group member to embellish.
- Another directive asked members to pick a photo that expressed a feeling, then add to it to enhance the feeling.

Richard, a 48-year-old man diagnosed with Schizoaffective Disorder, depressed type, had had many hospitalizations for psychotic symptoms, had low self-esteem, and was fearful in social relationships. He was anxious about handling the camera, and his hands shook unsteadily due to medication. Thorn helped him to practice different ways of holding the camera, which enabled him to gain a new sense of control in using it. He was apprehensive about traveling to new places, but once engaged in shooting, he relaxed and his fears diminished. Richard initially stayed close to Thorn on photo excursions, but as his confidence grew, he became more independent. He began to interact more freely with other group members, as well. Figure 8.18 shows an example of his work. His stories contained strong, confident, masculine characters. Thorn reports that the activation of Richard's imagination through art and photography enabled him to respond to and interpret the world in a whole new way. He gained new skills, improving his outlook on his abilities, and increasing his self-esteem.

FIGURE 8.18   Photography, art, and writing by 48-year-old man with Schizoaffective Disorder.

Shannon, a 30-year-old woman with a diagnosis of Post-Traumatic Stress Disorder and Borderline Personality Disorder, had a history of physical and sexual abuse, several rapes, and a number of suicide attempts, with hospitalization for the first two attempts at age 13. She suffered intense flashbacks of the experience of the rapes, had engaged in self-mutilation by cutting her arms and stomach, had low self-esteem and difficulty interacting with others, and was often overwhelmed by her feelings. Nevertheless, though initially introverted in the group sessions, she became actively involved and offered creative suggestions for photo excursions. Her involvement was reinforced when the group selected one of her suggestions for a field trip. Shannon was also familiar with the train routes, and the group often turned to her for travel information. She began to experience herself as a valuable group member, and her feelings of self-worth and confidence increased. When another group member pointed out Shannon's ease in working with the camera and her ability to find creative subject matter, Thorn suggested that the two of them work together. They continued their partnership and worked together on subsequent field trips, as well. Shannon's growing confidence and sense of security within the group also promoted her freer participation in group discussions.

The group's trip to a cemetery, which reminded Shannon of her mother's death, was very significant for her. Through the distance of the camera lens and within the security of the group, Shannon was given an opportunity to look at death without becoming overwhelmed by her emotions and loosing control. In following the directive to pick a photo that expressed an emotion and to enhance its expression with art, Shannon chose a cemetery shot looking up at the branches of an old tree losing its leaves. Working intently, she mounted it askew onto a black mat board, added an image of a dark sky behind it, and attached leaves she had collected around it (Figure 8.19). She described the feeling as loneliness and told the group that this was what she experienced in the cemetery. Ordinarily, she became agitated when discussing such feelings, rocking back and forth, but in this case the art seemed to ground her, allowing her to explore and express difficult emotions without becoming overwhelmed. In creating a story from a photo, Shannon chose another cemetery picture, a tree that had fallen on a grave in a recent storm. Again she created a collage, adding images and text. A girl embraced by a woman is saying "Don't Cry" in large words, with flowers drawn between the words and the grave. Her story was about a girl attending her mother's burial who describes feelings of loss, sadness, and anger. Indirectly, she was dealing with her own mother's death in a way that did not overwhelm her or cause her to lose control.

Through photography, art, and writing, members of Thorn's photo group learned new skills that fostered a sense of mastery and confidence. They increased their socialization, took risks in traveling to unfamiliar places,

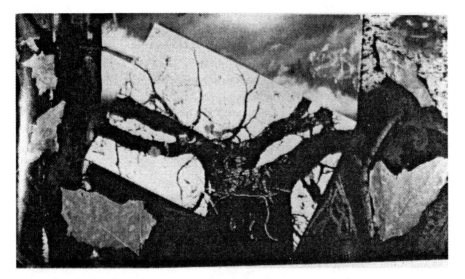

FIGURE 8.19   Collage from a photograph of a trip to a cemetery by a 30-year-old woman with Post-Traumatic Stress Disorder and Borderline Personality Disorder in reaction to her mother's death.

developed their creativity, and dealt with difficult emotions. All these accomplishments enhanced their self-esteem.

Summary

In an explosion of creativity, art therapists have been able to design a wide range of projects for working with clients with chronic mental illness. Working in neighborhood mental health clinics and psychosocial rehabilitation programs, art therapists can schedule several sessions a week and work long-term with many clients. Nevertheless, the progress is sometimes remarkable given the emotionally impoverished and often abusive backgrounds of the clients coupled with the low level of functioning that many of them have. Socialization is an important goal for these clients, whose lives are often lived in isolation. The art therapy with this population pulls out all the stops in experimenting with a range of media and ways of working. Much of it explores ethnic heritage as well as personal issues. In their creative experiments, art therapists have often stepped beyond the traditional boundaries of art therapy projects and ventured into art history, craft work, writing, and photography, as follows:

- Sally Lindberg (1991) used construction both as a slowed-down physical process for her clients and as a process symbolic of the building necessary in healing.
- John Bolde (1989) explored three-dimensional work using clay, wood, and mobile making. He found that making clay renditions of the family of origin elicited the most emotion. Mobiles made from branches and personal objects were a more playful activity.
- Beginning with a Victorian dollhouse, Bonnie Bluestein (1995) encouraged her clients to build environments. Rooms of personal significance built for the dollhouse were particularly interesting.
- Melissa Kistner (1999) arranged furniture refinishing for clients to make special objects they desired for their home environments.
- Laura Safar (1998) utilized slides of artworks by famous artists that depicted people in order to stimulate an interest in art among her clients. As a result, their interest increased and they began to depict people meaningful to them in their art.
- Judith Podmore (1991) took her Spanish-speaking group members to a variety of art exhibits that reflected their cultural heritage. They made art responses, including masks, large cardboard figures, environment constructions, and musical instruments.
- Colleen McNally (1996) explored women's issues by taking her women's group to an installation of her own feminist art and showing slides of artworks by famous female artists. The women in her group responded in art to the abuse and suffering they had experienced, which reflected themes in the art they had viewed.

- Erik Engel (1992) explored gender issues in a men's group dealing with relationships among men.
- Deva Suckerman (1999) combined poetry writing with art in her group. Members worked on joint projects and exchanges, but as the group developed, they worked more independently on their own art and poetry.
- Jutta Ohl (1992) facilitated the publication of a magazine of art and poetry by clients at the drop-in center where she worked. The clients took responsibility for every step in the process, from creation of the material to preparation for publication and distribution.
- Bettina Thorn (1998) organized a photography group that selected various locations for photo field trips, modified the photographs with art, and wrote stories about them. Clients learned new skills, took risks in venturing to new places, increased their socialization, explored personal issues, and increased their self-esteem.

Conclusion

Work with the psychiatric aftercare population of patients with chronic mental illness is an especially fertile field for art therapy. In many programs where clients spend most of the day several days a week, art therapy is a major part of the programming. By participating in groups they select themselves, clients are likely to be motivated to try the creative projects the art therapists develop. The innovation and creativity of some of the projects that have led art therapists into adjacent fields, such as art history and furniture restoration, might raise questions about the fluid boundaries of the art therapy profession. Although this question has raised controversy in the field, strict demarcation would not serve any useful purpose. All the art therapists presented here have been thoroughly trained; they are skilled in working in a variety of ways according to the many challenges they meet. Although Mel Kistner found furniture refinishing useful for one group, for example, for another she was conducting traditional art therapy. Laura Safar, who utilized art history, is a psychiatrist who put her thorough clinical training to use in her work with clients while encouraging their artistic creativity through the stimulation of viewing paintings by famous artists.

The benefit that many aftercare clients derive from art therapy is the sustained art making that is often labeled "art as therapy" in the field. This categorization is too limited. Hopefully, the case material presented in this chapter shows that there is a wide variety of benefits to be gained from the many ways of working with this population. Sustained art making can also yield very productive results artistically, as well as therapeutically. Recently I attended an opening in a gallery for outsider art. It was organized by Joanne Ramseyer and the other art therapists in the art therapy program at the Community Counseling Centers of Chicago (C4) psychosocial rehabilitation centers. The exhibit

FIGURE 8.20   Art exhibit at Intuit Gallery, Chicago, from the Outpatient Art
Therapy Program at Community Counseling Centers of
Chicago (C4), spring 1999.

FIGURE 8.21   Announcement of the art exhibit in Figure 8.20.

was one of the best I have ever seen, showing fantastic originality and technical skill in paintings, life-size sculptures, banners, and very tiny objects (Figure 8.20). Figure 8.21 is a photograph of the show's announcement. In full color, golden glitter emanates from the eyes of this unique face. Figure 8.22 shows a large banner suspended from the ceiling that was made by a group of participants.

FIGURE 8.22   Large banner made by a group, suspended from ceiling, from exhibit in Figure 8.20.

ART THERAPY PROJECTS

Projects discussed in this chapter are described further in Chapter 15, "Art Activities and Materials":

- Constructions (Lindberg, 1991; Podmore, 1991; and Engel, 1992)
- Mobiles (Lindberg, 1991; Bolde, 1989)
- Clay family of origin (Bolde, 1989)
- Environments (Lindberg, 1991; Bluestein, 1995; Podmore, 1991)
- Furniture refinishing with mosaic tiling (Kistner, 1999)
- Art history (Safar, 1998; McNally, 1996)
- Collage (Safar, 1998)
- Museum and gallery visits (Podmore, 1991; McNally, 1996)
- Masks (Podmore, 1991)
- Life-size cardboard figures (Podmore, 1991)
- Musical instruments (Podmore, 1991)
- Murals (Engel, 1992)
- Body tracings (Engel, 1992)
- Enactment and movement (Engel, 1992)
- Writing poetry (Suckerman, 1992; Ohl, 1992)
- Photography, photo collage, and photo stories (Thorn, 1998)

Chapter 9

Displaced Persons

A hand-tracing mural made by homeless women at a drop-in shelter.

Marigold adjusts her pink-rimmed sunglasses and smiles her toothless grin as the clay forms itself in her hands. She's made two faces on either side of a head, one with bulging eyes and a gaping mouth, the other with sunken eyes and a crooked scowl. She'll leave it for today; it's time for a little nip. After good-byes all around, she leaves the shelter wondering what those two faces will talk about when she returns tomorrow. Her walk is wavy as she heads down the night-enfolded street.

In earlier times, people displaced from their homes were rare. Today in cultures such as that in Bali, in which the family cares for its own, displacement is still rare. In our present society, however, there are numerous groups of people who have been removed from their homes, and their number continues to rise. The reasons for displacement are varied. Some populations are immigrants from other countries who have come to the United States seeking opportunity, as did the ancestors of most Americans. Others have come because they have been driven out by violence, torture, and war in their native lands. However, our homeless population is composed of native-born citizens, for the most part, who have been exiled from their homes by poverty. Another displaced segment of our society is composed of those incarcerated for criminal activity or suspected criminal activity. (People who have been removed from their homes due to illness, infirmity, or the need for hospice care in the face of impending death are discussed in separate chapters.)

A major problem for displaced persons is that of adjustment to a new and unknown culture and sometimes to a new language, as well. Adjustment problems may be compounded by poverty, as is the case for homeless people and some immigrants; trauma, as experienced by survivors of war and violence; and mental illness and substance abuse, as is frequently seen among homeless and imprisoned populations. Adjustment reactions may cause depression and isolation. The societal problems these individuals face are often substantial, and the service systems available to them are inadequate in the face of their often overwhelming needs.

Immigrants

Naoko Takano, a native of Japan who came to the United States to study art therapy, readily understands the need for cultural awareness and sensitivity in working with populations from other cultures. She questions Western concepts in working with Asians (Takano, 1992). For example, she cites the Japanese concept of *ma*, the space between people, which is highly valued. It leads to less direct and less confrontational relationships. This is an important attribute of a society that functions largely on consensual decision making. The concept of *ma* can be found in Japanese art, such as in Sumie pictures, which might appear too spacious to Western eyes, and in art therapy might be interpreted as indicating defensiveness. But to the Japanese, such art is aesthetically appealing. Both in interpersonal relations and in art, *ma* provides an example of how a lack of sensitivity can lead to misunderstanding.

However, Takano found art therapy to be similar to Japanese culture in that communication is mediated through the artwork, creating a certain space between the therapist and the client that can allow for less direct confrontation and less perceived threat to the client. Takano worked in this country with Cambodian refugees who had been victims of torture. Most showed symptoms of Post-Traumatic Stress Disorder (PTSD): inability to sleep, recurrent nightmares, flashbacks to experiences of torture, nervousness, hyperactivity, robotic behavior, lack of trust, sexual dysfunction, inability to enjoy normal life experiences, and tendencies toward suicide and violence. Adjustment problems included separation from their families, loss of livelihood, diminution of social status, and difficulty with the English language. There was often conflict between members of older and younger generations, as the former tried to retain vestiges of their native lifestyle, culture, and heritage, and the latter tried to become Americanized through school and media influences. All of these problems were compounded by poverty.

Takano worked with a Cambodian women's group, which had been functioning for several years at a refugee center that provided clinical, social, and legal services. The clients suffered severe PTSD, which often included somatic problems. Many had lost family members during the years of the Khmer Rouge regime, while others still had family members in Cambodia. Self-expression was difficult for these women for several reasons. There were culturally imposed inhibitions on sharing problems outside the family, and there was a general wish to spare others from learning of the enormity of the horrors they had endured in Cambodia. Due to the inhuman experiences they had suffered at the hands of other Cambodians, distrust was strong, and there was little sense of community or mutual support. It was necessary for Takano to work with the group through an interpreter, which also increased communication difficulties.

Ha Luc Tho overcame the prohibition against sharing problems and cried after drawing a picture of herself on which she wrote, "I hope God help me!" She complained about her daughter, who she said cared more about her boyfriend than her mother. She drew herself with no color and no hands, and seemed to be expressing her feelings of helplessness.

The women often drew their houses in Cambodia, raised on stilts because of the frequent flooding there. Mien Hoy drew steep black mountains in response to a group discussion in which the interpreter and others were speaking about the fears and difficulties they experienced when they crossed the mountain range to enter Thailand and escape from Cambodia.

Bin Chom drew trees after a discussion by her close friend, sitting next to her, of her suffering under the Khmer Rouge, her escape, and the loss of her children in the process. Bitterly, Bin Chom said, "People have to die. Trees have to die too."

Many of the women drew trees and flowers. Being sensitive to Asian culture, Takano came to realize that flowers represented a tangible prayer or offering for the women and therefore carried a deep spiritual significance. When Sui Phon spoke of considering suicide, Takano suggested that they make flowers together (after precautions against suicide had been taken). Takano taught her how to make flowers out of tissue paper. At the next session, Sui Phon came early and said she wanted to make more flowers. She then taught flower making to other women, which seemed to elevate her mood and increase her self-esteem. Soon the group became absorbed in flower making in a way that Takano had never seen before (Figure 9.1).

Typically, Cambodian women do not express their problems to non–family members. Nevertheless, Sui Phon was able to do so in a body tracing. She was asked to locate the painful parts of her body on the paper. She was then asked to depict her feelings there. She drew a snake that she said was poisonous. She drew several more and said that she did not feel safe and wanted to kill the snakes. Poisonous snakes are common in Cambodia, and being bitten by one

FIGURE 9.1 **Paper flowers made by adult female Cambodian refugee.**

POST-TRAUMATIC STRESS DISORDER (PTSD) SYMPTOMS IN WAR SURVIVORS

- Depression
- Anxiety attacks
- Memory loss
- Intrusive recollections of torture
- Distressing dreams
- Difficulty in concentrating

---

is a palpable threat there. She then drew a container for the snakes, but still did not feel safe. She requested some aluminum foil, covered the picture of the snake container, and said that she then felt safe.

Despite cultural conditioning that prohibits expressing pain or problems to people outside the family, these women, who had suffered extreme trauma, were able to overcome their inhibitions and express some of their suffering in art therapy. Even working through an interpreter, Takano was able to promote group connection by respecting their culture. She recognized that in Cambodia, illness—both physical and mental—is believed to arise from a bad soul, a condition for which one is not responsible. Therefore, confronting problems as is done in Western psychotherapy is not always an effective approach in working with Eastern peoples. Art therapy can be an effective mode in its use of metaphor and image. The paper flower making that Takano instituted in the group was beneficial in several ways. It is a Cambodian custom to make paper flowers to offer to Buddha in Buddhist temples. For the women it was an offering, a prayer, a traditional activity. It was also similar to traditional arts and craft work that may have been a part of the women's lives in a happier time. The repetitive folding required, similar in technique to Japanese origami, can be a very soothing activity.

Takano notes that almost all of the art creations made in the Cambodian women's group represented images from the women's native country rather than their present life in the United States. As pointed out by Moreno and Wadeson (1986), people who have immigrated from their native lands draw inspiration from their own cultures. Ethnic identity incorporates individual and family continuity.

Barbara Baker also worked with survivors of torture and war, at a refugee center for victims of torture. She developed a proposal for working with Bosnian refugees (Baker, 1997). The goals of the program were to increase the refugees' social interaction, reduce their isolation, and promote Bosnian culture. Weekly art therapy, field trips, and an art exhibit were planned to implement these goals.

More than 2.5 million Bosnians have been forced from their homes by the worst destruction and atrocities in Europe since World War II. Displaced Bosnians have suffered torture, massacre, ethnic cleansing, internment, rape, physical injury, and loss of family and friends. For these refugees, war traumas are exacerbated by the stress of adjusting to a new and different culture, finding work, and learning a new language. The post-traumatic stress symptoms they experience include depression, anxiety attacks, memory loss or intrusive recollections of torture, distressing dreams, and difficulty in concentrating. Many are isolated and have poor social interaction within the community. The circumstances of war have changed the traditional structure of the Bosnian family in that the male head of the household may no longer be able to support the family. This change often brings about role reversals that cause family conflict. Many of the activities Baker planned centered on prewar occupations and experiences in order to recreate the Bosnian culture that had been lost to these survivors.

An open studio was planned in addition to the structured art therapy sessions in order to provide opportunities to work on art outside the regular sessions. Art therapy activities were to revolve around gender roles, such as needlework for women and stone carving and woodworking for men. Traditional Bosnian crafts were to be encouraged in the groups. Creative needlework is an important cultural heritage for Bosnian women. It is a significant mode of self-expression. Projects would consist of embroidery, needlepoint, crochet, knitting, needle-lace, quilting, and weaving. In addition to individual work, a quilt about Bosnia was planned, for which each woman would complete a segment combining needlepoint and embroidery. Bosnian men traditionally have worked the land and have used tools to work stone and wood in building structures. In addition to their own carving, the men would build easels, frames, tables, and tapestry frames for the women's group.

For those grieving the death or disappearance of loved ones, the creation of symbolic or actual memorials would be introduced. Through such work, they could deal with their feelings of loss and sorrow.

Because many of the Bosnian refugees were quite isolated in their daily

---

PROBLEMS OF IMMIGRANTS

- Language
- Cultural differences (especially regarding art traditions and the discussion of private matters)
- Disruption of life patterns
- Changes in family relationships
- Generational differences in relation to the dominant culture
- Lowered social status
- Poverty
- PTSD among survivors of trauma (see separate box)

lives, field trips to such places as museums and cultural events would be planned. Outdoor activities such as picnics and garden tours would also be scheduled.

In order to inform the public about Bosnian culture, an art exhibit and gallery installation with Bosnian music and food was to be planned by the refugees and the center's staff. It was hoped that this event would lead to greater public understanding and acceptance of the Bosnian population.

The Korean immigrants with whom Sue Lee worked did not come from a background of trauma and war. They were adolescents who had immigrated to the United States with their parents. As a Korean immigrant herself, Lee was very sensitive to their needs. She was also able to speak with them in their native tongue (Lee, 1993). She notes that in 1902, 121 Koreans left their country and settled in the United States. Now there are more than 1 million Korean immigrants living in this country, not counting temporary residents and their families, such as those who have come to study or for business purposes. The transition to American life is especially difficult for adolescents, who are undergoing significant developmental transitions, as well. Most of them struggle alone and have little guidance, because they have been raised to be humble and to avoid the expression of emotions.

Lee introduced the group to the young people as an art discussion group and avoided the designation of therapy. She thought this group would be especially helpful for the adolescents, who were not verbally expressive and who had never experienced any form of therapy or counseling. She met with them privately, and because they traveled a long distance to participate in the evening group, she served them dinner beforehand. The group was composed of four adolescents who were from middle-class backgrounds and had been brought to the United States by their parents in early adolescence. Lee shared some of her own difficulties in being a Korean American with the group.

Lee structured the group to include the following art projects in order:

- Family of origin
- Feelings about retaining Korean culture in America
- Most stressful issue as a Korean American immigrant
- Identity issues through self-portrait masks
- Feeling of belonging by creating a safe space
- An ending project

The group members participated cooperatively in the projects, but Lee found them to be much less talkative than those in other groups she had led. They responded to questions and spoke only when they thought it was necessary.

Kyung, an 18-year-old who had come to the United States at age 10, was discouraged from making Korean friends by her parents because they wanted her to adapt to American culture quickly. For a long time she thought she had actually become "white." A year prior to joining the group, she finally realized that this would never happen, and she joined a Korean group despite her parents' objections. There she found some value in being Korean. In representing her stress in being Korean American, she drew herself screaming, with her hair half black and half curly blonde (Figure 9.2). In the middle of her body is her real self, frightened and trapped inside. She had tried to transform herself according to her parents' wishes for her by coloring and perming her hair and wearing lots of makeup. All the other group members related to her experience. They all felt torn by their parents' expectations. Many of their parents were under stress from working hard to support their families, often holding several jobs. They did not want their children to undergo similar hardships, so they tried to force them to become successful in the dominant society. Some of the young people felt guilty because their parents had told them that they had immigrated to give their children greater opportunities, and they often reminded them of how hard they were working for their children's benefit.

The self-portraits that emerged showed a lot of identity confusion. Youngsik, a 20-year-old who had immigrated with his family at age 15, drew his face half black and half white. His stick figure has a robotic look. His body is a crossword puzzle, he said, because he did not know what fit in each blank box (Figure 9.3). As he explained his image, he burst out laughing so hard that tears came to his eyes. His laughter sounded empty, and a heavy silence followed it. Everyone stared at the floor. Youngsik then expressed his relief that he had opened himself to the group and apologized for making others uncomfortable with his laughter. Group members told him that they related to his pain and that they felt confusion, too. The others discussed their own lost

FIGURE 9.2 Conflict over Korean heritage by adolescent 18-year-old girl.

FIGURE 9.3   Conflict over Korean heritage by adolescent 20-year-old boy.

identities and talked about supporting one another to fill in the blank boxes
they all had in their lives.

Sungkyu's self-portrait is more realistic (Figure 9.4). A nineteen-year-old
who had come to this country at age 12, he was a college student planning to
attend medical school. He explained that he used to think that study was the
only way to overcome the stresses in his life and has shown himself walking a
tightrope, which is the edge of the world. He is walking very carefully, always
worrying if he is succeeding academically, always thinking he should be
studying harder. Although he pleased his parents by studying hard, he was
probably denying other important issues in his life. He had no role models to
show him other ways of coping. Lee suggested to the group members that
they recognize the strengths within each of them, that they search within to
identify their needs, and that they learn communication skills and new ways
of coping.

FIGURE 9.4   Tightrope of studying by 19-year-old Korean American boy.

The group devoted two sessions to mask making. The group members found the experience of creating them, by putting plaster gauze on each others' faces, to be very relaxing, and they were amazed at how the hardened product resembled their own faces. They became very attached to their masks and wanted assurance from Lee that the masks would be well cared for until they returned the next week to decorate them. Lee encouraged them to spend some quiet time with their masks before beginning to embellish them, even though they were eager to get started right away. They worked on the masks for about 4 hours (Figure 9.5). Lee suggested that they enact their masks, but they refused. They were much too embarrassed. Youngsik filled his mask with white and gray cotton (Figure 9.5, upper left), saying it was a cloud, which meant freedom to him. It could go wherever it wanted and be gentle, yet show anger. It had the power to bring rain, and it could disappear, sending down light. Kyung made her mask realistic in order to be herself rather than trying to be someone else (Figure 9.5, upper right). She said she now loves her Ori-

FIGURE 9.5   Masks of self-identity by Korean American adolescents.

ental features. Nineteen-year-old John (who had changed his name when he came to this country) found so much energy deep within himself that his mask is exploding, he said (Figure 9.5, lower left). He painted the energy in the center of his face and added glitter to emphasize it. He said that he was in control of how to utilize the energy. Sungkyu used natural objects to decorate his mask (Figure 9.5, lower right), because he loved nature and wanted to live on a farm someday. Each person treated his or her mask very carefully, and it was clear that the group members had become very attached to their masks. Lee felt that she had seen the gentle and vulnerable sides of these tough, cool, quiet young people. When they reluctantly left their masks with Lee to be photographed, they said they felt that they were leaving a part of themselves.

In drawing his safe place, Youngsik made an underground refuge, which was very different from the sky image in his mask (Figure 9.6). He said it was like an ants' nest, with several entrances and places to stay, but he was the only one who knew how to get in and out. He still seemed isolated and lonely. Sungkyu found peace in his heart and did not need to go anywhere else to feel safe. Youngsik agreed that that was where he belonged also, adding that, as a result, he could go anywhere and feel safe. The group members liked this activity, finding peace and enjoying the quiet time for introspection. They were pleased to be doing something to care for themselves, rather than for others. Many adolescent Korean American immigrants are confused about their sense of belonging, feeling that they belong in both cultures, either culture, or neither one. This exercise helped the group members to recognize that a safe space could be anywhere they wished and that they could create a safe space within themselves.

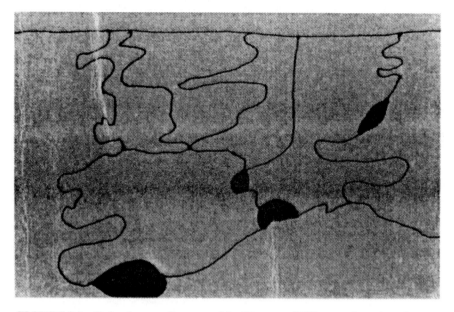

FIGURE 9.6 Safe place underground by 20-year-old Korean American boy.

The final project was a group mural. They decided to make a big, healthy tree in the middle and have everyone write a word that was important to them. They called the mural *1.5 Generation*, the phrase used by Korean Americans to denote immigrants who came here with their parents at a young age. Sungkyu drew the outline of the tree; Youngsik added a white cloud; Kyung drew a butterfly; and John wrote the title. In working together, they realized that they were not alone. At the close of the session, after 8 weeks of meetings, they ended by holding hands in a circle and singing a Korean folk song. Then the members exchanged hugs in the American way.

People of Hispanic origin compose the largest minority in the United States. Spanish-speaking therapists, therefore, are in much demand, especially in urban Latino neighborhood centers. Leslie DeVera, of Filipino origin, speaks Spanish and worked in a high school with a predominantly Latino student body. Like Sue Lee, she helped her adolescent clients to explore their cultural identity. DeVera notes that adolescents from ethnic minority groups face the major task of ego identity achievement, which includes making sense of the often contradictory knowledge, experience, attitudes, and images that derive from their ethnic social context (DeVera, 1999). The students with whom she worked were referred by teachers and counselors due to behavior problems, academic difficulties, or family and emotional trouble. Many were dealing with issues of unemployment, gang affiliation, and drug trafficking. DeVera introduced art therapy into a special education art class twice a week in order to explore cultural background and self-awareness. The group was composed of four males and two females, age 14 and 15, who had been assigned to special education because of a learning disability, an emotional or behavioral disorder, or both. After several sessions spent in experimenting with the media, DeVera introduced the following activities to focus on ethnic heritage and identity:

- *Family of origin and cultural background drawing.* DeVera showed an example of her own drawings of her Filipino heritage and spoke of how her cultural background had affected her development. The students were able to use atlases to draw their countries if they wished.
- *Flag making.* Using fabric, dowel rods, wood plugs, and fabric paint, the students created symbols representing their cultural backgrounds, family roles, school, and interests.
- *Self-portrait.* After being introduced to the work of Mexican artist Frida Kahlo through a brief biography and one of her self-portraits, the students were given mirrors with which to work.
- *Doll making to represent themselves.* DeVera brought in a doll she had made that had black hair and dark skin like her own that was different from the dolls of her childhood. She had dressed her doll in Filipino attire. She demonstrated how to construct a doll and provided fabric and decorations such as beads, buttons, sequins, and feathers.
- *Final presentation.* At the last session, the students gave an informal presentation of their artwork as it focused on ethnic heritage and identity.

Richard had been transferred to special education for threatening his teacher and classmates. He had had a history of behavioral problems since he was 11, and he was often loud and disruptive in class. He had witnessed much domestic violence directed toward his mother by his father, and he had begun to dream about it at a young age. His parents were divorced, and he no longer had contact with his father. In his family of origin and cultural background picture, Richard drew both the Puerto Rican and Mexican flags. He explained that his mother was Mexican and his father was Puerto Rican. He began drawing family members, but did not finish. In discussing his art, he said that he was proud of his cultural background and that his drawing made him happy. He put a cross on the Puerto Rican flag to symbolize his hope that his father was doing well, as he no longer knew where he was. He was grateful to have his mother, who had always been there for him, he said. At the next session, Richard made two flags. On the first, he began by making a Puerto Rican flag on the left and then smeared it over. On the right, he painted a black mask with glitter on it. On his second flag, he made the mask again, added a large signature, and drew a rat at the bottom. Both the masks and the rat represent the sneaky side of his personality, he said. He used the mirror to create his self-portrait and worked on it industriously. It was very realistic compared to all his other artwork. Richard was very pleased with the result. When it came to making the doll, he said that he wanted his doll to look crazy, so he gave it a "crazy" cape and only one eye. He said its name was Don Corleon and that he was a very rich man who could fly. He appeared to be expressing his grandiose wishes.

DeVera helped this group of troubled teenagers to recognize the importance of their ethnic backgrounds and to take pride in them.

Family life is strong in Latin cultures, so Hispanics often immigrate to this country as families, although not necessarily all together. Family work with this population is discussed in Chapter 5, "Family Art Therapy." For additional material on cultural issues in art therapy with immigrants, see Wadeson, Durkin, & Perach (1989).

Incarceration

Kathleen Terra worked with psychiatric patients in a jail (Terra, 1996). She found collage to be especially useful in helping to overcome resistance among members of this very difficult population. Terra notes that approximately 1.5 million people are incarcerated in the United States. Mental illness is common among them, and suicide is the leading cause of death in jails. Contributing factors include social alienation, cognitive distortions, poor adaptive resources, depression, and hopelessness, coupled with the intense environmental stress inherent in crowded conditions. Jail crowding has led to increased violence and decreased access to mental health services, with increased inmate mental health problems, decreased staff morale, and decreased resources for inmate training and education. The high incidence of suicide is an ever-present problem in correctional institutions. It is associated with in-jail isolation, incarceration for low-level offenses, and intoxication. Often the means is by hanging, and the occurrence is usually within the first 24 hours of incarceration.

As mentioned, Terra found magazine collage to be a particularly useful project in a jail setting. Many of the inmates had had little experience with art expression, and the prospect of having to produce an art piece was often daunting. Choosing personally appealing photographs was far less threatening. Art materials were strictly controlled within the jail. Monitoring of supplies, such as brushes, pencils, markers, and glue, was constant. Some materials were forbidden altogether, such as clay, knives, chisels, stone, and any wood other than brush handles. Prior to the sessions, Terra precut a large supply of photos from magazines, keeping in mind the interests of the inmates she was seeing. Because many of them were from a low socioeconomic segment of society, she was careful to select images that could reflect their experience. She included multiracial themes and images that showed a variety of emotions. She also included some from advertisements that were in sharp contrast with other themes of impoverishment. She recognized the paradox in selecting "beautiful" images, in that they might satisfy some hunger for beauty, yet might simply reinforce the inmates' misery regarding what they lacked in their lives.

In working with a men's group on a unit for prisoners with subacute conditions, Terra's goals were to encourage greater comfort with art expression, group cohesion, increased self-confidence, decision-making skills, emotional containment in the art, and decreased social isolation. Diagnoses included Schizophrenia, Bipolar Disorder, paranoia, Psychotic Disorder, and Cognitive Disorder. Criminal charges included battery, theft, aggressive sexual assault, criminal trespassing, and parole violation.

Nick was a 34-year-old man diagnosed with Bipolar I Disorder with a recent hypomanic episode who had been charged with battery. His parents had been slain, execution-style, by Mafia members. He had become a ward of the state and had suffered much upheaval in his life as a foster child. He had ended up in jail from time to time because of fighting when inebriated. Occasionally, he taught other group members collage technique. At one session, he jumped onto a bench to gain the group's attention for discussion of his collage. He glued the phrases "Think Big" and "Relive the Glory" on his paper and added photos of a group of people saluting the flag, a scene of ocean waves, and a rose blossom. He then drew a face with tears running down it. He spoke of the loss of his family and said that the rose stood for funeral flowers. His experiences of family difficulties, he said, were as deep as the ocean, and "reliving the glory" referred to the memories he had. The weeping face was his grief for his losses. Other group members responded by saying that they, too, had lost family members and that they shared his feelings. Some were surprised to learn that there was a commonality of experience, in that others had suffered loss.

Terra found that magazine collage was also useful in identifying suicidal ideation. Tim, another member of the group, was 33, had been diagnosed with somatic disorder, and had been charged with armed robbery. He spoke in the group of having a plan for getting out of jail. He pointed to the sky in his collage and said, "That's where I'm going." He claimed that he knew all about what happens after death and bragged that he had been clinically dead seven times. Terra brought her concerns about Tim's risk for suicide to the attention of the staff. During the next 2 weeks, Tim made three suicide attempts and was put in restraints and kept under close observation. Gradually, he was given incentives for good behavior, and once again was allowed to attend art therapy. He was able to take on the responsibility of instructing some of the other group members in art therapy procedures. He began to explore some more challenging art media and expressed the desire to learn computer-aided design and eventually open his own business. Terra encouraged him in these objectives. His suicidal ideation was replaced by other options. In a later collage, *The Struggle between Life and Death* (Figure 9.7), he placed an infant upside down, saying that sometimes one gets off to a bad start in life. He also spoke of the masks people wear, with which they struggle until their deaths. A subsequent collage shows various birds that stand for different ideas: An owl represents wisdom, eagles represent strength, and ducks represent freedom. Religious figures represent spirituality. By the time he made these pictures, his suicidal behavior had subsided.

FIGURE 9.7   Collage by suicidal 33-year-old male prisoner.

Terra points out that in working under the difficult conditions of a jail set-ting, with group members who may be very hostile, necessitating constant vigilance, she found that adopting a nonauthoritarian stance (as opposed to that of other staff members) tends to minimize competition for leadership and control of the group. Although some inmates might continue to view the art therapist as part of the correctional staff and therefore remain hostile, most do not do so. Terra also points out the importance of treating the inmates with respect and courtesy. For additional discussions of art therapy with prisoners, see Wadeson (1987) and Wadeson, Durkin, & Perach (1989).

Homelessness

Art therapy is a central activity in working with homeless women in several associated shelters. One offers transitional living space, another is an emer-gency overnight shelter that provides dinner and breakfast, and a third is a daytime drop-in facility with showers and a laundry. Lunch, telephones, and bus tokens are provided there, as well. It is a large, open loft-type area with an adjacent kitchen and small smoking room. The shelter serves 30 to 40 women daily. The walls of the main area are covered with art made by the women (Figure 9.8). Art materials are available whenever anyone wants to use them, and the kiln is fired once a week. Some women need shelter for only a short time, but many have been coming on a regular basis for years. The women live

FIGURE 9.8   Homeless women's shelter decorated with art by shelter clients.

under conditions of extreme poverty, and often have substance abuse problems, mental illness, or both. Some are in the late stages of chronic alcoholism.

Art therapy under these circumstances is practiced very differently from the more structured sessions seen in other kinds of facilities. Art therapy can happen at any time during the day, for as long or as short a period of time as there is interest. Others can watch, join in, walk away, or never participate at all. A woman may choose to work with the art therapist or not. In other words, there are no art therapy sessions as such. The work is generated as needs and desires arise. Usually, however, at least one person is making art at any time in a given day. The physical openness of the setting and the availability of art materials on open shelves are consonant with the shelter's approach of no schedules, requirements, or compulsory treatment sessions.

Art therapists coming to work at this shelter are challenged in their usual conceptions of how art therapy operates. Such was the experience of Suzanne Canby, who questions this approach (Canby, 1992). She notes that because the women in the shelter have no space of their own, their space in the shelter is respected; if a woman leaves an unfinished piece of art and some material unattended, they are not disturbed. Paint-filled brushes, dirty paint water, used paper towels, or whatever a woman might have left where she was working are not touched until she cleans it up herself, which may not be until several days later. Many of the women have had negative experiences with therapy and hospitals, so *therapy* and *therapist* are not popular terms at the shelter. The art therapist is therefore part of the daily routine and has no desk or office that is set

apart. Canby observes that the nature of the interaction between the art therapist and the women is often something like "parallel play," in which the art
therapist may sit at a table with a woman making her own art, or chatting, or
both. Staff members and volunteers are also welcome to make art.

Canby describes her group work at the shelter as being very different from
conventional group art therapy. One example is a leaf project she instituted.
She took three interested women to the woods to observe the fall colors and
collect leaves, acorns, seeds, and wildflowers. They made a bouquet to share
with those who did not come. After they returned, Suzanne spread a large
sheet of paper on a table, put out some acrylic paints, and invited the women
to make leaf prints. She demonstrated by painting a leaf with several colors
and printing it on the paper. Two of the three women who had gathered the
leaves joined in. Another woman who had watched them making the bouquet
also participated. The actual completion of the mural took several hours, as
the women would start and stop, get coffee, make phone calls, or just rest.
Eventually, seven people worked on the mural, but no more than four at any
one time. There were periods when no one worked on it. Everyone was careful not to intrude on another person's print. When the paper was sufficiently
filled, the participants agreed that it was finished, and it was hung for display.

Art making appears to be contagious at the shelter—and, indeed, the leaf
project had a ripple effect. One woman wrote a poem about the day, taking 3
weeks to do so as she looked up words in the dictionary and typed it out in
verse form. Another woman drew a tree on a card for a friend and taped some
of the collected leaves to it. A woman who frequently wrote lists of words from
the Bible with markers decorated one of her lists by taping leaves to it and
writing about them, as well. A woman who usually does not interact with
others asked for Saran Wrap, a Styrofoam cup, and markers. She made a
flower from the Saran Wrap, added green leaves, colored the cup reddish
brown with the markers, and stuck the flower in it, then put her "potted plant"
on the table. She was animated and smiling as others complimented her on her
creativity and skill.

Another group project was making a hand mural. An art therapist traced
her hand and arm in several places on a large sheet of brown butcher paper,
which generated no interest for several days. Then a few more people added
their own hands and colored in the outlines with designs made with markers
and oil pastels. The mural was pushed aside from time to time, but each day it
gathered several more hands. Slowly it began to fill up and attract attention.
Women would ask each other if their hands were on it and if they could identify them. Eventually it was filled, the background was colored in, and the
mural (shown on page 255), was hung in a prominent place, where it engendered further interaction.

One woman liked to use a walking stick made from a broken-off broom
handle to help her travel down the street. But one day, she arrived with an aluminum crutch instead. She said she wanted to paint it, but because paint would
not adhere to it, the art therapist suggested that it be wrapped with different-

colored wool. The woman directed the therapist and received the finished product as a prized gift from a respected and caring friend. She is shown with the crutch in Figure 9.9, dressed in the creative and dramatic attire she would fashion for herself as wearable art.

Sarah Frahm worked at the shelter several years later (Frahm, 1995). As a white, middle-class, educated young woman, it was not always easy for her to connect with older, black, impoverished women. Lily was an African American woman in her 50s with mischievous eyes behind her sunglasses, and no teeth. She had been coming to the shelter for 9 years, and her art covered the walls. She drank alcohol daily, and she sometimes drank milk from a baby bottle. Her paintings were built up of many layers, and her clay pieces depicted men and women masturbating, women giving birth, and fantasy creatures. Frahm asked Lily if she could draw one of Lily's expressive clay heads (Figure 9.10 shows an example). Lily assented, and over the course of a week Frahm drew Figure 9.11 while Lily and others watched. As Frahm and Lily grew

FIGURE 9.9   Homeless woman's wrapped crutch.

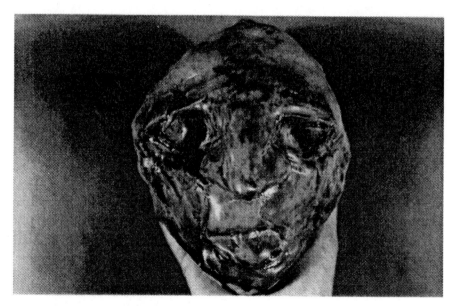

FIGURE 9.10   Clay head by homeless woman.

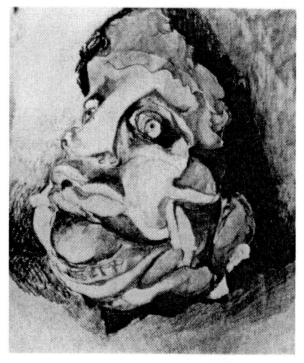

FIGURE 9.11   Art therapist's drawing of clay head
by homeless woman.

closer, Lily said, "I will mold you. I will teach you how to work with me" (p. 12). When Frahm returned to the shelter after an absence due to illness, she couldn't find her drawing of Lily's sculpture, which had been hanging on the wall. When Lily opened her locker, however, Frahm saw it hanging inside. Lily said, "Oh, that's nice isn't it? I like it there" (p. 13).

Amy was a Caucasian woman of indeterminate age who kept herself at a distance from others. She was not particularly interested in the artwork. When Frahm was embroidering, however, she approached her and asked her about it. Eventually, she began to talk about her life. They started to get to know each other. Later, when Frahm was leading an exercise in relaxation followed by body tracing, Amy was eager to try it. She said she wanted to trace Frahm. They colored it in together for the next hour, Amy giving Frahm a wedding band and a rose that has yet to open (Figure 9.12). "You know what's great about this," she said. "You don't have to be an artist. You got me to forget

FIGURE 9.12 Body tracing of art therapist by therapist and homeless woman.

about my problems for a while." Amy said that working together had been "a loving experience" (p. 19). She held Frahm's hand as she talked about her drinking problems.

Jean Durkin is the art therapist who established art therapy at the shelter's various locations. Although she had been offered a position at the state psychiatric hospital where she interned as a student, Durkin recognized that such a large bureaucracy was not the sort of place where she would feel comfortable and be able to have a maximum effect. In carefully reading the mission statement of the organization that operates the shelter program for homeless women at the time she joined it, Durkin recognized the program to be fertile ground to support her beliefs and to give her an opportunity to make an impact on the agency and its work. She sees her own mission as an art therapist as extending beyond the individuals and groups with whom she works to the neighborhood, the city, and, hopefully, to the world at large (personal communication, 1999).

One example of public art is a mural the women painted on the outside of the agency's building. Durkin describes it as "making a mark on an outside wall, making a public, self-determining, willful, self-identifiable image that will last a very long time." A woman with addictions who is actively delusional invited the alderman to the ceremony to celebrate the completion of the mural. He held the ribbon that encircled the building for another woman with addictions to cut. The woman with the scissors walked right up to the alderman, then veered sharply to the left and cut the ribbon where she wanted to, several yards away. Durkin describes the alderman as looking on "in puzzlement while most of us in the audience shook our heads in amusement, grateful for her decision to wear clothing for this event, suspecting that she chose this new spot because of the proximity to her portrait of one of our founders." (Social protest art made by homeless women at this agency is discussed in Chapter 10, "Women.")

Working in a shelter with homeless women is a challenge. The women may be hardened and despairing. Many of them abuse drugs constantly and are in poor physical health. They come to a shelter to get in out of the cold, to have a meal, to get some rest. They are not seeking therapy. Their needs are very basic. Yet art therapists have seen ways they may be reached through art. For some, such as Lily, art becomes a way of life. Suzanne Canby asks, is it therapy? For this population, art therapy can provide support, understanding, connection, self-expression, and a creative outlet. It is therapy and then some. Jean Durkin makes it a public statement, as well.

Summary

Displaced persons include immigrants, some of whom have come to the United States for greater opportunities and some of whom have come to escape the war, violence, and torture in their home countries; those who are incarcerated for criminal activity or suspected criminal activity; and those who are homeless. Many of the people in these groups have difficulty adjusting to the dominant culture, many live in poverty, and some are treated as societal outcasts. Art therapists have been able to work with them around the following issues:

- Naoko Takano (1992) pointed out the need for cultural sensitivity in her work with Cambodian women who were victims of torture and suffered the loss of family members during the Khmer Rouge regime.
- Barbara Baker (1997) developed a program for Bosnian refugees, also survivors of war and torture, that focused on traditional Bosnian arts and crafts.
- Sue Lee (1993) worked with Korean American adolescents with cultural identity issues.
- Leslie DeVera (1999) worked on cultural identity issues with adolescents in a high school with a predominantly Latino student body.
- Kathy Terra (1996) used magazine collage in art therapy groups in a jail setting.
- Suzanne Canby (1992) worked in a nontraditional, unstructured way with homeless women in a drop-in shelter.
- Sarah Frahm (1995), working in the same homeless women's shelter, found unique ways to make connections with the women through art.
- Jean Durkin (personal communication, 1999) worked with homeless women to make public art.

Conclusion

Historically, art therapy served populations with psychiatric conditions, primarily in hospitals. In our present society, however, various social ills have displaced many people from their homes and left them in need. Some have suffered severe trauma. For many of them, societal problems are intertwined with mental problems, and it is not always evident which has been the cause and which has been the effect. For some groups, such as people who are homeless and those who are incarcerated, substance abuse may be prevalent, as well. Many displaced persons have depleted their resources, both internally and in relation to others. There may be no family or community to which they can return. Certainly, these groups provide major challenges for our society in general, and for the human service professions in particular. Art therapists have done some impressive work with these groups of very needy people.

ART THERAPY PROJECTS

Projects discussed in this chapter are described further in Chapter 15, "Art Activities and Materials":

- Construction of paper flowers (Takano, 1992)
- Body tracings (Takano, 1992; Frahm, 1995)
- Masks (Lee, 1993)
- Murals (Lee, 1993)
- Paint applications, for making flags (DeVera, 1999)
- Dolls (DeVera, 1999)
- Magazine collage (Terra, 1996)
- Leaf printing (Canby, 1992)
- Group hand mural (Canby, 1992)
- Wrapping (Canby, 1992)
- Large public art (Durkin, personal communication, 1999)

Chapter 10

Women

Woman's reaction to menopause, seen as a barren time.

Lulu swaggers in, her long dark legs dangling beneath her black leather miniskirt, a cigarette dangling from her lips. She dumps her bag and curses at the run in her stocking. Then she sees her doll. It is almost finished. She smashes out her cigarette and picks up Little Lulu tenderly, cradling the stuffed sock in her arms. Singing softly, Lulu sews on button eyes and adds a ribbon to the doll's black wool hair.

The issues that women face in a society in which they are beginning to emerge from diminished status in almost every sector of their lives are vast and various. No one chapter could contain them all, nor are they separate from other problems women face that are treated in therapeutic and rehabilitation services. For example, the oppression of women can contribute to substance abuse. Poverty can lead to prostitution. Sexual abuse can cause disassociation. Many of these conditions are addressed throughout this book, as well as in this chapter. What follows here is a discussion of art therapy designed to deal with issues specific to women. Because treatment for sexual abuse has become such a large component of care, it warrants a chapter all to itself and is not addressed here.

Private Practice

In my own private practice over the years, I have seen far more women than men. Most have been well-functioning individuals, but many have experienced problems specifically related to their status as women. (A number of my clients have been survivors of childhood sexual abuse; this topic is discussed in Chapter 11, "Sexual Abuse.") Betty was a woman in her 50s who had come into therapy after having made a second and very serious suicide attempt. She was married to a man who was prominent in the small town in which they lived. Because of his position, he insisted that his wife provide the perfect image of what he thought she should be. She felt constrained to be the perfect wife and mother. He squelched her if she was too loud in a restaurant, pressured her to lose weight, and generally disparaged her. Betty's affect was flat, and she was little in touch with her feelings. Art gave her an access to them, and in her pictures she murdered and mutilated her husband many times. In time, she had ventilated her anger sufficiently to become relatively content in her marriage. She had been raised to be a "good girl" who did not make a fuss. Much of my work with her was of an educational nature, helping her to see that all of society had conspired to make her the self-sacrificing woman she had become. Betty came to enjoy art making so much that she set up a studio in her house, took art courses, and began selling her work. For the most part, she painted landscapes and made wooden craft items. She spoke of her "inside" and "outside" art. The former was what she made in art therapy, which was often raw and primitive. The latter was carefully executed, "pretty" art. Because I was seeing Betty privately, we had the luxury of working together for several years. Under these circumstances, the art therapist is privileged to participate in real personality changes by the client. For a more detailed account of my work with this client, see Wadeson (1997). That chapter concludes with the following statement:

> For this "traditional" woman whose culture had taught her to serve her husband, children and parents and to deny her own needs and feelings, art therapy became both the key to unlock her awareness and the door through which her long-closed-off feelings could flow (p. 236).

Menopause

Nancy Biederman, approaching menopause herself, established a menopause art therapy support group (Biederman, 1988). In order to encourage intimacy, she limited the size of the group to eight members. These women were functioning well in their families and in the community. The group was designed for support, rather than for treatment. Because the women were not experienced in art, the first part of each session was devoted to experimenting with the materials. After everyone had assembled, Biederman gave a directive, and the group worked on their projects for about an hour. They then moved from the art studio to a sitting room to discuss their work for an hour and a half. The directives Biederman utilized grew out of the women's concerns, as expressed in the first session when they were asked to draw what came to mind when they thought of menopause. The directives were as follows:

- *First session: Draw what comes to mind when you think of menopause.* The content of these pictures showed the women's concerns and therefore formed the basis for what followed in subsequent sessions. The issues that came up were their physical and emotional symptoms, how their roles in their families were affected, and how others perceived them.
- *Second session: Create a collage depicting how menopause has affected your life.* A variety of collage material was provided.
- *Third session: Close your eyes and locate that part of your body where you experience menopausal symptoms. Draw an outline of your body and locate that area on it. Cut it out and turn it into a painting.*
- *Fourth session: Draw how others perceive you on the left of your paper and how you perceive yourself on the right.* Additional kinds of collage materials were provided.
- *Fifth session: Depict your role in your family and how menopause has affected it.*
- *Sixth session: Draw how you have been affected emotionally by menopause.* The group planned for the termination session.
- *Seventh session: Visualize the group and depict it on your square.* The group had chosen to make a joint project, fabric squares that could be sewn together for a hanging. The group also decided how to bind it.

In addition, Biederman provided the group with information about menopause, including reference material and handouts. In conjunction with each session's subject matter, she gave information on such topics as the physical components of menopause, facts about hot flashes and osteoporosis, bone and muscle strengthening exercises, nutritional guidance, and sexuality for aging women.

In the first session, the group members were very open in imagining their reactions to menopause; as mentioned, their pictures formed the foundation for the subsequent art directives. Maggie drew menopause as a bridge that is a connecting transition from chaos to calm. Teressa experienced it as a barren time and drew herself as a pale nude, shown on page 279. She saw it as ghost-like, with the reds in the background making it appear to be on fire. Chris made a collage to represent a sense of renewal in which she was freed from the restraints she had placed upon herself when younger, but she also added a picture of a drag queen to represent her fears of losing estrogen and experiencing an increase in testosterone. She had tried hard not to lose her femininity. Biederman drew a grave with a cross and growing branches, but with shedding leaves (Figure 10.1). The closed door signifies the part of life that is over, youth and fertility. She described the sun on the horizon as brilliant and lively, giving her energy to go on. Kate's collage represents the tree of life. She wondered how she looked to others. On the left is her young self, and in the middle is herself as she looks now, "full, plump, and not very attractive" (p. 15). At the lower right is death. Teressa expressed similar feelings, which she said reminded her of adolescence, when she felt awkward, gawky, and ugly. She

FIGURE 10.1 Art therapist's reaction to menopause, the end of youth and fertility.

covered photos of her young self and present self with lots of pieces of paper in her collage to represent how she felt—frantic, hurried, not connected. She said she tried to keep busy so that she couldn't think about how she was being affected. Linda drew a pale representation of herself to show how extended and lifeless she felt. She was afraid of becoming bitter because menopause made her realize how little time she had left and how she had spent most of her life divided between being a single parent and working fulltime. Early on, these group members expressed their fears and their predominantly negative feelings about their present stage in life.

Another topic of concern was hot flashes. Maggie drew her head experiencing a hot flash and wrote, "The heat is on" (p. 16). She noted that the face has a small smile, which indicated that she could get through this. Kitty painted a large conflagration, which represented her hot flashes at night. Mary expressed another physical concern. All her art contained large areas of red, which she said represented her heavy periods and physical pain. Although she was in frequent contact with her physician, she felt that she did not receive the emotional support from him that she needed; however, she did find it in the group. Weight gain was another concern for some of the members. Joint pain and backaches were other common symptoms. These problems were given prominence in their pictures. Susan, who had never married and was childless, now faced the realization that she would never have children.

In the session examining how menopause affected their families' perception of them, Linda made a collage representing her family on a mountain vacation (Figure 10.2). The mountains and her family (foreground) are dark,

FIGURE 10.2 Woman's collage representing how menopause affected her family, shown on vacation.

she said, because she found herself to be too controlling, easily getting upset with them. When she looked at her picture, however, she saw it as serene, which made her feel better. Several others drew images symbolizing mood swings and easy upsets, as well. Biederman drew herself as two people (Figure 10.3). On the left is the mother, wife, and responsible woman. On the right is an animal, angry and defensive. These striking alterations occurred abruptly for her.

After six weeks, the group members felt very connected to one another. The representations of the group they made on their squares for the final wall hanging included the infinity symbol; female symbols interlocked with flowers around them; women standing by a book, indicating the knowledge that had been gained; a rainbow, representing shared and connected feelings; and overlapping hands, representing support. The group members decided to sew the squares together with white thread that matched the background so that they would all blend together. The outer edge was to have red binding since this color appeared so often in their art. Binding the squares together was symbolic of the cohesion and the emotional connection that the group had built.

After the final session, Biederman arranged individual meetings with all of the women to obtain feedback about their experience in the group. All expressed positive reactions, although one was intimidated by the art making. The women spoke of getting in touch with their feelings, enjoying making the art, becoming more knowledgeable about menopause, becoming more insightful about themselves, communicating and feeling supported, learning

FIGURE 10.3   Art therapist's depiction of herself as two people in relation to her family.

new coping strategies, and, especially, feeling good about themselves. Linda stated that the art making was a more personal way of understanding one another. Lisa said that her husband could see a difference in her after she had been attending the group. He said she was more relaxed and communicated better.

The members of Biederman's group, though not seeking treatment as such, were women who were having difficulty with menopause. Before joining the group, they had been dealing with their problems on their own. For the most part, they were able to function well in their day-to-day lives, but the group gave them a more reality-based perception of their stage of life, the support of others with similar experiences, and better feelings about themselves. The art making facilitated self-expression, provided a cathartic outlet, and enhanced their understanding of themselves and the other group members.

This time-limited art therapy group is an example of how art therapy may be conducted in private practice. In this case, however, because she was dealing with menopause herself, Biederman chose to cast herself in the role of facilitator and participant. In most other private practice groups, the art therapist would be the leader and facilitator, as usual.

Women Who Have Surrendered Children for Adoption

Another population of women who need emotional support consists of those who have given up their children for adoption. Like those with whom Nancy Biederman worked, the women discussed in this section were not a part of a treatment population. In contrast with Biederman, however, art therapist Angie Runyan was not a participant in the group she was leading. (She had not surrendered a child for adoption.) Runyan notes that more than 1 million women in the United States have relinquished children for adoption at birth (Runyan, 1992). Many experience an ongoing sense of loss, guilt, anger over the limited alternatives available, and a negative impact on their marriages and subsequent parenting. Adoption workers should therefore facilitate, rather than discourage, mourning for the surrendered child. Runyan found that the art making process provides a container for the expression of the deep grieving that often goes unacknowledged in women who have relinquished their children for adoption.

Due to public secrecy and legally closed birth and adoption records, the numbers of adoptees, birthparents, and adoptive parents in the United States remain unknown. The most widely accepted figure is 5 million adoptees. A nationwide network, Concerned United Birthparents, was formed to help both men and women understand how relinquishing their children for adoption has affected their lives. The organization operates through support groups and works for both adoption reform and personal problem resolution.

Runyan conducted art therapy for birthmothers who attended a Concerned United Birthparents support group. (The term *birthmother* is used to designate women who have given up their children for adoption.) She offered them both individual art therapy and a workshop for the group as a whole. Although some sessions were left open so the women could choose a personal subject related to surrendering a child for adoption, other sessions were focused on specific directives. These included the following subjects:

- A self-portrait or self-introduction art piece of yourself as a birthmother
- The pregnancy
- Relinquishment
- Your life following relinquishment
- Your decision to search for the adult child or not
- The search, if that was your decision
- Your feelings related to the adoption process

The women were free to choose to follow these directives or not.

A sense of community had been well established through participation in the support group prior to the introduction of art therapy. Two of the women in the workshop were dealing with having sought out their now-adult children. Barb, 39, had relinquished two children for adoption as a teenager. Now in the process of developing relationships with them at ages 20 and 22, she made collages to explore her experience with each (Figures 10.4 and 10.5). She included images of them as the young children she had never known, as well

FIGURE 10.4   Woman's reaction to experience of reconnecting with adult son given up for adoption at birth.

FIGURE 10.5 Woman's reaction to experience of reconnecting with adult daughter given up for adoption at birth.

as religious symbolism to indicate the influence of the church in her decision about the adoption. Her present relationships with her children figure prominently in the pictures. Her adult son is symbolized by an eagle and her daughter by a field of flowers with many lovely and intricate details to explore. Barb told the group that she felt a sense of relief after the search was over. Birthmothers' reunions with the children they have relinquished for adoption are often healing in bringing closure to their unresolved wondering about the child's fate.

Not all outcomes are as happy as Barb's, however. Joan, 38, expressed despair in locating her 22-year-old daughter. She had not met her daughter because the daughter refused to see her and claimed to have no interest in her. Joan made a collage in which she placed a woman with her back to an empty bassinet. She added the phrases "buried treasures" and "body snatcher" to the two images, respectively. "Caught in the middle" represents her ambivalence. At the bottom, in bold letters, is the word "boundaries." Joan told the group that she maintained certain boundaries in her relationships as a result of her experience with adoption. She was exploring the current usefulness of those boundaries.

The group art experience offered birthmothers an opportunity to recognize similarities and differences in their experiences and to understand one another more fully. Creating art together solidified group cohesion and provided inspiration for future work. Each participant requested that art therapy be an ongoing part of the support group.

The women who requested individual art therapy were highly motivated to deal with the effect that surrendering their children for adoption had continued to have on their lives. All described a sense of isolation and loss. They had not discussed their experiences before joining the support group.

Lynn, 34, had given up her infant son 12 years before. At the present time, she and her husband were waiting to adopt a child. The adoption process brought back memories of surrendering her son for adoption. Figure 10.6 shows a drawing she made to represent the isolation she had felt during pregnancy. She is separated from her family and friends by a chasm. The only people on her side, left, are the adoptive parents, silhouetted against a church. Raised Catholic, Lynn's unplanned out-of-wedlock pregnancy was considered sinful. Runyan notes that many of the women with whom she worked included religious imagery in their art about the adoption process. Adoptions were commonly arranged through church-affiliated organizations, and some of the birthmothers had been persuaded by clergy to give up their children. This option was often presented to the birthmother as a way to right the wrong committed in becoming pregnant. The product of the woman's transgression was thus removed to a safe and secret place. In Figure 10.7, Lynn has not included herself, only her hands holding her baby and, to the right, the adoption papers. At the upper right, the adoptive parents wait with outstretched arms, and a yellow ray of light is directed toward the child, which Lynn explained as representing hope for his well-being. Since participating in art therapy, Lynn and her husband have adopted a baby girl. They are committed to maintaining contact with the birthmother.

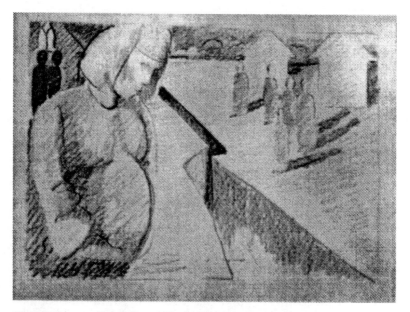

FIGURE 10.6 Depiction of isolation felt during pregnancy by woman who gave up infant for adoption.

FIGURE 10.7 Baby, adoption papers, and adoptive parents by woman who gave up infant for adoption.

Cathy, 40, had relinquished her daughter for adoption at birth when she was 22. Her collage introducing herself as a birthmother (Figure 10.8) shows Cathy in the center, pregnant, and without a head or arms. She appears again on the left, looking not happy, but not depressed, either, she said. On the right is an African sculpture of a mother and child. The father was African, and the phrase "In Black and White" refers to the child's mixed racial heritage. In another picture, Cathy drew a woman floating through an open window to represent the limited support she received during her pregnancy. She added two continents, hers and the father's, with the phrase "meeting of the bodies."

The grief that women who have given up their children at birth experience is frequently unresolved. Unlike the eventual end of mourning for a newborn lost through death, there is no finality in adoption. The birthmother may continue to wonder what has become of her child for the rest of her life. For this reason, meeting the adult child has been beneficial for many birthmothers. Giving up one's child often leads to guilt and sometimes to regret, as well. In many cases, the women were very young when they gave birth and may have been influenced by older, and supposedly wiser, respected elders.

The women with whom Runyan worked had experienced a profound sense of loss that markedly affected the rest of their lives. They found a means of expressing their feelings in their art, enabling them to understand themselves more deeply and at the same time to step back and gain perspective on their lives. Those who were adopting children themselves made commitments to maintain contact with their children's birthmothers so that those women would not have to go through the same agony of secrecy and separation.

FIGURE 10.8   Self-introduction as birthmother by woman who gave up infant for adoption.

Pregnant Women Hospitalized for Psychosis

Art therapy with pregnant women hospitalized for psychosis, most of whom also give up their babies for adoption, is very different from Angie Runyan's work. The mass deinstitutionalization of patients with mental illness in the 1960s led to a dramatic increase in the birth rate among women with chronic mental illness, and it has continued to increase since. Women with mental illness may respond to pregnancy with extreme ambivalence, noncompliance with prenatal care, psychotic denial of pregnancy, or psychotic behavior that may pose a threat to themselves and to their unborn babies.

A large university hospital with a 20-bed psychiatric unit reserves 5 beds for pregnant patients. Their length of stay is up to 4 months, and they are often readmitted for postpartum care. The patients are treated in collaboration with the obstetric, labor and delivery, neonatal, and pediatric units. Referrals are made to the psychiatric unit for episodes of mental illness that cannot be managed in outpatient treatment due to threats to the safety of the patient, of others, and especially of the fetus. Most patients suffer acute psychosis and have a history of multiple hospitalizations. Due to their pregnancies, they are maintained on the lowest possible doses of antipsychotic medication.

Joyful Freeman conducted an art therapy group for pregnant patients on the unit (Freeman, 1993). She notes that pregnancy poses a developmental challenge to the mother-to-be in accepting her pregnancy, forming an emotional attachment to the fetus, preparing for birth and mothering, and developing a reality-based perception of her infant. For the woman with mental illness, this developmental task may become increasingly problematic, especially when she is faced with the realistic likelihood that she will not be allowed to retain custody of her child. In such cases it is common for the Department of Child and Family Services (DCFS) to remove the baby from the mother's custody and place it in foster care—either temporarily, until the mother is deemed capable of caring for her infant, or permanently. Unfortunately, DCFS does not investigate the alternatives until after the child has been delivered, so it is impossible to prepare the pregnant woman for its decision. Knowing that there is the possibility that their babies will be taken from them causes these women extreme anxiety and makes their task of attaching to their unborn infant very difficult. Many respond with disinterest, anger, or psychotic denial of the pregnancy. Potential risks include lack of prenatal care, precipitous or unassisted delivery, fetal abuse, neonaticide, and postpartum emotional disturbance. Caretakers face the difficult task of helping these women to become attached to their unborn babies in order to facilitate a safe pregnancy and birth, and at the same time preparing them for the possibility of having their infants taken from them.

Freeman established the OB Art Therapy Group, scheduled to meet weekly for 45 minutes because that was the maximum time most group members could tolerate. The group included both pregnant women and those who had returned for postpartum care. If there were new members, each woman introduced herself to the group. Freeman encouraged them to propose issues to address in the group, but they were reluctant to do so. Generally, she introduced several relevant activities for the group members to choose.

When beginning treatment, each patient was asked to make a self-portrait that showed her current stage of pregnancy. A full-length mirror was provided for this purpose. Mable, an artistically talented 36-year-old woman diagnosed with Schizoaffective Disorder and Borderline Personality Disorder, had been admitted in her second trimester. She had a long DCFS history that included having her previous three children removed from her custody numerous times. It was therefore difficult for her to face the possibility of losing yet another child.

Mable had voluntarily admitted herself to the unit in a severely delusional state in order to protect her baby. When asked about her self-portrait (Figure 10.9), she became angry about the personal questions and began shouting obscenities. She calmed down when Freeman assured her that she didn't have to answer any questions she didn't want to. Freeman thought that the truncated body in Mable's picture was consonant with the fragmentation she was experiencing in relation to her pregnancy. Gradually, Mable began to express her ambivalence and fears regarding her pregnancy. She became anxious when the group turned to the subject of DCFS, and she wondered aloud if she should "kill the baby" (get an abortion) before it was taken from her.

Mable's pregnancy remained highly charged with overwhelming feelings

FIGURE 10.9   Self-portrait by pregnant patient with psychosis showing current stage of pregnancy.

of grief, anger, and despair, making it difficult for her to accept the reality of
being 5 months pregnant. Her picture of herself pregnant helped to ground
her in that reality. The art therapy group also helped her to begin expressing
her fears and concerns verbally.

Mable's later self-portrait, toward the end of her sixth month of pregnancy, is a diagram showing her increased awareness of her baby's development and individual human existence (Figure 10.10). The form at the left in

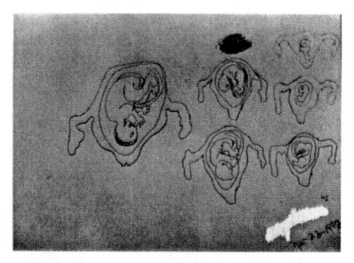

FIGURE 10.10   Fetus is more developed and individual-
ized in image drawn a month later by
woman who drew Figure 10.9.

Figure 10.10 is more recognizably human than the one depicted in Figure 10.9. Mable did not include herself, other than her reproductive system.

As Mable became more aware of her baby, she became increasingly delusional about the infant and became a less active participant in the unit's many activities. The only group she would attend was OB Art Therapy, although she would leave if the subject of losing one's child was brought up. She became painfully aware that DCFS would question her ability to care for her child, and the more attached she became to her infant, the more aware she was of the possibility of separation. In preparing for birth and motherhood, Mable drew *Dream of a Mother*, showing a bottle releasing a cloud that is the genie who will grant her wish of keeping her infant and her other three children.

As Mabel progressed into the final weeks of her pregnancy, she became even more attached to her unborn baby and focused on her dream of keeping it. Keeping her child was a motivating factor in following her treatment team's recommendations, complying with her medications, and increasing her therapy. Both her grasp of the reality of her situation and her mental condition improved. At her last art therapy group session, in response to the directive to draw herself on the day she would leave the hospital, she drew herself alone, shown from the back, taking a giant step toward a road leading over the horizon. She described it as walking by herself into an unknown future. Her ability to accept the possibility of a future by herself was a sign of her improved condition. DCFS allowed her to keep her baby. Mable made a copy of *Dream of a Mother* as a gift to the unit. On it she wrote, "Dreams Do Come True! Thanks 8-East!" (p. 25).

Anita, a 25-year-old woman diagnosed with Schizophrenia, maintained that she was not pregnant despite the visible evidence. She claimed she was gaining weight from eating sweets. She drew herself in the immature fashion of a young child's art development between the preschematic and schematic stages. Her drawing suggested the possibility of developmental delay. She was tested and was found to have mild mental retardation. In what was a breakthrough after a week of hospitalization, she drew her belly containing the fetus with very faint lines, although it was separated from the rest of her body. In a later self-portrait, she was able to connect her pregnant belly to her body. She participated in the group with Mable and identified her portrait as "more real, like Mable's." Mable's picture (Figure 10.9) served as a model to help ground Anita in reality and help her foster a connection with her unborn child. This is one example of how sharing images can enlarge a patient's experience, in this case, a sense of reality.

Lolly, a 40-year-old woman diagnosed with chronic Schizophrenia, Paranoid Type, drew herself lying on a large hospital bed, ready to deliver, and calling her doctor. She had made this picture in response to a directive to draw herself in labor. Because there is a high incidence of precipitous deliveries among women in this population, Lolly's drawing demonstrated to the treatment team that she was prepared to take responsibility for alerting the staff when she went into labor. Lolly had lost custody of her six children, but drew numerous pictures of herself with her child, such as one in which they are going to the park. Although she was able to envision giving birth and mothering the infant, she was not yet able to envision separation.

In an effort to help the women in the group organize their experiences chronologically in a life transition, which can be problematic for those with schizophrenia, Freeman asked them to make a triptych of images of themselves—in the past, before pregnancy; in the present, during pregnancy; and in the future, after the baby is born. Lolly's triptych chronicles the changes in her body as well as changes in her life. Her first panel shows her as a "pretty, skinny lady" (p. 23) with her boyfriend. The second shows the baby protruding from her belly. She titled it *After Got Pregnant No Man*. The third, after having the baby, restores her waistline but not her boyfriend, nor does she have her baby. Although Lolly's art is quite primitive, through making it she was able to integrate her experience, prepare for her delivery, and place her pregnancy in a realistic chronological context.

Suzanne Rozgonyi had conducted group art therapy with pregnant women on this unit several years earlier. She observed that women with schizophrenia can find a moving fetus so intrusive and disturbing that they deny its existence or behave in a manner dangerous to the fetus. In addition to the dangers mentioned by Joyful Freeman, Rozgonyi notes that self-induced abortions may result (Rozgonyi, 1991). Soon after a pregnant woman had been admitted to the unit, Rozgonyi would ask her to draw a full-body self-portrait in order to assess the patient's ability to organize her self-perception and sometimes her attitude toward her pregnancy. After a trusting therapeutic alliance had been formed, Rozgonyi would often ask the patient to make a life-size body tracing in order to foster an accurate self-perception during this period of bodily change. She would trace the patient's body in whatever pose the patient wanted, and then the patient would complete the picture by filling in the figure and adding a background if she wished. Margaret, a 29-year-old woman diagnosed with Schizoaffective Disorder, was the only one to choose a profile in order to show off her figure. She was also the only woman in the group who had planned her pregnancy and had found the father to be sup-

---

PSYCHOTIC REACTIONS TO PREGNANCY

- Ambivalence
- Noncompliance with prenatal care
- Denial of pregnancy
- Psychotic behavior that is dangerous to the fetus
- Self-induced abortion or neonaticide
- Precipitous or unassisted delivery
- Postpartum emotional disturbance

portive. Body tracings were Rozgonyi's patients' favorite activity. They were intent on making their features representational and often relied on a mirror to make their drawings accurate. They were pleased when others could identify them.

Sometimes perceptual distortions appeared in the artwork of the patients with psychosis. For example, Rachel, a 36-year-old woman diagnosed with Schizophrenia, Paranoid Type, drew *The Zoo* (Figure 10.11). She said she felt trapped on the unit, like an animal in a cage. She made several animals inside one another. Each time she described the picture, she named different animals, and the largest was not necessarily on the outside. Initially, she said that the outermost was a pig, and that an elephant was inside it. This drawing indicates that Rachel was confused about bodily boundaries and probably had no clear concept of her relationship with her fetus.

Many of the women in Rozgonyi's group expressed fears and anxieties about labor and childbirth. Staff members provided education and trips to the newborn nursery and the labor and delivery units to dispel misinformation. One patient was convinced that she would die during childbirth and that her child had to be killed prior to term. As was the case with Freeman's patients, the women in Rozgonyi's group also were concerned about keeping their babies. Denise, a 17-year-old hospitalized for postpartum depression two weeks after giving birth to her first child, painted a picture of herself with her baby to express her wish to be reunited with the child, who had been taken from her. Emma, another 17-year-old, was 6 months into her second

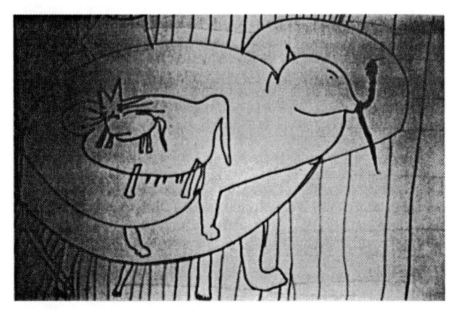

FIGURE 10.11 *The Zoo* by pregnant patient with psychosis, showing perceptual distortions.

pregnancy when she was hospitalized for psychotic behavior. Her firstborn was in foster care. Emma was well in touch with her anger when she drew Figure 10.12, *The Dead DCFS Worker*. At the top she is shooting him, and at the bottom he is in his grave. She is crying because she doesn't want to kill him and realizes that it is not his fault that she is ill and is unable to care for her children.

The pregnant women with psychosis in these groups point up a major problem in our society. Short hospitalizations don't provide the ongoing treatment these women need. They become part of the revolving-door syndrome in the mental health system, returning to the streets between admissions. They become pregnant and are unable to care for their offspring. Their grief and anger at losing their children only compound their misery. The children are placed in foster care, often being shifted from one home to another. Many become the troubled children and adolescents who populate the special schools and treatment centers described elsewhere in this book. Drugs, violence, and crime are a way of life for many members of this population. These children grow up to become the next wave of adults to pass through the revolving doors of the mental health system. At present, there are few hopeful signs of imaginative planning to intervene in what has become a most vicious cycle that is placing an enormous drain on both our economic and human resources.

FIGURE 10.12 *The Dead DCFS Worker* by pregnant patient with psychosis fearful of losing her baby to DCFS.

Prostitution

Another problem that grows out of poverty, the drug culture, and physical and sexual abuse is prostitution. In Chicago alone, an estimated 35,000 to 40,000 women are engaged in prostitution, not including those under 18 who are soliciting on the streets. In working with members of this population, Beth Black notes that the words used to refer to prostitutes—*whore, slut, tramp*—are uniformly derogatory, and little attention is given to the human beings who wear the title (Black, 1994). Black worked at a home founded by a missionary in 1984 to provide shelter and support for women who wanted to give up prostitution. The home operated for both crisis intervention and long-term care, with drop-in as well as residential services. Its goals were to provide the following services:

- Shelter, clothing, food, and support for women seeking refuge
- Long-term residential treatment for women seeking to leave the life of prostitution
- Education and awareness about safe sex and drugs
- A voice both locally and nationally to raise awareness of the issues of prostitution and to change the political, legal, and social systems that help to perpetuate prostitution

The house arranges for substance abuse treatment and coordinates with other agencies to find alternative housing and shelter for women who have completed a detoxification program. During the 18-month residential stay, the women attend Narcotics Anonymous and Prostitutes Anonymous meetings weekly, in addition to receiving various other support services. Many are helped to finish the requirements for a high school diploma or college degree and to find a new way of life.

POST-TRAUMATIC STRESS DISORDER (PTSD) AND RELATED PROBLEMS FOR PROSTITUTES

- Low self-esteem
- Depression
- Dissociation
- Leaving body when turning a trick
- Suicidal ideation
- Shame
- Stigma of prostitution
- Complications of arrest records
- Drop in income when moving to other jobs

Black began art therapy at the house by offering both crisis and long-term residents a structured program. She had intended to schedule tasks of exploring sexuality and making self-portraits and life-size body drawings in both individual and group art therapy. The women were resistant and informed Black that they did not speak about themselves to one another. Black scheduled individual sessions in which she gathered background information. She discovered that of the 27 women with whom she would eventually work, all had a history of sexual abuse beginning when they entered puberty at age 12 or 13. The perpetrator in all cases except one was the woman's father. In the exception, it was her mother. All had been homeless and all had polysubstance addictions. All claimed to leave their bodies when they turned a trick. Black observed various symptoms associated with Post-Traumatic Stress Disorder (PTSD)—low self-esteem, depression, dissociation, and suicidal ideation. Recovery was one of the greatest challenges of their lives, including as it did battling substance addiction, reconstructing lost memories of childhood, and finding a new career. The latter often meant accepting work at wages far below what they had been earning as prostitutes. For many there were the complications of arrest records, the stigma of prostitution, and enormous shame and pain.

On the first day of group art therapy, no one came. Black took some art materials out to the backyard and made a mask. One by one, the women became intrigued by what she was doing, and soon four were making masks of their own. Black had felt like a failure and had made a mask as a symbolic form of protection, a way to hide. The women appeared to need this sort of protection, too, to keep themselves at a distance, to defend against vulnerability. One woman named her mask Mozart. It represented her musical talent, which she had hoped to use after she graduated from high school. She explained that a man had stolen all the songs she had written, and as a result, she had become a drug addict. Black felt that the woman, like the other women in the group, wanted to be seen for her abilities rather than as the stereotype of an addict and a prostitute. Black found it necessary to learn about the individual masks before she could come to know the women further. The women had spent many years hiding their true selves. Most had kept their prostitution secret from their families. The subculture of prostitution does not allow for trust, as competition for territory and dates erodes the likelihood of trust among peers. One woman said, "We are hookers, liars, and thieves" (p. 12).

An initial goal of art therapy was to build trust in the group members, both among each other and within themselves. But even in individual sessions, pictures portrayed trees and birds, not feelings. If by chance a woman did reveal anything in her art, she would scribble over it with an explanation that she hadn't meant to draw that. The women usually destroyed their art, including, in one case, a card a woman had made for herself in honor of having maintained sobriety for 3 months.

Black had thought that her group would continue after the mask-making incident. But once again, no one came. On one occasion, the house director mandated attendance. Seven women came begrudgingly. They were calm while making the art, personalized paper dolls from enlarged Polaroid photos, a project that Black hoped would foster integration of the self. But when it was time for discussion, the tension rose, and the group became chaotic. Black was aware that the root of the tension was lack of trust within the group and fear of self-disclosure. She also noticed that the group was divided, with the residents forming one faction and the women in crisis, who came and went, another. Their issues and commitment to change were at very different stages. As a result, she divided them into two separate groups in order to promote group cohesion in each.

Nevertheless, Black felt that she needed to provide opportunities for the women of both groups to interact with one another. She also wanted to give them as much control over their art as possible so that their apprehensions regarding it would decrease. Toward these ends, she established an open studio. The women could come and go as they pleased and make whatever projects they wanted. This format was far more successful than the others she had tried. If a woman wanted individual sessions, she could request them week by week.

Recognizing that initiation into adulthood at an early age and the painful loss of childhood were common themes, Black worked on creating a piece from her own childhood, a stuffed cat made from an old sock. She left it in the studio. At the next open studio session, Gwen, a resident, asked Black to show her how to make a doll, too. In only a few minutes, all five women present were busy making dolls. They were stuffed with batting from old pillows and decorated with buttons and yarn. Clothes were made from patterns drawn by hand and cut from fabric. The dolls' significance to issues of childhood, mothering, nurturing, and femininity broke down barriers of distrust and competition. The women shared supplies, patterns, ideas, and help. All the dolls turned out to be female. The soft fabric objects allowed the women an opportunity to show their tender, caring sides without feeling ashamed or intimidated. They spoke of and to their dolls tenderly, carried them on their shoulders or placed them in their laps, never left them behind, and made certain they were safe. Clearly, the women identified with their dolls and gave them the care they had not received themselves. The dolls also led the women to tell stories of their childhood and to express their feelings about body image. Making the clothing promoted discussions of fashion and what they wore on the streets.

Gwen, 46, had attended only one art therapy session, always having an excuse to miss her individual sessions. She had become involved in prostitution when she was 16, and she had a history of alcohol and cocaine abuse and arrests for shoplifting. She spent 4 hours making her doll (Figure 10.13), talking to it as herself as she worked on it: "Now Gwen, your legs are too thin . . . you're acting like a whore . . . you need to put some clothes on" (p. 22). When asked about her experience, Gwen said, "The only thing I've ever completed in my life was a good high. Now I've completed this doll and I am proud of it. . . . It's the first time in my life I've ever done anything artistic. I never

FIGURE 10.13   Female doll by formerly resistant woman at shelter for prostitutes.

thought I could" (p. 23). Nor had she ever sewn before. Later, she called her doll "the whore and drug addict." Gwen's first doll gave her the confidence to make some more. Her second doll portrayed her ethnic side. It was more complicated, with African clothes. Her third doll was even more complex (Figure 10.14). This doll is a male, with removable clothes fastened with snaps and buttons. As Gwen worked on her successive dolls, she examined aspects of her own identity, speaking of herself as a mother in relation to the first one, as an African American in relation to the second, and about her relationships with men in relation to the third.

Melanie, a 30-year-old woman who had tried unsuccessfully to quit prostitution three times, had a college education. In art therapy she drew pleasant pictures of flowers, stating that they expressed the way she felt—just fine. Her doll was the monkey she had wanted to have as a child. She named him Marvin and would speak through him, saying such things as, "Marvin is sad today . . . Marvin had bad dreams last night of being hurt" (p. 28). Melanie had been sexually and physically abused by her mother. Two months after making the monkey, Melanie came to Black with a request to make a quilt. Black had been discussing ways of making a personal quilt with the women. Figure 10.15 shows the square Melanie made to represent her addiction. She is

FIGURE 10.14   Male doll by woman who
made doll in Figure 10.13.

FIGURE 10.15   Quilt panel by prostitute representing flames of addiction in her life
story.

being consumed in flames. She explained that one reason she had entered prostitution was that on one level it made her feel loved. She said she became obsessed with needing to feel this way and had become addicted to sex, drugs, money, and danger. Figure 10.16 shows a scene from her childhood—she and her best friend are about to ride their new bikes. When the two grew up, they became engaged, but he died. Melanie created the square on the twelfth anniversary of his death. Another square showed a bedroom that had been a safe place when she was a child. A final square showed another bedroom, this time a hotel room she used for prostitution, with money scattered on the floor. The sheets are wrinkled, and a Bible rests on the nightstand. The quilt took Melanie many weeks to make. There were times when she avoided the painful scenes. The quilt's planning, execution, and completion allowed Melanie to gain a perspective on her life, to understand how one decision led to another, to integrate the various aspects of her life, and, finally, to come to terms with who she was and how she got to be the person she was. The project took patience and dedication. It was a story of her life of which she could be proud.

It was through her own art that Black initially connected with the women of the house. Her response of making a doll grew spontaneously out of what she perceived as the women's lost childhoods. Fabric is a traditional medium for women. The slow and repetitive process of sewing can be very soothing. Working together gave the group the feeling of a traditional quilting bee, hardly the usual activity for women who have engaged in prostitution.

Teresa Walker also utilized fabric art in working with this population. She helped the women examine issues of self-image through making wearable art (Walker, 1993). Supplying donated clothing, Walker encouraged the women to select what they wanted and decorate the clothing to suit themselves. After mounting a mirror on a larger wood backing and decorating it for a frame,

FIGURE 10.16   Quilt panel by woman who made panel in Figure 10.15 of childhood scene with deceased fiancée.

Melba made an "anger vest." Melba used fabric paint on the vest. At first, she had planned butterflies, but became frustrated and turned them into "the birds from hell." A red cloud represents hell. She painted it in a frenzy and seemed to experience a catharsis from making it. Melba was proud of her vest and told others about making it. She didn't think she would wear it, however. On a black T-shirt, Melba painted an Indian goddess of protection. She worked on it diligently, explaining that she was part Cherokee. She would wear this one, she said, or perhaps frame it. Subsequently, Melba chose a slice of tree trunk that had once been a clock from the found-objects box. She painted it to represent her web of addictions. There is a very tiny figure at the far right that appears to have escaped the web.

Ximena Salomon focused on the chemical addictions of women with a history of prostitution (Salomon, 1992). Nevertheless, she dealt with all their recovery issues in her work with them at the residence. Most came from backgrounds of extreme poverty and in some cases had used prostitution to support their drug habits. Many had been referred to an outpatient facility for substance abuse treatment. At the time she worked with them, the women had been staying at the residence for 6 months to 2 years.

The examples shown here are by women who had been in recovery from addiction for at least 18 months. They were more open to exploring their personal issues in their drawings than were the initially resistant women previously discussed. An important focus of the art therapy for them was the exploration of self-image. Val, a 32-year-old woman with two children, drew a self-portrait that reminded her of her anorexic episodes as she noticed her ill-defined body representation. Tears stream from the eyes. She drew black around the figure to represent the feelings of emptiness and emotional entrapment within her own body "when [her] wall goes up," she said (p. 16). One of her goals in treatment was to form more realistic views of relationships. Val came from a chaotic family of alcoholics and tended to idealize present relationships in an effort to create a "normal" family. Figure 10.17 shows her final good-bye to an emotionally abusive ex-husband. He is the bottom figure with green oozing from his mouth. At the top, right, is his "normal" self that she idealized, despite his responsibility for some major tragedies in her life. Her children are represented by the small heads, and she has portrayed herself as a smiling angel, denying her anger. She continued to use the art to give form to her feelings, and as she did so, her confidence in her abilities increased.

Dawn became involved in prostitution in order to sustain a drug habit. She had been married to an ex-convict who had physically abused her severely. He also used her earnings from prostitution for his own drug habit. At the time she was at the residence, he was in prison, and during her stay she divorced him. She represented herself with an enclosed bleeding heart that is surrounded by forces that compel her to protect herself. This picture, completed early in her treatment, became a focal point for Dawn's exploration of her role and responsibility in relationships. It also helped her to look at her own needs. Dawn progressed well in treatment and was able to get a peer

FIGURE 10.17   Woman's depiction of final good-
bye to emotionally abusive hus-
band.

counselor certificate, which had been a priority she was able to establish in her
therapy.

Salomon observes that the popularity of 12-step programs has resulted in
an absence of other approaches to recovering from chemical dependency. Noting the fundamental therapeutic premise of treating clients at their particular
stage of psychological development, she found 12-step programs to be limited
by their adherence to an unchanging structure.

The women wanting to give up prostitution with whom Black, Walker,
and Salomon worked were people living in desperate straits. Coming from
backgrounds of poverty and, often, violence and abuse, they had sought
refuge in drugs. Most lacked training in career skills and resorted to prostitution to support their habits. Some had arrest records as well. Seeking recovery
from substance abuse and training for a career change required great dedication, effort, and commitment. Making the change necessitated more than sim-

ply giving up previous habits. The women underwent changes in their sense of self, which required that they explore their lives and the influences that had directed them toward drugs and prostitution. Art therapy facilitated both this exploration of the past and support for an emerging new sense of self.

Battered Women

According to Stephanie Haddon (1989), conservative estimates put the number of women beaten by husbands or boyfriends in the United States during a single year at 12 million. In developing an art therapy program for a battered women's shelter, she used the art to help the women meet the following goals:

- Reorganize their lives during a time of crisis.
- Overcome the effects of victimization.
- Learn about domestic violence.
- Tap into personal resources for support and healing.

The shelter provided emergency housing for women and their children seeking refuge from an abuser. It was a safe place for women who lacked the financial, family, or community resources necessary to leave an abusive situation on their own. They stayed for periods ranging from 1 night to 3 months. Most of the women were from lower socioeconomic groups and were, therefore, in need of financial assistance, legal advocacy, and employment, as well as counseling and emotional support. Many of the women were depressed and lacking in motivation when introduced to art therapy. They entered the shelter at a time of crisis, and their immediate priorities were concrete and external—legal advocacy, employment, and childcare. Most were not ready for art therapy until they had made some attempt at restructuring their lives.

Initially, Haddon set up a weekly half-hour morning group session to motivate the women to use their day constructively and to introduce them to art therapy in a nonthreatening way. The art tasks, therefore, were brief, enjoyable, and easy to master. Haddon was fearful at first that this design might trivialize art therapy, but the women enjoyed the relaxed atmosphere as well as the art making. Those who were highly motivated in art therapy were given individual sessions. These often focused on family relations, so, when indicated, Haddon included the women's children, as well. Haddon also incorporated art therapy into a weekly support group for residents and walk-in clients who had left or were considering leaving an abuser. The group focused on the concepts of the cycle of violence and the abuser's power and control. Through the articulation of these concepts, the women were educated toward the goal of empowerment. The artwork allowed them to express painful feelings that might not have been acknowledged otherwise. The power of the image could make the reality of their experience concrete and lessen the likelihood of their minimizing the intensity of their abuse in the future. Art making served a cathartic purpose as well, giving the women a safe way to release their anger.

It was clear to Haddon that the women were seeking an opportunity to ventilate their rage. This became evident in their interest in inviting a man to the group, presumably to find out what made him abuse a woman. Because men were not allowed in the shelter, Haddon supplied a life-size papier-mâché man. This project grew out of Lagorio's work (Wadeson, Durkin, & Perach, 1989). First, the group members were asked to list the characteristics of their abusers. They named the following: liar, jealous, possessive, insecure, unfaithful, and violent. They were then asked to express these characteristics with papier-mâché or paint. The figure was then introduced for them to work on. They created facial features, including "a big red mouth for all the lies he tells" (p. 12), and a question mark at the top to ask if he has a brain (Figure 10.18). Marie, a woman who had contemplated homicide before escaping from her abuser, made a papier-mâché dagger and stuck it in the ribs. She added a black heart for his evil, a chain in his hand for his need to control her, muscles for

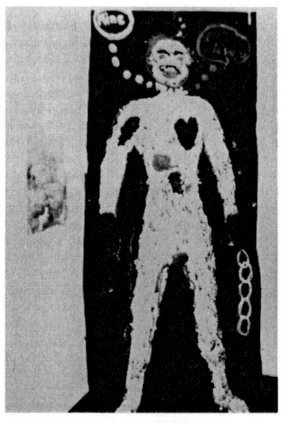

FIGURE 10.18 Life-size papier-mâché man to which battered women added characteristics of their abusers.

physical strength, and boxing gloves for his propensity to fight. "I love you" and "mine" are written in balloons to indicate his possessiveness and jealousy. Jan, who seldom spoke in groups, carefully constructed a wire and papier-mâché penis, which she painted red to represent her blood. She attached it and said, "That's what he did to me" (p. 13). Afterward, she told the group several times how great she felt. When they had finished with the man, the group members wanted to move on to *their* needs and leave the abuser behind. Sharing this very intense experience with one another made the catharsis even more beneficial.

The cycle of violence concept posits that battering follows a predictable course from the *tension-building phase* to the *battering incident*, ending with *loving contrition*, often referred to as the *honeymoon phase*. Then the cycle begins again. Haddon asked the women to make drawings representing what the cycle was like for them. Her purpose was to help them appraise their relationships by recognizing the phases they experienced and assessing whether the benefits of the honeymoon phase were worth the battering. She hoped that the women would ultimately confront their own minimization of the abuse they had suffered. Sandy drew the violence as a thick black ring around her relationship, inside which she was trapped (Figure 10.19). Inside is a tropical paradise, representing the honeymoon phase. At the center is the worst part for her, the tension-building phase, represented by two smoking volcanoes that will eventually erupt. Puzzle pieces around the volcanoes depict her confusion during the tension, in which anything she did could unleash her hus-

FIGURE 10.19   Cycle of violence by resident of a shelter for battered women.

band's rage. She told the group of how her coming home late because of a flat tire had triggered an acute incident of battering by her husband. Other group members empathized and shared similar experiences. Another member drew a cannon shooting a cannonball. She had been very quiet in the group and needed much encouragement to participate. Her picture enabled her to reveal for the first time that her abuser had shot her. She received much support from the group and became more open with the other women. Others spoke of their fears of being killed, as well.

Ambivalence about leaving an abuser is a common phenomenon. Most women leave six times before they effect a permanent separation. June, an Asian woman who had difficulty with English, had come to the United States only 5 months prior to entering the shelter. Haddon saw her in individual art therapy. Her cultural background encouraged imitation rather than original expression in art and discouraged self-revelation. Haddon did not push her, and in time she became more expressive in her art. June used clay to make a family sculpture of her husband, her baby, and herself. She manipulated their positions to show their present relationships and how she wanted them to be. At first they were close, and she spoke of the happy reunion she would have with her husband. Later, she discovered that he had deceived her about child custody, and she made a collage with a nativity scene to express her agony regarding her custody battle. When confronted with her clay figures standing together, she grabbed the figure of her husband, broke it, and threw it in the garbage. She was finally resolved to leave him. She placed the figures of herself and her child together and took them with her to keep. June had used her art to overcome her language barrier and to express her emotions. She had also learned that others could accept her anger.

Battered women often suffer greater depression after they have left an abusive relationship than while they are in it. The women in the shelter needed to mourn the loss of their relationships, their role identity, and their security. Loneliness, fatigue, grief, and depression were common among them. Tina drew *Old Man* (Figure 10.20), with whom she identified. She saw loneliness, isolation, and hopelessness in him. Like him, she felt cold and far from home. Having decided not to return to her abuser and her child, she was facing up to her grief at losing them. Haddon notes that grief is usually the most

---

CYCLE OF VIOLENCE FOR BATTERED WOMEN

- Tension-building phase
- Battering incident
- Honeymoon phase of loving contrition
- Repetition of cycle

FIGURE 10.20 Woman's depiction of loneliness, isolation, and hopelessness identified with separation from abuser.

suppressed of all emotions for women who have left an abuser. Society, she states, expects them to be angry and relieved, not grief stricken.

Marie used art to move from a position of victimization to empowerment. In an early picture she drew herself as armless and behind bars. A gun represents a failed attempt to protect herself with a weapon. She titled the picture *Hate* and wrote "burns, no escape, scars, low self-esteem, murder" on it. In a later picture, she drew herself and her daughter among trees carrying balloons. Another image of herself, this time with arms, is seated in front of bars. Marie usually presented herself with a tough exterior, confident and aggressive. She dropped her tough façade to show another image of herself crying. Nevertheless, she covered it with a black sheet of paper, but then cut a door in it, through which the crying face can be seen. Although she still showed her strong side most of the time, she could allow her vulnerability to be seen selectively by those who helped her to be more open. Marie was proud of her visual expressiveness. It showed her that she had choices and didn't have to remain imprisoned by her abuser.

Like the women leaving prostitution, women leaving an abuser are taking an enormous step in reordering their lives. Many have young dependent children and few resources for support. Art therapy can help them to confront these painful realities and set about restructuring their lives. Particularly significant for them is the anger they have and the opportunity to ventilate it in a safe way that art can provide. (Work with children in shelters for battered women and children, is discussed in Chapter 3, "Outpatient, Shelter, and Residential Treatment.")

Homeless Women and Social Protest

Even women who are among the most disadvantaged in our society can use their art for social protest against the conditions under which they live. Jean Durkin established art therapy at a shelter for homeless women in 1987. Its several centers offer both day programs and transitional living arrangements. The main facility serves 30 to 40 women daily. Many of them suffer from mental illness, poor physical health, and substance abuse. Art therapy is central to the agency's life, though practiced differently than in most settings. There are no art therapy sessions as such. Art materials and a large space to work in are always available, and the women make art as they choose. The walls are decorated with art made by the women (see Figure 9.8). (Art therapy at this facility is discussed further in Chapter 9, "Displaced Persons.")

Durkin sees her own mission as an art therapist as extending beyond the individuals and groups with whom she works to the neighborhood, the city, and, hopefully, to the world at large (personal communication, 1999). The benefits of joining others in making and exhibiting art for social awareness and protest have been substantial for the women with whom Durkin works, for the student interns she supervises, and for herself.

Durkin recognizes that "having hundreds of supportive onlookers applaud and praise the art you have created is a rare experience for anyone," but she and her clients have had that experience at rallies and marches. Although she is aware of the dangers in the unpredictability of crowd reactions at such events, she has seen significant therapeutic benefits in planning, preparing for, and participating in these social action demonstrations.

Each year her agency supports an annual march and rally sponsored by a peace and justice organization and supported by approximately 50 other such organizations. The nineteenth annual march and rally was held on Good Friday using the 10 stations of the cross as a model, with each station highlighting a social justice issue. Durkin and her group created a station to highlight women's rights. More than 20 of the women worked on the preparations. They wanted to focus on several issues: the right to appreciate all women as beautiful, the right to walk safely in the streets at night, the right to receive equitable pay, the right to live without verbal abuse, and the right to have better communication between genders. Seven panels representing these issues were created from weatherproof materials: acrylic paints, felt, and found objects applied to 3- by 4-foot pieces of muslin. They were edged in green and sewn together to form a 3- by 30-foot banner that could be folded together like a map and then unfurled dramatically.

The banner was begun with the central panel, depicting the beauty of women. Durkin drew seven ovals on the unprimed muslin surface after securing it to the table with masking tape. She started to paint a face in one of the ovals. She was soon joined by three of the women and one of her interns. They painted together and discussed what makes women beautiful. Durkin often engages the women in this nonverbal way by simply beginning a project;

others then join her. They painted faces of women of various ages and ethnic backgrounds showing different emotions. Another woman had her own ideas about the verbal abuse panel, so Durkin followed her lead. The women planned it carefully, drawing some of the parts on paper first. Because of its success, this woman then felt confident enough to work on the equitable pay panel with minimal help on the rough draft design. Another woman needed only a little help in making the image of a woman walking alone at night without fear. This image had special significance to the participants, as several women had recently been murdered in the neighborhood. They began accompanying each other when walking from the shelter at night.

At the rally, it was a big moment when a dozen of the women unrolled the banner before hundreds of supportive onlookers (Figure 10.21). One of the woman spoke into a microphone, calling out a reading she had composed, to which the others and the crowd responded:

Seventh Station: Jesus Meets His Mother
READER   This is our vision: A world where women step out after dark and go where we want free of attack and the fear of attack.
ALL   This is our vision.
READER   A world where women embrace and celebrate our bodies and selves, free of society's demands that we mutilate our bodies, emotions, and spirits.
ALL   This is our vision.

FIGURE 10.21   Thirty-foot banner made by homeless women to rally for women's rights.

READER   A world where women receive a just wage for our work, free of sexual harassment and economic exploitation.
ALL   This is our vision.
READER   How will we make our vision a reality?
ALL   By learning to respect each other as equals. By looking for the beauty in each other. By putting our gifts together and working as one. By supporting each other.
READER   Women united in sisterhood stand strong!
ALL   This is our vision.

The woman who wrote and led the call and response said, "The reason I led it so good was because it was from my heart. . . . The experience gave me more confidence to do things. My favorite word when I was growing up was 'I can't.' The experience helped my self-esteem. . . . It's one of the many things I'm doing for myself. I'm going to school. I'll get my GED. . . . Then I'll be ready for the Career Exploration Class. I'm seeing a therapist. She helps me."

Art such as this banner is both therapeutic and political. It is a significant expression for the artists, comparable to the individual expressions of grief in the AIDS Names Quilt, and it is a political statement made to the society at large in an empowering effort to bring about social change. The AIDS Names Quilt is a good example of collective individual art that has made a difference. Women, even the most disadvantaged, can find a voice and rally for their rights. Art made in the service of social protest is a piece of the whole in helping women to change their lives and change their world.

Summary

Although women are discussed throughout the book, this chapter focuses on issues that are unique to women. The chapter begins with well-functioning middle-class women, including those facing the predictable life transition that menopause brings; moves toward women living under drastic circumstances; and ends with women subjected to domestic violence and homeless women demonstrating for social justice. (Because childhood sexual abuse is so prevalent in the backgrounds of adult women, a separate chapter is devoted to that subject.)

This chapter and Chapter 11 demonstrate the enormity of the societal problems women face. Art therapy can be effective in helping women to identify their own feelings, the sources of their oppression, and resources for restructuring their lives. The art activity can become a cathartic vehicle for the ventilation of rage, and the art therapy group provides a context of support and understanding for the sharing of images of deep personal pain. Art can also join women (and others) in rallying for social change to eliminate oppression.

The material presented here covers the following issues:

- Nancy Biederman (1988) formed an art therapy group for women facing difficulties with menopause, including physical problems, fears about aging, and relationships with others. The group was both educational and supportive.

- Angie Runyan (1992) provided art therapy for members of a support group for women who had given up children for adoption. Some were working on relationships with these now-adult children.
- Joyful Freeman (1993) and Suzanne Rozgonyi (1991) formed art therapy groups for pregnant women with psychosis on a hospital psychiatric unit. Some of the women had delusions about their unborn children. Most were evaluated as being unfit to care for their babies, who were then placed in foster care. Grief over the loss of their children was a salient issue for these women.
- Beth Black (1994), Teresa Walker (1993), and Ximena Salomon (1992) provided art therapy at a shelter for women with a history of prostitution. Most came from backgrounds of poverty, sexual abuse, and chemical dependency. Working with fabric, creating dolls, quilts, and clothing, was beneficial for many, as was using the art to confront their substance abuse.
- Stephanie Haddon (1989) designed an art therapy program for a shelter for battered women and children. The women used art to ventilate their anger at their abusers, to examine the cycle of violence they had experienced, to deal with their ambivalence regarding leaving their abusers, and to move from victimization to empowerment.
- Jean Durkin (personal communication, 1999) worked with residents of a shelter for homeless women to create a 30-foot banner on women's rights, which they carried in a social justice demonstration, accompanied by a related reading.

Conclusion

For the most part, the women presented in this chapter are dealing with severe problems, not of a strictly psychiatric or internal nature, but rather resulting from societal oppression. Even the relatively well off women having difficulty with menopause discussed at the beginning of the chapter have suffered the subtle prejudices against aging women in our culture. Although art therapy can be beneficial to women who have lived under oppressive circumstances, clearly the major challenge facing our society is in prevention. Poverty, violence, crime, and drugs are so intricately interwoven in our culture, along with the victimization of women connected with them, that it will take major changes in societal values and in the availability of resources for the less advantaged to bring about the massive improvement that is needed. In our present climate of budgetary constrictions, too many of the women with whom art therapists work return to the environments that caused their oppression. (For further discussion of work specific to art therapy with women, see Hogan, 1997.)

ART THERAPY PROJECTS

Projects discussed in this chapter are described further in Chapter 15, "Art Activities and Materials":

- Collage (Biederman, 1998; Runyan, 1992)
- Quilting (Biederman, 1998; Black, 1994)
- Sock dolls (Black, 1994)
- Wearable art and clothing (Walker, 1993)
- Banners (Durkin, personal communication, 1999)

Chapter 11

Sexual Abuse

Strong woman photographed by incest and rape survivor.

Pam sits still and quiet, her eyes glazed but seeing more than the blank paper before her. Slowly she dips the brush in water and soaks the paper. She adds a puddle of blue and rims it with a ragged black edge. Coating the brush with as much red as it will hold, she splatters the painting. The colors bleed together as the tears stream down her face.

The once secret shame and denial of sexual abuse has become the focus of scrutiny and controversy in recent years. Sexual abuse takes many forms, from incest suffered during childhood to rape in adulthood. It may be a one-time incident or a recurring experience. The abuse may be violent or more subtly coercive. As is now common knowledge, it is more about power than sex. The perpetrator may be a trusted adult, such as a parent, or a stranger. Date rape has become a relatively common phenomenon among adolescents and young adults. In the past, children who complained of sexual abuse were frequently disbelieved, and females of all ages were often blamed for enticing those who victimized them sexually. Males were let off the hook with a general "boys will be boys" attitude or a belief that their sexual passion was uncontrollable in the face of female allurements.

Statistics regarding the occurrence of sexual abuse are unreliable because so many instances go unreported. Nevertheless, it is estimated that 1 out of every 5 to 7 women and 1 out of every 7 men have been sexually assaulted before the age of 18 (Voices in Action, 1985). The aftereffects of sexual assault often result in Post-Traumatic Stress Disorder (PTSD) and may include depression and disassociation. Reports of repressed memories have led to the concept of *false memory syndrome*, a very controversial issue—therapists have been taken to court for allegedly suggesting to clients who previously had no memory of such events that they were victims of childhood sexual abuse. Conflict within both the therapeutic and legal communities has raged as professionals have taken sides "believing the children," on one hand, and defending "wrongly accused" parents, on the other.

Private Practice

When I first began seeing clients privately, they did not present histories of childhood sexual abuse. In more recent years, however, many have done so. I believe the difference is that more women with such histories now feel validated and supported in their efforts to deal with the trauma and aftereffects of abuse, rather than being hushed or disbelieved. Art therapy has become a voice for many clients who have had experiences they could not articulate in words. The clients I have seen have come into therapy with full recollections of their experiences, so there was never any issue of false memory syndrome. In only one case did more memories surface during treatment. This was a woman whose father had molested her for a number of years, beginning when she was very young. Making art brought back memories of ritual abuse, as well. She had made art on her own before coming into art therapy, but as the memories surfaced, making art became too frightening for her while she was alone, so during this period she confined her art making to our sessions.

Another survivor of ritual abuse used the art to create elaborate rituals to ventilate her anger. In one, she made clay figures of her perpetrators, cut off their penises, threw them down the stairs at her home, and put the pieces in her kitty litter box.

Although girls are the primary victims of childhood sexual abuse, I have seen several men who were abused as children, as well. One, molested by a neighbor in early adolescence, became a perpetrator himself, estimating that he had had sex with approximately 50 little boys. (A discussion of art therapy for perpetrators follows in this chapter.) Another client, who had been forced to have sex with an older brother, used the art well to express his depression and to deal with his sexual conflicts.

The survivors of sexual abuse I have seen privately have all been very bright, and many have held highly responsible positions. Nevertheless, most had considerable relationship difficulties, finding it hard to trust anyone. Others were not able to function very well. One believed that almost everyone she met was a member of a cult and therefore posed a danger to her. Another was suicidal. Many suffered Borderline Personality Disorder, and as a result, the people in their lives shifted rapidly from being perceived as saviors to being seen as evil. I was one in a long chain of therapists for these clients. The work with some of these clients is so very intense and demanding that it is difficult for a therapist to work with more than a few of them at any one period of time.

Rape

Although I have worked with a few women who have been raped, they had not sought art therapy with me specifically to deal with issues of rape. Despite the horrific nature of the rape experience, which left a significant aftermath in their lives, the therapeutic work related to the rape experience was very much embedded in their total treatment. Ann McCullough, however, has conducted art therapy with women who had sought treatment specifically for rape counseling (McCullough, 1991). McCullough provided art therapy at a rape crisis center to which clients were referred by hospitals after an assault. Other clients sought counseling there because a recent event had triggered memories of rape which led to a crisis.

McCullough notes that rape is unique in the "privatized" nature of the violence, in which sex is the weapon used to assert power over the victim (p. 4). Its context is a sexist society in which power is distributed unequally along lines of gender, race, and class. It is most frequently perpetrated on women by men. In McCullough's experience, art expression enables rape survivors to refocus from what happened during and after the assault to the significance these events held for them. Survivors struggle with issues of loss, guilt, shame, trust, humiliation, helplessness, fear, anger, sexuality, and changes in values and the perception of self, especially along lines of vulnerability. Naturally, these issues differ from client to client, depending on many factors, such as how long ago the rape occurred, previous experience of victimization, and the nature of the rape itself. Art therapy provides a visual validation of the client's experience and helps her to regain a feeling of control of her own life. During a period of disruption of a sense of self and the loss of a sense of safety, the process of creating images can furnish a container for the chaotic emotions that often follow in the aftermath of rape.

Wanda, a 26-year-old woman who had been raped at college by an ex-boyfriend when she would not accept his proposal of marriage, had sought redress by asking the college to reprimand him. It did not do so. Three years later, when she told her mother of the assault, her mother replied that she probably deserved it. She entered counseling because the trial of a man who had raped a friend was approaching, and her own fear and anger were reactivated. She wanted to feel more in control of her feelings. Initially, she discussed herself very intellectually and drew a courtroom, which she described quite logically as reflecting her experience of the trial of the man who had raped her friend. She did not express her feelings. McCullough directed her toward using looser media and making abstract images. She asked Wanda not to tell her what she thought about her picture, but just to describe it. If she had a thought, she should express it visually first. This was a slow process that eventually became a way for Wanda to access and express her emotions. She painted an image representing her anger. At first she spoke of it as frustration, but after making the picture she began to explore its source. She traced it back to feeling powerless as a child, as well as to being a rape victim. At the end of

---

RAPE SURVIVORS' ISSUES

- Shame
- Guilt
- Loss
- Humiliation
- Sense of helplessness
- Fear
- Anger
- Changes in sexual desire
- Changes in values
- Changes in perception of self, especially regarding vulnerability
- Loss of a sense of safety

her course of art therapy, she commented that she had learned to accept herself more by making art.

Twenty-four year old Susan had been raped by a stranger who broke into her apartment. She did not see him and was unable to identify his voice in a police lineup. Her family and friends stopped talking about the rape shortly after the media coverage ceased. Susan was referred to the center by the hospital where she had been treated for the rape. She said that she thought it should affect her, but it didn't. Her problems, she said, were in telling others about it and in being unproductive at work. Susan was unable to get in touch with the impact the rape had had on her until a friend died of AIDS. She drew an image representing her sadness. She showed bad things taking pieces out of her and buckets of tears. She said that it was easier for her to draw her feelings than to talk about them. For most of McCullough's clients, art therapy was a means of identifying, validating, and controlling their chaotic feelings following the rape.

Alexandria Elliot-Prisco, a photographer herself, utilized photography in art therapy with rape victims (Elliot-Prisco, 1995). She was the primary therapist for women and children at a not-for-profit agency for counseling and crisis intervention. All her clients had been sexually abused in childhood. At 24, Margaret had kept two rapes by an acquaintance when she was 13 secret for 11 years. She had seen two male therapists 7 months prior to her work with Elliot-Prisco, but had found it too difficult to reveal the rapes to them because of their gender. She appeared to be depressed. At her fourth session, Elliot-Prisco introduced phototherapy, using a single-lens reflex 35-mm camera and black-and-white film. Figure 11.1 shows Margaret's photographic self-portrait prior to the rapes, a tightly closed pink rosebud. Margaret related the color pink to a little girl's fragility. She said that the rose never bloomed and that she became an old dead flower after the rapes. Indeed, Margaret looked old beyond her years, with a withered appearance. She had felt neglected as a child and had never disclosed the rapes to her parents. After disclosing the rapes to Elliot-Prisco through her photographs, she developed the strength to tell her husband and to let him know her needs. Through her therapy, she began to demonstrate an increasing capacity to trust herself and others and to experience greater self-sufficiency.

Incest

Alexandria Elliot-Prisco (1995) also used photography in art therapy with incest survivors. Donna, 39, who had been in therapy most of her adult life, had been molested by her maternal grandmother at age 5 and by her stepfather from age 8 to 11. At 15 she had been raped by an acquaintance, and at 16 she had an abortion. When she discovered that she was pregnant for the second time, she had married her high school boyfriend, and she now had a daughter, age 18. Donna suffered chronic depression; had been hospitalized three times,

FIGURE 11.1 Self-image photographed by rape survivor who felt she had never bloomed.

the last two for suicide attempts; and currently suffered isolation, interpersonal difficulties, fear of intimacy, and sexual dysfunction. She hoped to gain increased self-confidence through therapy. Elliot-Prisco felt that learning a new skill by using the camera and having a visual reference to remind her of her accomplishments would enhance her confidence. The picture on page 315 was her favorite of a black-and-white 24-exposure roll she shot. Donna had said that she wanted to have her own power and strength, and that having physical strength would help her to feel safer. She associated her photo of a reproduction of a Greek caryatid with a strong woman who is part of something larger than herself. Donna said that the woman is holding up the building, that she is society, holding up men's institutions. The men leave her out in the cold elements while they are inside and don't notice her or have anything to do with her. She could walk off into the air, Donna said, and be on her own, be creative, be different, be anything she wants to be. Through capturing meaningful images, Donna was able to gain a sense of mastery. She said that the camera gave her some control and power, and that to her it was magical.

Donna Mills conducted group art therapy at a community sexual assault crisis center for adult survivors of childhood incest (Mills, 1992). The group met for 2 hours and 15 minutes weekly for a 10-week course of treatment. Mills organized the group around specific art tasks each week:

1. Self-representation, feelings about being in the group, and expectations from the group

2. Differences between others' perceptions of you and your perception of yourself
3. Yourself as a child
4. Aloneness
5. Anger
6. Your relationship with your husband
7. Defenses and how they can help and hurt you
8. Safety
9. The ending of the group and what you learned from it
10. Feelings about the ending of the group

In the first session, the women made collages and noticed a similarity in their images showing that, for all of them, life had never felt predictable or safe even as adults living in their own homes. In the second session, they made an inside/outside project showing on the outside how they presented themselves to others and on the inside aspects of themselves others did not see. One of the women made a book that contained inner self-disgust. The theme of the group members' discussion of their art was the need to wear a mask to hide one's real self. They spoke of shame and fear that friends would discover how horrible, ugly, and dirty they were. There was fear of truly feeling all the stored-up, intense, ugly things locked inside. They described many masks, one existing under the other, to be removed only very slowly and carefully. Even the deep layers contained masks covering the real horror of the incest and the damaged self underneath.

Although the next session was to focus on defenses, the group members had been so opened by the previous session that they continued with expressions of their pain. This led to a focus on isolation and the word *alone*, which became the subject of the next session. Some drew themselves alone as children in order to be safe. One stated that as a result of the incest, she did not know how to be close to people, and when she tried she experienced shame and fear. The women were surprised at the depth of the sadness their art was revealing, and each cried while sharing her own picture. They grieved for their loneliness and lost potential for relationships, both past and present. Toward the end of the session, the sadness began to change to anger, the subject of the next session. They worked on large paper, standing up, smearing paint, saying "I hate you" aloud and writing it on some of the pieces. Each woman made three or four pieces, moving from controlled anger, to freedom of expression, to exhaustion.

The most difficult area of focus for the women was their relationships with their husbands. In their art, all of them confused their husbands with their fathers. They wanted intimacy with them, but were afraid and ashamed; they had to isolate themselves in various ways to feel safe. Three of the four women in the group refused to have sex with their husbands. As a result of these recognitions, they chose to work on their defenses at the next session. Isolation, once again, was a common characteristic. One woman drew herself in a fetal position trapped in what she called her box. She said she had built the box herself for protection from the horrors of abuse to which she was constantly subjected. As a result of all the expression of deep-seated feelings, one woman felt exposed and no longer safe within the group. Safety, therefore, became the focus of the next session. The women drew places where they felt safe. After sharing their drawings, they agreed sadly that they all experienced safety only in a small space where they could be alone and undisturbed.

The last two sessions were spent in dealing with the group's termination. The women expressed sadness, and one made a black picture showing the end of a book with "The End" written in large letters. They felt they had grown and had developed a better understanding of their own dynamics, except for one woman who was angry because she thought she had not come as far as the others. They pointed out to her that she had revealed less of herself and had done so later than the others, so that she was in a different place from them. They offered her their continued support, and all exchanged phone numbers. Obviously, in addition to facilitating the expression of strong feelings and further self-understanding, the group countered the isolation so prominent in the lives of incest survivors.

Katie Klitchman's art therapy work at a crisis-counseling center for treatment of sexually abused women and children was somewhat different from that of the others. Recognizing that the conventional therapy for these women often included remembering and reliving the abuse, grieving and mourning for their childhood, feeling their anger, and experiencing much suffering, Klitchman formed an art therapy group to give them a break from all this pain (Klitchman, 1991). It was clear to her that too much therapy could be overwhelming to the women. Her weekly 2-hour group was warmly received by the women. The purpose was to explore positive feelings. The goals were to increase self-esteem, empowerment, creativity, and self-expression; to play; and to develop "healthy selfishness." Music accompanied the sessions to provide a relaxed atmosphere, and the women kept journals about their artwork.

The first project was a self-introduction collage. The women also made found-object collages. Interestingly, all three women in the group chose to use lace doilies to represent their femininity or sexuality. Another activity consisted of drawing pictures representing different emotions. They drew representations of such feelings as peacefulness, loneliness, and harmony. One woman's favorite picture was her sunset, representing peacefulness. She hoped to become as peaceful as it looked to her. Another woman spoke of her peaceful woodland picture as a place to calm her down and rest her soul. After this experience, one of the women began making art outside the sessions; one piece represented feeling happy and exuberant. In order to enhance the women's positive self-regard, Klitchman asked them to make valentines to themselves, because the group meeting was on Valentine's Day. One woman used hearts, metallic paper, and jeweled beads for her inner child and her grown-up self. She cushioned the little heart for her inner child with feathers and surrounded it with glitter for protection and safety. In her journal she wrote,

In this life that has had this black hole beneath and dark clouds above, this group has helped me see, feel, and express a side that has been a long time coming. It feels really good to do a piece of art and realize you have expressed positive feelings. No telling how long they had been there, but there was no way to tap into them. (p. 30)

One of the group's final projects was to create a container for either feelings that were not validated in childhood or were restricted, or feelings that they would like to increase in their lives. The goal was to create a safe place. Klitchman provided boxes, but the women were encouraged to bring any containers they liked. One woman made two boxes, one for positive feelings, painted white, and the other for negative feelings, painted black. The latter resembled a coffin, to bury them, she said. A final task was to make a gift for oneself. All used clay. One woman made a peaceful mountain; another created a silly figure that made her laugh. For another woman, the process of molding the clay was very soothing.

At the end, the women evaluated their experience in the group. For one woman, finally feeling understood after sharing her artwork each week was very valuable to her. She had also created much art at home during this time as a result. Another woman felt that she could succeed and accomplish things based on the group's support and understanding. She had looked forward to the group all week because she could do what she wanted and didn't have to please anyone but herself. The third woman had discovered parts of herself that brought her joy rather than pain. The women had come to enjoy the creative, spontaneous, playful, humorous parts of themselves that they had lost in childhood.

Child Abuse Survivors with Addictions

Vicki Polin notes that adult survivors of childhood sexual abuse will use whatever means they can to anesthetize the pain resulting from the trauma of their abuse. Many do so through drugs and disassociation. The art process can be a way for them to communicate their pain instead (Polin, 1991).

Marc was a 34-year-old recovering addict, a survivor of childhood sexual abuse, and an ex–street gang member. He had recently been diagnosed with multiple personality disorder. Abandoned by his mother as a toddler and subjected to neglect and physical and sexual abuse by his father, Marc proclaimed that he was the product of our great foster care system. He had had numerous treatment failures, including hospitalizations for suicide attempts. After several art therapy sessions, Marc came in very angry one day, so Polin suggested that he throw clay on the table and say whatever came to mind. Various personalities emerged, including Little Marc, a 4-year-old who needed to feel safe and be nurtured. One of the other personalities made an image of Little Marc from the clay, and a more aggressive one came out and wanted to smash it.

The figure was protected, and other personalities came out and worked on it. At the end of the session Marc asked if he could leave Little Marc in Polin's office so that he could be safe. Little Marc continued to be used in treatment. He was changed from age to age by various personalities. One of Marc's personalities was a gang member, as Marc had been in early adolescence. The gang had been the only kind of family he had had. Although representing gang symbols is forbidden in many treatment settings, particularly in group work where it might incite conflict between members of different gangs, Polin allowed free expression in her individual sessions with Marc. It was important to him that all his personalities be accepted. The gang personality created a collage, titled *Love and Peace*, to represent "The Folks" (his gang). In the center he made a six-pointed star formed from glitter. A peace symbol within it was Marc's wish for peace among the gangs. The image was on blue paper covered by yellow cellophane, his gang colors. Marc developed various strategies to prevent triggering events, usually anniversaries of painful experiences, from leading to drug usage, illegal acts, or suicide attempts. Marc said:

> I'm a drug addict. This is around my tenth treatment attempt. I was sexually abused by several relatives since I was around four. . . . I could never talk about that before! . . . I kind of thought it was my fault. When I was fourteen I got into prostitution. It was the easiest way to support my habit. That art stuff really helped me to tell my secret. (p. 4)

(Female prostitutes who also had addictions and were survivors of childhood sexual abuse are discussed in Chapter 10, "Women.")

Joanna, 63, a recovering heroin addict who had also been sexually abused as a child, felt guilt over her neglect of her own children. Though usually mild-mannered, she was able to use the art to express her rage at her childhood abuser. Her anger was triggered by her daughter's revelation that she had been abused by the same man. Joanna made a series of drawings showing herself fighting with the man. She called him names and drew herself strangling him. She drew other pictures of shooting and stomping him to death. The art was an excellent vehicle to allow her to express her fury safely.

Robert, 45, a survivor of incest, was recovering from polysubstance abuse (alcohol, heroin, and cocaine). He had lost his medical license because of his illicit drug use. Diagnosed with Obsessive Compulsive Disorder as a child, he had made two violent suicide attempts. Nevertheless, he had not been treated for incest trauma as a child. Robert used the art to disclose his history of incest and to explore a recurring nightmare. He drew pictures of blood, gore, and cutting. In one, a body is being cut and there are dark clouds above it. In another, a hand is ripping a body apart. In a final drawing in this series, he is a young boy sacrificing a woman at the direction of another person, and it is important that he follow the directions exactly. He relapsed after this session, but unlike his previous relapses, he was hospitalized before attempting violence against himself or others. After his discharge and return to outpatient art

---

RESULTS OF SEXUAL ABUSE TRAUMA

- Fragmentation
- Dissociation
- Numbing
- Anxiety
- Depression
- Rage
- Guilt
- Shame
- Substance abuse
- Disturbed dreams
- Post-Traumatic Stress Disorder (PTSD)

---

therapy, he was able to connect his relapses with feelings related to his abuse as a child. He realized that he didn't want to look at the feelings that were in his pictures.

Polin helped incest survivors with chemical addictions, both men and women, to use art to express their very strong emotions instead of anesthetizing them with drugs. These individuals had long histories of social and psychological problems with many attempts at treatment in the past. The art therapy was a first step in awareness and trust for many of them. Most had been treated for substance abuse issues, but few had revealed the incest they had suffered.

Perpetrators

I have been a consultant to a child sexual abuse treatment agency where the therapists used art with the children. In addition to consulting with them, my own interest was in treating perpetrators. It is obvious that simply teaching children to say no will not eliminate or even significantly decrease childhood sexual abuse. My interest was to inform myself regarding the issues that lead adults and adolescents to abuse children sexually. Although the agency's clients were primarily children referred by the Department of Child and Family Services (DCFS), there were also a few perpetrators referred by the courts.

Harold was a very large, imposing man of 35 who had no teeth, and who had been abused himself at age 13. As an older adolescent, he began seeking out young boys for sexual contact. He lived in the working-class neighborhood where he had grown up, and he assisted the police as a volunteer in maintaining a safe community, especially for the juveniles. Harold estimated that he had probably sexually assaulted about 50 young boys in this capacity. Although he had been picked up for this several times, he described himself as "the king of the bullshitters" and was able to talk himself out of being charged each time. Finally, when he attempted sex with the sons of the police chief and the lieutenant police chief together, he was caught. Harold acknowledged that in attempting such a risky ploy, he had been inviting arrest.

Although initially resistant to making art, Harold was eventually able to use it to examine his issues, primarily his relationships with his father and brother, who lived nearby. Harold was unemployed and had never been able to hold onto a job for very long. His family of origin was still very enmeshed, and he felt like a failure compared to his father and brother. It was very clear that his relationships with young boys fulfilled a need to feel powerful among males. Occasionally Harold frequented gay bars and expressed fears that he might be homosexual. He was able to separate his sexual activity with boys both from those concerns and from his relationship with his own young sons. He stated that if anyone had done to them what he had done to other boys, he would kill him. Through his art, he also explored his relationship with his wife, who was very ill and unable to function as a wife and mother. Utilizing his art to explore options, Harold enrolled in a computer course, and found that he enjoyed it and was very good at it. At the end of our work together, he was on his way to developing a career in computer programming and was feeling much better about himself.

The agency's funds for consultants were eliminated, so I was unable to complete my work with Harold. A very interesting aspect of his history emerged that we were unable to explore further. At one of his last sessions, he was particularly agitated. He had been dealing with fears of homosexuality and said he had something to tell me, but couldn't bring himself to do so. I saw another client after his session, and when I was finished, Harold was outside my door waiting for me. He said that he had to talk to me. I had an appointment in a nearby building, but I told Harold he could walk there with me. As we crossed the parking lot, he blurted out that when he had been in a Vietnam prison camp with his best friend from childhood, his buddy had died there. Harold had cannibalized him. When he returned home, he had had all his teeth pulled. I related this information to the two male psychologists who were seeing him in a group for perpetrators, hoping that they would work with Harold on this issue, because I was leaving. They didn't believe that he had even served in Vietnam. This incident of horror was even more bizarre in the context of art therapy with another perpetrator I was seeing at the agency.

Bill had been convicted of sexually abusing his wife's two daughters from a former marriage. They were white; he was black. Bill claimed that he was innocent, that the children had framed him, but that he had pleaded guilty because a black man accused of molesting white girls would not stand a chance in court. He, too, was a large imposing man with serious employment problems. He presented himself as a person who always tried to do the right thing. He was very bright and an excellent artist. His pictures centered primarily on his family life. He also was a Vietnam vet and began drawing pictures of his war experience. Finally, the following story emerged.

Bill had been raped and beaten when taken prisoner by an enemy soldier. After escaping and returning to his own unit, he searched for his captor for 3 months. The enemy soldier then showed up in a group his unit had captured. Bill asked his comrades to let him take care of this prisoner. He took the man out into the woods, where for 2 hours he mutilated him. Finally, he stuck his pistol up the prisoner's rectum and shot him. This story, too, surfaced just before I left the agency.

Although my experience in working with child molesters was very limited, I was surprised at the concordance between these two men. Both felt inadequate and had a strong need to prove themselves. Both were very large, imposing men. Both were Vietnam vets with harrowing experiences as prisoners and perpetrators of violence. My own reaction to these horror stories was very strong, and it was difficult for me to get them out of my mind. It seemed to me at the time that what we call civilization is a very thin veneer covering raw and primitive responses to very real threats to survival. For many men who served in Vietnam, the horrors they witnessed and experienced tore away the shreds of civilizing influences that contain the wild and uncontrolled urges that may be provoked by extreme conditions. Perhaps there are parallels in the lives of both victims and perpetrators of sexual abuse. (For further discussion of these clients in the context of art therapists' using their own art to process their reactions to their clients' horror stories, see Wadeson, Marano-Geiser, & Ramseyer, 1990.)

Like Bill, many of Steve Ploum's clients denied molesting their victims. Ploum works in a program for the treatment of juvenile sexual offenders. Such programs are extremely important because of their efforts to thwart what can become lifelong patterns of abuse for juvenile offenders. Ploum states that denial is a symptom that is usually the first obstacle to therapy in working with offenders. Therapy focuses on helping them to recognize and understand their sexual assault cycles and to develop means to stop before they engage in harmful behavior (personal communication, 1999). Therapy is designed to break down their denial and help them develop an understanding of the emotional states that lead to sexual aggression. Therapists working with juvenile sexual offenders often need to strike a balance between two seemingly contradictory forms of interaction, Ploum has found. On one hand, they must actively confront the denial and challenge the lies and manipulations that are common among these offenders. It is important that they be held accountable for their behavior so that they can experience a cognitive restructuring that allows them to feel empathy for their victims and the appropriate guilt and remorse. On the other hand, in order for therapy to be effective, these clients need understanding and a traditional empathy-based approach to deal with the issues of low self-esteem, depression, and separation and loss that many of them face.

Paul, a 17-year-old African American ward of the DCFS, had been referred to the juvenile sex offenders program for forcing another adolescent male to

---

JUVENILE SEX OFFENDERS' ISSUES

- Denial
- Accepting accountability for their actions
- Identifying triggering feeling states
- Developing empathy
- Modifying responses to triggering feelings

---

perform oral sex on him. He had been removed from his biological parents at age 8 due to neglect and had lived in many foster and group homes. Ploum saw Paul in both individual and group art therapy. Paul claimed that the other boy had initiated the activity and that his own mistake had been in "allowing the kid to suck my penis." When Ploum tried to explore sexuality further, Paul presented himself as asexual, stating that he had never had sexual fantasies, or masturbated, or ever even had an erection until the incident in question.

In order to break through this type of denial, Ploum has developed some art therapy tasks that can reveal a lot more than the verbal explanations. One exercise is to draw a picture of what happened before, during, and after the offense, which is referred to as "the situation" in order not to arouse the client's defenses further. Ploum offers colored pencils and markers so that the client can feel a sense of control in making the drawing. Clients are asked to include as many details as they can remember, such as objects in the room and clothing, and to sign the artwork to reinforce ownership of what has been depicted. Ploum asks clients to make this drawing again over several intervals so that any discrepancies can be identified and challenged. Paul's initial response to the task was a pale pencil drawing with little detail or commitment to any subject. There is a very small and minimal image of the fellatio, with Paul as the larger figure. He admitted that the picture seemed to show him as the one in control of the situation. When asked to repeat this task in a group session, his avoidance was even greater, with emphasis placed on the room and no figures in the drawing. Reasons for denial became the focus of therapy, with opportunities for Paul to express thoughts about others who were sexual offenders. Ploum indicated that he would always welcome "improvements in memory," in order to break down Paul's denial without causing a heightened sense of vulnerability.

Paul made an inside/outside box to show his inner and outer self. Inside were black and red bars that contained his "inner fire." Discussion revealed fears of embarrassment. Ploum felt that Paul was beginning to recognize his problem as being dangerous to others for the first time. As he experienced Ploum's unconditional positive regard, Paul began to explore his emotional states, especially regarding rejection and loss in being neglected by his parents and in being placed in more than a dozen foster placements and group homes. There were limited opportunities to form satisfactory relationships, which impacts on the ability to feel empathy for others. As Paul became more comfortable in therapy, he was able to admit to more realistic and developmentally appropriate sexual urges, along with some deviant sexual fantasies. Eventually he also admitted the sexual offense, saying that he had threatened the victim physically and adding that he had committed other sexual offenses three or four times, also by threatening violence as a means of coercion. He had also fondled and digitally penetrated his younger sister three or four times. Paul knew that these admissions would require Ploum to report the offences to DCFS, which ultimately resulted in an extended probation and more restrictions. Nevertheless, Paul's disclosures of his sexual offenses indicated that he now held himself accountable and responsible for his actions, a huge step forward in his therapy.

The focus of therapy turned toward developing insight into the feelings that triggered sexual aggression. Paul was moved to a favorable foster home, which he liked, but as the family was planning to move, he was worried that they might not take him and he would be placed in another substandard home. Steve asked him to make an art piece to depict his worry. Paul built a robot from wood, working hard on the piece. Initially, he was going to make a prison. He changed his mind, switching from an object that represented powerlessness to one that had power. He said that the robot was powerful and "offensive-minded," with an arsenal of a sword and guns on its chest and grenade packs on its back. Ploum helped Paul to see that worry set off feelings of powerlessness that were then compensated with feelings of power and aggression. They worked on developing ways to resolve feelings of worry in a healthy, nonhurtful manner.

Toward the end of treatment, journal work is often used with sex offenders. Adolescents, however, are seldom trusting of writing down their secrets, but they may be willing to keep a drawing journal. Figure 11.2 shows a drawing from Paul's journal that he brought to therapy. He related to it in terms of assuming power. A lengthy discussion followed around appropriate and inappropriate uses of power and control. Figure 11.3 shows his next journal entry, demonstrating his connection between sex and aggression. Although Paul claimed both pictures were originals, it is likely that he copied them, as he often presented himself as being more capable than he really was.

Like many juvenile sex offenders, Paul suffered depression and a sense of incompetence and powerlessness. Attempts to gain power by taking it from others often satisfied immediate urges. Art therapy helped him to take the initial steps in holding himself accountable for his actions, identifying his states of feeling, and increasing his feeling vocabulary. He learned how certain feelings can create a sense of powerlessness and trigger a responsive reaction in order to gain a sense of power.

Ploum reports that art therapy is often used to develop empathy for sex

FIGURE 11.2   Journal drawing about assuming
power by juvenile sex offender.

offenders' victims by asking them to draw their victims or to find images for a collage among magazine photos of children. In groups, they are asked to respond to one another empathically rather than aggressively. Many of these youngsters come from such unstable backgrounds, as did Paul, that they need training in healthy human interaction in order to prevent them from continuing in a life of violence toward others.

Working with sexual abuse perpetrators can be very demanding. Beyond dealing with lies and manipulation, therapists must be able to feel empathy for their clients and care about them. Prior to working with offenders, I wondered if I would even be able to like them. I realized that if I could not, I would not be able to help them. Childhood sexual abuse is such a heinous crime that it requires that therapists, without denying their own values, be able to accept the offender as another struggling human being with his or her own needs, vulnerabilities, and strengths.

FIGURE 11.3   Sex and aggression in journal drawing by juvenile sex offender who
drew Figure 11.2.

Art Therapists' Self-Processing

As is evident in the examples presented in this chapter, working with clients
who have been sexually abused is extremely demanding and sometimes horrific. Therapists are often inundated by fragmentation, dissociation, numbing,
anxiety, depression, rage, guilt, and shame on the part of their clients. Art
therapists see the horrifying images that accompany the shocking stories of
people who had lost control of their bodies as children and were completely
vulnerable to exploitation by those more powerful than themselves. Secondary trauma or vicarious PTSD has been identified as a condition that therapists may experience from their work with these clients.

Jennifer Swerdlow experienced an impact on her perception of the world,
as the stories and images of her clients, with their constant reminders of vulnerability and the threats of violence in our society, aroused anger and fear in

her. In order to contain, explore, and understand her own traumatic countertransference to her clients and the effects of secondary PTSD on herself, she utilized the multiple steps of quilting to process her reactions (Swerdlow, 1996). Swerdlow notes that the properties of the materials used in quilting are intrinsically soothing, both visually and tactilely. The methodical, rhythmic, ritualistic, sensory nature of the process provided a kind of self-care that she found necessary in order to continue treating her clients. In designing and constructing quilting squares, Swerdlow placed herself in the tradition of women who, for centuries, have given voice to their own personal narratives through the medium of quilting. As an artist and as a feminist, Swerdlow followed in the tradition of women who have expressed personal histories in the stories told in the quilts they have made. This project gave her the time, structure, and process to assemble pieces of her experience with women who had survived sexual abuse.

Swerdlow worked at a women-staffed not-for-profit agency that uses a feminist empowerment model in treating women and children who have been sexually or physically abused. In addition to counseling, the agency provides court advocacy and abuse education for individuals and communities. Swerdlow worked with clients individually and in groups, and she offered an open studio format. Clients came for both short-term crisis intervention and long-term treatment. Many had been referred by rape victim advocates and hospital emergency rooms after a sexual assault. Swerdlow served as a primary therapist for some and worked adjunctively with others who had been referred to her by their primary counselors. Most presented with symptoms of PTSD, including flashbacks, nightmares, avoidance of abuse-related stimuli, dissociation, emotional numbing, and increased arousal. Additional features included depression, low self-esteem, hopelessness, isolation, and impaired relationships. The art experience provided a safe way to express powerful emotions, a means of communication, a tangible record of the healing process, and enhanced self-esteem. Group work encouraged socialization, as well.

In order to create consistency in her quilt, Swerdlow decided in advance to use a black cotton background and black thread for each 12-inch square. She purchased a range of fabrics in various colors to appliqué on each square. Usually she worked on them at home immediately after returning from work. Sometimes she worked on them at the agency while answering the crisis hotline. Swerdlow began work on a square when she had a specific question about a client or was experiencing strong feelings that she didn't understand in relation to a client. For some squares, she came up with a design in advance; for others, the design evolved as she worked on it. Designs were drawn on paper first, drawn directly on the fabric, or cut freehand. Cutting technique varied from careful trimming to hurried chopping. After the pieces of fabric to be appliquéd were cut, they were pinned on the background in various positions until Swerdlow got the composition she wanted. Because quilting is a time-consuming process, these first steps were usually the only ones completed in a first sitting for a particular square. Sewing was done after Swerdlow had established some distance from her initial feelings, during which time she reflected on her own internal processes. Throughout the process of creating each square, she dialoged with it, and after it was completed, she wrote in her journal, exploring her reactions further.

Linda, a 53-year-old well-educated woman with a history of childhood abuse who had been recently assaulted, was Swerdlow's first client at the agency. She presented herself as an authority on many matters, acted as though she had all the answers, discounted Swerdlow's empathic responses to her current complaints, and stated that she did not want to discuss her assault or the abuse by her father or the abandonment by her mother. At the same time, she questioned Swerdlow's competence and experience. Swerdlow became progressively more tense and quiet in the sessions and found herself doubting her own abilities as an art therapist. Feeling drained after her second session with Linda, she created a quilt square in response. She worked for 3 hours, completing the square in one sitting (Figure 11.4). She selected red gauze to represent herself and applied it in horizontal stripes without folding the edges under so they remain loose and unsecured. On top are shards of red, fuchsia, and silver satin, representing Linda. These pieces are sewn with a satin stitch completely covering the edges of each piece. The frayed edges of the Swerdlow pieces express how she was feeling, raw and undefended. Linda's pieces, on the other hand, are tightly secured, flattening and covering Swerdlow. She described herself as feeling overwhelmed and constricted by

FIGURE 11.4 Art therapist's quilt square representing her difficult relationship with a sexually abused client.

Linda. The shards of Linda reminded her of being stabbed and penetrated, whereas the strips representing herself suggested a brick wall with rows that did not quite meet. She reflected that her silence in the sessions was a way of defending herself, yet the spaces between the bricks left her vulnerable to Linda's criticism. Swerdlow experienced Linda as draining and impossible to please. Nevertheless, in the 3 hours it took to complete the square, Swerdlow noticed a transformation in her feelings. She no longer felt overwhelmed. The intense colors and smooth soft textures of the gauze and satin were soothing to her. Cutting the fabric was a cathartic release. The rhythmic quality of the sewing machine and the evenness of the stitching calmed her. Swerdlow slowed herself down as she worked, and came to see that she was responding to Linda's damaged relational style more than to her trauma. She decided to work on distinguishing the roles between therapist and client and on establishing authority over the structure of the sessions. In the next session, Swerdlow directed Linda in developing and exploring the images she had drawn, suggested that she bring her own art materials since she had found fault with those supplied by the agency, and discouraged conversation during art making. As a result, Linda became engaged in the art process and gained meaningful insight from her work. Swerdlow became more comfortable in her role and came to respect Linda's strengths as a survivor.

Swerdlow was cofacilitating a group with the agency director. Although this was not an art therapy group, the director and Swerdlow agreed that she would introduce art activities in the sessions. Nevertheless, each time Swerdlow suggested one, it was flatly dismissed. Only a few art therapy techniques that the director had used in previous groups were allowed. Swerdlow was relegated to conducting check-ins and check-outs and collecting payments from the members. Although she was encouraged to enter into the discussions in what turned out to be mostly verbal group sessions, there was seldom an opportunity to do so. At one session, the director introduced a new group member to everyone present except Swerdlow. At another, while Swerdlow was leading an art activity, the director conversed with one of the members throughout. Swerdlow became increasingly withdrawn in the group and found her attention wandering. The director was too busy to discuss the sessions outside of group time.

Prior to the seventh session, Swerdlow was waiting for the director to update her on the group because she had missed the previous session. She was scheduled to lead an art activity as a follow-up to a member's disclosure of abuse, but she did not know what had transpired. The director was nowhere to be found, and Swerdlow began to feel panic. She started painting to soothe herself, but she became choked up and began to cry. She wanted to leave, but the director finally showed up and encouraged her to observe the group. It was an intense session, and Swerdlow went home exhausted and full of emotion. She felt broken and fragmented, and especially vulnerable because she had cried in front of the director.

Swerdlow began a quilt square (Figure 11.5). She started with a single

FIGURE 11.5   Art therapist's quilt square representing her feelings in working with abused women.

piece of purple silk, which she cut in the shape of a head. She then cut out eyes and cut the head apart to express the fragmentation she felt. Her intention was to sew it back together to make herself whole again. To her surprise, as she pinned the pieces, they did not match up. She sewed them securely as they were. She cut out tears from icy blue satin, but did not pin and sew them that same evening; she did so on three occasions over the following 2 weeks.

When Swerdlow stepped back and looked at the head on the first evening, she was shocked to discover that it was not a head at all, but a cracked and wounded mask. She recognized that she had been wearing a mask for the past 7 weeks to protect herself from her reactions to the horrible atrocities the group members described. On the evening of the seventh session, the mask could no longer hold her powerful emotions.

Swerdlow realized that the anger she felt toward the director stemmed from her wish to be taken care of by the director as the group members were. She did not feel that the director valued her presence in the group or that she had anything to offer to the group. Swerdlow saw that her inability to stay present and focused in the group was a form of dissociation, similar to what abuse survivors adopt to flee a situation in which they feel powerless. By waiting to sew on the tears, she allowed herself time to reflect on what they were about. At first, she thought she was crying for the group members. As she reflected while she sewed, she understood that there was a woman beneath the mask with her own painful past. Each time she sewed a tear, she remembered some of her own pain. Waiting to sew the tears helped Swerdlow to separate her own grief from that of her clients. Bearing witness to the horrors in their lives had triggered feelings that echoed her own past sorrows.

Swerdlow's final observation was that by selecting the purple silk, the most expensive and visually satisfying and tactilely soothing fabric she had purchased, she had conveyed to herself that her own needs and feelings were valuable and that she deserved to be nurtured and soothed. She had wanted the director to fill a nurturing role for her, but she was finding a way to do it for herself. From her integration of her experience in the group through making the quilt square, Swerdlow was able to establish direct communication with the agency director and to give herself a voice in the group. The director agreed to schedule more time for planning and processing the group sessions with Swerdlow.

Judy, a 28-year-old woman who had been a victim of gang violence, was receiving court-mandated counseling after her four children had been removed from her household due to witnessing domestic violence between her and her partner. Judy's only goal was to retrieve her children, and she did not understand why she was required to have therapy. Swerdlow knew that Judy's caseworker expected her to make progress reports that would affect her case. Judy had missed several sessions. Whenever she did express her feelings, she would pull back and deny them. Swerdlow found herself frustrated with Judy's lack of engagement and feeling guilty that she was not able to help her get her children back. She decided to make a quilt square to explore their relationship.

Swerdlow used a thin, shiny, orange piece of fabric to signify a caution or a yield sign to represent Judy. For herself, she chose a thick, soft, mustard-colored piece of felt. It is a neutral color, which she thought she was. Judy's fabric piece had a segment cut out of the middle. Swerdlow's shape had tentacles and took up more space. It was holding a tool, which she related to a poker, paintbrush, or spoon. Swerdlow saw her figure as being more grounded, whereas Judy's was cut open and was exposed and undefended on the side facing Swerdlow. The edges on that side were loose and frayed. The piece cut out of Judy represented her backing away from Swerdlow. The "long, monstrous tentacles," intended to be reaching out to Judy, were pushing her with the tool instead. Swerdlow was reminded of how she tried to get Judy to express her emotions and how she felt like a mother "spoon (force) feeding her" (p. 24).

Swerdlow realized that she had avoided exploring Judy's trauma and PTSD symptoms and that she had been leading Judy instead of responding to her needs. A trusting relationship had not been established. As a result of the insight she gained from her quilt square, Swerdlow set about making changes in the way she worked with Judy. She called Judy's caseworker and explained that it was not her role to assess Judy's fitness as a parent. Next, in her sessions with Judy, she allowed her to take the lead in the issues they explored. In order to develop a more trusting relationship, Swerdlow suggested that they make art together. Swerdlow was careful to respond empathetically in her own art to the images Judy drew. The foundation for a relationship of trust that was laid in this way led to more effective treatment.

In her various quilt squares, Swerdlow was able to notice the reoccurrence of several themes, including boundaries, client-therapist roles, and issues of power. The multi-step process of quilting provided an outlet for different levels of experience. Cutting was a catharsis. Assembling and pinning provided a sense of ordering. Sewing offered a period of quiet reflection. The completed squares were statements that gave Swerdlow further insight, and new directions in her work arose from them. Throughout this book, there are various examples of art created by art therapists, but Swerdlow has used a unique process in creating quilt squares and utilizing the several stages of their construction to examine her own issues as a beginning therapist. The reflections this process and the resulting images produced led Swerdlow to an understanding of the dynamics in her relationships with clients and staff members and enhanced her effectiveness as an art therapist.

Summary

Working with sexual abuse survivors can be very demanding because the trauma they have experienced can make it very difficult for them to trust anyone. They often suffer impaired interpersonal relationships, depression, dissociation, and other symptoms of PTSD. Some have abused drugs in order to anesthetize the pain of their abuse. Therapists may be affected by vicarious trauma and suffer secondary PTSD. Art therapy can be useful in helping survivors express their strong emotions safely; in some cases survivors have disclosed the abuse for the first time through their art. It can also be helpful in working with perpetrators of abuse. Work discussed in this chapter includes the following:

- I have noticed in my private practice that in recent years clients have reported sexual abuse, whereas this was not the case in the past. I believe that this experience is now met with validation, rather than skepticism and disbelief.
- Ann McCullough (1991) found that survivors of rape could more readily express their feelings in their art.
- Alexandria Elliot-Prisco (1995) used photography in working with both rape and incest survivors.
- Donna Mills (1992) formed an art therapy group for incest survivors that facilitated expressions of loneliness, insecurity, isolation, and anger.
- Katie Klitchman (1991) developed an art therapy group for incest survivors in order to give the women a break from the intense therapy they were undergoing regarding their abuse issues. They felt safe and well understood in this group.
- Vicki Polin (1991) worked with both men and women who had chemi-

cal addictions and were sexual abuse survivors. Some had multiple personality disorder.

- I have worked with child molesters who had committed bizarre acts during the Vietnam war.
- Steve Ploum (personal communication, 1999) worked extensively with juvenile sex offenders. He found that art therapy is effective in breaking through their denial, helping them to accept responsibility for their acts and to identify feelings that trigger their aggressive behavior.
- Jennifer Swerdlow (1996) used the several steps in quilt making to examine her own relationships with clients and staff members. She gained insight into her own position in the dynamics of her therapy relationships, which helped her to become a more effective art therapist.

Conclusion

It is evident from the scenarios presented here that sexual abuse is a multifaceted problem. In all its forms, whether incest or rape, it involves a power differential, with the weaker, more vulnerable person (usually female) being exploited, sometimes violently, by the other person (usually male). In the case of childhood abuse, the power differential is that of an adult or adolescent in relation to a child. The aftereffects of sexual abuse are generally life altering to a very significant degree. Many problems may develop as a result, such as dissociative disorders (including multiple personality disorder), PTSD, depression, and substance abuse. Art therapy has become an important mode of treatment in giving voice to what has been unmentionable for many sufferers. It has also been used successfully, though less extensively, with perpetrators of abuse.

ART THERAPY PROJECTS

Projects discussed in this chapter are described further in Chapter 15, "Art Activities and Materials":

- Collage (Mills, 1992; Klitchman, 1991; Polin, 1991)
- Bookmaking (Mills, 1992)
- Boxes and containers (Klitchman, 1992)
- Photography (Elliot-Prisco, 1995)
- Inside/outside box (Ploum, personal communication, 1999)
- Quilting (Swerdlow, 1996)

Chapter 12

Sexual Orientation and AIDS

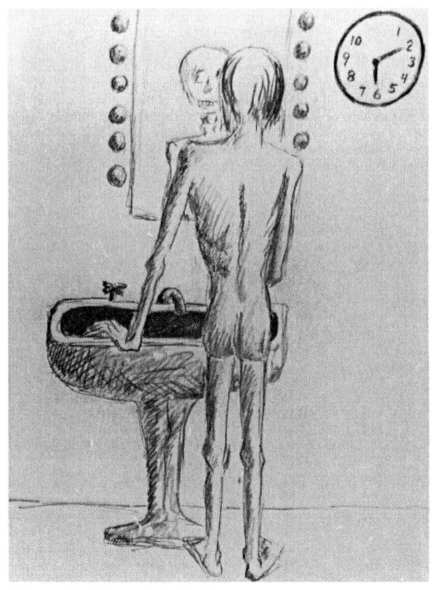

Self-portrait by dying patient with AIDS, showing his wasted body, skeletal reflection, and time running out.

The house that Roger rented on Fire Island stands empty, except for the ghosts. His slippers make a swishing sound accompanied by the rattling of his rolling IV apparatus, which has become a permanent appendage, as he shuffles down the hall to the art room. He'll make a collage today, the anniversary of Buddy's death. He puts on a tape of La Traviata, Buddy's favorite, and searches the magazines for a tennis racket, sports cars, and booze. He tears out pictures of a Porsche, a bottle of Stolichnaya vodka, and a German shepherd. After arranging them on the paper so that the dog is drinking the vodka while riding in the car, he glues them down and scrawls For Buddy *across the bottom. Then Roger closes his eyes and listens to Violetta sing* Gran Dio! Morir si giovane *(Oh God! To die so young).*

Same-sex coupling has been viewed in many ways over the millennia. Plato honored it (for men); Sappho celebrated it (for women). During the Victorian era, women were not viewed as sexual beings; if there was no man involved there was no issue of sex between women. Nevertheless, gay life has a stained history of persecution and shame. Tchaikovsky is reputed to have been ordered to take poison as his punishment for same-sex affairs. The Nazis imprisoned and tortured gay people, and in our own country, until fairly recently, exposure of homosexuality was so consequential that gay people were considered to be security risks.

Sexuality became nasty in the Victorian era, and Freud, a Victorian himself, based his ideas of human functioning on irrepressible sexual libido. With the rise of psychoanalysis, same-gender sexual activity became a perversion, and with the advent of psychiatry, an illness. Until the last three decades of the 20th century, treatment of homosexuality was geared toward the elimination of homosexual behavior and desires. There were even conditioning programs designed to make the opposite sex attractive and the same sex sexually repulsive to the patient.

During the latter half of the 20th century, gay people began to organize, many coming out of the closet to fight for their rights. I was actually present at the major turning point in the elimination of homosexuality from the categories of mental illness. I was attending the American Psychiatric Association (APA) conference in San Francisco in 1970 when gay activists stormed the halls to demonstrate against such categorization. Subsequently, the APA's *Diagnostic and Statistical Manual of Mental Disorders* (the bible of the profession) dropped homosexuality from its third edition.

Although homosexuality is now much more visible, especially in urban centers, there is by no means universal acceptance of homosexuality. The acquired immunodeficiency syndrome (AIDS) epidemic has been a momentous factor in the coming out of the gay community (as discussed in this chapter). Like many other clients with whom art therapists work, gay and lesbian individuals present a mixed picture of the same sorts of syndromes as others, which might include psychiatric symptoms, substance abuse problems, and problematic interpersonal relationships, for example. Nevertheless, there are some unique ways in which problems associated with feelings of differentness, rejection of one's lifestyle by family and others, social stigma, and shame associated with internalized homophobia can exacerbate or create problems for members of this population.

For example, several clients in my private practice come to mind. One is a 70-year-old highly successful corporate executive. She grew up feeling different because she was attracted to other girls, rather than the boys she was dating. In college, she entered psychotherapy in order to change—to no avail. Throughout her professional career she remained closeted, feeling she was leading a double life. Only in the last few years, as she has prepared for retirement, has she introduced her female partner to her colleagues. She has been surprised to find acceptance and feels that the world has truly changed. Another client is a Catholic priest whose shame over his gay sexual activity has led him into cocaine abuse. He is currently in a residential rehabilitation program for Catholic clergy. Another is a tall, handsome woman in her 40s. She reports that when she takes the train home at night, teenagers sometimes mistake her for a man and yell "fag" at her. She, too, sought therapy at a local hospital while in college in order to deal with her homosexuality. Her psychiatrist used her as a demonstration in grand rounds to show the staff a specimen of a lesbian. She was thoroughly humiliated.

In addition to whatever has brought them into treatment, gay and lesbian clients may also have to deal with coming-out issues, shame associated with internal homophobia, and social stigma. Many wonderful autobiographical books have been written about these experiences. Especially moving is the National Book Award winner *Becoming a Man: Half a Life Story* by Paul Monette (1992). When he died of AIDS in 1998, I felt as though I had lost a friend. Another good book is *Cures: A Gay Man's Odyssey* by Martin Duberman (1991). Art therapists who have little first-hand knowledge of gay and lesbian people's experience can learn a great deal from these books.

The Lifestyles Group

Art therapists are most likely to encounter gay clients in treatment programs for psychiatric problems and substance abuse. Petra Miskus conducted a lifestyles group for gay men, lesbian women, and bisexual individuals at a psychiatric hospital (Miskus, 1996). There were instances in which patients admitted themselves to the hospital solely for the lifestyles program. That the hospital recognized the need for such a group gave a powerful message about its importance. Of course, this was meaningful to those who felt like invisible outcasts of society. Miskus found that the group members felt more comfortable bringing up their issues in this group than in the other hospital groups they attended.

One of the pressing questions for such a group is the sexual orientation of the leader. The members indicated that they preferred a gay leader, rather than one who was not one of them, who wouldn't understand them, or who might be judgemental. For a gay or lesbian therapist who does not want to come out, conducting such a group can pose a serious problem. Ordinarily, a therapist's sexual orientation is none of the clients' business, but in a case such as this, it is a reasonable question. This is the sort of issue that therapists need to think through ahead of time. A gay or lesbian therapist who comes out to his or her gay and lesbian patients cannot expect the matter to remain confidential. Coming out to anyone at an institution means coming out to everyone there. The consequences may be unexpected and harmful. For example, a student who came out as a lesbian to staff of the hospital unit where she was interning was asked to leave the hospital. In a discussion of therapist transparency in a supervision group I was leading, a student said he would not anticipate his response to difficult questions from clients, but would react out of his feelings at the time. I advised against this approach. On the spur of the moment, one might not realize the ramifications of one's reaction. He then acknowledged that he would not want to disclose that he had served a jail sentence. Although there is seldom prejudice against heterosexuality, straight therapists might also be reluctant to reveal their sexual orientation to gay clients lest they be perceived as "other." Miskus handled the lifestyle group members' questions by discouraging them from labeling people.

Therapist transparency is tricky business. Hopefully, in the future, same-sex sexual orientation will not elicit prejudice, but for the present, therapists working with gay clients need to be comfortable with their own attitudes toward homosexuality, regardless of their own sexual orientation. Comfort in revealing one's sexual orientation is a very personal matter, and there are no clear guidelines for handling this question in working with gay clients. I am familiar with several gay art therapists' work with homosexual populations, some of whom are out and some of whom are not.

Miskus recognized that the question of how internal homophobia affects recovery issues would be an important focus of the lifestyles group. Because patients' hospital stays were not long, the group's membership changed from session to session. Some of the members were human immunodeficiency virus (HIV) positive. One was Sam, a 31-year-old man with a diagnosis of major depression and cocaine and alcohol abuse. He displayed emotional lability, saying that he didn't know whether he felt like living or dying, but he didn't want to feel the hurt. He drew a knife, a tombstone, a broken heart, and a crying eye on black paper to express the death side of his feelings. In another session he recognized his need to love himself in order to create intimacy. He drew a picture representing his need for love, in which he is a large rose basking in the sun that symbolizes love. Through the group's almost daily meetings, Sam became friendly with Craig, who was also HIV positive. Craig let Sam know that he was not alone. Craig was married and the father of a daughter. No one in his family knew of his HIV status, his gay sexual orientation, or his alcohol problem. Craig and Sam created a body tracing together in which Craig chose a fetal position and Sam drew around him. Craig said the position represented his need for safety. Sam added blue to symbolize the energy Craig brought to their friendship. Both Sam and Craig were discharged shortly thereafter. Sam had several relapses with AIDS complications and was rehospitalized. Craig continued in outpatient art therapy, exploring the issue of ending his marriage and establishing an intimate gay relationship. He did so and has continued to function well.

Kelly, a 38-year-old suicidal lesbian who had been sexually abused by her mother at age 4, had also been violently raped three times. Her female partner of 7 years, with whom she had expected to live for the rest of her life, had died in her arms. Kelly was an emergency room nurse who concerned herself with the problems of others and intellectualized her own feelings. Although Kelly had initially resisted art making, when Miskus suggested a collage to the group, Kelly used it to express her feelings about herself as a woman along with images representing her own death. One of the images was a woman without a mouth, representing her silence about her victimization. After a period of making collages, she began using chalk, finding it to be a breakthrough in the development of her creativity, which she described as a discovery of herself. Additional collages were very positive. She felt that she was retrieving the innocence of her inner child and identifying ways to have fun and to gain a sense of inner peace through appreciating nature. She was discharged, continued in the outpatient program, and eventually developed a new relationship. She reports that she is living with more wisdom and confidence in herself.

Although Sam and Craig worked on gay-related issues, specifically HIV and the matter of adopting a gay relationship instead of marriage, Kelly's issues were more universal. I have found in my own private practice that homosexual clients' issues and heterosexual clients' issues have been more similar than different. Even in therapy with gay couples, the issues have been similar to the usual relationship problems that couples present.

AIDS

Although art therapists are likely to work with gay and lesbian clients in treatment programs for psychiatric and substance abuse problems, HIV and AIDS have been by far the primary instigator of art therapy for gay men. Who would have dreamed that in the scientifically advanced 20th century, the world would experience a plague of proportions unknown in previous centuries? Who would have suspected that a virus from the remote jungles of Africa would spread death throughout the civilized world? The gay men who were among its first victims were often treated as lepers. Many were refused treatment out of fear of contagion, and some were even refused air transportation to be taken home to die. Just as the gay community was coming out of the closet as a visible and viable social force, just as the community was beginning to develop a sense of pride, it was being decimated. Some thought it was the wrath of God punishing gay men for their wicked ways. Others, particularly celebrities, began raising money for AIDS research. The extensive losses in the arts have also been visible—deaths from AIDS have highlighted the considerable contributions gay people have made to the visual arts, dance, drama, music, and film. The public has had to face the irony that some of its favorite romantic movie idols have been gay. There have been numerous dramas in theater and film about people with AIDS. Particularly noteworthy are the play *The Normal Heart* by Larry Kramer, an early AIDS activist, and the movie *Philadelphia*, for which Tom Hanks won the 1993 academy award for Best Actor.

Although not all HIV and AIDS patients are gay, art therapy with this population is included here because the stigma of homosexuality has been such a significant factor in our society's response to the disease. There was an initial reluctance to allocate funds for research on a "gay disease"; more specifically, the method of transmission through sexual contact has led to the resulting isolation and prejudice that AIDS patients have suffered. As time has passed, hospital AIDS units have included more women and heterosexual men, many of whom are intravenous drug users, and their sexual partners. There are also children who are HIV positive, many of whom contracted the virus from their mothers prior to birth. Despite the fact that sexual orientation is not an issue for these patients, they are included in this chapter because familial homosexuality and homophobia often enter into their treatment. As mentioned, homosexuality is still associated with the disease. (Paradoxically, it is probably accidental that the first patients in this country were gay, although the disease is more readily spread through sexual contact by males than by females.)

Publicity has paid off in increased funding for AIDS research, and new medications are helping people with HIV to live longer. Earlier therapy for AIDS patients often was focused on easing their deaths. More recent work is directed toward helping people to live with HIV.

AIDS Art

In 1987, when the need for psychological services for AIDS patients and those close to them was beginning to be recognized, Wendy Pollack established an art therapy program on a hospital AIDS unit where treatment was primarily medical (Pollack, 1988). Because the patients' hospital stays were short, it was difficult to develop the group cohesion necessary for the sense of community in dealing with AIDS-related issues. Pollack established two groups. One was structured around thoughts and feelings related to AIDS, with appropriate directives and a discussion period following art making. The other group featured an open studio for long-term projects and further investment in art expression.

Common themes in the art were depression and isolation as a result of AIDS. There was grief over the loss of friends, lovers, jobs, family, and, most common, loss of control over one's life. The images expressed anger, fear, and sadness. Nevertheless, there was also joy in being able to be creative.

In her work with a patient Pollack designates as C., it is evident that art expression and the trust and understanding that this patient developed through the relationship with his art therapist helped him to counter his isolation and fear. C. was a 35-year-old computer operator who had recently been diagnosed with AIDS and had been admitted with a severe case of pneumonia. During the course of his illness he was forced out of his job due to rejection by coworkers and some supervisors. His affect was flat, and he was quiet and withdrawn. Pollack learned that C. had little outside support; he was estranged from his family, had no love relationships, and had few friends. He indicated that he felt totally alone and trusted no one. C. had been an art major in college, and when Pollack invited him to join the art groups, he seemed to brighten at the prospect. He became an active member and continued to work with Pollack in individual art therapy as an outpatient after his discharge.

Figure 12.1, titled *Unreachable*, was drawn with markers. C. explained that although he wants help, he does not reach out because he trusts no one. Here, although trying to reach, he has no hand. Again using markers, C. drew Figure 12.2, *Struggling against Fear*. Still alone, the man may be beginning to find his way out of the entangling structure. In another marker drawing, *I'm Hiding behind a Wall of Masks* (Figure 12.3), C. showed how he defended himself against the possible pain involved in revealing to others how he felt. Paradoxically, however, the artwork was enabling him to do just that. In *The Human Mobius Strip or Back to Where I Started*, C. expressed his frustration with the progress of the disease, but more important, he also communicated his feeling

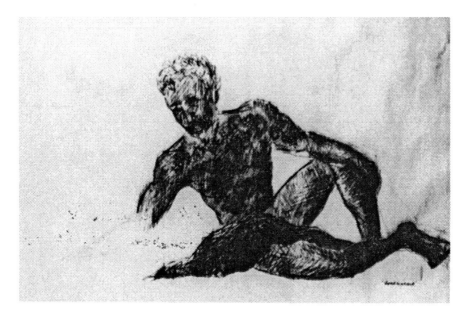

FIGURE 12.1 *Unreachable* **by patient with AIDS shows self as unable to reach out to others because of lack of trust.**

FIGURE 12.2 *Struggling against Fear* by patient with AIDS.

FIGURE 12.3 *I'm Hiding behind a Wall of Masks* by patient with AIDS.

of being let down by those he had finally come to trust, hospital staff members who had not informed him of their holiday leaves. He felt abandoned by them and once again felt isolated.

In his work with Pollack, C. gradually let down his guard and communicated feelings through his art that had initially been too painful to reveal. Over the period of their work together, his affect brightened considerably, and he became sufficiently trustful of others to bring his knitting projects to the unit when he came for individual outpatient art therapy. He showed his work to other patients and to staff members, trusting them sufficiently to show a side of himself that he had not revealed while he had been an inpatient. He decided to visit his family and tell them of his illness. There had been little contact previously, and he had not informed them of his hospitalization. C. used art making to explore his feelings in preparation for his visit home, and he was able to let go of old issues that were rooted more in the past than in the present.

Pollack reports that C.'s developing ability to take risks and explore his inner world through art prompted her to do the same. As their relationship grew closer, she was inclined to pull away and distance herself emotionally. She knew that she would be leaving the facility and moving to another city. But perhaps even more threatening were her mixed feelings about developing a close and trusting relationship with someone who was likely to die shortly. Nevertheless, she states that, "C. was my inspiration to continue on the path that I was on and not alter my course emotionally. I was aware of both of our losses in this relationship, yet the net gain was far greater for both as well" (p. 20).

At the end of her internship on the AIDS unit, Pollack curated a showing of the patients' artwork. It was a gala and significant event for the members of the gay community, many of whom were in attendance. The interest and the pride of those present were visible. A local restaurant donated refreshments, and there was a warm social feeling despite the suffering illustrated in much of the art. C.'s pictures were the centerpiece of the show, both because of the number of works he produced and the clarity of his images. C. was able to accept the overwhelming response to his pieces with pride. They stood as a tangible testimony to his reaching out to others and revealing his inner self.

The Art Room

In 1990, at a time when most patients with AIDS died of the disease, Russell Leander set up an art room on a hospital AIDS unit (Leander, 1991). The unit's population was composed largely of Caucasian middle-class gay and bisexual men who had contracted HIV through high-risk sexual activity. There was also a growing percentage of heterosexual male and female intravenous drug users who had contracted the illness from contaminated needles. Leander recognized that "combating anxiety and the loss of 'self' in an institutionalized setting called for a space that provided an escape from sterile lighting, cold linoleum, paging systems, and the smell of disinfectants" (p. 5). The space

Leander was given for art therapy was an empty hospital room with fluorescent lighting and a window that faced a brick wall. He set about deinstitutionalizing the room by gelling the lights with deep pink cellophane, covering the bare walls with panels of warm colored burlap, and hanging silk plants from the curtain tracks on the ceiling. Leander furnished the room with comfortable chairs, a supply cabinet, and a long work table. Unit volunteers and staff members responded generously to his request for contributions of fabrics, buttons, magazines, and other materials useful for art making. The art room also acquired an electric pencil sharpener for those who might be too weak to crank the manual kind and a supply of folding table easels suitable for bedside art making. Finally, the art room was equipped with a boom box and a large assortment of tapes, a sewing machine that had been donated, an electric tea kettle, and a keyboard and headset that were on loan. Because many of the patients spent sleepless nights, the art room was left open 24 hours a day, and there were no locks on the supply cabinet.

Having now worked on the unit for 8 years, Leander lectures students that patients with AIDS are in much greater danger of contracting disease from their caregivers than vice versa, due to the opportunistic nature of the many sources of infection to which patients with AIDS are vulnerable. As a result, it is necessary to be careful in the selection of art supplies. For example, Leander points out that chalk dust can be hazardous to those whose respiratory systems are compromised. Cutting blades can also be dangerous to those with blood-clotting impairment, in addition to posing a threat of disease contagion, because blood carries the virus. Other inappropriate materials include aerosol

---

ART MATERIALS FOR AIDS PATIENTS

Do Not Use

- Chalk
- Sharps
- Aerosol fixatives or adhesives
- Toxic cleaning solvents
- Hot glue guns
- Model airplane glue
- Permanent ink
- Sand trays

Substitutes

- Berol Art Stix
- Nontoxic fumeless markers
- Spring-loaded cutting tools with retractable blades
- Oatmeal trays

fixatives and adhesives, toxic solvents for cleanup, hot glue guns, model air-plane–type glues, and permanent ink. Instead, Leander has used dustless, wax-based Berol Art Stix, nontoxic and fumeless markers, and spring-loaded cutting tools with retractable blades.

Leander also points out to students that AIDS is not a single disorder, but a constellation of illnesses resulting from a single immunological impairment. Manifestations can include loss of vision, loss of mobility, dementia, fatigue, and disfigurement. There is often an increasing reliance on medication and medical apparatus. Obviously, the art therapist must be sensitive to the unique condition of each patient.

One of Leander's first patients was Ken, a 31-year-old man who had been diagnosed with AIDS 3 years earlier. He gave Leander some advice: "You'll need to be assertive. We're mostly just a bunch of sick old queens who are bored and angry and afraid. Don't be afraid to kick down a door and say, 'Get your ass out of bed! Try doing some art. If nothing else, it's fun' " (p. 7). Leander thought of this advice later when he took his final leave of Ken as he lay in a fetal position with bandages over his blind eyes. Above Ken's bed was hung his last art piece from his final art therapy session—a series of weak scribbles, which was all he could manage by then.

Not all of the unit's patients visited the art room spontaneously. Leander found that building a therapeutic alliance with some of the patients entailed meeting small needs, such as bringing water or an extra blanket, or dropping off the day's newspaper in a patient's room. A second step might be stopping in to ask if the patient would like a change of scenery and then offering the art room as a different environment. Sometimes patients would then pick up some art materials.

Such was the case for Robert, a 41-year old businessperson who had become depressed and withdrawn shortly after his admission for an AIDS-related infection. He drew an exotic flower and behind it an object that Leander could not identify (Figure 12.4). Robert explained, "It's a lawn mower. The flower is me. The lawn mower has a full tank of gas and it's barreling down. I know nothing can stop it. That's how I feel" (p. 16). In this way, Robert was able to emerge from his withdrawal briefly and express how he felt.

Juan, a 29-year-old waiter whose spleen had been removed the previous day, created a collage about being hospitalized for the first time. He asked Leander to help him search the magazines for the word *death*. Juan explained, "Even though my family and friends are supportive, we have an unspoken rule never to use the D-word. It's kind of nice finally getting to say it" (p. 22). He and Leander found variations of the word *death, dead,* and *dying.* From a choice of six, he selected *dying* and glued it onto his collage. Art therapy provided Juan an opportunity to express his feelings about death.

In addition to working with individual patients in the art room and some-times in their bedrooms, Leander did some group work. It was almost impos-sible to achieve group consistency. There were frequent admissions and discharges; patients became too weak to attend group sessions; and patients

FIGURE 12.4   Depiction of self as a flower about to be mowed down by lawnmower by patient with AIDS.

died. Because there was also scheduling gridlock—other treatments took precedence over art therapy—Leander had to be flexible. The availability of open studio time in the art room increased the opportunities for art therapy.

In one group there were four men with full-blown AIDS and one who was diagnosed HIV positive. During the session, the patient with HIV sat across the table from a patient who had severe Kaposi's sarcoma lesions on his face, and he became increasingly withdrawn. Leander sought him out later. He asked Leander if that was what would happen to him. The patient said he was looking into a mirror and seeing his future, and he began to cry. From then on, Leander offered him one-to-one sessions at his own request that provided him with an opportunity to express his feelings and to soothe himself by painting with watercolors. This experience taught Leander to recognize the significant difference between an HIV-positive condition and full-blown AIDS.

Although group work posed various difficulties, there were instances in which Leander's patients reached out to one another. Clyde, a 29-year-old dressmaker who was slowly losing his vision to cytomegalovirus retinitus, taught several patients how to use the sewing machine and assisted them in making Christmas presents such as pillows and stuffed snowmen decorated with buttons and glitter. He also made decorations to hang on each door of the unit. His help was especially important to patients who were unable to buy gifts.

Dave, a 30-year-old pinball machine designer, expressed himself in highly charged, eloquent artwork throughout his hospitalization. He also introduced some much-needed humor to the unit. While enduring a severe bout of neuropathic swelling in his feet, making them too sensitive to tolerate even the slightest touch, he drew Figure 12.5, *Neuropafeet.* His picture evoked much laughter from both patients and staff members. Upon his discharge, he presented the unit with a framed drawing of several patients and the legend "AIDS. Support each other" (p. 9). It was hung on the unit as a reminder of Dave and his work in art therapy.

Leander found that he was assisting his patients in possibly the most intimate experience of their lives, making preparations for death (see the drawing on page 339, in which time has run out for the emaciated patient who views his skull-like reflection). Nevertheless, he warns that one should not use work with terminally ill patients to come to terms with one's own fear of disease or death. The therapist must be constantly aware of the countertransference issues commonly reported by those working with HIV-infected individuals: fear of death, fear of contagion, helplessness, homophobia, overidentification, anger, and the need for professional omnipotence. (See the work of Stephanie

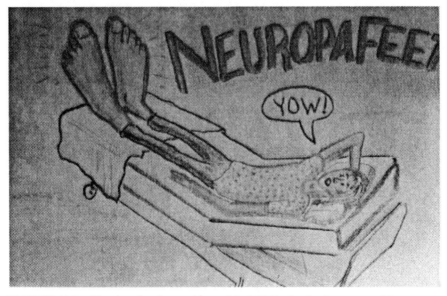

FIGURE 12.5   *Neuropafeet* **by patient with AIDS who had neuropathic swollen feet.**

Zentz, discussed later in this chapter, for measures to deal with some of these issues.) Obviously, a censorial, moralistic, or judgmental attitude regarding various lifestyles or personal belief systems by the therapist can be undermining to what might be a patient's last chance to find acceptance in a world in which he or she has been an outcast.

Finally, Leander has worked with some of his patients' grieving survivors, both before and after their deaths. Keeping the patients' artwork for their loved ones served to comfort the survivors. They could see that "in a large hospital in a large city their 'loved ones' individuality was recognized and valued" (p. 20).

The Art Room Improved

The new art room, which opened in 1993, was funded from a large bequest for strengthening art therapy willed by a former patient on the unit in recognition of its significant benefit to him. Located at the very center of the unit, the art room is easily accessible. It is a large room with plenty of natural lighting and a hardwood floor (instead of the usual hospital tile), leading onto an atrium that is filled with plants and comfortable chairs. In addition to an abundant variety of art materials, hundreds of cassettes have been added as well as a guitar, and the room is available to patients' visitors and to staff members. Upon admission, each patient receives a pamphlet describing the art room's services and is personally invited to come in and take a tour.

In 1994, when Mary Beth Seefelt began her internship under Leander's supervision, the population on the unit was changing, with an increase in the numbers of African American and Hispanic American patients, including more intravenous drug users of both genders. Most of the patients were dying (Seefelt, 1995). Seefelt saw her goal as using art therapy to help make the transition between living and dying more peaceful and less frightening for her patients. She found that many of them were able to work through their feelings of anger, denial, fear, and sadness and ultimately reach an attitude of acceptance.

Seefelt's introduction to the unit was a baptism of fire—her entrance was accompanied by the screams of John, age 38, "a skeleton of a man writhing in fear and pain on his hospital bed" (p. 2). He wrote the following poem:

> *Help me, please!*
> *I don't want to die.*
> *Please, somebody, help me!*
> *I'm not ready, oh God,*
> *I'm so scared.*
> *I'm dying,*
> *Oh God, I'm dying!*
> *Won't someone help me?*
> *I'm dying! (p. 2)*

Peter, a 36-year-old homosexual man who had contracted AIDS through high-risk sexual activity, had been hospitalized for weakness and confusion from toxoplasmosis, a complication of AIDS that causes inflammation of the brain. He was also suffering withdrawal symptoms from coming off an antianxiety medication, Ativan, to which he had become addicted. Peter painted representations of his feelings of anger and his wish for peace. He continued art therapy three times a week as his condition stabilized. Nevertheless, he was having trouble with both short- and long-term memory. Diagnosed with dementia, a frequent result of toxoplasmosis, he expressed his anxiety and frustration over his increasing lapses in memory to Seefelt. She suggested that he keep a daily journal, which he did, recording questions for his doctor and directives from the nurses. After a week of keeping the journal, he happily observed that his notebook had become his memory.

Two days before his discharge, Peter painted a galaxy of stars with a "happy smiling man" (p. 14) floating among the constellations. He explained that he was making a place for himself where he would go one day. In the meantime, he felt peaceful about his stabilized condition and his ability to return home. He had hired a round-the-clock caregiver so that he would not have to burden his family. Peter died a month later in his own apartment.

Doug, a 31-year-old gay man, had been involved in both high-risk sexual activity and intravenous drug use. He had been hospitalized for pneumonia associated with AIDS. In his art he expressed his anger and frustration at having spent most of his life feeling ashamed of his sexual preference. He had sought relief in drugs and promiscuity. He wanted to speak to adolescents about being happy with who they were rather than worrying about what others thought of them. He said that if he could share his story to warn others, he would not die in vain.

Doug was a musician who wrote songs, and one came to him as he drew the picture titled *Too Much* (Figure 12.6). He explained that the physical and emotional pain were too much: too much pain, pity, ugly smells, and nasty tastes. He said he had nothing to look forward to but death. He envied his friends who were already dead, because they didn't have to suffer alone and wake to gray days. They had left him behind, he felt. The triangle represents the battle in his body against the virus. He thought it looked like a maze with no escape. He outlined the triangle in red for his anger, which would crush the virus. Doug expressed his anger again in a collage, made in a later session, in which he used the phrase, "Get real mad, very Doug." Among the many images was the Virgin Mary holding a Visa card, representing his mockery of religion, which he said had excluded him for being gay. Doug was very pleased with his collage, finding it a good reminder of what his life was like and observing that "being mad can be all right" (p. 18). Anger obviously felt better than helplessness and despair.

Gwen was a 36-year-old woman who had contracted HIV through sex with her husband, an intravenous drug user. He had also given her hepatitis B prior to his death 4 years previously. At that time Gwen and the youngest of

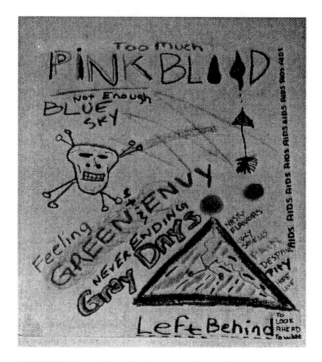

FIGURE 12.6 *Too Much* by patient with AIDS depicts pain, pity, ugly smells, and
nasty tastes.

her nine children (all under 16) were diagnosed as HIV positive. Gwen was
hospitalized for strep pneumonia associated with AIDS and liver failure from
the hepatitis. She had had eight hospitalizations in 4 months, and throughout
Seefelt's internship, she was in and out of the hospital almost weekly.

Gwen was shy and apprehensive upon beginning art therapy. She was
besieged with worries about her children and her current eviction from her
apartment. Her drawings were of pleasant memories from her childhood,
which she enjoyed as a distraction from her fears. As her health deteriorated,
she began to express her fears in her art. She drew herself as the central tall figure in a picture, with her youngest child attached to her. Large circles around
her are the four children she worries about the most. In the corners are the four
who can easily survive without her. She feels herself drawing up within herself, she said. Her spirit is reaching toward heaven.

Gwen spent the last month of her life in the hospital, eventually becoming
too weak to sit up. Her last piece of art was a collage she titled *The Precious
Things of Life*. They were memories and hopes for her children, that they
would grow up to have their own families, that they would live long healthy
lives, that they would appreciate nature and not experience prejudice. She had
made arrangements for them to be cared for by her mother and sister. In her
final 2 weeks, Gwen had Seefelt hang all her artwork on the walls of her hos-

pital room, saying that she had always wanted to have her own art gallery. Reviewing the art with Seefelt and her family, she pulled Seefelt aside and said, "Always remember how important art therapy is to people like me in a place like this" (p. 21). The artwork helped Gwen to take control of her life, and when she was ready to let it go, to take control of her death. Gwen found the courage to say good-bye to her children, who now have her artwork.

HIV-Infected Children

As AIDS infects more women like Gwen, it also claims more children, most of whom are infected perinatally or congenitally by a mother who is an intravenous drug user or whose sexual partner is an intravenous drug user or is bisexual. Art therapists working with such children face some unique problems.

In her work with children infected with HIV, Krista Nelson found that the themes expressed in their artwork often focused on medical procedures and hospital personnel (Nelson, 1991). The majority of the children came from extremely disadvantaged families that were suffering the ravages of AIDS in the deaths of other family members. Because their parents had died or had become unable to care for them, many of the children were abruptly thrust into a new family environment of other relatives or foster parents. Some who remained with their biological parents were exposed to substance abuse, poverty, neglect, and criminal behavior. In some cases there was isolation, as well, because extended family members and friends withdrew when told of the HIV diagnosis.

Nelson worked in a hospital child life program, where she saw HIV-positive children who were waiting for medical examinations and treatment. Sometimes she worked with their siblings, as well. At any one time there was a wide range of ages among the children, and they were called into the examining rooms intermittently, so that it was necessary for Nelson to have a flexible approach. She provided some structured group art activities as well as an open studio. She developed ongoing relationships with some of the children, with whom she arranged one-to-one time in a corner of the clinic.

Nelson had expected the children to be extremely ill and perhaps incapacitated. Most, however, did not have full-blown AIDS and appeared to be healthy and energetic. Because only a few of the patients, mostly teenagers, knew of their HIV diagnosis, themes of life-threatening illness were not expressed in their artwork. More common were themes of painful medical procedures, such as injections and intravenous infusions, and family issues, such as the death of a parent, placement in a foster home, or other family problems.

Lana, a 4-year-old who was waiting to receive an injection, drew *Bad Witch and Good Witch*. The bad witch is wearing a nurse's cap. Eddie, an 8-year-old who had attended the clinic for several years, asked Nelson to guess what the objects that he was adding to the girl he was painting were. First he added red tears, and when Nelson asked why she was crying, he painted a syringe going into her arm. He had received an intravenous infusion several hours earlier. Next, he painted a bubble of comic strip heroes that his figure thought about when getting the IV to help her be brave and strong. Eddie acknowledged that these were thoughts he conjured when getting an IV or an injection: "It helps me to be brave" (p. 11). Although both these children had been subjected to numerous medical procedures, they still found them frightening.

An example of the family violence present in the lives of many of these children was painted by Jesse, the older brother of a clinic patient. He rapidly covered the figure he had painted with red paint. He explained that the man had been shot. Later, Nelson learned that his stepfather had been shot and killed within the past year. Although a number of children depicted their homes in turmoil, some drew positive family relationships. When asked to draw one of his favorite things, Eddie drew himself playing Nerf ball with his foster father. Eddie is throwing the ball into a hoop as his foster father catches it for him.

The children used art to express grief over family losses, as well. Eddie and Nelson played a game with an Etch-A-Sketch. First, he drew a lone figure on the right, "a space guy named Eddie." She created a similar figure, though larger, on the left. He said Nelson's figure's name would be Maria, which had been his mother's name. When Nelson asked him to tell a story about her, he said she had lived in Puerto Rico and used to sing to him in Spanish. She had gotten sick, he said, and gone to the hospital where "she must have had a heart attack or something" (p. 22) because she died and he never saw her again. Eddie refused to talk further about her and moved away from Nelson to play with the other children. Abruptly ending discussion of a painful loss was typical for these children. Maria had died of AIDS when 3-year-old Eddie was in protective custody. He was later told that she had died of heart failure.

Despite the anxiety in the waiting room atmosphere of the clinic's art therapy studio, as well as the interruptions when children were taken into the examination rooms, Nelson saw that art therapy provided many benefits. In addition to the obvious possibilities for self-expression and emotional support, the program gave children opportunities for interaction with one another. Some of the children did not attend school or have siblings. Because of their backgrounds, some had had little experience with art materials and the sort of imaginative play they stimulate. Art making was an occasion for mastery and resulting self-esteem.

Video

During his first year working on the AIDS unit, Russell Leander made a video that showed the art room he set up and the art of some of the patients, with voiceovers by the patients discussing their work and the importance of art therapy in their lives. Many of these people are now dead. The video, which was professionally made with musical accompaniment, is an impressive testimony to what art therapy can bring to the population of patients with AIDS.

Perhaps influenced by Leander, William Kasser also used video, but in a different way and for a different purpose (Kasser, 1998). In 1997, Kasser began his internship on the AIDS unit under Leander's supervision. By this time there had been important changes in AIDS treatment. The virus could be reduced to undetectable levels in the infected person's blood, with the patient contracting few or no opportunistic HIV-related infections. Kasser points out that this shift in disease prognosis caused a major shift in the expectations of those living with HIV or AIDS. What was once a death sentence can now be replaced by daily struggles with disease management. Whereas Mary Beth Seefelt's goals were to help people with AIDS to have a more peaceful and less frightening transition from life to death, Kasser's work has been directed toward helping people live with HIV.

Kasser notes that the composition of the population infected with HIV continues to change, the incidence of infection decreasing among gay men, but increasing among heterosexual women, resulting in an increase in the number of children born with HIV. Although the death rate is decreasing, there is a rise in the number of those infected. Safe-sex education in the homosexual community is paying off, but among the indigent and some minority populations there is little access to safe-sex education, condoms, clean needles, and counseling. Even with the success of the new protease inhibitors, some patients fail to comply with their medication procedures because of the cost and the strict demands of these regimens. In addition to taking an abundance of medications daily, most people living with HIV must have monthly blood tests and make frequent trips to the doctor. As opposed to aiding in preparing for death, Kasser undertook to assist people living with HIV to reflect on the nature of their lives under these conditions.

As a now-familiar lens to record life events, Kasser found that video also helped his subjects to distance themselves from their daily lives in order to offer a more reflective perspective. The people with whom he worked came from the hospital AIDS unit where he interned, an alternative health care facility offering adjunctive therapies such as acupuncture and massage for people with HIV, and a group housing agency for people with HIV. Kasser invited each participant to record a day in his or her life. They were given the option of doing their own taping or directing Kasser in the taping. They began by listing the circumstances of their lives and the activities of a typical day. These were then visualized on a storyboard to serve as the plan for the taping. Each participant's video might include shots from several locations. Finally, they selected music and voiceovers for the accompanying soundtrack. Each participant reviewed the rough cut and the soundtrack and selected changes for the final video footage, which was then given to him or her. Obviously, a major benefit of the video-making process was the relationship each participant developed with Kasser as he entered their lives, followed their directions, and heard and saw their reactions to the conditions of their lives.

Jim was a 32-year-old gay Caucasian who had been diagnosed with HIV 2½ years before. He and his partner of several years had recently moved into a new apartment. At the same time, he began a new medicine combination as a participant in a new protease inhibitor study. The drugs had reduced the amount of HIV in Jim's system, giving him a more positive attitude toward life, along with a very stringent daily regimen of oral medications that required strict adherence in order to prevent viral resistance. Jim was feeling stressed by his job, living with his partner, housework, and nausea from the new drug program. He found himself becoming obsessive about household cleaning. These concerns were the focus of his video. His storyboard was specific in its images of his broom, pills, and other paraphernalia. He enjoyed directing Kasser in taping himself sweeping, the television, and his partner. Jim was an enthusiastic participant and did some of the taping himself. Upon viewing the rough cut later, he commented that "It probably helped me address some issues I was getting hung up on" (p. 11). At a time when he was feeling overwhelmed by the new conditions of his life, the video process helped him to put his reactions in a more balanced perspective. After making the video, Jim reported that his compulsive behaviors of sweeping and cleaning mirrors had abated.

Orlando, a 35-year-old gay Latino who could not read or write in English or Spanish, had had very little education. It was unclear whether his HIV status, diagnosed 4 years before, was affecting his thinking in the early stages of dementia. He was not cognizant of the medications he was taking nor very compliant in taking them. Orlando had suffered a severe accident as a child, leaving him partially paralyzed, and he currently needed a wheelchair because of a sprained ankle that would not heal. He required a great deal of guidance in the video project due to his physical and mental limitations. Orlando could not write a list of activities, nor did he create a storyboard initially. Nevertheless, he chose the thrift-store art in his room in the group home, his medications, the phone, his stuffed animals, his medical alert system, stacked dirty dishes representing the dish duty he disliked doing, and his foot pushing his wheelchair for the taping. Only after the scenes were taped did he produce a storyboard (Figure 12.7). It showed detailed depictions of activities he used to enjoy: driving, building a snowman, going on picnics, dating, drive-in movies, and church. Kasser suggested taping these scenes in the future.

Archie, a 39-year-old African American, died from complications due to AIDS during the video project. Prior to meeting with Kasser, he had planned his video. He wanted scenes of himself sitting on a bench and walking down the street against traffic with the Same Cooke song "A Change is Gonna Come" playing. Archie's health was failing, and he was easily fatigued, so Kasser helped him with his storyboard. He was not strong enough to go outside in the cold windy weather, so Kasser suggested using a stand-in. Nevertheless, Kasser was able to take indoor shots of him looking out the window and playing a record on his turntable. Archie was not able to finish his video

FIGURE 12.7 Storyboard for video by HIV-positive man showing activities he used to enjoy.

or view the rough cut. The night before he died, he told Kasser how sorry he was not to be able to complete the project. Archie had a strong sense of purpose and a clear focus in planning his video. It was a way for him to leave his mark. Kasser completed Archie's video for him, utilizing the shots of him and his stand-in accompanied by a soundtrack of the music he had chosen (Figure 12.8).

For Argenis, a 38-year-old HIV-positive man from Venezuela, the process of the videotaping itself was more important than the product. A social service worker who had been diagnosed with HIV 10 years before, he was currently almost free of the virus as a result of the protease inhibitor/antiretroviral combination he was currently taking. He wanted Kasser to do the taping while he directed. He had set up a shrine in his dining room including documents of his academic accomplishments, favorite books, family photographs, pictures and statues of role models, and trophies and medals from sports competitions. He had constructed this shrine and videotaped it a few years earlier to help him tell his family of his HIV status. (The video is now being used for educational purposes in Venezuela.) After taping the shrine, Kasser was directed to tape Argenis's daily yoga, meditation, tai chi, and relaxation practices. Then followed shots of his bedroom, daily medications, family photos, and his arrival home from work. After 3 hours of taping, Argenis seemed exhausted. Throughout the taping, he and Kasser had been discussing the issues that the subjects of his video brought up for him. He shared his poetry with Kasser as well, using it to stimulate more ideas for the video. Prior to viewing the rough

FIGURE 12.8 Frame from video by patient with AIDS who died before its completion.

cut, Argenis said that for him the video process was "great, like revisiting a place I was before. Rarely do we go back to parts of our life to remember and focus on things with a different perspective. . . . Directing you gave me the space and the power I needed over all the ideas and thoughts I was having all at once" (p. 19). Kasser felt a deep communication with Argenis, whom he found to be a spiritual person. He discovered that they shared similar views of life, destiny, art, love, and death. Their discussions served to remind Kasser of issues from which he had distanced himself in recent times.

Kasser's project was very interesting in a number of ways. There is a paradox of immediacy and distance. Taped mostly in the participants' own homes, the video brings the viewer (including the protagonist) into intimate contact with the subject. Yet the process of viewing allows one distance. For Argenis, for example, creating the video brought him back to the experiences from which his objects were derived (photos, trophies, etc.), while viewing it provided distance. Mostly, Kasser took direction from the participants in recording a segment of their lives. There was much discussion as they brought Kasser into the intimacy of the world they inhabited. For them, the connection and catharsis were significant. The fact of the video project itself was very significant to them as well, giving importance to their daily lives. And finally, the relative permanence of their creations, which would likely outlive them—particularly for people facing imminent death, such as Archie—gave them an opportunity to make a mark by leaving a record of themselves behind.

Care for Caregivers

As is evident from the connections between art therapists and clients implicit in all the work described in this chapter, working with patients with HIV or AIDS is extremely demanding emotionally. To provide support, Stephanie Zentz began an AIDS caregivers' art therapy group (Zentz, 1994). She states that stress results from adjusting to multiple losses, recognizing one's own mortality, fear of contagion, helplessness, anger, irrational unfulfilled rescue fantasies, decreased job satisfaction, and possible stigma associated with the AIDS population, which may result in professional isolation and lack of support from family and friends. Early on in her work with patients with AIDS, Zentz recognized the stress she was bringing home after a day of work, often feeling she was riding an "emotional roller coaster" (p. 6). She began utilizing her own art and keeping a journal to process her reactions. She and her supervisor, also an art therapist, looked at the work together. Out of this experience grew the idea of forming an art therapy group for interested staff members. Of the six Zentz approached, five joined: the two art therapists, a hospital chaplain intern, a case manager, and two volunteers. All were working with HIV-infected children, whose suffering and death were especially painful to the caregivers. The group met for 14 weeks immediately after a clinic day each week.

Zentz's art therapy supervisor, Krista Nelson, created a three-dimensional piece in relation to 8-year-old Amy, who, unlike some of the children, knew of her AIDS diagnosis and had planned her own memorial service. Nelson had worked with her for 3 years and had witnessed her suffering from her illness as well as from many losses of family members and friends to AIDS. After one of her sessions with Amy, Nelson needed to express her feelings about her struggles in working with Amy at a time when her condition had worsened to the extent that imminent death was possible. Nelson selected a small box, covered it over with black tissue paper, and placed pieces of colored tissue paper and feathers inside it. As she closed the sides, giving it a houselike appearance, the colored paper and feathers squeezed out of the box. Finally, she wrapped string around the box in all directions. She described the piece as representing her reaction to Amy's resistance in their previous session. The colored tissue and feathers are the strong emotions held inside Amy. Because so much was held in, Amy was difficult to reach. The string represents the defenses wound tight around the feelings to hold them in as Amy continued to survive the multiple losses in her young life. Nelson wanted to cut the string and picked up scissors, pretending to do so, but she recognized Amy's need for her defenses. This art piece helped both its creator and the rest of the group members to vent their frustrations and sadness.

Zentz utilized the art group in dealing with the difficulty she was having in her treatment of another AIDS-infected child, 7-year-old Marie. The child was unaware of her diagnosis because her family did not want her to know.

THERAPISTS' ISSUES AND AIDS

- Fear of death
- Fear of contagion
- Anger
- Over-identification
- Multiple losses
- Helplessness
- Rescue fantasies
- Need for professional omnipotence
- Homophobia
- Stigma of AIDS

She had developed chronic thrombocytopenia, a blood disorder caused by the medication she was given to treat AIDS. This disorder is life threatening; if untreated it can cause bleeding to death. Marie was unaware of this danger. In her artwork, she expressed her experience of loss, finding in art expression a powerful means of communicating with Zentz. They developed a very strong and understanding relationship.

Marie's life was shrouded in veils of secrecy. Because of the stigma of AIDS, she had not been told of the death of her mother, who had died of AIDS when Marie was 6 months old. Marie was living with her paternal grandparents, who had adopted her and who had led her to believe they were her parents. Her father, also infected with AIDS, had come to live with his parents and daughter in the final stages of his illness; he had died 6 months earlier. Marie had been told he was her brother. Shortly before his death, he told her he was her father. When she related this to her grandparents, they said he was crazy. Nevertheless, during their time together, Marie established a strong bond with him. Because her grandparents told her that she was not to speak of the dead, she used her drawings to express her loss of him. For months after her father died, she wrote his name in many places around the clinic. Marie needed answers to her questions, but her grandmother, fearful of what she and Zentz might discuss, was always present when Zentz was working with Marie. It was difficult for the grandmother to keep her stories straight, which left Marie very confused. For example, she didn't know whether a relative of her own generation was a cousin or a nephew.

After spending almost a whole day with Marie and her grandmother, Zentz needed to deal with her frustration through the art support group. The process of art making proved to be particularly meaningful for Zentz. On a base of red construction paper, she began tearing and layering pieces of colored tissue paper. She left some partially unattached so she could slip pieces of black construction paper with oil pastel scribbles underneath them. An area of glitter to the left suggests even more layers to the depth of the tissues of Marie's life. With purple yarn and a large needle, Zentz sewed around the layers of tissue paper to represent the grandmother's efforts to keep the truth hidden. Next, Zentz placed a large piece of yellow tissue paper over the layers and added pieces of black construction paper to magnify the small pieces she had inserted earlier. The image resembled a fish, so she elaborated the image further (Figure 12.9). Figure 12.10 shows a detailed view of the layers of tissue paper beneath the fish. Zentz's association of the fish was probably stimulated by the Play-Doh fish Marie had made in art therapy earlier in the day. Zentz saw the picture as representing the secrets in Marie's life that were below the surface. The fish is trying to bite the black form that represents the pieces hidden from view. Zentz smashed a mirror and attached its shards to indicate that Marie was reflecting on her life and beginning to ask for some well-deserved answers. But the image at the upper right indicates not only the family's secrets, but also the trail of questions and answers that would likely follow from the disclosure of her illness: "How did I get the illness?" would lead to disclosures of her parents' identities and their deaths from AIDS, which would lead to, "Am I going to die?" Zentz found both the deception and the possibility of disclosure extremely disturbing. She recognized the broken mirror as representing not only reflection, but also dangerous sharp slivers that could cause Marie to bleed to death. It was emotionally difficult for Zentz even to talk about Marie. Creating the artwork about the child was very helpful to her.

FIGURE 12.9   Tissue-paper collage made by art therapist in reaction to difficult feelings from treatment of HIV-positive child and her grandmother.

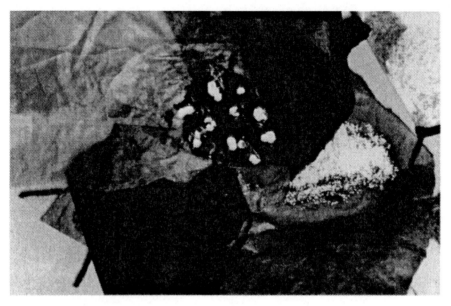

FIGURE 12.10   Detail from Figure 12.9 showing layering.

The caregivers' group became very supportive for its members and pro-vided a relief from their trying days at the clinic. In addition to loss, grief, and worry about particular patients, members shared with one another through their art each one's unique view of death and mortality. For example, a case manager explained that her collage of childrens' faces with feathers above them depicted "somewhere between heaven and earth" (p. 18). She continued, "The children are not here with us and not there (heaven) yet. The children are like spirits. . . . One day the children are happy and playing, and the next day they're gone." On the other hand, Zentz's supervisor's portrait of death show-ing a central skeleton is more severe (Figure 12.11). Around the central bust of a skeleton are three mourning figures. Black paint is dripped around them.

Summary

With the rapid changes in treatment of HIV and AIDS in recent years, both medically and socially, there has been greater progress in the work with gay clients than in that with most other populations.

- Petra Miskus (1996) worked in an early hospital program that recog-nized the special needs of gay and bisexual patients. Participants in her groups and in individual sessions focused on internal homophobia and relationship issues.
- Wendy Pollack (1988) began her work with hospitalized AIDS patients

FIGURE 12.11   Portrait of death by art therapist working with HIV-positive children.

in 1987, when there was little in the way of emotional services for them. The art-making and relationship opportunities she offered them provided an outlet for the expression of painful feelings. The showing of her patients' artwork was of benefit not only to them and those close to them, but also to the members of the gay community at a time when there was much less cohesion and fewer opportunities to come together to share feelings and pride in expressing themselves.

- Russell Leander (1990) set up an art room in 1990, initiating a growing and highly successful resource on a hospital AIDS unit. At the time, most of his patients were dying from AIDS-related conditions. He developed his program around their unique medical and emotional needs. He often worked with their loved ones and survivors, as well.

- In 1993, Mary Beth Seefelt (1994) began working in the new art room, funded from the generous bequest of a deceased patient, under the supervision of Russell Leander. Her focus was the transition from life to death for patients. The population on the unit was changing to include many more African American and Latino patients, including women and intravenous drug users.

- Krista Nelson (1991) worked in a hospital child life program utilizing art therapy. With an increase in the number of female patients with AIDS, more children who had been prenatally infected with HIV became patients. Most of the children were symptom-free and unaware of their diagnoses. They focused on painful hospital procedures and family problems in art therapy.

- In 1997, William Kasser (1998) found that advances in treatment were enabling many patients with HIV and AIDS to live for many years with the disease, so that therapy could be directed toward living with a strict medication regimens, rather than toward preparing for death. He developed a video project in which people with HIV documented a day in their lives.
- Stephanie Zentz (1994) began an art therapy group for caregivers to help them use art expression to deal with the emotional strains of working with HIV-infected children.

Conclusion

AIDS is not simply a "gay disease," as it was viewed by many in the 1980s. Although it is still potentially lethal, people are now living with AIDS (under strict medication regimens) for many years. Although there has been increasing success in fighting the disease, it is still a major plague of epidemic proportions. Caregivers are still faced with losing their clients to death, as did William Kasser when Archie died before the completion of his video. Death of those close to us and the eventual confrontation with death that each of us must face remain the ultimate mystery of our lives. Those working in the arena of HIV/AIDS encounter it on a daily basis.

Mary Beth Seefelt (1995) concludes her summary of her work as follows: "I still recall the cries of John. They will forever echo through my mind, serving as a reminder of the humbling pain and suffering AIDS inflicts on its prey" (p. 25).

ART THERAPY PROJECTS

Projects discussed in this chapter are described further in Chapter 15, "Art Activities and Materials":

- Body tracings (Miskus, 1996)
- Art exhibits (Pollack, 1988)
- Collage (Leander, 1990; Seefelt, 1994; Zentz, 1994)
- Writing in journals (Seefelt, 1994)
- Video making (Kasser, 1998)
- Boxes and containers (Zentz, 1994)

Chapter 13

Older Adults

Ghost made with fabric stiffener on gauze by 52-year-old man after a cerebral contusion.

Virginia hobbles in, planting her walker hard on the floor with each measured step. She eases into a chair at the table, nodding to the others, who have already begun tearing colored tissue paper for collages. It's spring, and the group is making flower petals and leaves. "I need a magazine," she says. "It's prom time, and I want a picture of young people dancing. I was the prom queen, you know." Faintly she hears strains of "Stardust" and hums it softly as she leafs through Time *magazine.*

Work with older adults requires sensitivity to their unique physical, mental, and emotional conditions. There may be compromises in physical and mental abilities as well as emotional responses to impairment. In addition to these losses, there are likely to be abundant other losses, as well. These may include deaths of loved ones, termination of a career, loss of youth; but perhaps of greatest significance is the loss of a sense of self as an independent, fully functional adult. Problems of dependency may loom large, and family relationships often alter greatly in this regard. Overlying all of this may be an anticipation of death. Belief systems vary widely about death, so that its meaning to each individual must be considered by caretakers.

Art therapists generally see older clients in nursing homes or day care centers where they may spend several or most days of the week, giving family members some relief from care and providing the participants social, recreational, and educational activities. In these settings, therapy is not the sort of psychotherapy art therapists provide in psychiatric facilities. Nevertheless, the life problems older adults face may be considerable, as mentioned. The ways that art therapists provide treatment are likely to be more subtle and less direct than in psychotherapy. The work may or may not be insight oriented, depending on the interests and functional level of the client. Treatment goals are often centered on improvement in current quality of life, which may include socialization to counter isolation, self-expression, adjustment to current life conditions, and increased self-esteem.

Physical limitations require not only sensitivity on the part of art therapists in providing materials that can be used without difficulty, but in some cases, resourcefulness as well. For example, art therapist Cherie Natenberg devised a Velcro strap for an 83-year-old woman with severe arthritis whose hands were frozen into fists. The strap was wrapped around her hand with a paintbrush secured in it. Natenberg placed the paints in a flat dish and the water in a low bowl so they could be easily reached with the brush. After a few sessions, the client developed good control in her brushwork. The woman had been an artist in her younger days but had not painted in years. Previously isolated and withdrawn, she now began to blossom, both expressively and socially, not only in art therapy, but in other areas of her life, as well. When she died a couple of years later, tribute was paid to Natenberg at her funeral for the importance of her work in adding to the quality of the woman's final years (Wadeson, 1987).

Countertransference issues may take on a more universal kind of identification than is the case with some other populations; if we are lucky, we will

---

LOSSES ASSOCIATED WITH AGING

- Physical impairment
- Deaths of family and friends
- End of career
- Loss of independence
- Loss of sense of self as a fully functioning adult

---

grow old. Expectations about old age may be modified by work with older adults. In some cases, especially in long-term work, art therapists may witness the decline and death of clients. In such instances, the art therapist shares in the client's losses. However, many students want to work with older adults as a result of their own positive and loving relationships with their grandparents. Reciprocally, some older adults are especially happy to receive the attentions of a young person, perhaps recreating a relationship with a child or grandchild, or reliving their own youth to an extent. Attachments can be very warm and gratifying to both parties.

Life Review

In 1963, Robert Butler wrote a seminal paper contending that older adults are naturally inclined to talk about their pasts in an effort to resolve previous conflicts and reach a state of peace in old age (Butler, 1963). As a result, life review has become a frequently used structure in work with older adults. In her work at an adult day care facility, Janet Stallman encouraged reminiscence art therapy groups in which her clients reviewed their lives (Stallman, 1996). Many of her clients experienced depression with a sense of hopelessness, despair, loss of identity, isolation, frustration, and anger due to profound loss associated with the deaths of loved ones and the loss of physical abilities. Some of them suffered from aphasia, so Stallman hoped the art would become a means of communication of personally meaningful experiences. She intended the group art making to furnish an opportunity for socialization and a sense of connection. She also hoped to pose a challenge to perceptions of the past and thereby identify previous behaviors and perceptual patterns used for adaptive problem solving that might serve in the present.

One of Stallman's groups consisted of eight people ranging in age from 57 to 80. Each was experiencing depression, but otherwise was high-functioning cognitively. Stallman's major goal for this group was the integration of life events to achieve a true sense of identity. The group met weekly for 75 minutes for 14 weeks. Typically, the first 40 minutes were devoted to artwork, and the remaining 35 minutes were spent in discussion. For the members with aphasia there was little verbal participation and explanations were minimal. The art-work was especially important to them, as their life review would have been nearly impossible without it.

Stallman began the first session with a directive to create an image about a significant event from the past. She set out white construction paper, water-colors, pastels, markers, and collage materials and offered to provide any other art materials the group members requested. Subsequent sessions began with a review of the previous week's images and a suggestion to create a pic-ture from a memory of a significant life experience 5 years from the time of the previous week's image. Or, the client could choose an aspect of the previous piece to emphasize. Stallman had planned to encourage each individual to develop a series of related images that would eventually address each of the life stages delineated by Erik Erikson (Erikson, Erikson, & Kivnick, 1986). She found, however, that when common issues emerged among the members, it made more sense to provide a relevant group directive than to continue the self-directed serial images. Of course, one of the major advantages of group work is this sort of recognition of universality. Nevertheless, the group issues fit into the themes of the series in Stallman's life-stage approach. At the culmi-nation of the group, the images were mounted onto heavy black paper, arranged chronologically, and bound together in book form.

Bill was a 66-year-old man who had suffered a cerebral vascular aneurysm (stroke) 8 years before, leaving him with paralysis on the right side of his body, which made walking difficult for him. Although high functioning cognitively, he exhibited moderate expressive aphasia, communicating verbally in a limited manner, which had resulted in the loss of his career. Bill's wife had died 10 years earlier and he lived with one of his four daughters in a close-knit family. Stall-man's goal was to help him to express his feelings about his considerable losses.

In his first group session, Stallman suggested creating a personal time line and then developing an image from a pivotal point in the time line. Bill depicted his wife reading the results of his bar exam to him while he worked on a construction site as an electrician (Figure 13.1). Bill explained that his family had expected him to continue in the family business as an electrician and scoffed at his attending law school. The ensuing discussion focused on how Bill pushed himself beyond others' expectations of him, relating his suc-cessful law career to the way he had pushed himself after his stroke to walk and talk, surpassing his doctors' expectations. His picture shows his wife's support while other family members were not so supportive.

During the following two sessions, Bill drew pictures about his profes-sional achievements. At the fourth session, however, he returned to his wife and created an image of her funeral (Figure 13.2). She is shown in the casket; dabs of color around her indicate the guests at the funeral. The triangle repre-sents the church, and a yellow design is light coming in the windows. Bill described the details of the funeral and discussed aspects of his wife's person-ality and her death. He was becoming more personal in revealing himself to the group. At the next session, he became angry with another group member,

FIGURE 13.1   **Life-review drawing of wife giving support for career change by 66-year-old man after a stroke.**

Myrna, who was discussing the death of her sister. Bill yelled at her to shut up. He was surprised when Stallman brought out his picture of his wife's funeral. From that point on, he became apologetic to Myrna. She had evoked a strong emotional response from Bill that he could not control, probably related to his difficulties regarding the loss of his wife.

The group members were spontaneously drawing pictures about the losses they had experienced, especially in relation to disabilities from stroke. Stallman suggested that they create two self-images, one before the stroke or brain injury and one afterwards. On one side of his paper, Bill drew his young family, including his wife. On the other side, he drew himself waking from his coma, with his daughters around him.

His next picture was of the family vacation house (Figure 13.3). His wife and four daughters have their arms outstretched. On the other side of the picture is Bill, also with outstretched arms, standing beside his car, and at the top he has written "12:00 Sat to 12:00 Sun," indicating the 24 hours he spent with the family on summer weekends. Bill told the group that he had sold the house after his wife's death because it was too painful to be there without her. He described their last vacation together shortly before she died of cancer. The next week, he drew a picture of their wedding and told the group about his in-laws. Bill continued to explore his relationship with his wife and to share this very personal and supportive connection, both in the art therapy sessions and

FIGURE 13.2 Life-review drawing of wife's funeral by man who drew Figure 13.1.

FIGURE 13.3 Life review drawing of family separation at vacation house by man who drew Figures 13.1 and 13.2.

in informal gatherings outside the group. He now had to face the obstacles in daily living caused by the stroke without her support. It was clear that he missed her immensely. The group art therapy sessions enabled him to become less isolated in dealing with his current difficulties.

Sara, a 57-year-old woman, had suffered a left-hemisphere aneurysm 12 years before, resulting in right-side paralysis, blindness in her right eye, severe expressive aphasia, and some receptive aphasia. Her husband had died 13 years before, and she lived with her daughter, a sister, and a niece. Cognitively, Sara was high functioning and typically presented herself with pleasant enthusiasm. When asked how she was, she consistently replied, "Fantastically!" Nevertheless, physical limitations were a source of frustration for her.

Sara's initial artwork evidenced some resistance and superficiality. Her fifth drawing, however, was more personal. She drew herself as a 15-year-old girl with a piano floating over her head. It was out of her reach, as was her ability to play it at present due to her paralysis. It had once been an important part of her identity; Sara said that nobody had to force her to practice on the piano. The image facilitated a discussion of Sara's life pattern of self-sufficiency and independent achievement that applied not only to her past piano playing, but also to the committed and independent manner in which she worked on increasing her vocabulary. Figure 13.4 shows her comparison drawing of before and after the stroke. Before the stroke, she is shown as a stiff but strong figure occupying most of the space. After the stroke, the boxlike

FIGURE 13.4   Life-review drawing comparing self before and after stroke by 57-year-old woman.

shape in the picture represents her wheelchair holding a smaller representation of herself. Discussion centered on how that confined figure would feel. Sara imitated herself saying, "Fantastically!" followed by a sarcastic, "Yeah, right, fantastic." She felt sufficiently safe in the group to give up her enthusiastic façade.

Sara's images became increasingly more personalized and expressive. She drew a picture of her wedding (Figure 13.5), genuinely depicting a time of joy as she and her husband danced together. Sara's final picture was a response to the directive to draw how others see you (Figure 13.6). The figure has a worried look and one arm is smaller, consistent with Sara's unilateral paralysis. She described it as a happy little girl. This self-representation reveals fundamental changes in her sense of identity in terms of how she thought others perceived her. She had spoken previously of her dependence on her family and of feeling as though she was considered a child rather than a woman. As Sara's artwork became more expressive, her verbal participation in the group also became more authentic and personal. Participating in the art group with others who also felt the loss of physical abilities and important components of their identity enabled Sara to move past superficial pleasantries in dealing with her changed life situation. The art was important in providing freedom of expression beyond the limits of her expressive aphasia.

Another stroke survivor, Frank, introduced himself as an award-winning and well-paid commercial artist. Nine years previously, he had suffered a cerebral vascular aneurysm, leaving the left side of his body paralyzed. He could

FIGURE 13.5   Life review drawing of dancing with her husband at their wedding by woman who drew Figure 13.4.

FIGURE 13.6 Self-portrait as "a happy little girl," the way others see her, by woman who drew Figures 13.4 and 13.5.

walk with difficulty using a quad cane, but at the day care center he moved about in a wheelchair. Frank lived at home, where his wife was his primary caregiver. He also had three adult children. Although he had expressed interest in the art therapy group, it was difficult to engage Frank in art activity. As a successful commercial artist, he may have been experiencing performance anxiety regarding what he said was his inability to represent his ideas visually.

His initial art was schematic, often including only stick figures. Nevertheless, he was an eager participant in the discussions of others' images and experiences, frequently interjecting insightful comments. Frank brought his own art materials to the center, but easily became frustrated with preliminary sketches he made to try to get the image correct. He said that he had lost his motivation to make art and spoke of his disappointment at not winning a recent design contest. Frank's alternations between excessive flattery of others' work and boastful comments about himself made interaction with him difficult. Although he spoke little of his art productions, sometimes leaving the session before the discussion, his pictures became more personal and expressive. In response to a directive to the group members to draw an image from their wedding day, Frank drew himself and his wife with cartoonlike faces inside a stylized heart. Their arms looked as though they were pushing against the edges of the heart, changing its shape. They appeared to need more space. Perhaps Frank was feeling confined in his present dependent relationship with his wife. In Figure 13.7 he drew himself more expressively, with a large cloud hanging over his stiff figure. Although his engagement in the group remained somewhat tangential, Frank derived some benefit from the interaction.

The last thing that most people want to hear from incapacitated older adults is a list of complaints about their condition. Nevertheless, these are people who have suffered profound losses at the most basic level of functioning and in some cases, such as Bill's, have lost those dearest to them. The art therapy group allowed them to be themselves and to express their feelings to others in similar circumstances who could understand how they felt. This sort of recognition of universality of experience is one of the most moving factors in group therapy. For these individuals, who suffered communication compromises because of aphasia, the opportunity for self-expression through art facilitated community and connection and countered isolation. Further, having lost many of the pillars of their self-esteem, such as a law practice for Bill and the ability to play the piano for Sara, the pride in accomplishment that making art can provide is a significant benefit for older adults with handicaps.

FIGURE 13.7   Self-portrait under a cloud by older adult man after a stroke.

Three-Dimensional Art

MaLinda Johnson, who worked in an adult day care center, found that three-dimensional art projects were beneficial to older adults with physical and mental impairments because of the heightened sensory experience they can provide (Johnson, 1998). The focus of her work was on the strengths and functional abilities of her clients, rather than on their disabilities, with the goals of maximizing their experience of sensory and motor functions and helping them to experience success in these endeavors. Although the clients may have had little or no control over their physical and mental capacities, the art provided them with an opportunity to take control of whatever they wished to create. The art was intended to improve the clients' quality of life, as well. Clients at the center had suffered physical or mental impairments due to brain injury from accidents, strokes, dementia, and other related disabilities. They attended the center from 1 to 5 days each week. Johnson's art therapy group met twice weekly for 90-minute sessions. A classical music radio station played in the background at the request of the members.

Betty was a 73-year-old widow who had suffered aphasia and right hemiplegia from a stroke. Her two-dimensional artwork was composed of repetitive themes of houses and trees. When she was given plaster gauze and other construction materials and instructions in how to use them, she jumped right in enthusiastically. She took pleasure in constructing her familiar motifs, working the plaster gauze and paints with great care. Her house and trees appear to come to life in their new three-dimensional world (Figure 13.8). When Johnson gave Betty a mask form, she approached it with the same zeal. She applied three layers of plaster gauze, painted it red, and glued a flower on the forehead and feathers and other found objects at the mouth. The three-dimensional materials afforded tactile stimulation and further expressive possibilities. When Betty gave her usual subject matter three-dimensional form, she was motivated to move beyond her usual images and venture into more dramatic self-representation.

David, 52, had suffered a cerebral contusion from an accident that resulted in compromised cognitive abilities, aphasia, and weakness in his left extremities. He had been a teacher until the accident had truncated his career. He lived with his wife and two children. When the group was making pictures, David avoided investment in the projects and remained on the sidelines observing. Prior to Halloween, Johnson introduced a cheesecloth ghost project. David playfully put the cheesecloth on his head and said boo several times. The group members were to paint the cheesecloth with fabric stiffener, but David continued his interactive playfulness and dipped his cheesecloth into the bowl of stiffener. He massaged it in the bowl before draping it over a plastic form to create a ghost shape. He molded the saturated cloth further, exerting control over the materials. The tactile nature of this three-dimensional project engaged David so that he became invested in his creation and dropped his typical pas-

FIGURE 13.8 Three-dimensional construction in plaster gauze by 73-year-old woman after a stroke.

sive response to the group. After the cloth had dried, he removed it from the form and added eyes and a mouth (see page 367). He was pleased with his whimsical ghost and was eager to show it to his wife. Subsequently, Johnson introduced clay in the group, and once again David participated actively. He was able to roll and smooth the clay with his impaired arm as well as his functioning arm, and showed much interest in the range of sculpture tools.

Johnson has found that although adult day care clients may suffer physical and mental disabilities, their sensory functions are still intact. Those with cognitive impairments may have difficulty interpreting all they see, hear, touch, and smell, but they can still derive pleasure from these senses and use them to communicate. Betty's and David's projects are quite striking and brought them feelings of pride, accomplishment, and heightened self-esteem. Both these clients were more impaired cognitively than some of the other members of the group. The active participation encouraged by the sense-stimulating media brought them closer to the functional level of the other members.

Sensory Stimulation

The often quasi-medical environment of nursing homes lacks sensory stimulation for residents who may be mostly confined there with little or no opportunity to go elsewhere. Sensory stimulation is often a prime objective of art therapy in these settings. Deborah Del Signore has found that olfactory stimulation may facilitate memory retrieval, as well (Del Signore, 1999). Del Signore notes that everyone has had experiences of scents recalling a time and place. She explains that the olfactory sense is the only one that is directly connected to the limbic system in the brain, which is the seat of emotions. She also states that studies have shown that an odor is never forgotten.

Del Signore formed an aroma group at the nursing home where she was working. It was composed of both cognitively high-functioning older adults with physical impairments and residents who were beginning to show signs of dementia. Generally, the group members began with a discussion of a given scent she had brought—identifying it and discussing where they had smelled it before and whether they liked the scent. Specific activities included the following:

- Potpourri collage, in which members were given an assortment of potpourri of various scents, heavy paper, and glue. Large pieces of potpourri of various colors and textures were used, and residents were encouraged to create the collage with the scents in mind.
- Response to a specific aroma, in which the group members were asked to make an art response to specific aromas, such as those of tea, mint leaves, scented fabric, and candy.
- Bounce screen, utilizing a silkscreen method, by painting over fabric softener sheets onto paper. The sheet's scent stimulates memories of laundry.
- "You Are What You Eat" mask, in which the group members decorated masks with dried fruit and spices, producing highly aromatic and textured masks.
- Edible still life, in which Del Signore brought in a basket of oranges. The group members smelled them, painted a still life picture of them, and then peeled and ate them.
- Mystery aromas, in which Del Signore tied various aromatic objects into pieces of fabric and gave one to each group member, then asked them to make a picture of whatever it suggested.

Initially, members were resistant to making art in this unaccustomed way, so that it took several attempts before they were willing to try Del Signore's suggestions.

Natalie, a 65-year-old woman who was confined to a wheelchair because of multiple sclerosis, had also suffered an extreme loss of vision and showed early signs of dementia that produced difficulties in verbal communication. Perhaps due to her vision impairment, her sense of smell was particularly acute. She laughed while making her potpourri collage, saying that the smells were beautiful and making jokes about the various textures. She overheard others talking about the pine potpourri and asked for some. This was unusual for her, as she was generally passive in groups. Her face lit up, and she said she had to include it in her collage. She explained that it reminded her of the camp that she and her husband had owned in Wisconsin. Others became interested and asked for details. Although it was usually difficult for other residents to understand what Natalie was saying, now she was leading the discussion, naming a number of lakes in the area. Soon the entire group was sharing experiences they had had in that area. Natalie was eager for her collage to dry so she could hang it in her room and "smell the camp."

The potpourri collage made by Rose, an 84-year-old woman who suffered severe depression and was beginning to show signs of dementia, represented a woman under the sun (Figure 13.9). Responding to the scent, she said that the dried apples reminded her of the sun. The first time Rose ever showed any pleasure in the group was in response to the smell of peppermint in scented fabric. She yelled, "Quick, get me a crayon!" It was the most animated and energetic response Del Signore had seen from her. She created a winter scene (Figure 13.10). She told the group that as soon as she smelled the peppermint, all she could think of was winter, and that she wanted to draw it before she forgot what she was going to do.

Rose continued to respond positively to the olfactory stimulation until she smelled the spices Del Signore brought for the "You Are What You Eat" masks. She found the oregano especially unpleasant. She painted her mask and decorated it with yarn instead of the spices. At the end, however, she glued oregano onto the nose and titled it *A Nightmare*. Shortly after making the mask,

FIGURE 13.9 *Woman under the Sun,* **potpourri collage for sensory stimulation, by 84-year-old woman with severe depression and signs of dementia.**

FIGURE 13.10   Winter scene stimulated by scent of peppermint drawn by
woman who made Figure 13.9.

she had a significant decline in functioning, with increased disorientation,
lowered energy, and decreased socialization. Perhaps the mask expressed her
notice of her cognitive decline. Prior to this, however, the olfactory stimulation
had seemed to decrease her isolation, as she had socialized more with the
group. Her self-esteem had increased in the group, and she was proud of her
ideas. Although she was suffering the early stages of dementia, the stimulation seemed to help her mind to work better.

The olfactory stimulation helped to evoke visual imagery and memory
recall for nursing home residents, even those with dementia. The stimulation
also led to increased socialization within the group. There is one caveat that
Del Signore points out, however. For some people, the aging process dimin-
ishes the sense of smell. There were moments when she noted that some group
members clearly could not smell a scented object being passed around. It was
certainly counter to the aroma group's purpose of stimulation to remind members of their deficiencies. Obviously, an art therapist must be sensitive to such
possibilities. On the whole, however, it was apparent that most of the group
members benefited from the olfactory stimulation.

Alzheimer's Disease

Work with patients with Alzheimer's disease is generally custodial in nature,
as little hope is given for those stricken with the unrelenting progressive men-

tal deterioration brought about by this condition. The first and most noticeable symptom of Alzheimer's is memory decline, which often leads to frustration, anxiety, and self-blame on the part of the client. The memory decline also leads to an inability to process and learn new information, so the client may ask repetitive questions. Loss of language ability makes communication difficult with inappropriate remarks ensuing at times. Many clients are confused and disoriented.

Four million people in the United States have Alzheimer's disease. The Greater Chicagoland chapter of the Alzheimer's Association has estimated that the number in the Chicago area has more than doubled since 1980. It is the fourth leading cause of death in adults, and 1 out of every 3 families has a member with the disease or a related disorder. One-half of all nursing home residents have Alzheimer's disease or a related dementia-type disorder (Blass & Bloom, 1980). Alzheimer's disease is progressive and irreversible. There is no known cause or cure for this condition. In addition to its obvious impairments of dementia, there may be aphasia, apraxia (motor disturbance), agnosia (failure to recognize objects), and inability to perform executive functioning, such as planning, organizing, sequencing, and abstracting.

Given the low functional level of clients with dementia and the hopelessness of their condition, one might question the feasibility of using art therapy productively with this population. Despite the extreme limitation imposed by the condition, art therapists have developed effective programs with these patients. For example, Linda Mathews created an art therapy program at a nursing home and wrote a grant proposal for funding (Mathews, 1997). She describes the objectives of art therapy with Alzheimer's patients as follows:

1. Maintaining interaction and communication skills through:
   • Small social support groups to counteract isolation
   • Nonverbal communication through making art
2. Maintaining cognitive and functional abilities by providing:
   • Opportunities to make simple choices
   • Opportunities to use remaining functional abilities
   • Opportunities for productive behavior to develop a sense of pride and dignity
   • Opportunities for release of emotions.

Brenda Brecht worked with clients with Alzheimer's disease in individual art therapy sessions at a day care center (Brecht, 1989). Sessions lasted 30 minutes to 1 hour, depending on the client's ability to stay relatively focused. Brecht identified the three stages of the disease and designed the art therapy to suit the conditions and needs manifested in each stage of the progressive effects of Alzheimer's disease. Reisberg (1983) identifies three broad clinical phases; (1) the forgetfulness phase, (2) the confusional phase, and (3) the dementia phase. In the *forgetfulness phase*, the individual recognizes increased difficulty in recalling names of places and objects that had been familiar. There may be a heightened irritability and shame over the forgetfulness. In the second or *confusional phase,* forgetfulness becomes more pronounced, and there is failure to remember recent or past events. The individual may become lost when going to a familiar place, and concentration becomes diminished. Concern and shame turn into feelings of helplessness, and a flattening of affect may occur. The final or *dementia phase* is characterized by worsening of memory to the point where daily living tasks become extremely difficult or impossible. Left on their own, patients probably would not survive. The eventual end of this phase is the loss of most or all personal abilities. Although Brecht encouraged her clients to create "free" pictures, most responded more readily to structured directives. Music playing in the background was an encouragement, as well.

Hannah is an example of a woman who showed signs of both the forgetfulness and confusional stages. She failed to recall names of objects and became frustrated with herself. She realized that her memory was failing and became confused and ashamed. Nevertheless, she was still able to use most art materials with little or no direction. In her initial sessions, she drew free pictures, but became discouraged that she could not "do art," as she put it. Therefore, because she was ashamed over her memory loss, Brecht gave her tasks that redirected her attention toward her abilities rather than her deficits. She was given precut construction paper shapes of various colors from which to create a collage. Hannah became very interested in this project and was proud of the result, which she signed and hung on the wall (Figure 13.11). A similar task with different material was arranging ceramic tiles on a framed cardboard surface. Once again, she was very pleased with the result. Both pictures looked very beautiful to her. These projects helped to raise her self-esteem.

Although Fran had reached the dementia phase, she was able to use art materials with direction. She enjoyed creating a magazine collage. When she added a picture of the Sphinx, she commented that she would like "to visit a place like that before I go." Fran also made a tissue-paper collage. After pasting two pieces of tissue paper down, she asked for drawing materials, and she

---

STAGES OF ALZHEIMER'S DISEASE

1. *Forgetfulness phase.* Difficulty recalling names of familiar objects and places, shame over forgetfulness, irritability
2. *Confusional phase.* More pronounced forgetfulness including recent and past events, diminished concentration, shame, feelings of helplessness, flattened affect
3. *Dementia phase.* Worsening of memory, unable to live alone because daily tasks of living become too difficult or impossible, eventual loss of most abilities

**FIGURE 13.11   Collage from precut forms by woman
with Alzheimer's disease.**

was delighted with her completed mixed-media construction. Sometimes
Fran was too agitated to concentrate. On one such day, Brecht suggested painting to the rhythm of music. Fran made two paintings, although she spent only
a short time on them due to her anxiety. She was pleased with the result, and
left the session calmer than when she had come in. She explained that she had
feelings inside that bothered her, but making art helped her feel better.
Because Fran could not remember what she had done from one session to the
next, display and review of her work was very important for her. She was
delighted when Brecht reminded her that she had created the paintings.

Joyce's dementia had advanced to the extent that she no longer remembered how to use art materials. Brecht asked Joyce to direct her in creating the
work. In making a magazine collage, Joyce hunted through the magazines for
pictures of flowers, which Brecht then cut out and pasted on the page according to her direction for placement. She commented that there should be grass

beneath them, so Brecht directed her in using a green oil pastel, which she added in small delicate strokes. Another joint project was made from tissue paper. Joyce drew a flower pattern, and Brecht cut it out of the bright-colored tissue paper Joyce chose. She deliberated over where to place it and was very pleased with the finished project. Most of Joyce's pictures were signed by both Joyce and Brecht. Working together enabled Joyce to experience some success and pride and helped her to build a strong relationship with Brecht.

Shirley's difficulties from dementia were compounded by her visual and hearing disabilities. Nevertheless, art therapy offered her an opportunity to express herself. She made magazine collages representing her family. There was illness and death in her family at the time, and the artwork allowed her to express her concerns during a difficult period. Nevertheless, she became frustrated when her pictures were fragmented or unrealistic, so Brecht presented her with tasks centered on creating a design, such as using paper shapes and ceramic tiles to create collages.

Jane was Brecht's lowest-functioning client. She could not use the art materials or remember a direction from moment to moment. She was very anxious during the sessions. Brecht found that playing music helped her. She skipped and dotted the paint brush across the paper to a lively song, and in another session she made a string painting to music.

Brecht recognized that her work with patients with Alzheimer's disease was of necessity supportive, not insight oriented or curative. In general, she found that tasks that centered around abilities her clients still possessed were most beneficial for the first phase of Alzheimer's disease. During the second phase, she added more structure and direction to simple tasks that were within the clients' capabilities. In the final phase, she tried to provide relaxing tasks that were not overstimulating. Throughout, Brecht tried to maintain her clients' dignity while encouraging their creativity in order to promote a sense of accomplishment and raise their self-esteem.

Clients with Alzheimer's disease made up half the population at the day care center where Deborah Ruland worked, and there was a separate program for them. Her goals for her group members were to improve their quality of life and to increase their self-esteem. She found that the completion of a successful art project became a visual reminder of accomplishment when it was displayed.

Ruland worked at a very slow pace with her clients, kept directions short and simple, and repeated them often. She minimized noise and disruptions because the clients were easily distracted. They required a calm environment in order to stay focused. It was important to keep the tasks within the functional limitations of the clients. Directions had to be broken down into single steps that were concrete and understandable. Some of the projects she used that were successful included tissue-paper collages, seed mosaics, magazine collages, and simply filling pages with color. With staff assistance, she was able to introduce glue, but scissors were too difficult, so she encouraged the

---

ART ENGAGEMENT

Supportive art therapy at a slow pace with directions kept simple, broken down into single steps with concrete, understandable instructions, repeated often

1. *Forgetfulness phase.* Tasks centered on abilities
2. *Confusional phase.* More structure and direction added
3. *Dementia phase.* Relaxing tasks, not overstimulating

Source: Stages of Alzheimer's disease from Reisberg (1983).

---

clients to tear the paper. She found that messy materials such as papier-mâché and clay were not appealing to her groups. Less messy, but still tactile and three-dimensional, was Play-Doh. An advantage Ruland found in working with this group was that they had fewer inhibitions in expressing themselves through art than other older adults, and in some cases they were more creative, as well. Exhibiting the finished work provided the clients with a reminder of their achievements.

An example of this sort of creativity can be seen in the seed mosaic made by Jenny. Ruland drew a circle on a piece of paper for each member of the group and gave them seeds to glue onto it. The other group members filled in the circle, but Jenny made it into a face (Figure 13.12). Alice's work is another

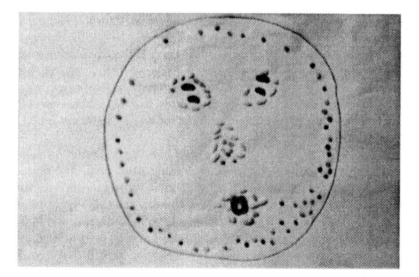

FIGURE 13.12 Seed mosaic by woman with Alzheimer's disease.

1ˢᵗ LAW OF THERMODYNAMICS

- If system does work, internal energy of the system decreases because that energy is going somewhere else

- If work is done **to** the system, internal energy increases because the system is taking "energy" in (+W)

- REMEMBER, cannot destroy or create energy, only transform it!

example. Ruland planned a Play-Doh mobile for the group and invited them to make balls, cylinders, and other shapes from Play-Doh. Alice made hers into a tree, and after it was baked she painted it.

Many patients with Alzheimer's disease are confused and unable to follow directions. Mary is an example. Her attention span was short as well. Nevertheless, there were some activities that she enjoyed. She liked to paint with string, dipping yarn into a bowl of paint and creating a design by dragging the yarn across the paper. Mary could make her own designs with little assistance. She smiled readily when she was complimented on her work.

Two men in the group were having difficulty making a macaroni collage, so Ruland suggested that they work together. With her assistance, one man placed the macaroni on the paper and the other glued it down. They were able to accomplish the task together, and they experienced social interaction.

Another group effort resulted from the absence of a staff member. Because group members were confused by this unexpected change, Ruland suggested that those who could do so tear out magazine pictures of smiling people for a large collage. Ruland wrote "We missed you today" in the center of the collage, and the group members chose a location to hang it where the absent staff member could see it the following day. The collage served as a visual reminder that she would not be in that day, but that she would return the following day, thus allaying some of the anxiety about her absence. (For additional material on art therapy with patients with Alzheimer's disease, see Wadeson, Durkin, & Perach, 1989.)

Hospice Care

As a child, I was told that people eventually died of old age. Later, I realized that old age is not a cause of death—the diseases of old age are. Now, after having witnessed the deaths of my parents in their 90s, I believe that they *did* die of old age, even though their diagnoses were heart failure and Alzheimer's disease. Medical advances that extend life mean that we may die later and differently from our predecessors. Advanced medical treatment and life-support technology may extend not only life, but also the dying process.

These conditions have changed the approach toward death from an effort to prolong life under any circumstances to an awareness of the importance of quality of life. Many people are writing living wills expressing their wishes to be spared invasive medical procedures when there is no hope for recovery. In this same vein, the hospice movement has developed to provide support and care for dying persons and their families. Hospice care is instituted when there is no hope for recovery with the aims of making the dying patient as comfortable as possible, providing relief for family caregivers, and improving the patient's quality of life as much as possible. There are residential hospices as well as hospice care that is brought to the patient's home. Although such services are available to dying patients of any age, most often it is older adults who need them.

Art therapy can contribute to the hospice objective of elevating the quality of life for the dying patient and for family members. In developing an art therapy program for the terminally ill hospice patients, Cheryl Denz's goals were to increase the patients' activity levels, autonomy, and communication (Denz, 1997). She focused on their remaining physical and mental strengths and the expression of their feelings. Experiences of accomplishment can enrich the patients' lives. Denz notes that many who are terminally ill face boredom, powerlessness, and loneliness. Her research indicated that more than 92% of terminally ill individuals have no control over their environment and little control over their bodies, which leaves them feeling useless and stripped of their dignity. As she puts it, "many have 'died' before they are actually dead" (p. 4). Making art provides an opportunity for autonomous decision making that can counter this sort of powerlessness to some degree.

Denz's clients began to look forward to the opportunities to create art that she provided in her biweekly visits to their homes. Many spent their days watching television and welcomed having "something to do," as they put it (p. 4). Their creations were self-expressions, gifts and messages for others, and sometimes decorations for their rooms.

Many terminally ill patients experience social isolation. Denz's visits brought social interaction as well as art-making opportunities. Each session ended with a discussion of the artwork. Even when a patient's physical deterioration precluded making art, Denz continued her scheduled visits until the patient's death in order to prevent feelings of abandonment.

As discussed in Chapter 12, it is often important to dying patients and their families that they leave something they have created as gifts and tangible memories for their loved ones. One patient chose to make necklaces, each one a gift to a specific family member. With Denz's technical assistance, she rolled strips of paper to form various sized oblong beads. As her body grew weaker, her mind remained sharp and her spirit strong as she focused on slowly threading each bead. After completing each necklace, she expressed her joy and feeling of accomplishment. For her, the necklaces represented pieces of her life and love that her family could hold onto after she was gone.

Summary

In working with older adults, art therapists must be sensitive to their unique physical, mental, and emotional conditions. The clients are generally seen in nursing homes and day care centers, rather than in therapy facilities. The goals of treatment focus more on quality-of-life issues than on therapeutic change. The element of loss is often predominant, particularly the loss of loved ones and loss of abilities. Art therapy can enhance the maintenance of dignity and self-esteem in the face of such losses. Even clients in the advanced stages of Alzheimer's disease can benefit from art making. For further discussion of work with older adults, see Wadeson (1987).

- Janet Stallman (1996) employed a life-review approach in group work with older adults in an adult day care facility. Helping clients to identify former adaptive patterns helped them to deal with the depression and, in some cases, feelings of hopelessness they were encountering. Recognizing the universality of their experience fostered a sense of connectedness within the group. The artwork provided a framework for viewing pivotal experiences in their lives.
- MaLinda Johnson (1999) utilized three-dimensional media for sensory stimulation in her work at an adult day care facility. Despite cognitive and physical losses, her clients benefited from three-dimensional art experiences in managing their anxiety, lessening their isolation, investing themselves further into the art process, and expressing themselves.
- Deborah Del Signore (1999) utilized olfactory stimulation by organizing an aroma group for nursing home residents both to add to their sensory stimulation and to facilitate their memory recall. Among other things, the group made potpourri collages, drew pictures in response to scents, and decorated masks with spices. Specific scents reminded residents of various experiences. The stimulation increased socialization within the group, as well.
- Linda Mathews (1997) developed an art therapy program at a nursing home and wrote a grant proposal for funding. Noting that Alzheimer's disease is the fourth leading cause of death in adults, her goals were to preserve residents' ability to make choices; help residents preserve a sense of pride and dignity and maintain independent functioning where possible; provide a nonverbal means of communication; develop a social support group; and to facilitate the release of emotions that accompany severe loss.
- Brenda Brecht (1989) designed art projects at an adult day care center to meet the needs of clients in various stages of the progression of Alzheimer's disease. Tasks in the first phase, forgetfulness, centered around abilities the individuals still possessed. More structure and direction were provided for simple tasks in the second, or confusional, phase. In the final phase, dementia, there were relaxing tasks that did not provoke overstimulation. Where necessary, Brecht assisted the client in a joint effort that could be successful.
- Deborah Ruland strove to improve the quality of life and increase the self-esteem of clients with Alzheimer's disease at an adult day care center. She found that their successful art projects became visual reminders of their accomplishments.

- Cheryl Denz (1997) used art therapy to enhance the quality of life of terminally ill hospice patients and found that it offered opportunities for expression, communication, socialization, autonomy, and accomplishment.

Conclusion

Many art therapists feel that it is a privilege to work with people nearing the end of their lives. There are often opportunities for some very tender relationships if art therapists are sensitive to the unique needs of their clients. The momentous losses some of the individuals have experienced can leave them feeling hopeless and depressed. There can be significant satisfaction in helping to allay some of these feelings. When functional abilities have been severely diminished, art expression can still provide an opportunity for creativity and a sense of pride. Most of us who have the fortune to live to an old age will suffer some degree of loss of our former abilities and perhaps will outlive those who are dearest to us. Working with clients at this stage of their lives gives us a perspective to help us live our own lives as well as we can.

ART THERAPY PROJECTS

Projects discussed in this chapter are described further in Chapter 15, "Art Activities and Materials":

- Directed life-review drawing (Stallman, 1996)
- Plaster gauze (Johnson, 1999)
- Masks (Del Signore, 1999; Johnson, 1999)
- Cheesecloth and fabric stiffener (Johnson, 1999)
- Sensory stimulation (Del Signore, 1999)
- Printing with Bounce screen (Del Signore, 1999)
- Collage (Brecht, 1989; Del Signore, 1999; Ruland, 1988)
- Painting with yarn (Ruland, 1988)
- Mobiles (Ruland, 1988)

Chapter 14

Self-Exploration through Art in Community

Applying makeup for ritual celebration at the University of Illinois Annual Art Therapy Summer Institute at Lake Geneva, Wisconsin.

Alissa closes her eyes and lets the images float by. Her grown daughters dance before her as they did as children. Her mother smiles at her and dies. Alissa's life flings itself in her face. How to sort it all out? As the week glides by, her mother speaks to her from a watercolor portrait. Alissa's eyes fill with tears as one of the members of her small group remarks that the woman she has painted looks like herself. Later, she speaks to her portrait, telling her mother how she wishes she had lived to see her grandchildren grow up, how she missed sharing with her the joys and sorrows of raising them.

Most of the work described in this book has involved clients with painful, often tragic lives. I would like to end on a more upbeat note. Not everyone with whom art therapists work is in difficult circumstances, although it is certainly true that most art therapy positions are to be found in facilities serving people with rather severe problems. There are also well-functioning people seeking to use art for personal growth and reflection.

Every summer for a number of years, I have conducted a workshop on using art for self-exploration at the University of Illinois Annual Art Therapy Summer Institute on the shores of Lake Geneva, Wisconsin. The workshop is not a course in the conventional sense, in that hardly any didactic material is presented. Nor is it therapy, as there is no therapeutic relationship or responsibility offered. It is a guided opportunity for self-exploration through art. In earlier years, it was more guided than it has since become. I felt some responsibility for providing structure. Participants created "a safe place" from which to begin their self-journeys. They made inside/outside boxes. They did body tracings to explore both positive and negative identities influenced by their families of origin. They created life-story books. They made plaster gauze masks of all sorts, and images of their "shadow" sides, what others saw, and their fantasy selves. Throughout the years, participants have worked very creatively and uniquely with an abundance of media.

More recently, however, the workshop has taken a different tack. Although the workshop is open to all interested people, most of those who come are busy professionals with little extended time for self-reflection or art making. So the workshop is now offered as a time and space to do just that. On the beautiful wooded shores of Lake Geneva, we gather each morning to the sound of an Indian drum used throughout the workshop to call us all together. We begin with relaxation exercises, followed by a suggestion to watch the images that come behind closed eyes in that relaxed state. Participants then create an art piece of whatever they want to pursue in their art and self-reflection for the week or two of the workshop (it has varied in length). We are called together again and we walk silently, holding our art and looking at the art each of us has made. Then everyone forms groups of four based on their responses to one another's art. This, too, is done in silence.

Everyone has charted their course and found their own small group within which they will share their art throughout the workshop. The remainder of the time is spent creating a body of work, meeting as a whole at the beginning and end of each morning and in the small group before the final gathering of each morning. Participants are encouraged to work alone, rather than socializing during art making, so that they can be most deeply in touch with themselves. Many work outside or on the large veranda of the spacious old building we use. An important part of their reflection on their art is keeping a journal, especially dialogs. Participants are encouraged to speak to their images each day and to let their images speak back. There have been many surprises and increased awareness from these dialogs. Some participants have written poetry, as well.

The small group meetings are not the usual sharing of art. The members are discouraged from explaining their work. Instead, they follow the *pursuit of the image* approach to responding to the art (Wadeson, 1987). Each art piece is discussed in turn, first by the other members of the group and then by its creator. Responses are limited to what each person finds intriguing, exciting, interesting, or puzzling about the piece. In other words, responses are emotional rather than intellectual and are based solely on visual information. From these reactions, including one's own, participants develop another art piece. Sometimes they develop a particular aspect of the artwork that has been discussed. The discussion may stimulate a new direction in their art. Or they may disregard the comments altogether.

On the last day of the workshop, each participant creates an installation of his or her work, and everyone visits each one as a group and hears the story of its development.

The initial suggestions given are few, but they are important. Some of the participants are inexperienced in art. The workshop stresses the importance of following their own way, wherever it will take them, rather than believing that there is a right way to make art. Most often, their own way takes them both to self-discovery and pleasure in making art. We discuss the paradox of intentionality and spontaneity, encouraging both. It is helpful to have a direction, to chart a course. It is also enlivening and broadening to surrender to one's own images, to let them lead the way. Many have discovered that their images have had far more to tell them than their initial quest asked. A direction may be broadened or changed altogether.

Added to the key words of *intentionality* and *spontaneity* is *community.* What has been described in the art making and journal keeping could as readily be done alone. Community adds another dimension in several ways. Although participants are encouraged to work on their art and journal by themselves so they won't be distracted, they cannot help but be influenced by one another's art. We have found that the stimulation of working near other creative art makers has been enormously enhancing. Although we are not directly interacting as we draw, paint, sculpt, and construct, we are somehow supporting one another's efforts. Most of us grew up believing that copying was shameful. Yet there can be concrete advantages in learning from one another, such as seeing a new use of materials or a theme worth exploring. Most obvious is the support of the small groups, which often become an intimate home for sharing personal images and reflections, a place to be known and to know the others. Sharing images can bring about a level of intimacy that can go deeper than words alone. Often there is time after the initial pursuit-of-the-image responses for further discussion in which the members share their life issues.

Examples

One group member commented that hearing the drumming and forming a circle created a warm and comfortable beginning and ending ritual each day to contain the exploration process for her. Another found that the art making had a life of its own, and that she was following rather than leading it. A participant who was accustomed to art making discovered the dialoging to be the most interesting part of the process for her. She had never allowed her artwork to convey messages to herself in such a direct way. She was surprised at how freely answers flowed from the questions she asked. She said that she thought she had given her unconscious a voice and herself a device for listening, creating a communication channel for discoveries previously unrecognized.

As one participant began a magazine collage, the images she selected formed into the theme of her daughter's recent engagement. She became aware that it was impacting her more than she had initially realized. She experimented with a variety of materials and repeated the engagement theme in a jute hanging. She used beadwork to denote the high points of her own life. In the process of constructing it and adding Stars of David made from Popsicle sticks painted gold, representing her daughter's religious conversion, she recognized that it had been difficult to accept her daughter's transition to adulthood. Dialoging with the art helped her to understand how to be supportive without being intrusive. Arranging her art pieces for the culminating installation helped her further in seeing parallels between her own life and her daughter's.

When another group member closed her eyes in the relaxation exercise, she saw lines. Using vivid inks, her drawings of the lines reminded her of the fences that line the vast outback of her native Australia. The lush colors began to change the lines to the familiar rainforest of her childhood backyard. Successive drawings of the lines behind her eyes took her to the formation of a face that gave her reassurance about her future and to a suppressed issue that she had been avoiding. Each time she had tried to draw the issue previously, her heart and mind had frozen, she said. She was amazed to find how she had now become free with her few random marks. She made an X with a circle around it, which reminded her of how she signs letters with a kiss and a hug. Newly married, she thought of the letters she had exchanged between herself in Australia and her husband-to-be in America. Over her drawing she wrote a letter to him and one she had wished to receive from him before their marriage. This was a cathartic experience that brought closure to an issue she had been unable to tackle before. On the last day of the workshop, her lines took her back into the lush greens of the wet tropics and the deep colors of her childhood. They evoked a sadness, missing what she had once taken for granted. She had come full circle.

In another member's first image, she saw her brain overtaking her heart. She used to be more spontaneous in her artwork, she felt, but her art training had caused her to become less so. She drew many images in the workshop and found that her favorite was a spontaneous image of a tumultuous ocean with a large ship plowing through its cresting waves. She wrote in her journal, "wherever there is a sea (in my art), there must always be a ship." She pondered why she liked this unintentional image so much and concluded that it represented a freedom from the anxiety that accompanied her intentionality in her art in the form of performance fear. She rediscovered the spontaneity she thought she had lost. She also identified with the ship. It might travel through treacherous waters, but it was seaworthy and strong. As her confidence in her spontaneity increased over the course of the workshop, she felt that the authenticity in her art increased, as well.

Bereavement

Each year, there are other workshops at the summer institute, as well. Russell Leander conducted one on bereavement. The participants made ritualistic icons to deal with their feelings about the death of someone significant to them. One was especially important to its creator as she tried to mediate her ambivalent reactions to her father's recent death. She had brought a picture of him as a young man, the way he had looked when she was a child. Some of her cherished memories were of him taking her sailing, so she created a boat, glued his picture to it, and set it to sail in a tub of water. Upon his recent death, however, the family learned that he had led a double life, which was now causing them hardship. For this participant, creating the sailboat for her father in the midst of her current shock, anger, and disappointment with him brought back the happy times and reminded her of what a good father he had been.

In my workshop, one participant worked lovingly on a puppet she had learned to craft from a previous workshop on puppet making taught by Anne Canright. This glowing green frog (Figure 14.1) came to represent her recently deceased father, who brought her comfort and guidance. She felt that in times of need her frog could be a source of solace.

Rituals

Although I have used ritual creation in individual therapy, it comes to serve a community purpose when developed by a group. Individuals in my private practice have created some elaborate rituals—for example, to mourn the death of a mother who committed suicide when the client was 10, and for empowerment to release anger at perpetrators of sexual abuse. In the workshops at the

FIGURE 14.1 Consoling frog puppet by workshop participant.

summer institute, the rituals have been of a more celebratory nature. Traditionally, rituals serve to mark important transitional events and thereby to bind the community in their support. Cultural rituals include seasonal markers such as harvest festivals, joining of families through marriage, births and deaths within the community, and the ascendance of leaders. At Lake Geneva, various teachers have conducted ritual workshops using a number of expressive modalities and celebrating such events as the summer solstice and the creation of community. These celebrations have involved group planning and creativity, often utilizing costumes created for the purpose (Figures 14.2, 14.3, and 14.4), music and dancing (Figure 14.5), elaborate makeup (page 391), and the setting up of a special place. Creating rituals together enhances group cohesion and sparks group creativity. Some of the rituals orchestrated by Clay Bodine have included torchlight processions, life-size cardboard puppets (Figures 14.6 and 14.7), and large structures the groups have built, such as a castle (Figure 14.8) that was later set on fire as part of the ceremony.

Environments

The creation of environments by small groups within the large group is similar to the group process involved in creating some of the objects used in rituals. These are made outdoors, with the group usually deciding to include individual spaces created by each member and common space for all. Figure 14.9 shows an example of one. After they are completed, all the workshop

FIGURE 14.2   Ritual costume at summer institute.

members visit each one in turn. Often, the small groups provide welcoming rituals in their spaces for the visitors. All kinds of materials can be used. The use of space is important in serving the needs of the participants, both for demarcating private and shared space and for forming the boundaries of the environment. Obviously, aesthetic considerations are important, as well. The groups are very careful not to deface or permanently change the natural environment in any way. The experience of making art to surround oneself and to form a group space is very different from the usual art projects. Like ritual creation, building environments develops group cohesion with particular attention to group and individual needs and preferences.

Is It Therapy?

Should this sort of work be considered art therapy? Certainly it is art, and it is therapeutic. The leader, however, functions more as a facilitator than as a therapist. The leader makes art along with the others and shares personal reflections

FIGURE 14.3 Ritual costume at summer institute.

FIGURE 14.4 Ritual masks at summer institute.

FIGURE 14.5   Ritual dance in costume at summer institute.

FIGURE 14.6   Life-size puppet in ritual procession
at summer institute.

FIGURE 14.7   Larger-than-life dragon head in ritual procession.

FIGURE 14.8   Castle for ritual drama at summer institute.

FIGURE 14.9   Environment created by small group of workshop participants.

with them. There is no effort to assume therapeutic responsibility or to form a relationship in which there is therapeutic dependency. With this sort of blurring of definition, it is important to make expectations clear. Because personal material is revealed in such groups, we suggest that all agree on confidentiality. Beyond that, participants share with one another in their small, intimate groups and do not look to the leader for therapeutic intervention or responsibility. This experience is time-limited, and there is no expectation that any particular problem will be solved. Participants explore and get what they can from their own journeys of art making and journal keeping. Usually they get much, and often they are surprised. Some have said that the experience has changed their lives.

Although the journey of self-discovery that these workshops provide might be beneficial to almost anyone, they tend to attract professionals in the helping professions and graduate students who are interested in art expression. Because they are offered by a university, there is a charge, which restricts them to people who can afford them or whose employers pay their tuition. Art therapists must recognize that it is a great luxury to be able to work with highly motivated people eager to explore themselves and to find expression in art. Many of the participants are very creative, and their creativity is contagious. In a more perfect world, these attributes would characterize more of our clients. Of course, these are the characteristics of most art therapists themselves. In their training, if not before, they experience the joy and enlightenment they find in their own art making. Working with actual clients usually opens their eyes to a very different world of grimmer realities for people who may be struggling just to survive. The opportunity of working with highly functional creative people, including art therapy students, can provide an inspiring change for art therapists whose day-to-day work is with people who are in much greater need.

Summary

Art therapy can utilize community support to enhance personal self-exploration and development among those who are not in treatment. Residential workshops provide opportunities for the expansion of creativity and the luxury of self-focus uninterrupted by daily responsibilities. Included are the following:

- Harriet Wadeson has conducted workshops on self-exploration through art for a number of years at a retreat center.
- Russell Leander conducted a bereavement workshop at the same retreat center.
- Workshops included creating community rituals.
- Environments were created, as well.

Conclusion

Although the work described in this chapter cannot be considered therapy, these workshops have been life altering for some participants. Short of that, for many they have produced profound insights in addition to the joy of expanding their creativity in a very supportive and intimate community. Working with the high-functioning creative professionals and students who attend these workshops can be a welcome change for art therapists who ordinarily work in the trenches with people whose problems and needs are most severe.

ART THERAPY PROJECTS

Projects discussed in this chapter are described further in Chapter 15, "Art Activities and Materials":

- Sequence drawings in pursuit of the image (Wadeson)
- Altars and memorials (Leander)
- Rituals (Wadeson)
- Puppets (Bodine)
- Wearable art (Bodine)
- Life-size cardboard figures (Bodine)
- Environments (Wadeson)
- Masks (Bodine)
- Writing dialogs (Wadeson)

PART III

Art Therapy Projects

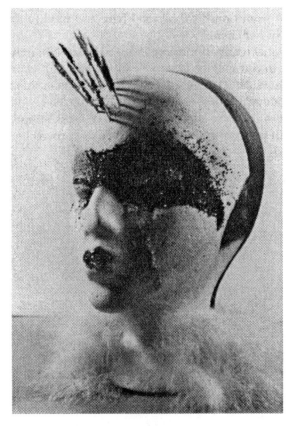

Styrofoam head construction.

This description of art projects used in art therapy must begin with a very important caveat. Although the art therapists highlighted in this book have developed many innovative projects in their work with varied populations, the emphasis must always remain on the client's process, not on the product created. The art project is a means, not an end. The projects described often served to develop creativity, to promote pride in accomplishment, to increase the ability to remain focused and concentrate, and, by these many means, to elevate self-esteem. Nevertheless, the desired goals were these results, not the completion of the project itself. This is a very important distinction between art therapy and art education. Although both may achieve similar results, the focus of *art education* centers more on the meaningful and aesthetically developed product. In *art therapy,* a simple drawing often facilitates therapeutic goals as readily as an elaborate art production.

The art therapist's thinking about the work is crucial in this regard. *First* the therapist must set the goals, *then* think of the means to achieve them. Hopefully, readers will not approach the project descriptions by being attracted to a particular art process and then figuring out how it might be used in practice. My hope is that the reader might recognize the value of a specific project for promoting specific goals in working with a particular population. The reader might gain ideas from projects described here and modify the project to suit the needs of his or her clients.

Art therapy is a creative endeavor in every sense. Not only do we strive to foster creativity in our clients; creativity is a significant characteristic of the way in which we work with them. The art therapists in this book have been creative in their development of art projects to suit the needs of their clients. Hopefully, readers will find these art therapists' work stimulating in designing innovative art projects to meet the needs of their own clients.

Chapter 15

Art Activities and Materials

Whimsical mask performance.

This chapter describes many of the art projects used in the art therapy described in this book. Some are original; some are modifications of projects frequently used in art therapy; and some are tried and true old standbys. Obviously, this cannot be an exhaustive categorization. A further reservation is in the descriptions of the projects themselves. There may be additional possibilities for ways of creating a particular object that are not mentioned here. There is no attempt to present an exhaustive discussion of any of the media used or the techniques involved. For that sort of information, many arts and crafts books are available. The purpose of these descriptions is to give some guidelines and stir of the creative soup that nourishes the field of art therapy.

Collage

This chapter begins with collage because it is one of the least threatening activities that can be presented to those new to art therapy who may be fearful of committing themselves to the creation of an image. Collage is a process of assembling and arranging materials. It is especially advantageous for people who may be either intimidated by the prospect of drawing or painting or for those who may be physically unable to do so. For elderly patients with Alzheimer's disease, for example, Brenda Brecht provided precut shapes and in some cases helped to glue them down (Chapter 13). Generally, strong paper, such as poster board, is best for the background. But objects can be collaged as well, such as the inside and outside of boxes, cardboard, or wood. Most any kind of glue can be used on most paper. Glue sticks are easiest and least messy to manipulate.

Magazine Collage

Magazine collage provides preformed pictures for use. The particular magazines provided will determine the nature of the photos, so art therapists may select them deliberately—for example, by supplying sports magazines, those showing a diversity of ethnic types, illustrations of children, or animals. Debra Paskind keeps a face file for her hospitalized psychiatric patients with pictures of faces showing various emotional expressions (Chapter 7). Self-identity can be readily expressed through found magazine images. A self-introduction collage can be a useful icebreaker for members of a group that might initially find drawing threatening. (For examples, see the work of Monique Prohaska with special education adolescents in Figures 1.3 through 1.7, and Kathy Terra's work at the jail in Figure 9.7.) As with other collage objects, magazine images can be precut for those unable to cut them—for example, young children or those in the advanced stages of Alzheimer's disease (Chapter 13). Clients who are unable to glue can direct the art therapist in the arrangement of the images. Mary Lou Hasara's hospitalized adolescent patients made *speech/thought collages* in which they added bubbles of words and thoughts to the magazine figures (Chapter 2). Beth Black and Lorelie Swanson used *image cards,* full-page magazine photos glued to stiff paper to stimulate responses among the members of the families of the children at risk with whom they worked. Clients selected cards for various purposes, such as expressing a feeling, representing the family, showing how they would like the family to be, making up a story, and more. The therapists found the image cards to be a good introduction to working with images (Chapter 5).

Tissue-Paper Collage

Tissue-paper collage offers the advantages of mixing colors and layering. When wet, colored tissue paper bleeds, producing interesting effects. In layering colors, those underneath may show through. Texture and color changes are also provided by wrinkling the tissue paper. Elmer's glue mixed with water in a 50-50 ratio works best to encourage bleeding. Stephanie Zentz used tissue-paper collage to process her reactions to working with an HIV-positive child (Figures 12.9 and 12.10).

Found Objects

Found objects, such as leaves, bark, and other material that can be glued may be used. Deborah Ruland's patients with Alzheimer's disease made macaroni and seed collages (Figure 13.12), and those working with Brenda Brecht used ceramic tiles. A hot glue gun is useful for many found objects, such as leaves, bark, and grass. Deborah Del Signore utilized scented objects, such as premixed potpourri on heavy paper, for olfactory stimulation for older adults in a nursing home (Figure 13.9). Similarly, the residents glued spices to masks in a you-are-what-you-eat project, resulting in highly aromatic and textured masks.

Mixed Media

Mixed media can provide interest in almost limitless ways. For example, magazine images or photographs can be enhanced by drawing with markers, oil pastels, or ink. Shapes of colored construction paper can be used with other materials. Colored or clear cellophane covering the images can give a veiled effect, with or without images glued to it. Kathy Osler's family scrapbook in Chapter 5 combined magazine photos and drawings, as did Anne Coseo's racial reactions in the Chapter 1 frontispiece, page 21, and Figures 1.13 and 1.14. Dee Ann Foss's work with clients with developmental delay utilized feathers and pom poms in collage (Chapter 6).

Group Interaction

Group interaction can be stimulated by round-robin collage making, as in Debra Paskind's work with patients hospitalized for psychiatric conditions. One project was a pass-around collage, in which group members each had different colors of construction paper, which they tore up and glued to large sheets of white paper that were passed around, round-robin style. They also made round-robin collages with precut magazine images they selected (Chapter 7).

Constructions

Like collage, construction offers the advantage of preformed materials that can be combined. The materials themselves may suggest objects to create. The range of materials is extensive, including wood scraps, foam core, fabric, pipe cleaners, wire, Popsicle sticks, tongue depressors, twine, Styrofoam cups, tiles, and cardboard of all sorts, such as boxes, egg crates, and tubes from paper towels and toilet paper rolls. Objects may be combined by using nails, glue, and tape, as appropriate. A hot glue gun is useful for decorations (such as encrusting objects with shells). The constructed product may be painted, covered with fabric, or collaged. Often clients, especially children, are very pleased with their results. Complex constructions are usually created in stages, often over several art therapy sessions. Though more complex than collage because of the structural elements involved, construction also offers an opportunity for experimentation with arrangement. Many children who are resistant to creating two-dimensional art take to construction and are able to concentrate on a piece over several sessions (Chapter 3). Children from backgrounds of neglect and poverty, some of whom may be diagnosed with Attention Deficit Disorder, often have difficulty conceptualizing a drawing when faced with a blank piece of paper. Having objects that they can pick up and arrange helps them to create by allowing them to utilize one piece at a time. Remey Rozin found that encouraging some adolescents with neurological impairment to write a step-by-step plan for making a construction enabled them to complete their projects without becoming confused (Chapter 2).

Boxes and Containers

Boxes can be made into many imaginative containers. In working with families, Gian Luca Ferme encouraged the family members to build a house together out of cardboard boxes (Figure 5.4). This was a good task to see how the family distributed responsibilities. Betty Wolff's patients with substance addictions created a message in a box to give to a special person in their lives (Chapter 7). Stephanie Zentz describes a box filled with feathers and wound tight with cord to represent a child with AIDS who held in her feelings (Chapter 12).

Foam Core

Foam core can be easily cut and glued to make a base on which other objects are mounted; in addition, it can be used to make upright constructions. It is an easily worked material for building houses and environments—for example, the house built by Gail Wirtz's child client (Figure 5.1).

Musical Instruments

Musical instruments can be made by filling containers with rice, seeds, nails, or pebbles, and then painting them. Oatmeal boxes, cans, and plastic cups taped together are a few examples of containers that can be used. Various kinds of sticks are useful for hitting together or for banging a hollow container. See Judith Podmore's work with clients with chronic mental illness in an aftercare program (Figure 8.14).

Self-Boxes

Self-boxes are very popular for representing what is seen by others on the outside and what is private on the inside. The contrasts are often very telling. The boxes may be painted or collaged, and objects can be placed inside. For examples, see Monique Prohaska's work with adolescents in a special school (Figure 1.3) and Alexandria Elliot-Prisco's work with sexually abused girls and women (Chapter 3 frontispiece, page 86, and Chapter 11).

Rooms and Environments

Rooms and environments are constructions that can be of almost infinite variety. Bonnie Bluestein purchased an old Victorian dollhouse, and her aftercare clients with chronic mental illness built rooms in it (Chapter 8). They used felt, paint, wood scraps, ceramic tile, cardboard tubes, wallpaper, wire, magazine images, Styrofoam, and other found objects. Removable cardboard walls, ceilings, and floors were inserted into each dollhouse room so that the clients could remove their rooms in order to work on them at the studio table. They could also take their rooms home and reassemble them. Bluestein provided a toy train track around which clients could create an environment as well. Michele Drucker also instigated a room project for adolescent boys with behavior disorders with whom she worked. In working with families, Beth Black and Lorelie Swanson asked the family members each to make a clay animal to represent themselves and then to create an environment in which they could all live together harmoniously (Chapter 5). The environment was made in a large box, and various materials could be added or made for it (Figure 5.11). Paul Menzes, a summer institute participant, created a small outdoor environment of soil, sticks, and stones to represent himself (Figure 15.1).

Furniture Refinishing

Furniture refinishing using mosaic tiles provided a creative outlet for the clients with chronic mental illness in aftercare with whom Melissa Kistner worked (Chapter 8). Selecting or requesting furniture from a resale shop that could be used in their homes motivated these clients to work with dedication

FIGURE 15.1   Self-representation environment.

on their projects. The clients chose the tile, cut it, arranged it, glued it down, applied grout over it, and cleaned off the grout (Figure 8.4).

Altars and Memorials

Altars and memorials are often important in bereavement work. They may be made from boxes or crates on which are placed significant objects. Candles and incense can be added, and the altar may be set up in a special place. One of the HIV-positive men with whom William Kasser worked had created an altar and memorial (Chapter 12).

Styrofoam Heads

Styrofoam heads were used by Anastasia Limperis in work with children hospitalized for medical problems (Chapter 4). Life-size heads used for holding wigs can provide a sense of completion for short-term work when there may be limitations of time or ability. The heads can be painted and materials can be stuck into them or glued on (Figures 4.5 and 4.6). The result is often impressive and provides a feeling of accomplishment (Part III frontispiece, page 403).

Mobiles

Mobiles can be made of a variety of materials. John Bolde's clients with chronic mental illness in aftercare used branches, from which they hung favorite and found objects (Figure 8.2). Deborah Ruland's patients with Alzheimer's disease hung forms they had made from Play-Doh on their mobiles (Chapter 13).

Newspaper Construction

Newspaper construction is a quick and inexpensive process, involving nothing more than newspaper and masking tape. In a spirited group project, the various group members make different parts by wadding and taping the newspaper, then combine them together with the tape.

Piñatas

Piñatas are made by blowing up a balloon and covering it with papier-mâché, with a hole left to insert small gifts. Conical cups may be attached and covered with papier-mâché also. After it has hardened, cut tissue paper can be glued on for a decorative fringe, as in Figure 5.15, showing a piñata made by a Mexican-American family with whom Alicia Contreras worked. Traditionally, children are blindfolded and given sticks or bats to hit at the suspended piñata until it has broken open and the gifts fall out. It can also be hung as decoration and not broken up.

Other Materials

Other material for construction can be seen in the junk art material Michele Drucker gave the children with whom she worked and the cones the same children used for making rockets in work with Holly Rugland (Chapter 3). Other useful materials include Popsicle sticks and tongue depressors, used by Remey Rozin in work with adolescents with neurological damage (Figures 2.10 and 2.11); the found objects Anita Yeh offered children for construction (Figure 1.1); and tissue paper, used to make flowers by the Cambodian refugees with whom Naoko Takano worked (Figure 9.1). Sturdy paper can be used for construction as well, such as in Ruth Evermann's work with children hospitalized for psychiatric problems (Figures 2.1 and 2.4). Egg cartons can be cut up and made into various forms, for example faces (Figure 15.2). Tooled wooden decorations can be assembled into a sculpture (Figure 15.3).

Three-Dimensional Shaping

In contrast with materials that can be assembled for constructions are those that can be shaped. Clay is the most common. Its scent and tactile properties make it attractive, though there are a few people who find these characteristics repugnant. Clay can be fired and glazed, although many art therapy services do not have the necessary equipment. Most clay is softened by working it with the hands or adding water. Plasticine is an oil-based clay that does not harden, so that it can be reused. It comes in a variety of colors and is easier to manipulate, thus making it appealing to children. Clay is especially desirable for its forgiving nature. It can be reworked indefinitely. It is also useful as a receptacle for the expression of strong feelings, in pounding it, tearing it, or cutting

FIGURE 15.2   Egg carton faces.

into it. A series of clay objects can be moved around to form varying relation-ships with one another.

Clay Family

Clay can be used to show family members symbolically by portraying their various characteristics through size and shape. They can be moved in relation to one another or changed to show how the client would like the family to be. Examples are the work of Kimberly Rakestraw with families in Chapter 5 and of John Bolde with outpatient clients in Chapter 8 (Figure 8.1). Figure 15.4 shows group members discussing their clay families.

Clay Heads

Ed Foss taught clients with substance abuse problems how to make heads using a pinch-pot method by combining two equal-size pots to make an egg-shaped ball that is already hollowed for firing. A hole to allow the air to escape

FIGURE 15.3   Tooled wood construction.

is made in the bottom or as one of the features, for example, the mouth. Features can be carved into the head or added onto it (Chapter 7).

Plaster Gauze

The same sort of plaster gauze that is used for medical casts can be cut into strips and formed into the shape of whatever it is molded around. (This material is sold as Paris Craft or Rigid Wrap at craft stores.) The strips are cut into the desired size, dipped in water, and applied in at least three overlapping layers to the mold. The plaster gauze alone can also be shaped to a certain extent. Armatures can be made of crumpled newspaper, aluminum foil, or Plasticine, which is then removed or scooped out after the form has hardened. Initial drying takes only a few minutes. Complete drying takes 24 hours. The dried object can be painted or decorated with beads, shells, feathers, fabric, yarn, or other materials. A hot glue gun works best. Examples are the house made by MaLinda Johnson's elderly client (Figure 13.8) and the doll made by Angie Taraceiwicz (Figure 2.16).

FIGURE 15.4   Group sharing clay families.

Poured Plaster

Poured plaster is also a possibility for construction, though it is less easy to control than clay unless it is poured into a mold. Holly Rugland worked with a child who used poured plaster to create a volcano, which he then painted to show lava cascading down the sides (Chapter 3). If a beach is handy, sand casting may be done by digging molds in damp sand and pouring in the plaster (Figure 15.5). The hardened plaster will pick up some of the sand. Objects may be embedded in it while it is still wet. If there is no beach nearby, a box of sand will do.

Sand Molding

Sand molding is an enjoyable beach exercise for creating a temporary sculpture. Figure 15.6 shows a group is forming mermaids from damp sand.

Cheesecloth and Fabric Stiffener

The use of cheesecloth is similar to molding of plaster gauze. It can be either painted with fabric stiffener or dipped into it. It, too, is molded on an object and takes its form when it dries. An example is the ghost made by MaLinda Johnson's older adult client, shown in the Chapter 13 frontispiece on page 367.

Dolls

Dolls have been significant possessions for humankind since prehistoric times. We imbue them with lifelike characteristics. For children, they are important

FIGURE 15.5 Poured plaster in sand molds.

objects in learning to relate to others; for some, dolls are their most valued possession. A doll that one fashions oneself can be particularly meaningful in representing the self or a desired other. Dolls offer not only possibilities for creativity in making them, but also opportunities for interactional enactment. There are many ways to make dolls, and a variety of materials can be used.

FIGURE 15.6 Group sand sculpture.

Felt Dolls

Simple dolls can be made from two layers of felt that are stuffed and stapled together. Prior to stuffing they can be decorated with marker or glued-on objects. To make the task even simpler, the felt can be precut for the client.

Sock Dolls

Sock dolls are made by stuffing a sock and decorating it with sewn or glued-on objects such as buttons, yarn, and fabric. Limbs can be made of fabric and tied on, with glued-on foam hands and feet. Beth Black found that the women recovering from prostitution with whom she worked took to doll making although they rejected other forms of art (Figures 10.13 and 10.14).

Wrapped Dolls

Making wrapped dolls can provide a very meditative process in the repetitive wrapping of yarn around a piece of material. A length of fabric is doubled and tied near the center to form a head, using a piece of twine long enough to extend as arms. The end of a ball of yarn is tied at the neck and wrapped around the doubled piece of fabric to form the body, around the separated fabric to form the legs, and around the twine for the arms (Figure 15.7). Objects can be glued on for features, yarn for hair, and fabric for clothes. Figure 15.8 shows a group of wrapped dolls made by Mary Ann Zent.

Plaster Gauze Dolls

Angie Taraceiwicz made plaster gauze dolls and decorated them by gluing on glitter and pieces of metal (Figure 2.16).

Life-Size Dolls

Life-size dolls even more realistically become another individual with whom one can interact. They can be made from fabric or paper. Gail Wirtz helped a child to trace his body onto fabric. Together they used a sewing machine to sew two layers of the cut-out fabric. They left an opening for stuffing it (Figure 5.2). Susan Kowalcyzk employed the same method in her work with children, except that they used paper, which they painted and stapled together (Figure 3.7). Ruth Evermann showed the children hospitalized for psychiatric problems with whom she worked in short-term treatment how to make life-size dolls from an assemblage of materials (Chapter 2). They began by tracing their hands and feet on foam rug padding. They connected boxes and plastic Kool Bursts bottles for the head, body, and limbs. The dolls were then decorated by gluing on yarn, beads, sequins, and fabric (Figure 2.3).

Other Materials

Gian Luca Ferme used other materials in his work with families (Chapter 5). They added decorations to cardboard paper towel tubes or construction paper

FIGURE 15.7 Wrapped doll.

glued behind a picture and mounted on a piece of an egg carton for a stand. In one exercise, he asked family members to make Polaroid portraits of each other and to pick an animal and glue its shape to the back of their own portrait. They were each to tell a story about the animal and then turn the doll around and tell the same story substituting themselves for the animals (Figure 5.4).

Puppets

Puppets are closely related to dolls. They are dolls to be worn on the hand and moved. The clients become their puppets as they make them move and speak.

Plaster and Papier-Mâché

Anne Canright uses plaster- or papier-mâché-covered balloons to make heads for puppets (Figure 15.9). The balloon is blown up to the desired size, secured,

FIGURE 15.8   Wrapped dolls.

FIGURE 15.9   Papier-mâché-covered-balloon puppets.

and covered with approximately three layers of papier-mâché or plaster gauze. A ring of cardboard is attached using the same material to serve as a neck, through which the puppeteer's finger fits into the head. After the material has dried, the balloon is punctured so the finger can fit through. Features may be added by building up the face with the plaster or papier-mâché, and objects, such as beads or shells, can be glued on. The puppet heads can also be painted. Fabric and yarn can be attached for clothing and hair. In her work with clients with developmental delay, Vickie Scescke used molded clay, rather than balloons, to form the papier mâché or plaster gauze (Figure 6.2). The advantage of clay is that it allows for shaping the head.

Styrofoam Balls

Styrofoam balls provide an even easier way to make the puppet head. Once again, fabric and other objects can be attached. Slender sticks operate the arms and hold the head (Figure 15.10).

Throwaway Materials

Throwaway materials such as cereal cartons and Styrofoam cups are effective for making animal puppet heads whose mouths can open and close. A Styrofoam cup served as the head for Holly Pumphrey's client's dragon (Figure 3.4). He cut it in half to form the jaws and attached it to a tube sock. He added fangs made from cardboard, inserts covered with felt for the roof and floor of

FIGURE 15.10   Puppets with heads made from Styrofoam balls.

the mouth, and a long tongue. He painted the head and made eyes from foam rubber. Small cereal boxes can be used the same way (Figure 14.1). Even a scrap of wood can serve as a head for an animal, as in Figure 15.11. Gian Luca Ferme's clients used paper towel tubes for puppet bodies (Figure 5.3).

Stockings

Stocking head puppets can have expressive faces. A stocking is stuffed with batting and stitched to shape the features. Features can also be painted, and objects such as beads or shells can be glued or sewn on. Stockings are also used for arms, and fingers can be sewn in. Fabric is added for clothing, and yarn or other material is used for hair and hats (Figure 15.12).

Finger Puppets

Finger puppets can be made by forming a head from plaster gauze or papier-mâché over one's finger or a small object. Plastic wrap is effective in covering the finger to keep the material from sticking. The dried head can be painted or decorated with glued-on objects and fabric can be added for the body.

Masks

Masks are intriguing because they allow us to become what we are not. Often clients are able to say from behind a mask what they would not dare to otherwise. Masks can express wishes, fears, and fantasies. They can be made out of

FIGURE 15.11   Wood-scrap puppet head.

FIGURE 15.12   Stuffed stocking puppets.

a variety of materials and are often very successful projects, even for clients with limited abilities. For those whose abilities are very limited, preformed masks can be purchased, or clients can use paper plates or precut cardboard forms, as did Vivian Ragis's clients with developmental delay (Figure 6.4). More elaborate cardboard masks were made for ritual processions in Clay Bodine's workshops (Figures 14.2 through 14.4). Masks can be worn, dialoged with (as another part of the self, for example), or hung. They can also be mounted onto stretched canvas to form part of a larger composition.

Plaster Gauze

Plaster gauze is an especially good material for mask making because it produces a lifelike reproduction when formed on a face. The maskmaker can then transform it into a god, spirit, magician, demon, angel, or whatever. And transformation is what therapy is all about. The material is also highly versatile. It can be collaged, painted, and decorated with glued-on or sewn-on objects. Highly expressive and creative masks can be made by those with no experience. Although it is possible to make a mask on oneself with the use of a mirror, it is much easier to form partnerships, with one person making the mask on the other. Children who are unable to concentrate or do not have sufficient dexterity may still enjoy a mask project when the art therapist makes a mask on them. Forms can also be made on other body parts, such as hands and feet (Figure 15.13). Care must be taken to cover the body part to be plastered thoroughly with Vaseline so that the plaster will not stick to the skin. The hair can be covered with plastic wrap or a plastic shower cap. Rolls of plaster

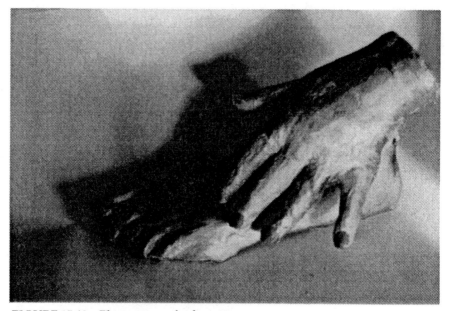

FIGURE 15.13   Plaster gauze body parts.

gauze are cut into strips, dipped into water, applied to the face by overlapping, and smoothed out (Figure 15.14). At least three layers are needed. The eyes can be covered so that objects such as buttons or shells can be glued on for the mask's eyes. Or, eye holes can be left so the mask wearer can see. Obviously, the nostrils should not be covered. After the mask is removed, that area can be covered and indentations can be made for nostrils. If the mask is extended upward to cover a portion of the hair, material such as yarn or raffia can be added later to serve as hair, or fabric can be added for a hat. The plaster sets up quickly, so usually the mask does not have to be left on for more than about 5 minutes after completion. It takes about 24 hours to dry thoroughly and can then be decorated. Because some people find covering the face to be frightening, great care should be taken to assure comfort. Remind them that they can pull the mask off at any time; they are never trapped in it. Some people might prefer to make half masks covering only a part of the face. On the other hand, many people find the smoothing action very comforting and the whole experience of the feel of the plaster and its changing temperatures and textures as it dries to be a very sensuous experience.

Figures 15.15 through 15.17 show examples of plaster gauze masks. Deborah Haugh made a nest inside a mask to represent her view of her relationship with a client (Figure 3.19). The photo on page 405 shows a whimsical use of a mask. Sue Lee's Korean American adolescent group members were very proud and protective of their masks (Figure 9.5).

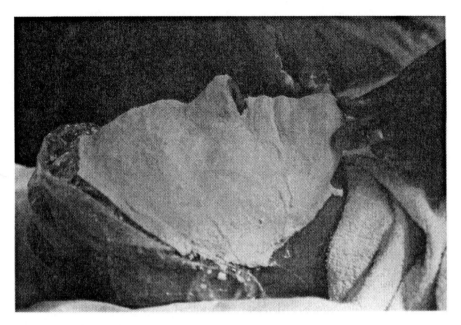

FIGURE 15.14   Making a plaster gauze mask.

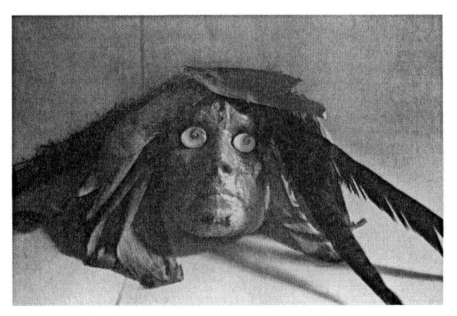

FIGURE 15.15   Plaster gauze mask made by author of her face with feathers, corn husks, and shells.

FIGURE 15.16 Plaster gauze mask with ribbons, beads, and shells.

Fabric

Fabric is useful for a myriad of other projects in addition to creating dolls and puppets and decorating constructions as just described. Fabric work is a traditional women's activity that can be introduced to engender a sense of female solidarity. It is not limited to use by females, however.

Wearable Art

Teresa Walker's clients created wearable art as they decorated donated clothing with paint (Chapter 10). Other materials may be glued or sewed onto the clothing, as well. As former prostitutes who were trying to change their lives, clothes were very important to Walker's clients. In workshops conducted by Clay Bodine, costumes were made for ritual celebrations using fabric, painted cardboard, and other materials (Figures 14.2, 14.3, and 14.5).

Wrapping

Wrapping with vividly colored yarn is a repetitive action that can be soothing and can provide pleasing results. In addition to using the wrapping method to make dolls as previously described, many other objects can be decorated by wrapping. Beads, shells, feathers, and such materials can be hung from wrapped twigs. The end of the yarn is tied to the object and wrapped around so that the object is completely covered. Colors can be alternated to form stripes. The end is tied off. A homeless woman with whom Suzanne Canby worked had her crutch wrapped (Figure 9.9).

FIGURE 15.17 **Plaster gauze mask with macaroni.**

Quilting

Quilting is a traditional women's project that often brought women together to socialize as they quilted. Some quilts told stories. In art therapy, material can be cut and appliquéd on the quilt square background, or it can be glued on. One of Beth Black's clients, a former prostitute, told her life story in her quilt squares (Figures 10.15 and 10.16). Nancy Biederman's women's group decided to make a quilt as the group's final project. Each woman painted a canvas square showing what the group had meant to her. They decided to bind the edges of the quilt with red fabric because red had been so prominent in their art about menopause (Chapter 10). Jennifer Swerdlow found quilting to be an expressive modality for processing her strong feelings about her work with sexually assaulted women in a traditional craft that women have used for a long time (Figures 11.4 and 11.5). She stated that by assembling pieces she reconnected with herself, her gender, her art, and her society. She used 12-inch black cotton pieces for the background and an appliqué method for sewing on pieces of different fabrics. The various stages of selecting the material, cutting it, pinning it to the square, and sewing it on became part of Swerdlow's reflective process.

Drawing, Painting, and Printing

Drawing and painting are the art therapist's stock and trade. Most often in art therapy sessions, clients and patients simply draw or paint whatever comes to them at the time.

Directives

For particular purposes, the art therapist might suggest a *directive*. Some that are included in this book are ideal- and reality-family drawings, used by Beth Gonzalez-Dolginko (Figures 5.6 through 5.9), "monster of addiction" drawings, used by Betty Wolff with patients with substance abuse problems (Figure 7.10); and life-review drawings, used by Janet Stallman with older adult clients (Figures 13.1 through 13.7).

Sequence Drawings

Images can form a serial sequence in which one leads to another, as in the pursuit of the image work of Harriet Wadeson (Chapter 14). Sequences can also be formed with separate cells on one sheet of paper. Debra Paskind asked her hospitalized psychiatric patients to work backwards in understanding their relapse triggers. They folded a large piece of paper into eight cells. They began drawing in the last cell, depicting their latest admission to the hospital, and proceeded backward in drawing the events leading up to their readmission, in order to determine what had led to their current hospitalization (Figure 7.1).

Scribble Drawings

To encourage spontaneity and the emergence of unconscious material, art therapists sometimes suggest the *scribble*, in which the client closes his or her eyes and makes a long continuous looping line on the paper. Susan O'Boyle encouraged her client with developmental delay to keep on scribbling to loosen up (Chapter 6). More often, art therapists encourage clients to look at their original shapes and to develop them into the objects they see in them, as Terry Lavery did in his own self-processing work (Chapter 2 frontispiece, page 53, and Figures 2.12 and 2.13).

Group Murals

Group murals encourage interaction and socialization. Large paper, such as that cut from a roll of butcher paper, can be placed on the floor or a large table, or hung on the wall. Drawing materials or paints can be used. A mural can be planned in advance by the group or it can develop spontaneously, like the work of Nina Benson's patients hospitalized for psychiatric conditions (Figures 7.2 and 7.3).

Round Robin

Group interaction can be encouraged through pass-around drawings. A round robin, in which each person works on a drawing for only a minute or two (timed) and then passes it to the next person, helps to overcome performance anxiety. Each picture is passed (usually around the table) until each person has worked on it, so all the pictures are the combined work of the whole group. This is a good icebreaker to help new group members relax with one another and feel more comfortable with making art. Variations include collage work, in which each person glues on a few pieces of colored construction paper or magazine images. A round-robin approach can be used in mural making; each person moves around the mural after a designated period (usually only a couple of minutes). Susan Kowalczyk used music in a musical chairs manner, so that group members switched pictures when the music stopped (Chapter 3).

Bookmaking

Pictures can be combined into books that may have a particular theme and can include writing, as well. Various materials can be used for covers, and binding can be accomplished through stapling, stitching, or punching holes and tying. Clients with developmental delay made books in their work with Anita Glover and Vickie Scescke (Chapter 6).

Paint Applications

Paint can be applied to various materials, as in the flag making by Leslie DeVera's high school students (Chapter 9) or the painting on clothing by the women with whom Teresa Walker worked (Chapter 10). Paint can also be applied with materials other than brushes, as in the yarn painting by Deborah Ruland's Alzheimer patients (Chapter 13) and the sponge painting and crayon with paint methods used by the women with developmental delay with whom Dee Ann Foss worked (Chapter 6).

Printing

Printing can be done on paper or fabric, with paint or ink, using a variety of simple implements, such as a carved potato, carved foam core, or found objects. Acrylic paint works well. Suzanne Canby's homeless women made a large leaf print mural from leaves they had collected on a fall outing and another in which they printed their hands (Chapter 9 frontispiece, page 295). Deborah Del Signore's older adult clients printed with acrylic paint by using

Bounce fabric softener sheets in a silk-screen technique. They drew simple images on the sheets, placed them on paper, and painted the images; the paint passed through the sheet and was transferred onto the paper. Scenes were created by using multiple images and a variety of colors (Chapter 13).

Large Art

Large art makes a strong statement and is often very impressive. Robin Lee Garber, working with patients hospitalized for psychiatric problems, secured large brushes into the splayed ends of 3- to 4-foot bamboo poles with rubber bands. She provided recycled coffee cans of tempera paint. Sheets of 4- by 6-foot paper were taped to the floor, which had been covered with a plastic drop cloth. Garber encouraged the patients to use their whole bodies in creating their paintings and to stand upright, using their legs to bend rather than their backs (Chapter 2). They were encouraged to make sounds as they worked. Some sang. Garber found that working large in this way aided clients in emotional release and body awareness, and that it countered the psychomotor retardation of depression.

Murals

Mural making by groups of clients provides an opportunity for socialization and cooperation (see preceding section). Mural making can also furnish information about group interaction. A mural can evolve without advanced planning, or the group can decide on a theme or even plan out the mural's design in advance. Figure 15.18 shows a group sitting next to a mural that evolved spontaneously. Even larger murals can become community art. Jean Durkin and the homeless women with whom she worked created a mural on the side of their building (Chapter 9).

Banners

Jean Durkin's homeless women painted a 3- by 30-foot banner for a social action rally. It was composed of seven panels made from weatherproof materials painted with acrylics and decorated with felt, found objects, and a border of green material that divided and framed each panel. Each 3- by 4-foot muslin panel was treated as an individual work until they were all joined together. The seven panels expressed different issues of women's rights, chosen by the women (Figure 10.21). A responsive reading on the seven issues accompanied the unfurling of their banner at the rally (Chapter 10).

Body Tracings

Body tracings are usually very successful art expressions. Mural paper is taped to the wall or laid on the floor. The client stands against it or lies on it

FIGURE 15.18 Group mural.

in a position he or she selects, while a partner or the art therapist traces around the entire body (Figure 15.19). Care must be taken not to be invasive in any way. For some clients, it may be necessary to avoid the genital area and leave that part of the tracing for the client to complete. The client then works from the outline, adding whatever is desired, including clothing, other people, and a background (Figures 15.20 and 15.21). The life-size result is often striking. The image may be a fantasy, the ideal self, or one's shadow side. Kama Shulte had members of the families she worked with make body tracings of one another, which they combined in a mural (Chapter 5). Sarah Frahm and a woman at the homeless shelter worked together on a tracing of Sarah (Figure 9.12).

Life-Size Cardboard Figures

Judith Podmore's aftercare clients with chronic psychiatric conditions made life-size cardboard figures in the style of the artist Ruffino Tamayo, whose work they saw at a gallery visit. Judith showed the group how to make a symmetrical shape out of folded newsprint. Individuals paired up to cut their large figures out of corrugated cardboard using paper cutters, knives, and scissors (Figure 8.13). Summer Institute participants made the life-size woman in Figure 14.6 and the large cardboard dragon in Figure 14.7 that were used in ritual processions. The castle in Figure 14.8 was also created for a ritual and was later set on fire as part of the celebration.

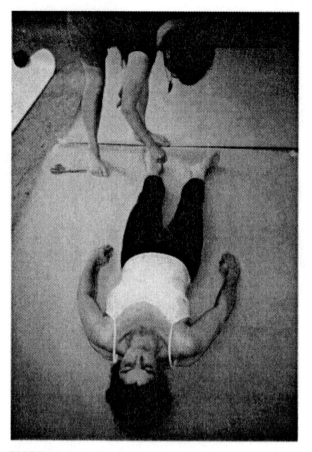

FIGURE 15.19   Drawing a body tracing.

Boundary Mats

Boundary mats are used in an exercise Beth Black and Lorelie Swanson developed in order to help members of families determine boundaries for their personal space and learn to respect the space of others (Chapter 5). Each family member is given a discarded bed sheet that is spread on the floor. He or she stands in the center, with the others at the perimeter. One by one they approach slowly from the edges. When each one has come as close as feels comfortable to the one in the center, he or she says to stop (Figure 5.10). The place is marked on the sheet. The places of all the family members on one's mat constitute the boundaries, and the mat is cut outside the marks, so that what is left is a boundary mat of one's personal space. The mat can then be decorated. The mats can be used both in discussion and in the actual designation of physical space. Family members learn to protect their own space and to ask permission before entering the space of another. This exercise is good for families in which there is little recognition of personal space and privacy.

FIGURE 15.20   Embellishing a body tracing.

FIGURE 15.21   Completing a body tracing.

Games

Gian Luca Ferme created special games to respond to the needs of the families with whom he worked (Chapter 5). The children, especially, learned to follow directions and to deal with winning and losing. From some of the games, they learned particular skills—for example, to avoid getting lost in detail. A group of boys who had been sexually abused, with whom Marjory Hamilton worked, created a board game, which included cards that helped them to deal with issues of abuse. In designing and making the game, the boys learned to cooperate with one another. They painted the board and used clay to make game pieces and reward tokens (Figures 3.5 and 3.6).

Art History, Gallery Visits, and Exhibitions

Viewing the work of artists can be used in a variety of ways. Examples described in the book include the following:

- Vivian Ragis took her primarily African American group of clients with developmental delay to view African art during African History Month in order to encourage their ethnic identity and pride. The outing was a significant event for them, and they made their own masks in response to those they saw (Figure 6.4).
- Judith Podmore took her aftercare clients with chronic psychiatric conditions to numerous exhibits, some supporting ethnic identity and some seasonal. The group members created art responses to each, including making masks (Figure 8.12), life-size figures (Figure 8.13), and musical instruments (Figure 8.14).
- Laura Safar, working with the same population, brought in art history slides and books to encourage the group members in the development of their art. She selected paintings that showed people interacting. Her clients' art reflected this influence (Figures 8.5 through 8.11).
- Colleen McNally, working at the same facility, took her women's group to a show of her own feminist art installation and showed slides of artwork by women. The group discussed the art in relation to their own issues, especially sexual abuse, and created their own art expressions of their painful feelings (Chapter 8).

Art Exhibits

Exhibits of clients' artwork are appropriate for some populations and not for others. Where issues of confidentiality are paramount and where self-expression is encouraged rather than the creation of a high-quality product, exhibiting the art could give the wrong message. Art therapists must be clear in their understanding of the purpose of an art exhibit and must communicate it to the clients. Generally, competition should be discouraged. It goes without saying that clients' art should not be used for the financial benefit of the facility or of anyone other than the client. Turning an exhibit into a financial enterprise is not in the clients' best interests, although there might be a few exceptions. For the most part, the purpose of an exhibit of clients' art is to raise the self-esteem of the clients. Such was the case for the children at the therapeutic school where Susan Kowacyck established an art therapy program (Chapter 3). A university facility for persons with developmental delay has had a tradition of annual art exhibits since the University of Illinois began assigning art therapy internships there a number of years ago (Chapter 6). An especially important event, which drew the gay community together in the early days of the AIDS epidemic, before the AIDS quilt was begun, was the art exhibit by patients with AIDS organized by Wendy Pollack (Chapter 12). Particularly impressive was an exhibit of works from the long-established art therapy program for clients in psychiatric aftercare originated and directed by Joanne Ramseyer. Some of the clients sold their work at the exhibit (Figures 8.20 through 8.22).

Electronic Media and Photography

Traditional photography, video, and digital imaging techniques can be used in many interesting ways.

Photography

Photography can become an occasion for expeditions, which were significant adventures for Bettina Thorn's clients with chronic mental illness at an aftercare facility (Chapter 8). The clients were supplied with disposable cameras. They enhanced their original photos by adding artwork, and they wrote stories about the scenes they shot (Figures 8.18 and 8.19). Alexandria Elliot-Prisco was able to get a nonprofit organization to donate 50 rolls of black-and-white film and some automatic 35-mm cameras. She developed the film herself to ensure confidentiality for her clients, who had been sexually abused (Chapter 11 frontispiece on page 315, and Figure 11.1).

Polaroid Photography

Polaroid photography offers the advantage of instant results and the disadvantage of a small picture. Enlargements can be made on a Xerox machine. The larger the image, the more grainy the copy. The copy can then be colored and otherwise enhanced. This is a good technique for producing an accurate representation (for example, a picture of a person) and then modifying it. Claudia Clenard's hospitalized adolescent patients told stories with their photographs, made art around them, and combined them into photo collages (Chapter 2). Alexandria Elliot-Prisco photographed an 11-year-old client in the poses the client chose for a story she composed. The figures were cut out and mounted onto cardboard and placed with clay figures the client made to represent her imaginary animal friends (Figure 3.2). In a similar fashion, paper dolls can be made from Polaroid shots mounted on cardboard, and paper clothes and environmental objects can be made for them. This sort of project can be especially useful in enabling children and adolescents to tell their stories.

Viewing Videos

Videos are important in Gail Roy's work with patients in a partial-hospitalization psychiatric program. She selects films that are relevant to their issues. After discussing their reactions, they make art responses (Chapter 7). Many of the films Roy has used deal with women's issues and feature themes of empowerment, such as *Shirley Valentine*, for women with depression, or *How to Make an American Quilt*, showing women's solidarity.

Video Making

William Kasser took on an ambitious video project with men who had AIDS (Chapter 12). First, the patients each created a storyboard about a day in their lives (Figure 12.7). Then they either taped the scenes or directed Kasser in doing so (Figure 12.8). They directed him in editing the rough cut and selected music or a voiceover. The final editing was done in a professional production studio with video-editing software. Kasser did most of the technical work, but the creative elements were the work of the men themselves.

Film Animation

Film animation can be executed with a variety of images. Magazine photos can be used, or figures can be drawn. Backgrounds can be drawn or painted. The figures are moved across the backgrounds. Characters can be cut-out figures, photos, dolls, puppets, pipe-cleaner creations, or clay figures, to name a few. Monica Dougherty made a film with institutionalized women with developmental delay who used real leaves floating across their pictures to represent autumn (Chapter 6). Each woman created an image of herself (Figure 6.5), which was then clothed appropriately for each scene. A special area of the room was set up that could remain undisturbed for the duration of the project. The camera was mounted on a tripod, and two photoflood lights pointed downward on the surface holding the images (Figure 6.6). A cable-release attachment controlled the shutter speed to shoot one frame at a time, and a stylus moved the figures across the background from shot to shot to create motion. Film can be transferred to videotape. Sound can be added with an audiotape, and by using two videocassette recorders, the sound and picture can be dubbed together on a second videotape.

Computer Art

Computer art continues to develop almost as rapidly as the computer industry itself. Facilities equipped with computers for their clients can offer possibilities for "drawing" and "painting" with the basic equipment. Scanners provide the capacity to combine pictures and insert photographs that can then be modified. Printers create a permanent version of the art. Many children and adolescents who resist drawing and painting are happy to create art on a computer. (See Wadeson, Durkin, & Perach, 1989.)

Digital Photography

Digital photography is a more recent technological development that offers many new possibilities. The digital camera uses a computer disk that can be loaded into the computer for viewing and altering photos. Unwanted photos can be erased. Prior to shooting, the image shows on the back of the camera. Gail Wirtz uses the digital camera in working with children, who shoot their own artwork, sometimes from various angles (Chapter 5). She also uses it for her own record keeping, loading the images into her computer and printing out two examples of the art for each day. She writes her notes at the bottom of one copy and adds the other to the client's file, which she shows to him or her at the next session. The computer also enables her to compare art pieces. For example, she dragged Michael's various head drawings onto the screen, allowing her to view them in sequence over the previous 6 months (Chapter 5 frontispiece, page 145). The digital photographic process helped Wirtz to show Michael's work to his teachers and parents, as needed. It also helped her to engage him in assisting her in recording the work, thereby helping him to form a relationship with her. Finally, it served as a method for taking case notes and as a resource for cataloging the art and pulling it up for later reference.

Other Modalities Combined with Art

Art expression can form interesting relationships with other modes of expression.

Enactment

Enactment is a natural progression from the creation of masks, puppets, and dolls. The creator can speak for the mask, puppet, or doll, or speak to it in a dialog. The epilog frontispiece on page 439 shows art therapy students acting out their masks' characters. Often, clients can say things in the voice of their creation that they cannot allow themselves to speak directly. An example is Holly Pumphrey's work with children in foster care (Figure 3.4). Imaginative costumes, masks, and life-size puppets may be created for more complex enactment, such as those shown in the Chapter 14 frontispiece, page 391, and Figures 14.2 through 14.9, from workshops conducted by Clay Bodine. The photo on page 405 shows a mask combined imaginatively with a costume for an enactment.

Movement

Movement can be a warm-up for art making (as in Susan O'Boyle's work with clients with developmental delay, Chapter 6) or the result of art-making (as in Erik Engle's outpatient clients with chronic mental illness dancing to their mural, Chapter 8).

Writing

Writing is a concretization of reflection on the art. Writing a dialog with the art often brings forth unrecognized meanings and realizations, as in the work of Harriet Wadeson with well-functioning professionals and students (Chapter 14). Mary Beth Seefelt suggested keeping a journal to a patient with AIDS who was having memory difficulties (Chapter 12). Riv Stein used journal writing in combination with her art to help herself process her negative feelings toward her clients with developmental delay (Chapter 6). Stories can be written about the art (as in Bettina Thorn's work with aftercare clients with chronic mental illness, Chapter 8). Poetry is an especially poignant form of writing in which pictures are often created in words. Deva Suckerman formed an art and poetry group at an outpatient clinic (Chapter 8), and Jutta Ohl's aftercare clients with chronic mental illness published a magazine of their art and poetry (Chapter 8). Lexi Mitchell utilized her own poetry in combination with her art to process her strong reactions to the difficult children with whom she was working (Chapter 1).

Sensory Stimulation

Sensory stimulation is lacking in the lives of certain groups of people. Vivian Ragis found this to be the case in her work with clients with developmental delay. She utilized music, scents, and still-life compositions of fruit that the group members then ate (Chapter 6). Deborah Del Signore encouraged older adult residents of a nursing home to make art in response to scents she supplied. Such scents as peppermint and potpourri brought back specific memories for some of the residents. Her clients also used herbs and other scented materials in creating collages (Figure 13.9) and in decorating masks (Chapter 13).

Guided Imagery

Guided imagery is useful in enabling clients to relax and focus. It can help to stimulate ideas and imagery that might not come easily otherwise. Holly Rugland asked children with behavior disorders and learning disabilities to relax, become aware of their breathing, and focus on any muscle tension. Once they were relaxed, she told a story consisting primarily of images involving as many of the senses as possible. They then created art from the experience (Chapter 3). One story involves the discovery of a door, leading the listener to imagine what is behind it (Figure 13.10). Other stories took the children to imaginary planets.

Rituals

Rituals usually are a group enactment to mark a special event. They can become very creative celebrations involving many expressive modalities, including music, movement, drama, and visual art. Their creation and performance are usually a powerful influence in underscoring and advancing group solidarity as in Clay Bodine's ritual workshops (Chapter 14 frontispiece, page 391, and Figures 14.2 through 14.8).

Environments

Environments can be small, such as shown in Figure 15.1, which was created outdoors from natural materials by summer institute participant Paul Menzes to represent himself, or Figure 5.11, a family project in which clay representations of each family member were placed in an environment where they could all live harmoniously (from Beth Black and Lorelie Swanson's work). Environments can also be large and habitable as in Figure 14.9. A group can work together to develop a space where each one's individuality is expressed and common space is designed to suit the group's needs. Space may also be provided for receiving visitors, and a ceremony may be created to welcome them. Like creating rituals, building an environment often enhances group cohesion.

Therapists' Postsession Art

Art therapists are fortunate to have their own art making as a resource for themselves as well as for their clients. Processing reactions to clients and the feelings aroused in particular sessions is essential, and facilitating reflection through image making enables less linear, unconscious material to surface. It is very useful for art therapists to make postsession art, both in quick spontaneous images and in more developed pieces for deeper reflection. The examples in this book illustrate several content areas and various approaches to making art to gain a deeper understanding of client issues, the therapeutic relationship, countertransference, and the art therapy process. The following are some examples:

- Anne Coseo used mixed-media collage to look at the racial biases she brought to her work with inner-city children (Chapter 1 frontispiece, page 21, and Figures 1.13 and 1.14).

- Lexi Mitchell wrote poetry then made art to help her deal with her reactions to the very difficult children with whom she worked (Figures 1.15 through 1.17).
- Angela Tarasiewicz worked in the style of one of her hospitalized adolescents and tried to envision her countertransference reactions (Figure 2.16). She also made drawings and collages from her feelings about them (Figures 2.14, 2.15, 2.17, and 2.18).
- Terry Lavery employed a several-step process to understand and accept the shock he felt in learning of the tragedies in the lives of his adolescent clients (Chapter 2). He made a quick abstract response immediately after a group session, then a scribble in pastels that he developed to see what emerged spontaneously. He then elaborated this in a very finished piece in colored pencils that involved a lengthy process of layering the pencil strokes, allowing time for reflection (Chapter 2 frontispiece, page 53, and Figures 2.12 and 2.13).
- Nina Kuzniak made clay heads and abstract forms to depict feeling states related to the hospitalized children and adults with whom she worked (Figures 2.19 and 7.11).
- Rita Nathanson let one image develop out of another in her reactions to her adolescent patients (Figures 3.12 through 3.14).
- Polly Cullen created art from a dream about her client (Figure 3.15).
- Deborah Haugh recreated images her clients made, then modified them to gain a deeper understanding of her relationships with them (Figures 3.16 through 3.19).
- Susan Gasman needed to make art in order to deal with the difficult feelings aroused by her work with dying children on a hospital oncology unit (Figures 4.10 and 4.11).
- Julie Marchand made art in order to ventilate feelings about a baby who had been sexually abused (Figures 4.12 and 4.13).
- Kathy Osler created a family scrapbook of photos, magazine collages, and drawings about her own family issues in order to prevent them from interfering in her work with families (Figures 5.16, 5.18, and 5.19).
- Riv Stein used art to help overcome the distance and negative feelings she was experiencing toward her clients with developmental delay (Figure 6.7).
- Jennifer Swerdlow created quilt squares to release the powerful reactions she had to the women who had been sexually assaulted with whom she worked (Figures 11.4 and 11.5).
- Stephanie Zentz formed a staff group to make art to help them grieve the plight of the HIV-positive children with whom they worked (Figure 12.11), including a many-layered collage Stephanie made (Figures 12.9 and 12.10).

Epilog

Art therapy students perform a mask enactment.

Writing this book has been an eye-opening experience for me. Although I was familiar with the work of many of the art therapists represented here, getting into the detailed nitty-gritty of what they actually did was almost overwhelming. Taking it all together, I was amazed at the astonishing creativity, ingenuity, and sheer variety in our profession.

The boundaries of art therapy have expanded in several directions. Art therapists now work with many other populations than heretofore. Modalities have blurred as visual art expression has blended with other art forms. In some settings, even the concept of therapy has stretched toward personal growth and creativity.

In addition to the pride I feel in being a part of this exceedingly dynamic, still very young field, I was also surprisingly saddened. As chapter after chapter unfolded, the aggregation of tragedy in the lives of those we treat began to weigh heavily upon me. As an art therapy educator with only a small private practice, I no longer work in the trenches, although I supervise those who do, including many whose work is described in this book. Nevertheless, I am removed from contact with the clients they treat and know them only vicariously. As these art therapists take in their stride daily confrontations with their clients, so do I, although at a distance, in supervising them. It is in this accumulated writing, however, that I see the courage and perseverance of these art therapists, the hopefulness they convey to their clients, their unrelenting giving to those who need the most. They give the gift of art and the gift of themselves.

The varied work of all these art therapists constitutes a very big picture. So does the work of any one of them.

References

American Psychiatric Association (1994). *Diagnostic and statistical manual of mental disorders* (4th ed.). Washington, DC: Author.

Baker, B. (1997). *Art speaks in healing survivors of war.* Unpublished master's degree thesis, University of Illinois, Chicago.

Bean, M. (1992). The poetry of countertransference. *The Arts in Psychotherapy, 19,* 347–358.

Benson, N. (1983). *Mural making: a group art therapy venture.* Unpublished master's degree thesis, University of Illinois, Chicago.

Biederman, N. (1988). *Art therapy with premenopausal and menopausal women.* Unpublished master's degree thesis, University of Illinois, Chicago.

Black, C. (1994). *The art of survival: Art therapy with women recovering from prostitution.* Unpublished master's degree thesis, University of Illinois, Chicago.

Blass, J., & Bloom, F. (1980). Neuroscience research program-stated meeting on dementia. *Neuroscience Newsletter, 11.*

Bluestein, B. (1995). *Art therapy with 3-D environments.* Unpublished master's degree thesis, University of Illinois, Chicago.

Brecht, B. (1989). *Art therapy for the varying stages of Alzheimer's disease.* Unpublished master's degree thesis, University of Illinois, Chicago.

Bolde, J. (1989). *The importance of 3-dimensional work in art therapy.* Unpublished master's degree thesis, University of Illinois, Chicago.

Bowen, M. (1978). *Family therapy in clinical practice.* New York: Jason Aronson.

Butler, R. (1963). The life review: an interpretation of reminiscence in the aged. *Psychiatry, 26,* 65–76.

Canby, S. (1992). *Shelter art: Is it therapy?* Unpublished master's degree thesis, University of Illinois, Chicago.

Cane, F. (1951). *The artist in each of us.* New York: Pantheon.

Cashdon, S. (1988). *Object relations therapy: Bridges to self psychology.* New York: W. W. Norton.

Center for Substance Abuse Prevention (1995). *Curriculum modules on alcohol and other drug problems for schools of social work.* Rockville, MD: Author.

Clenard, C. (1986). *A use of still photography with individual adolescents in a psychiatric inpatient setting.* Unpublished master's degree thesis, University of Illinois, Chicago.

Contreras, A. (1993). *Short term family art therapy with Mexican immigrants.* Unpublished master's degree thesis, University of Illinois, Chicago.

Coseo, A. (1997). Developing cultural awareness for creative arts therapists. *The Arts in Psychotherapy, 24*(2), 145–157.

Cullen, P. (1992). *Images of understanding: The use of post-session imagery to clarify countertransference issues.* Unpublished master's degree thesis, University of Illinois, Chicago.

Dalley, T., Case, C., Shaverien, J., Weir, F., Halliday, D., Hall, P., & Waller, D. (1987). *Images of art therapy.* New York: Tavistok.

Del Signore, D. (1999). *Smell the memories: The use of olfactory stimulation as a pathway to art making with older adults.* Unpublished master's degree thesis, University of Illinois, Chicago.

Denz, C. (1997). *The art expressions program: Artistic relief of the terminally ill hospice patient.* Unpublished master's degree thesis, University of Illinois, Chicago.

DeVera, L. (1999). *Art therapy in identity formation for minority adolescents.* Unpublished master's degree thesis, University of Illinois, Chicago.

Dougherty, M. (1991). *Lights, camera, action! The therapeutic use of film animation with the developmentally disabled.* Unpublished master's degree thesis, University of Illinois, Chicago.

Drucker, M. (1995). *"Junk" art therapy: working with behavior disordered children and adolescents.* Unpublished master's degree thesis, University of Illinois, Chicago.

Duberman, M. (1991). *Cures: A gay man's odyssey.* New York: Plume.

Elliot-Prisco, A. (1995). *Through the viewfinder: Focus on the ego of sexually assaulted females.* Unpublished master's degree thesis, University of Illinois, Chicago.

Engel, E. (1992). *Creating a community for men through art therapy.* Unpublished master's degree thesis, University of Illinois, Chicago.

Erikson, E. H., Erikson, J. M., and Kivnick, H. Q. (1986). *Vital involvement in old age.* New York: W. W. Norton.

Evans, D. (1985). *Art therapy with the hospitalized pediatric patient.* Unpublished master's degree thesis, University of Illinois, Chicago.

Evermann, R. (1994). *Enabling relatedness through creative art intervention with psychotic children.* Unpublished master's degree thesis, University of Illinois, Chicago.

Ferme, G. L. (1996). *Puppet interviews and formal games in family art therapy.* Unpublished master's degree thesis, University of Illinois, Chicago.

Fisher, L., Matthews, D., & Seals, J. (1992). *Brain electrical activity mapping (BEAM) in the explosive adolescent.* Paper presented at American Association of Children's Residential Centers Conference.

Foss, D. A. (1999). *From self-injurious behavior to sensory integrative behavior.* Unpublished master's degree thesis, University of Illinois, Chicago.

Frahm, S. (1995). *Living in a creative environment: Homeless women's connections through art.* Unpublished master's degree thesis, University of Illinois, Chicago.

Freeman, J. (1993). *Using art therapy with pregnant psychiatric inpatients to facilitate the mother-child bond and prepare for separation.* Unpublished master's degree thesis, University of Illinois, Chicago.

Garber, R. L. (1996). *When bigger makes better: A mural technique for healing.* Unpublished master's degree thesis, University of Illinois, Chicago.

Gasman, S. (1989). *Art expression for children with cancer: Working with children who might die.* Unpublished master's degree thesis, University of Illinois, Chicago.

Glover, A. (1991). *Bookmaking as a means of creative expression for developmentally disabled adults.* Unpublished master's degree thesis, University of Illinois, Chicago.

Graduating from state care. (1999, May 23). *Chicago Tribune,* sec. 1, pp. 1, 12.

Haddon, S. (1989). *Empowering battered women through art therapy.* Unpublished master's degree thesis, University of Illinois, Chicago.

Hamilton, M. (1996). *Art therapy with sexually abused boys: Creating a therapeutic communication board game.* Unpublished master's degree thesis, University of Illinois, Chicago.

Hannigan Blocher, L. (1988). *Art therapy with substance abusers within a psychiatric after-care population.* Unpublished master's degree thesis, University of Illinois, Chicago.

Hasara, M. L. (1993). *Garbage pail kids: Children whose living mothers gave them to their grandparents to be raised.* Unpublished master's degree thesis, University of Illinois, Chicago.

Haugh, D. (1994). *Multiple reflections: Exploring countertransference through a series of facsimiles of clients' art work.* Unpublished master's degree thesis, University of Illinois, Chicago.

Hogan, S. (Ed.). (1997). *Feminist approaches to art therapy.* London and New York: Routledge.

Hollinger, M. (1997). *Helping renal failure children help themselves.* Unpublished master's degree thesis, University of Illinois, Chicago.

Jacob, L. (1995). *Breaking hearts: The need to end recidivism.* Unpublished master's degree thesis, University of Illinois, Chicago.

Johnson, M. K. (1998). *Three-dimensional art therapy as sensory stimulation for adult day-care clients.* Unpublished master's degree thesis, University of Illinois, Chicago.

Johnson, S. (1985). *Exploring delusions in art therapy: Case studies.* Unpublished master's degree thesis, University of Illinois, Chicago.

Kasser, W. (1998). *Video journals: Images and HIV.* Unpublished master's degree thesis, University of Illinois, Chicago.

Kellogg, R. (1969, 1970). *Understanding children's art.* Palo Alto, CA: Mayfield.

Kimmel, P., Weihs, K., & Peterson, R. (1993). Survival in hemodialysis patients: The role of depression. *Journal of the American Society of Nephrology, 4*(1), 12–23.

Kistner, M. (1999). *Transforming furniture: An environmental approach to art therapy with chronically mentally ill adults.* Unpublished master's degree thesis, University of Illinois, Chicago.

Klitchman, K. (1991). *Taking a break: Art therapy with women survivors of childhood sexual abuse.* Unpublished master's degree thesis, University of Illinois, Chicago.

Koenig, C. (1992). *Listening to the silence: Art therapy with electively mute children.* Unpublished master's degree thesis, University of Illinois, Chicago.

Kowalczyk, S. (1988). *Integrating art therapy into the Sonia Shankman Orthogenic School.* Unpublished master's degree thesis, University of Illinois, Chicago.

Kuzniak, N. (1992). *Termination and short-term art therapy, a therapist's process.* Unpublished master's degree thesis, University of Illinois, Chicago.

Lavery, T. (1994). Culture shock: Adventuring into the inner city through post-session imagery. *American Journal of Art Therapy, 33*(1), 14–20.

Leander, R. (1991). *Drawing conclusions: Developing an art therapy program on an acute care AIDS unit.* Unpublished master's degree thesis, University of Illinois, Chicago.

Lee, S. (1993). *Art therapy as a third language for adolescent Korean-American immigrants.* Unpublished master's degree thesis, University of Illinois, Chicago.

Limperis, A. (1996). *Making headway: The use of pre-molded anthropomorphic styrofoam heads in a short term pediatric setting.* Unpublished master's degree thesis, University of Illinois, Chicago.

Lindberg, S. (1991). *Construction: A physical and symbolic process of restructuring the self.* Unpublished master's degree thesis, University of Illinois, Chicago.

Lowenfeld, V., & Brittain, W. L. (1970). *Creative and mental growth* (5th ed.). New York: Macmillan.

Marchand, J. (1993). *Surviving, healing, growing: An art therapy intern's journey as seen in countertransference exploration.* Unpublished master's degree thesis, University of Illinois, Chicago.

Mathews, L. J. (1997). *Creative arts for Alzheimer's and related disorders.* Unpublished master's degree thesis, University of Illinois, Chicago.

Matthews, D., & Fisher, L. (1992). *The neurobiology of juvenile violence.* Paper presented at the Second Annual Troubled Adolescent Conference.

Matthews, D., Williamson, B., Seals, J., & Fisher, L. (1993). *Treatment planning for violent juveniles.* Paper presented at the Annual Meeting of the National Association of Private Psychiatric Hospitals, Fort Lauderdale, FL.

McCullough, A. (1991). *Validation, empowerment and exploration: Dimensions of creativity with survivors of rape.* Unpublished master's degree thesis, University of Illinois, Chicago.

McNally, C. (1996). *An integration of art therapy and art history in work with chronically mentally ill women.* Unpublished master's degree thesis, University of Illinois, Chicago.

Mills, D. (1992). *Group art therapy with female adult survivors of incest.* Unpublished master's degree thesis, University of Illinois, Chicago.

Miskus, P. (1996). *Primary issues in inpatient gay-affirming group psychotherapy using art therapy as the central treatment modality.* Unpublished master's degree thesis, University of Illinois, Chicago.

Mitchell, L. (1995). *The use of verbal and visual images in helping the art therapist explore countertransference issues.* Unpublished master's degree thesis, University of Illinois, Chicago.

Monette, P. (1992). *Becoming a man: Half a life story.* San Francisco: Harper.

Moreno, G., & Wadeson, H. (1986). Art therapy for acculturation problems of Hispanic clients. *Art Therapy, 3*(1).

Morrill, A. (1992). Early interventions in the cycle of violence through art therapy. Unpublished master's degree thesis, University of Illinois, Chicago.

Nathanson, R. (1994). *Illuminating the path to empathy through personal images.* Unpublished master's degree thesis, University of Illinois, Chicago.

Neely, K. (1984). *Art therapy with gang-affiliated behavior disordered adolescents: Some effects of structure.* Unpublished master's degree thesis, University of Illinois, Chicago.

Nelson, K. (1991). *Art therapy in a pediatric outpatient HIV clinic.* Unpublished master's degree thesis, University of Illinois, Chicago.

O'Boyle, S. (1989). *Awakening creative expression in developmentally disabled adults.* Unpublished master's degree thesis, University of Illinois, Chicago.

O'Bryan, S. (1989). *Exploring the dually diagnosed individual through group art therapy.* Unpublished master's degree thesis, University of Illinois, Chicago.

Ohl, J. (1992). *Let the public share my pain and joy: Published works by mentally ill adults.* Unpublished master's degree thesis, University of Illinois, Chicago.

Osler, K. (1996). *A family scrapbook: Using art to promote therapist differentiation.* Unpublished master's degree thesis, University of Illinois, Chicago.

Podmore, J. (1991). *Ethnic group development using art therapy and museum exhibits.* Unpublished master's degree thesis, University of Illinois, Chicago.

Polin, V. (1991). *The art of healing: Using art as a tool to empower chemically addicted survivors of child sexual abuse.* Unpublished master's degree thesis, University of Illinois, Chicago.

Pollack, W. (1988). *Art therapy as a means of expression for people with AIDS.* Unpublished master's degree thesis, University of Illinois, Chicago.

Port, F. (1993). Worldwide demographics and future trends in ESRD. *Kidney International, 43,* S1–S7.

Prohaska, M. (1999). *Collage with emotionally and/or behaviorally disordered adolescents.* Unpublished master's degree thesis, University of Illinois, Chicago.

Pumphrey, H. (1999). *Using handmade puppets and masks to increase foster children's self-esteem and identity formation.* Unpublished master's degree thesis, University of Illinois, Chicago.

Ragis, V. (1987). *Group art and enrichment for the dually diagnosed urban adult.* Unpublished master's degree thesis, University of Illinois, Chicago.

Rakestraw, K. (1997). *Exploring family roles: Creating family representations in clay with sexually abused children.* Unpublished master's degree thesis, University of Illinois, Chicago.

Reisberg, B. (1983). *Alzheimer's disease, the standard reference.* New York: Free Press.

Rosenbaum, A., & O'Leary, K. D. (1981). Children: The unidentified victims of mental violence. *The American Journal of Orthopsychiatry, 5*(14), 692–699.

Rozgonyi, S. (1991). *Pregnancy and mental illness: Group art therapy for pregnant psychiatric inpatients.* Unpublished master's degree thesis, University of Illinois, Chicago.

Rozin, R. (1999). *Art therapy with neurobehavioral brain impaired adolescents.* Unpublished master's degree thesis, University of Illinois, Chicago.

Rubin, J. A. (1978). *Child art therapy.* New York: Van Nostrand Reinhold.

Rugland, H. (1999). *Sparking creativity: using guided imagery to stimulate self-expression for behavior disordered children and adolescents.* Unpublished master's degree thesis, University of Illinois, Chicago.

Ruland, D. (1988). *Using art therapy to facilitate self-esteem in clients with Alzheimer's disease.* Unpublished master's degree thesis, University of Illinois, Chicago.

Runyan, A. (1992). *Art therapy with women who have surrendered children for adoption.* Unpublished master's degree thesis, University of Illinois, Chicago.

Safar, L. (1998). *The utilization of art slides and books in group art therapy with chronic clients.* Unpublished master's degree thesis, University of Illinois, Chicago.

Salomon, X. (1992). *Reclaiming the self: Women recovering from addictions.* Unpublished master's degree thesis, University of Illinois, Chicago.

Scescke, V. (1990). *Kindling the imagination; stoking the heart: Storytelling in art therapy.* Unpublished master's degree thesis, University of Illinois, Chicago.

Seefelt, M. E. (1995). *"Help me I'm dying!" Using art therapy to build a bridge between living and dying with adult AIDS patients.* Unpublished master's degree thesis, University of Illinois, Chicago.

Schulte, K. (1991). *A pilot study: The family body tracing technique.* Unpublished master's degree thesis, University of Illinois, Chicago.

Simic, C. (1992). *Dime-store alchemy.* New Jersey: Ecco Press.

Stallman, J. (1996). *Using art for simultaneous reminiscence and life review with older adults.* Unpublished master's degree thesis, University of Illinois, Chicago.

Stein, R. H. (1994). *Self-exploration of hopelessness and dehumanization while working with mentally retarded persons.* Unpublished master's degree thesis, University of Illinois, Chicago.

Stevanus, K. (1997). *Taking the first step: A look at using art therapy in facing powerlessness.* Unpublished master's degree thesis, University of Illinois, Chicago.

Streeter, K. S., & Bell, L. (1991). Domestic violence intervention handbook. *Family shelter service.* Unpublished.

Suckerman, D. (1999). *Words and images.* Unpublished master's degree thesis, University of Illinois, Chicago.

Swerdlow, J. (1996). *Reassembling the pieces: Quilting in response to adult female survivors of abuse.* Unpublished master's degree thesis, University of Illinois, Chicago.

Takano, N. (1992). *Cross-cultural sensitivity in art therapy: A discussion with reference to Cambodian women refugees.* Unpublished master's degree thesis, University of Illinois, Chicago.

Tarasiewicz, A. (1997). *Exploring countertransference working with adolescents in art therapy.* Unpublished master's degree thesis, University of Illinois, Chicago.

Terra, K. (1996). *Exploring collage as a medium for self expression in the jail setting.* Unpublished master's degree thesis, University of Illinois, Chicago.

Thorn, B. (1998). *Picture this: Phototherapy with chronic mentally ill adults.* Unpublished master's degree thesis, University of Illinois, Chicago.

The Thresholds Lakeview Club (1991). *The Musing Place, 6*(2). Chicago.

U.S. Renal Data System (1991). USRDS 1991 Annual Data Report: The National Institutes of Health, National Institute of Diabetes and Digestive and Kidney Diseases, Bethesda, MD, August 1991. *American Journal of Kidney Diseases, 18*(2), 1–127.

Van der Ent-Zgoda, J. (1990). *Art therapy with children staying in a crisis center: "Draw where you live."* Unpublished master's degree thesis, University of Illinois, Chicago.

Voices in Action (1985). *Victims of incest can emerge survivors.* Chicago: Author.

Wadeson, H. (1980). *Art psychotherapy.* New York: John Wiley & Sons.

Wadeson, H. (1987). *The dynamics of art psychotherapy.* New York: John Wiley & Sons.

Wadeson, H., Durkin, J., & Perach, D. (1989). *Advances in art therapy.* New York: John Wiley & Sons.

Wadeson, H., Marano-Geiser, R., & Ramseyer, J. (1990). Through the looking glass: dark sides I, II, III. *Art Therapy, 7*(3).

Wadeson, H. (Ed.). (1992). *A guide to conducting art therapy research.* Mondelein, IL: American Art Therapy Association.

Wadeson, H. (1997). Many murders. In S. Hogan (Ed.), *Feminist approaches to art therapy.* London and New York: Routledge.

Walker, T. (1993). *Wearable art therapy: Making therapeutic choices.* Unpublished master's degree thesis, University of Illinois, Chicago.

Wolff, B. (1993). *Confrontation through image.* Unpublished master's degree thesis, University of Illinois, Chicago.

Yeh, A. (1997). *Exploring the lost and found: The use of found objects in art therapy.* Unpublished master's degree thesis, University of Illinois, Chicago.

Zentz, S. (1994). *An AIDS caregivers art therapy group: Self-examination and support for the professional.* Unpublished master's degree thesis, University of Illinois, Chicago.

Index